Luxury, Sensation and the Moving Image

LEGENDA

LEGENDA is the Modern Humanities Research Association's book imprint for new research in the Humanities. Founded in 1995 by Malcolm Bowie and others within the University of Oxford, Legenda has always been a collaborative publishing enterprise, directly governed by scholars. The Modern Humanities Research Association (MHRA) joined this collaboration in 1998, became half-owner in 2004, in partnership with Maney Publishing and then Routledge, and has since 2016 been sole owner. Titles range from medieval texts to contemporary cinema and form a widely comparative view of the modern humanities, including works on Arabic, Catalan, English, French, German, Greek, Italian, Portuguese, Russian, Spanish, and Yiddish literature. Editorial boards and committees of more than 60 leading academic specialists work in collaboration with bodies such as the Society for French Studies, the British Comparative Literature Association and the Association of Hispanists of Great Britain & Ireland.

The MHRA encourages and promotes advanced study and research in the field of the modern humanities, especially modern European languages and literature, including English, and also cinema. It aims to break down the barriers between scholars working in different disciplines and to maintain the unity of humanistic scholarship. The Association fulfils this purpose through the publication of journals, bibliographies, monographs, critical editions, and the MHRA Style Guide, and by making grants in support of research. Membership is open to all who work in the Humanities, whether independent or in a University post, and the participation of younger colleagues entering the field is especially welcomed.

ALSO PUBLISHED BY THE ASSOCIATION

Critical Texts
Tudor and Stuart Translations • *New Translations* • *European Translations*
MHRA Library of Medieval Welsh Literature

MHRA Bibliographies
Publications of the Modern Humanities Research Association

The Annual Bibliography of English Language & Literature
Austrian Studies
Modern Language Review
Portuguese Studies
The Slavonic and East European Review
Working Papers in the Humanities
The Yearbook of English Studies

www.mhra.org.uk
www.legendabooks.com

MOVING IMAGE

Legenda/Moving Image publishes cutting-edge work on any aspect of film or screen media from Europe and Latin America. Studies of European-language cinemas from other continents, and diasporic and intercultural cinemas (with some relation to Europe or its languages), are also encompassed. The series seeks to reflect a diversity of theoretical, historical, and interdisciplinary approaches to the moving image, and includes projects comparing screen media with other art forms. Research monographs and collected volumes will be considered, but not studies of a single film. As innovation is a priority for the series, volumes should predominantly consist of previously unpublished material.

Proposals should be sent with one or two sample chapters to the Editor, Professor Emma Wilson, Corpus Christi College, Cambridge CB2 1RH, UK.

APPEARING IN THIS SERIES

1. *Spanish Practices: Literature, Cinema, Television*, by Paul Julian Smith
2. *Cinema and Contact: The Withdrawal of Touch in Nancy, Bresson, Duras and Denis*, by Laura McMahon
3. *Cinema's Inter-Sensory Encounters: Krzysztof Kieślowski and Claire Denis*, by Georgina Evans
4. *Holocaust Intersections: Genocide and Visual Culture at the New Millennium*, edited by Axel Bangert, Robert S. C. Gordon and Libby Saxton
5. *Africa's Lost Classics: New Histories of African Cinema*, edited by Lizelle Bisschoff and David Murphy
6. *Agnès Varda Unlimited: Image, Music, Media*, edited by Marie-Claire Barnet
7. *Thinking Cinema with Proust*, by Patrick ffrench
8. *Blanchot and the Moving Image: Fascination and Spectatorship*, by Calum Watt
9. *Chantal Akerman: Afterlives*, edited by Marion Schmid and Emma Wilson
10. *Screening Work: The Films of Christian Petzold*, by Stephan Hilpert and Andrew J. Webber

Managing Editor
Dr Graham Nelson, 41 Wellington Square, Oxford OX1 2JF, UK

www.legendabooks.com

Luxury, Sensation and the Moving Image

Alice Blackhurst

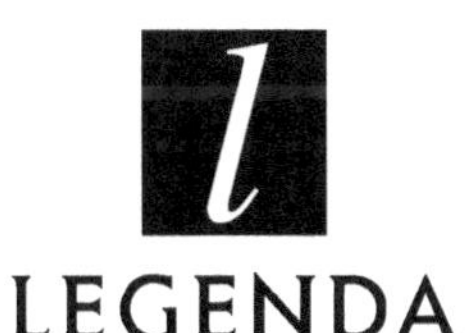

Moving Image 13
Modern Humanities Research Association
2021

Published by Legenda
an imprint of the Modern Humanities Research Association
Salisbury House, Station Road, Cambridge CB1 2LA

ISBN 978-1-83954-022-6 (HB)
ISBN 978-1-83954-023-3 (PB)

First published 2021

Copy-Editor: Charlotte Brown

CONTENTS

Acknowledgements ix

Introduction: A Sensual Relation to the World 1

1 Chantal Akerman: An Experience of Immersion and Duration 15

Voluptuous rupture, luxurious reprieve: *Jeanne Dielman, 23 quai du Commerce, 1080 Bruxelles* 17

Je, tu, il, elle: Languorous Unproductivity 31

Nomadic Ambling 37

Desire Unlimited 40

Conclusion: *l'éclosion du regard* 44

2 Annie Ernaux: l'écriture, un luxe 55

From the 'Community of Lovers' to the Exposure of Community: *Passion simple* 58

Se perdre: vivre une histoire 66

Conclusion: Vast Collective Sensation 73

3 Louise Bourgeois: Sensuous Matter 81

Mid-career Soft Sculptures: The Birth of Breasts 83

Fillette: Lateral Expansions 95

The *Insomnia Drawings*: Pleasure in Drawing 98

Conclusion: Metamorphosis and Mutability 114

4 Sophie Calle: The Luxury of Taking Care 123

Suite vénitienne: Submission, Surrender, Failure 125

Douleur exquise: Uncountable Experience 131

Prenez soin de vous: Community, Excess, Spectacle 140

Conclusion: A New Mode of Seduction 149

Conclusion: Living Otherwise 157

Bibliography 163

Index 181

ACKNOWLEDGEMENTS

This book originated as a PhD project supervised by Emma Wilson, and examined by Martin Crowley and Marion Schmid. To Emma Wilson I am extraordinarily grateful, for her unfailingly supportive, always inspiring, and profoundly kind guidance of many years. Without her belief in my work in all its different guises, this book would not have been able to exist.

I am also greatly indebted to Martin Crowley and Marion Schmid, who were excellent, engaged PhD examiners, and whose insights and generous thoughts about luxury since submission have been critical to the progression of ideas in the book. Christopher Prendergast and David Hillman were early, patient cheerleaders of my topic, and my gratitude to King's College, Cambridge for affording me the space and time to do further research on my subject as a Junior Research Fellow from 2016–20 is extensive. Aline Guillermet, Rory O'Bryen, and Iris Brey read early versions of early chapters, for which I am very thankful. Maggie Wright and Glenn Roepnack made a residency at the Louise Bourgeois Easton Foundation in Manhattan in July 2019 possible, which greatly enriched and enabled Chapter 3. Colleagues in the Departments of Film & Screen and French at the University of Cambridge such as John David Rhodes, Laura MacMahon, Jules O'Dwyer, Bill Burgwinkle, Zoe Angelis, Ian James and Nick White have also contributed to conversations and to the supportive intellectual environment which made this book possible. I am also grateful for the support of colleagues Elena Gorfinkel, Daniella Shreir, Rhiannon Harries, Amaleena Damlé, and Emily Apter further afield.

For the different ways in which they have supported and inspired over the years, I would also like to thank Eliza Apperly, Emma Mackinnon, Fiona Allison, Alina Khakoo, and Rebecca Liu. I am grateful beyond words to the members of my family who encouraged and supported the production of this book over the years: Matthew Blackhurst and Rosie Humble; John Blackhurst and Justin Porter-Blackhurst, amongst others. To my parents Keith and Olena Blackhurst, for everything, and especially for the environment which allowed me to bring this book to completion, I am immeasurably indebted. This book is dedicated to them.

A.B., January 2021

INTRODUCTION

A Sensual Relation to the World

Luxury as concept and idea attracts a wealth of definitions, an abundance of shifting historical and sociological resonances, and an ever-expanding constellation of proximate terms. Embedded in the French cultural imaginary, after Charles Baudelaire's poem 'L'Invitation au voyage', as an experience of 'calm voluptuousness', it evokes both appetites for orderly containment, satiation, and fulfilment but also longings for excess, transgression, and the boundless motions of desire. This inherent sinuosity and luxury's state of permanent suspension between order and abandon, stasis and insatiable mobility, resists conceptual capture or representational fixity. To commit to providing an account of what luxury involves, entails, or signifies is to confront its tendency always to exceed given definitions.[1]

The ambition of this book is to offer new, creative thinking about luxury, and ideas of the luxurious, as a material, embodied, affective, and indeed sensory value. It is to re-imagine luxury as a form of full, sensuous attention to works of art and to the phenomenal world; as a celebration of embodied multiplicity and sexual plurality; and as a state of possibility which opens spaces free of calculation, counting, and control. Such re-conceptualisations depart from the pervasive understanding of luxury through the lens of object fetishism, 'conspicuous consumption', and its typecasting as a complicit agent in capitalist processes of acquisition, exploitation, and gratuitous display.[2] To emancipate ideas of luxury from fetishistic grasping, deadening exchange economies, but also nihilistic notions of waste and dereliction is my project here.[3] Through immersive, intimate readings of artworks, to encourage new economies of pleasure and desire and develop an affirmative phenomenology of luxury which augments a sensual relation to the world, yet persists as a valence in excess of ordinary life, is my hope.[4]

A vital tenet of this study is that luxury's potentialities are amplified by its connection with the moving image in particular. The corporeal, gestural, and affective experience of going to the cinema has long been underscored as one of luxury,[5] whose decadence has been, at time of publication, even more accentuated due to the unprecedented impact of the coronavirus crisis. Even prior to the effects of a global pandemic, the act of going to the cinema has consistently been understood as a privileged means of making space for leisure independent of the working day,[6] of escaping labour, and even as an exercise in sumptuously 'wasting time', resonating with Immanuel Kant's 'purposeless purposiveness' ('zwecklose Zweckmassigkeit').[7] Roland Barthes, in an essay 'En sortant du cinéma', famously linked the cinema's 'diffused eroticism' to its architectural conceit of sheltering, cocooning and enclosure, positing how 'it is because I am enclosed that I work and glow with all my desire'.[8] The both literal and metaphorical 'screening off' of space enabled by traditional site-specific cinema, he argued, as well as the medium's trafficking in tropes such as engineered passivity, narrative transport, and synchronised, successive, and hypnotic bodily release, twinned the experience of film-going with luxury's historical conception as a form of lavish hedonism, idleness and indolence, or as a surrender to a languorous experience of comfort, pleasure, and consumption.[9]

The structural luxury of cinema is subject to revision, nonetheless, in an age of splintered screens and interrupted streaming: or in a time where the experience of going to the cinema, when it is even possible, chafes against the more convenient experience of watching something on a personal computer or a phone. As Nico Baumbach has acutely diagnosed, contemporary strains of the moving image, or what he calls the 'new cinephilia', are infected both with the condition of abundance and of scarcity:[10] or with the profusion of new methods and modalities of 'doing cinema' (as Girish Shambu has it), but also the encroaching, calculative force of the algorithm, or the creep of metrics, which dictate to us what we want to watch before we have ourselves become aware of such desires.[11] As a counter-force to the insatiable speed and surfeit of these new technologies,[12] the rise of what has come to be expressed as 'slow cinema' in the 2000s and the 2010s (marked by formal techniques such as the long take, extended duration, and the studious avoidance of montage, close-ups, or the fracturing jump-cut) has been read as an attempt to reinstate 'expansiveness, ongoingness and flow', to quote Elena Gorfinkel, or, in Tiago de Luca and Nuno Barradas Jorge's words, to 'rescue extended temporal structures from the accelerated tempo of late capitalism'.[13] Though slow cinema has alternatively been dissected as an arduous spectatorial mode of 'doing work',[14] or of straining to maintain attention amidst what Dan Kois infamously characterised an austere experience of 'eating one's cultural vegetables', in this book I argue that the quality of sustained, close looking, 'hyper-attention', and immersion in the present moment that slow cinema encourages cultivates a novel form of luxury not as passive consumption but as intentional, devotional form of spectatorial relationality.[15] My approach to luxury as *formal* quality throughout the book steeps the term in new ecologies of attention and perception. It methodically reframes 'the luxurious' as a quality of looking and attentiveness, rather than an overly thematic concern with surfaces, embellishment, annotation, and adornment.[16]

A reading of slow cinema as a relational, participatory, and surprisingly active mode of film spectatorship[17] avoids the trope of 'static gazing' that has dogged feminist and queer critics of the moving image since Laura Mulvey's seminal 1975 indictment of classical Hollywood's tendency to 'freeze' women subjects on screen.[18] The belief that slow cinema can foster an emphatic form of 'kinaesthetic empathy', to use Katharina Lindner's and others' phrasing,[19] also dovetails with dynamic work in film and cinema scholarship since the turn of the millennium on the moving image's encounter with, and enrichment by, the multi-scored environments of 'affect' and sensation.[20] In her book *Cinema and Sensation*, Martine Beugnet understands a 'sensuous' approach to reading film — partially derived from Gilles Deleuze's assertion of the time-image's ability to render thought immanent to the image[21] — as 'multi-directional' in import, seeking to engage with the full range of functions at work in the human sensorium (touch, sound, taste and intuition, in addition to the long privileged faculty of sight) in order to see texts as part of a material continuum, enmeshed in, rather than conferring meaning on, the sensate, relational, and phenomenological world.[22] For Eugenie Brinkema, writing on the potential intersection between an affective approach to reading film and the question of form, the co-extensive turn to affect in arts disciplines takes as combative object the ongoing prevalence of the semiotic and linguistic in critical encounters with artworks.[23] In the body of this book I employ an ethics and aesthetics of sensation to irradiate new practices of moving image and art scholarship untethered from a 'hermeneutics of suspicion' but also from a denial of formal properties. A re-imagining of luxury as an affection of the body, an expanding of the sensorium, and as the visceral desire for an intensity of sensuous experience further avoids, in our current, growing context of 'immaterial production' and 'cognitive capitalism', the trap of what I term luxury's 'experiential turn', eager to transform indeterminate experiences such as time, space, solitude, and contact into circumspect, substitute commodities.[24] An insistence on a deeply embodied, kinetic, and affective critical process of feeling with as opposed to looking at my assembled artworks avoids scopophilia, or what Sarah Banet-Weiser calls today's 'economy of visibility' invested in making networked subjects primarily 'available to the algorithm'.[25] It also, by highlighting co-presence, multi-sensory collaboration and the sharing of perspective between audience and artist, artist and critic, affirms a rigorously feminist approach to moving image scholarship, emancipated from the reductive contours of the heteropatriarchally-inflected 'gaze'.[26]

In inviting new readings of luxury I draw upon a corpus of four artists: Louise Bourgeois, Annie Ernaux, Chantal Akerman, and Sophie Calle. All four can be said to partake enthusiastically of a 'mixed media' approach, both resonating with, yet also stretching out beyond, the moving image. All four adopt a creative praxis of experimentation, and, eluding categorisation in terms of fixed paradigms of genre, work across film, literature, installation, performance, conceptual and plastic art. Looking to such artists' ludic and engaged expansion of generic categories, throughout the book I borrow from their interdisciplinary elasticity in order to affirm ideas of luxury as both grounded in material culture and closely defined frameworks of aesthetic matter, but also as a volatile and mobile value, reaching out to touch novel existential and aesthetic latitudes. In putting Bourgeois, Ernaux, Akerman, and Calle in contact, my motivation is not only to connect Francophone, early twenty-first-century artists with a similar insatiable, autonomous, and indeed sovereign approach to the question of creating artworks (as all four, indeed, faced substantial obstacles to the early actualisation of their lives as writers, filmmakers, sculptors and performers).[27] I aim, also, to identify a group of self-defining women subjects equally invested in the decadence of 'making one's life into a work of art', to rehearse a phrase of Michel Foucault, without disproportionate apology, self-diminution, guilt, or shame.[28]

Testimonies to my women artists' inexhaustible creative energy and expansive range of artistic output, indeed, helps to distance my account of luxury from consistent tropes of feminine passivity and indulgence and to sharpen its explicit feminist ambitions.[29] As well as conspicuously intermedial, experimental, and formally innovative, my corpus is exclusively composed of 'women-artists', who share concerns to document and render visible a certain experience of contemporary, quotidian, and what I will term 'obligated life' under the auspices of 'the feminine'. Whilst far from a historical, sociological, or overtly political investigation into the materialities of making art as a woman in the context of late capitalism, this study focuses on women artists in order to further explore this frequent and ingrained gendering of luxury as feminine — its pathologising of women as incorrigible 'consuming subjects' and its deemed opening of passive, recessive, contemplative, and therefore 'female' states of being.[30] Sharing Hélène Cixous's view, in *Le Rire de la méduse*, of the necessity of seeing Woman's functioning as an 'economy' that can no longer be expressed in 'economic' terms, my hope, in connecting luxury to a certain mode of feminine aesthetic production rather than consumption, fetishism, or recessive visuality, is to forge new circuits of exchange, discourse, and communication.[31] My hope is to cultivate new contexts out of which to think women's relationship to the aesthetic and to the embellishment of life through art and suggest that, as an affective state able to transport us beyond the boundaries of the self and open up new modes of sensuous relation with others, luxury might be remapped as a feminist ontology of sharing.

A thinking of luxury as a defiant proliferation of aesthetic media and styles further departs from persistent evocations of *le luxe* as, citing Pierre Bourdieu, a practice of elite 'domination' and class visibility, or a means of oppressive ostentation exercised by an elite class and staged via strategies of accumulation and possession.[32] Such accounts, of luxury as conspicuous expenditure or a social practice characterised by sumptuous spending in order to affirm a sense of rank or conspicuous prestige, privilege ideas of the luxurious as social tool, or as a sociologically transparent marker and distributor of time and space.[33] Etymologically rooted in unquestionably carnal, visceral processes of lusting, *luxure* and *luxuria*,[34] this evolution of the term from form of sexual exuberance to mode of socio-economic 'distinction', and luxury's now ubiquitous qualification in terms of a partnering luxury *product* — it being difficult to apprehend the term without an accompanying noun such as 'car', 'meal' 'hotel' or 'vacation' — traces the 'incitement of consumption and the constant production of a regulated and quantifiable pleasure'; and inventories ingrained symptoms of a capitalist culture heavily invested in amassing, exhibiting and accumulating goods.[35] These developments couch any understanding of excess, abundance, and what Slavoj Žižek calls 'pure surplus enjoyment' in possessive, quantitative, and serialised terms.[36] As Jean-Luc Nancy, whose thinking I return to throughout this book, speaking on the concept of *jouissance* or intense embodied pleasure in conversation with Adèle Van Reeth, observes, 'La jouissance se confond aujourd'hui en partie avec le profit [...]. L'excessif change de sens: d'exubérant il devient appropriatif' [*Jouissance* is confused today with the notion of profit... The excessive has changed meaning: from being understood as exuberant it has become appropriative].[37]

In March 2019, protests led in Paris by *gilets jaunes* activists selected as explicit target an iconic symbol of commodity capitalism and French consumer decadence: the internationally renowned and cathected Champs-Elysées. Smashing up the shop-fronts of super brands such as Hugo Boss, Louis Vuitton, and Nespresso, and setting fire to the liberal-elite favoured restaurant *Le Fouquet*, famously frequented by the president of 'bling', Nicolas Sarkozy, on his election victory in 2007, the scenes mounted a decidedly ambivalent relationship to early twenty-first-century luxury, and seemed intent upon defacing its entrenched centrality within the French national character.[38] Whilst not at all a sociological or economic investigation, one over-arching question of this book is to explore creatively what the future of luxury, as conceptual idea and experience, might look like both in a specifically francophone context (in alliance with the culturally French and French-speaking focus of my four assembled artists) and against a broader global backdrop of austerity, automation, underemployment, and the climate crisis, where questions of consumption are increasingly subtended by projected timelines of extinction. What shape might luxury assume in, as the poet Anne Boyer writes, 'our time of overwhelming and confused chronicity, when each hour is amplified past circadianism, quadrupled in the quarter hour's agenda, Pomodoro-ed, hacked, FOMO-ed, and productivized'?[39] Though aiming principally to inspire greater elasticity in how luxury is conceptually understood and engaged with, this book aims to contend with such dilemmas, with both the increasing 'luxurification' of everyday life in the hyper-curated,[40] personalized, and 'bespoke' digital age and, at the same time, the inevitable fragmentation of the term as we tread these ever-more immaterial contemporary waters.

A concern to exit an economy of parasitic, intransitive consumption, and to affirm instead a philosophy of vital production and the incessant 'productivity of desire' broadly characterises the thinking of Gilles Deleuze. Throughout the book, I draw recursively upon Deleuze's work to aid in extricating my elected corpus of artists from economics of negativity, and to instead insert them in creative networks of luxurious potentiality and fecund exchange. With support from thinkers such as Brian Massumi and Rosi Braidotti, I harness both Deleuze and Félix's Guattari's consistent emphasis on corporeal capacity and the inexhaustible amplification of affective and embodied life as a model for my re-imagining of luxury as a form of material connection and sensory 'immanence' (defined by Deleuze and Guattari as the radical encounter with the present moment, or the emphatic, molecular 'belief in this world').[41]

Drawing on Deleuze's efforts to articulate a novel 'logic of sensation', the thought of Nancy broadly seeks to explore the infinitely mobile nature of the sensible and sensuous — or what is generally referred to in his work under the broad term of 'sense' — from within the circumscribed parameters of our finite, shared, and emphatically material corporeal existence.[42] For the purposes of thinking about luxury, I employ Nancy's skill in folding a philosophy of the transcendent, that which eludes conceptual capture, alongside a philosophy of immanence, that which adheres strictly to the contours of embodied life, along the curve of this study, in order to advance my harnessing of the luxurious as both an experience of the excessive, incommensurable, and the incalculable (or in Derrida's words, that which interrupts all appearance of economy) but also of the senses, to remain in contact with the thick, precarious viscosities of embodied, sensate life.[43]

In his polemical 1949 work *La Part maudite*, Georges Bataille suggests that faced with 'a play of energy that no particular end limits, our only real choice is limited to how the wealth is to be squandered, to the form its useless consumption should take'.[44] Working at the juncture between literature, philosophy, socially-inflected economic theory, and anthropology, Bataille's thinking about luxury not only in *La Part maudite* but also novels such as *L'Histoire de l'œil* (1928) and the later essay *L'Érotisme* (1957) furnishes a crucial backdrop to the book's intention to imagine the luxurious beyond capitalist processes of commodity accumulation, and in novel terms of viscerality, extreme limit experiences and affective spontaneity. For Bataille, the fundamental materiality of human life in excess of symbolic elucidation is addressed explicitly as 'la part maudite' or the 'accursed share' imagined to consistently afflict every living being and to universally incite organic entities — both human and inanimate — towards processes of lavishing, sacrifice and expenditure.[45] Alternatively glossed as the experience of 'potlatch' edging primitive societies towards raucous stagings of community festivity, or the willed giving away of esteemed and precious goods, such a phenomenon — radically asserted as inherent to, or immanent within organic life[46] — hazards luxury as gratuitous and inexorable, and as a form of, in the poet Lisa Robertson's words, 'self-squandering'.[47] Taking distance from the more entropic, intransitive contours of Bataille's philosophy as fruitless exorbitance or 'negativité sans emploi' my focus throughout the book will centre more upon his thinking's project of ejection from the claustrophobic circuits of the 'servile' self, and what that project has to say to luxury's itineraries of release and rapture.[48]

Chantal Akerman, born in Brussels in 1950 and based for most of her adult life in New York and Paris, reportedly saw Jean-Luc Godard's *Pierrot le Fou* as a teenager and decided to become a film-maker 'that same night'.[49] Recalling in an interview with Nicole Brenez that Godard's film 'was like nothing I'd seen before. I didn't know that films could be like that',[50] a sense of breathless possibility and boundless creative dynamism informs all her projects, from the short, explosive debut feature made in 1968, *Saute ma ville,* right up until *No Home Movie* (2016), her last, singularly inquisitive film.[51] Often aligned with a structural, semiotic or explicitly politicized cinema,[52] Akerman in interviews makes defiant case for the inassimilable quality of her work, adamant that fundamentally 'I am making Chantal Akerman's films'.[53] Couched in an insistent, *auteur*-esque tradition, and moving across documentary, narrative cinema, musical comedy, and more arthouse offerings, her filmography performs a sinuous resistance to classification or pigeonholing. In Chapter One, on

Akerman, focusing on two works from the 1970s (*Je, tu, il, elle* of 1974) and *Jeanne Dielman, 23 quai du commerce, 1080 Bruxelles* of 1975) and developing the study's ideas about luxury as an experience of expanded affect and protracted temporality, I argue that her formally meticulous, inventive films activate a quality of 'thick' time and space which, via their at times obstinate stretching of spectator patience,[54] deliver the viewer back towards a deeply embodied and indeed voluptuous mode of being in the present.[55]

Moving from cinema and installation art to recent excursions in French autofiction, 'photobiographie', and self-ethnography, in Chapter Two I shift to an examination of the autobiographical *récits* and experimental texts of metropolitan French author Annie Ernaux.[56] Born in rural Yvetot in 1960, and later relocating to Cergy-Pontoise, outside Paris, Ernaux follows Akerman in eschewing fixed positionalities of genre and aesthetic purpose, publishing anthropologically-inspired surveys of the choreographies of her local hypermarket alongside bold accounts of personally lived love affairs and diaristically gleaned records of experiences such as going through an abortion, or caring for an ailing parent.[57] Outspokenly endorsing an 'transpersonal writing' or 'écriture transpersonnelle' which employs the props and markers of self-narrative in order to extend communal templates for how to theorise a thinking 'life' out to reading others, I exploit, via analysis of her 1992 text *Passion simple* and 2001's *Se perdre*, this portion of the study to appoint Ernaux's vision of writing a 'sociology of writerly vacation', where the ego-self, via means of passionate limit-experiences, is dissolved, in the act of self-exposure, to make room for more collective structures.[58] Though in *Passion simple*, luxury is initially understood as the ability to enjoy and accumulate 'les manteaux de fourrure, les robes longues, et les villas au bord de la mer' [fur coats, long dresses and seaside villas] as her work develops in maturity the concept, I argue in my chapter, becomes more fluid and open-ended, less enthralled to the seductive reign of the commodity.[59] Moving from Bourdieu's notion of 'distinction' to more Nancean models of community, sharing, and sensory exposure I trace the evolution of an 'aesthetics of expressive motion' in Ernaux's work and its possible allegiances with both luxury and the moving image.[60]

Extending a conversation about art as a material and sensuous engagement with the diffuse textures of embodied life, Chapter Three takes as object of scrutiny the diverse visual, plastic, and sculptural media of the late Franco-American artist Louise Bourgeois. Born in Paris, producing the majority of her art in Manhattan and globally recognised for her ability to imbue corporeal landmarks such as childbirth, sexual intercourse, and death, and inchoate affective landscapes such as grief, anger, and eviscerating jealousy with material and three-dimensional aesthetic form, Bourgeois is not the most obvious candidate to draw upon for a creative reinvigoration of ideas of luxury. Yet, while her work has long been circumscribed by psychoanalytic registers of the 'part-object', the cathected 'fetish', and debates surrounding the 'good' or 'good-enough' mother, my intention in this analysis of her work is to rupture this cycle of compensation and perceived 'reimbursement' for past trauma.[61] Reading her work through an alternative optic of joyful creativity, generic promiscuity, and material and sensual enjoyment, I suggest, yields productive, generative consequences not only for the criticism of Bourgeois's corpus but for the reception of art made by women more broadly. Through readings of her mid-career soft 'breast'-shaped sculptures and her later, under-theorised 'Insomnia Drawings', a recasting of luxury in Bourgeois's work less as mode of indulgent melancholy than as the ability to range across various aesthetic media and imagine new expansive templates for erotic, gendered life has, I argue, distinct feminist import and potential for revisions of art history.[62]

In Chapter Four, oriented around the work of French conceptual and performance artist Sophie Calle, luxury finds its way back to the object, and in processes of making art closely imbricated in collecting, displaying, arranging, and adorning. Moving fluently between the gallery space, the streets of Paris, and more intimate domestic arenas, Calle's twenty-year career, I argue in my reading of her work, bespeaks a rich and complex relationship to the commodity and to art as 'objet fétiche': both interested in staging relational and immaterial encounters with the artwork as affective field of intersubjective possibility yet at the same time attentive to a deliberately honed aesthetics of curation, ornamented framing, and the stylised registers of pop accoutrements and kitsch.[63] Titling the chapter 'Sophie Calle: The Luxury of Taking Care', I examine the motifs of craft, order, detail, and control which appear recursively across Calle's projects in counterpoint to her experiments' parallel desires to abandon, lose, and embed the self in outrageous, exhibitionist, and incendiary public exposures. Looking at three works in particular: *Suite vénitienne* (1980), *Douleur exquise* (2003), and *Prenez soin de vous* (2007), I argue nonetheless that the idea of 'care' develops as her work evolves, becoming more and more invested in curating the experience of others and in developing aesthetic practices of collaboration which transcend individual output. Departing from Foucauldian accounts of 'le souci de soi' as an ascetic attempt at self-mastery, then, I explore via Calle's work whether an alternative imaginary of luxury as a form of 'refined sharing' and respectful encounter with otherness, difference, and plurality can be claimed.[64]

★ ★ ★ ★ ★

In her study *Wayward Lives, Beautiful Experiments: Intimate Histories of Riotous Black Girls, Troublesome Women and Queer Radicals*, Saidiya Hartman suggests that:

> Beauty is not a luxury; rather it is a way of creating possibility in the space of enclosure, a radical art of subsistence, an embrace of our terribleness, a transfiguration of the given. It is a will to adorn, a proclivity for the baroque, and the love of *too much*.[65]

After Hartman, to find possibility within spaces of enclosure, and from within discourses of fetishes, commodities, cuts, and costs which codify contemporary life, is my hope for what luxury might signify in this both contracted and expansive 'digital age'.[66] Inscribing paths to the exceptional and the disruptive from within closed contexts has long been configured as what cinema might singularly 'do', or contribute to the everyday. Jolting us out of thoughtless repetition, moving images indeed extend to us emancipating templates for encounters with a more expanded life. My ambition in this study is that luxury, as reinvigorated 'conceptual sensation' or mode of gestural plasticity, might install the same: or that it might reveal, by encouraging phenomenologies of slowing down, immersing in, attending to, and languishing on, an experience of stillness from within the harried flows of networked, mechanised, automated experience.[67] In staging coalitions with artworks across disciplines and in reclaiming luxury as a feminist project of embracing both shared and solitary creative pleasures, my hope is that luxury might be returned to its etymologies of 'light', 'bodies', *lux*, and *luxuria*. Challenging its negative associations with the fetish and commodity, my desire is that it might become an instrument for the embellishment and amplification of embodied life, disrupt the staidly homogeneous, and irradiate inversions in perception which enrich the everyday.

Notes to the Introduction

1. For an account of 'le caractère mouvant et protéiforme du luxe' [the mobile and protean character of luxury] in its contemporary incarnation see Olivier Assouly, 'Introduction', in *Le Luxe: essais sur la fabrique de l'ostentation*, ed. by Olivier Assouly (Paris: Le Regard, 2011), p. 16, or Gilles Lipovetsky and Elyette Roux who argue that 'sphère désormais plurielle, le luxe a "éclaté": il n'y a plus *un* luxe mais des luxes, à plusieurs étages, pour des publics divers' [An increasingly plural sphere, the idea of luxury has 'exploded': there is no longer just *one* luxury but luxuries plural, at different stages and for different audiences] (*Le Luxe éternel: de l'âge du sacré au temps des marques* (Paris: Gallimard, 2003), p. 15).
2. This now axiomatic concept is derived from Theodor Veblen, *The Theory of the Leisure Class: An Economic Study in the Evolution of Institutions* [1899] (Lenox, MA: Hard Press: 2010).
3. An idea of luxury as negativity beyond dialectical utility (*negativité sans emploi*) can for example be found in Georges Bataille's *Le Coupable*, in *Œuvres complètes*, 12 vols (Paris: Gallimard, 1973–88), v, 289. (I owe the details of this reference to Martin Crowley, *Duras, Writing and the Ethical: Making the Broken Whole* (Oxford: Clarendon Press, 2000.)
4. Though Lambert Wiesing has already used this phrase in 'Toward a Phenomenology of Luxury', *Cultural Politics*, 14.1 (2018), 78–89, he does so in relation to the German eighteenth-century writer Friedrich Schiller, and not in relation to a feminist aesthetics, nor to the moving image.
5. See, amongst others, Jocelyn Szczepaniak-Gillece, 'Smoke and Mirrors: Cigarettes, Cinephilia, and Reverie in the American Movie Theater', *Objects, Exhibition, and the Spectator*, special issue of *Film History*, 28.3 (2016), 85–113, and Susan Sontag, who in an elegiac *New York Times* essay on 'The Decay of Cinema', evokes the 'erotic, ruminative' rituals of the 'darkened theater' (Susan Sontag, 'The Decay of Cinema', *The New York Times*, 25 February 1996 <http://movies2.nytimes.com/books/00/03/12/specials/sontag-cinema.html> [accessed 17 February 2020].
6. See John David Rhodes, 'Art Cinema's Immaterial Labors', *Diacritics*, 46.4 (2018), 96–116 (p. 97).
7. See again Szczepaniak-Gillece, 'Smoke and Mirrors', p. 92. Karl Schoonover ('Wastrels of Time: Slow Cinema's Laboring Body, the Political Spectator, and the Queer', *Framework*, 53.1 (2012), 65–78) has seen the 'time-wasting' inherent to the specific experience of art-house cinema as a potential, contrarian source of 'queer value', though Rhodes has queried whether queer experience and the conceptual import of 'value' are not in fact frictional experiences ('Art Cinema's Immaterial Labors').
8. Roland Barthes, 'Leaving the Movie Theater', in *The Rustle of Language*, trans. by Richard Howard (Irvine: University of California Press, 1989), pp. 345–49 (p. 346).
9. See Samuel Johnson, *The Fatal Effects of Luxury and Indolence* (London: J. Bradley, 1778).
10. See Nico Baumbach, 'All that Heaven Allows: What is, or was, Cinephilia? (Part Three)' <https://www.filmlinc.org/daily/all-that-heaven-allows-what-is-or-was-cinephilia-part-three-cinephilia-2/> [accessed 18 February 2020].

11. See Girish Shambu, 'For a New Cinephilia', *Film Quarterly*, 72.3 (Spring 2019), 32–34. For a cinematic manifesto against metrics see Elena Gorfinkel, 'Against Lists', *Another Gaze* <https://www.anothergaze.com/elena-gorfinkel-manifesto-against-lists/> [accessed 18 February 2020]
12. For explicitly political readings of how slow cinema's decelerated temporalities proffer 'forms of resistance' to late capitalism's pressurised velocities, see Lutz Koepnick, *The Long Take: Art Cinema and the Wondrous* (Minneapolis: University of Minnesota Press, 2017); Alanna Thain, *Bodies in Suspense: Time and Affect in Cinema* (Minneapolis: University of Minnesota Press, 2017); and Todd McGowan, *Out of Time: Desire in Atemporal Cinema* (Minneapolis: University of Minnesota Press, 2011).
13. Elena Gorfinkel, '*Wanda*'s Slowness: Enduring Insignificance', in *On Women's Films: Across Worlds and Generations*, ed. by Iwone Margulies and Jeremi Szaniawksi (London: Bloomsbury Academic, 2019), pp. 27–48 (p. 45). Tiago de Luca and Nuno Barradas Jorge, 'Introduction', in *Slow Cinema*, ed. by Tiago de Luca and Nuno Barradas Jorge (Edinburgh: Edinburgh University Press, 2015), pp. 1–21 (p. 3).
14. See again Rhodes, 'Art Cinema's Immaterial Labors'.
15. Dan Kois, 'Eating Your Cultural Vegetables', *New York Times*, 29 April 2011 <https://www.nytimes.com/2011/05/01/magazine/mag-01Riff-t.html> [accessed 23 August 2020]. This mode of deep attention and luminous absorption is distinct from what Mauro Resmini diagnoses as a 'phenomenology of immediacy' in relation to the *cinéma du corps* or 'New French Extremism' extremely popular in France in the early 2010s ('Reframing the New French Extremity: Cinema, Theory, Mediation', *Camera Obscura*, 30.3.90 (2015), 161–87 (pp. 163–64)) For such a movement, luxury is understood principally in negative terms of extremity; intensity; and as a form of revelling in visual excess, or 'access to a pure realm of sensation' detached from formal or relational concerns. (p. 164).
16. An overly thematic concern is the effect of John Armitage's chapter, 'Luxury and Cinema', in *Luxury and Visual Culture* (London: Bloomsbury Academic, 2019), pp. 119–48, where cinematic luxury is understood as the 'transformation of luxury lifestyles in contemporary cinematic cultures' (p. 125) and on 'luxurious cinematic selves having to deal with lavish choices', such as in Harmony Korine's 2012 *Spring Breakers* (ibid). In *Afterimages: On Women, Cinema and Changing Time* (London: Reaktion Books, 2019), Laura Mulvey notes how the commodity '[depends] on a glamorous surface, attracting the eye of the consumer while erasing any trace of the labour power that had produced the product' (p. 20). For contrarian ideas of luxury as a certain, 'queer' re-evaluation of the surface or abstention from (hermeneutic) 'depths', see Rosalind Galt, *Pretty: Film and the Decorative Image* (New York: Columbia University Press, 2011).
17. This is also somewhat argued by Koepnick (*The Long Take*), for whom extended shot durations are posited as powerful mediums for exploring different modes of perception and attention in our fast-paced world of mediated stimulations.
18. See Laura Mulvey, 'Visual Pleasure and Narrative Cinema', *Screen*, 16.3 (Autumn 1975), 6–18.
19. Katharina Lindner, 'Queer-ing Texture: Tactility, Spatiality, and Kinesthetic Empathy in *She Monkeys*', *Camera Obscura*, 32.3.96 (2017), 121–54.
20. See for example Giuliana Bruno: 'Film moves, and fundamentally "moves" us, with its ability to render affects and in turn, to affect' (Giuliana Bruno, *Atlas of Emotion* (London & New York: Verso, 2007), p. 7.
21. Gilles Deleuze, *Cinéma 2: L'Image-temps* (Paris: Minuit, 1985).
22. See Martine Beugnet, *Cinema and Sensation* (Edinburgh: Edinburgh University Press, 2007), p. 58. Laura U. Marks also makes this point in 'Thinking Multisensory Culture', *Cinema and the Senses*, ed. by Emma Wilson, special issue of *Paragraph*, 31.2 (July 2008), 123–37.
23. See Eugenie Brinkema, *The Forms of the Affects* (Durham, NC: Duke University Press: 2014), p. xii.
24. See, amongst others, André Gorz, *The Immaterial* (Chicago: University of Chicago Press, 2010); Maurizio Lazzarato, *The Making of the Indebted Man* (Los Angeles: Semiotext(e), 2012); and Michael Hardt, 'Affective Labor', in *boundary:2*, 26:2 (Summer 1999), 89–101. See Yann Moulier-Boutang, *Cognitive Capitalism* (Boston: Polity Press, 2012).
25. Sarah Banet-Weiser, *Empowered: Popular Feminism and Popular Misogyny* (Durham, NC, & London: Duke University Press, 2018), p. ix.

26. For more on such an approach see Alice Blackhurst, 'The Defiant Muse', *Los Angeles Review of Books*, December 2019 <https://lareviewofbooks.org/article/the-defiant-muse/> [accessed 18 February 2020], and Iris Brey, *Le Regard féminin* (Paris: L'Olivier, 2020).
27. In broad terms, I understand 'sovereignty' — a charged concept which recurs under various guises throughout the book — here in the sense of, as Georges Bataille writes, 'Attitudes souveraines, c'est-à-dire gratuites, sans utilité, ne servant qu'à ce qu'elles sont, jamais subordonnées à des résultats ultérieurs' [sovereign attitudes, in the sense of gratuitous attitudes, without utility, serving only what they are, never subordinated to ulterior results]. In *L'Érotisme*, 'sovereign life' is further defined as 'an existence free of limits' (see Georges Bataille, *L'Érotisme* [1957] (Paris, Minuit, 2011), p. 195.
28. Michel Foucault, 'Une esthétique de l'existence', interview with A. Fontana, *Le Monde*, 15 July 1984, p. XI. For an excellent account of twenty-first-century Anglophone women artist's projects of autofiction and life-writing and their relation to shame, see Kaye Mitchell, *Writing Shame: Contemporary Literature, Gender and Negative Affect* (Edinburgh: Edinburgh University Press, 2020).
29. For an account of the rendering of women into passive subjects under capitalism more broadly, see Lazzarato, *The Making of the Indebted Man*, p. 27.
30. See Elizabeth Kowaleski-Wallace, *Consuming Subjects: Women, Shopping and Business in the Eighteenth Century* (New York: Columbia University Press, 1997), who argues convincingly that 'in the historiography of capitalism written by men, there is an emphasis on the presumed feminine propensity for "unproductive expenditure," qualified economically as expenditures for clothing, movable goods, flowers, jewellery, elaborate cooking, and ornamentation' (p. 57). See also Anne-Lise François, *Open Secrets: The Literature of Uncounted Experience* (Stanford, CA: Stanford University Press, 2008), p. 13.
31. See Hèlene Cixous, *Le Rire de la méduse et autres ironies* (Paris: Galilée, 2010), p. 68: '[La femme] ne "sait" pas ce qu'elle donne elle ne le mesure pas; mais elle ne donne ni le change ni ce qu'elle n'a pas. Elle donne plus; sans assurance qu'il lui reviendra de ce qu'elle donne un bénéfice même imprévu. Elle donne à vivre, à penser, à transformer. Cette "économie"-là, elle ne peut plus se dire en termes d'économie'.
32. I refer here to Pierre Bourdieu, *La Distinction: critique sociale du jugement* (Paris: Minuit, 1979).
33. I cite here from the *Trésor de la langue française*'s definition of *le luxe* <http://www.cnrtl.fr/lexicographie/luxe> [accessed 4 October 2015] (para. 1 of 53): 'pratique sociale caracterisée par des dépenses somptuaires'.
34. See <http://www.etymonline.com/index.php?term=luxury> [accessed 4 October 2015].
35. Paul B. Preciado, 'Learning from the Virus', *Artforum* (May-June 2020) <https://www.artforum.com/print/202005/paul-b-preciado-82823> [accessed 23 August 2020].
36. See Slavoj Žižek, 'Surplus-enjoyment: Between the Sublime and the Trash', *Lacanian Ink*, 15 (1999) <http://www.lacan.com/frameXV6.htm> [accessed 4 October 2015].
37. Adèle Van Reeth and Jean-Luc Nancy, *La Jouissance* (Paris: Plon, 2014), p. 113. Translations from original French into English in the main body of the book are my own, unless otherwise indicated.
38. See Laurence Benaim, 'Has Luxury Become a Dirty Word in France?', *Business of Fashion* (March 2019) <https://www.businessoffashion.com/articles/opinion/has-luxury-become-a-dirty-word-in-france-gilets-jaunes-yellow-vests-protest> [accessed 23 August 2020]. For an account of the centrality of luxury to the French psyche see for example Joan DeJean, *The Essence of Style: How the French Invented High Fashion, Fine Food, Chic Cafés, Style, Sophistication, and Glamour* (New York: Simon & Schuster, 2005).
39. Anne Boyer, *The Undying* (New York: Farrar, Strass & Giroux 2019), p. 161.
40. See Armitage, *Luxury and Visual Culture.*
41. Though theorising a philosophy of luxury through Deleuze might initially appear at odds with the thinker's seminal diagnosis of capitalism, in *L'Anti-Œdipe*, as a cannibalistic system which, having exhausted production and manufacturing as paradigms, depends on mining credit to consolidate a debt economy and the condition of endebted man, I incline towards a reading of Deleuze's thinking as providing templates for experiments in living, installing an affirmative ethics invested in what bodies can produce when in sensual collaboration with each other. See

Kathrin Thiele, 'To Believe in this World, as It Is': Immanence and the Quest for Political Activism', *Deleuze Studies*, 4 suppl. (November 2010), 28–45 <https://www-euppublishing-com.ezp.lib.cam.ac.uk/doi/10.3366/dls.2010.0204> [accessed 23 August 2020].

42. For an extensive discussion of the centrality of sense and sensuous life to Nancy's philosophy, see Ian James, 'Jean-Luc Nancy: The Infinity of Sense', in *The New French Philosophy* (Cambridge: Polity Press, 2012), pp. 53–78, and *The Fragmentary Demand: An Introduction to the Philosophy of Jean-Luc Nancy* (Stanford, CA: Stanford University Press, 2005).
43. See Jacques Derrida, *Given Time: Counterfeit Money*, trans. by Peggy Kamuf (Chicago: University of Chicago Press, 1994), p. 7.
44. Georges Bataille, *The Accursed Share*, trans. by Robert Hurley, 3 vols (New York: Zone Books, 1988), I, 23.
45. See for example Georges Bataille, *L'Érotisme* [1957] (Paris: Minuit, 2011), p. 95: 'c'est en nous le désir de consumer et de ruiner, de faire une flambée de nos ressources' [there exists within us a desire to consume and ruin, to set aflame our resources].
46. Georges Bataille, *La Part maudite* [1949] (Paris: Minuit, 2011), pp. 30, 32.
47. Lisa Robertson, 'Rose: A Carnal Becoming', *Cabinet Magazine*, 48 (Winter 2012–13) <http://www.cabinetmagazine.org/issues/48/robertson.php> [accessed 23 August 2020].
48. See again Bataille, *Théorie de la religion*, pp. 289, 369, 564; *L'Érotisme*, p. 241. In an essay written with Judith Butler, 'You Be my Body for Me: Body, Shape, and Plasticity in Hegel's Phenomenology of Spirit', in *A Companion to Hegel*, ed. by Stephen Houlgate and Michael Baur (Oxford: Blackwell, 2011), pp. 611–40, Catherine Malabou also argues, via Jacques Derrida's *L'Écriture et la différence*, that 'according to Derrida's Bataille, sovereignty would be the genuinely detached attitude, whereas mastery would be only another name for a servile overattachment to life' (p. 613).
49. Élisabeth Lebovici, 'No Idolatry and Losing Everything that Made You a Slave: Chantal Akerman', *Mousse*, 31 (November 2011) <http://moussemagazine.it/chantal-akerman-elisabeth-lebovici-2011/> [accessed 24 August 2020].
50. Nicole Brenez, 'Chantal Akerman: The Pajama Interview', *Devils, LOLA Journal*, 2 (2011) <http://www.lolajournal.com/2/pajama.html> [accessed 5 October 2015].
51. For a celebration of Akerman's courageous intermediality, see Marion Schmid, 'Chantal Akerman: Filmmaker, Video Artist, Writer', in *Chantal Akerman: Afterlives*, ed. by Marion Schmid and Emma Wilson, Moving Image, 9 (Cambridge: Legenda, 2019), pp. 150–63. For a further homage to Akerman as a 'radical innovator of forms [...] spanning a dazzling array of genres and formats', see Marion Schmid and Emma Wilson, 'Introduction', in *Chantal Akerman*, ed. by Schmid and Wilson, pp. 1–6 (p. 1).
52. See Ivone Margulies, *Nothing Happens: Chantal Akerman's Hyperrealist Everyday* (Durham, NC: Duke University Press, 1996), p. 24, and Claire Johnston, 'Towards a Feminist Film Practice: Some Theses', in *Movies and Methods Volume II*, ed. by Bill Nichols (Berkeley: University of California Press, 1985), pp. 315–27; Brenda Longfellow, 'Love Letters to the Mother: The Works of Chantal Akerman', *Canadian Journal of Political and Social Theory*, 13.1–2 (1989), 73–90; and Judith Mayne, *The Woman at the Keyhole: Feminism and Women's Cinema* (Bloomington: Indiana University Press, 1990), p. 133.
53. See Chantal Akerman and Angela Martin, 'Chantal Akerman's Films: A Dossier', *Feminist Review*, 3 (November 1979), 24–47 (p. 24).
54. See for example Dirk Lauwaert, '23, quai du Commerce, Brussels: On Chantal Akerman', *Sabizian* (February 2019) <https://sabzian.be/article/23-quai-du-commerce-brussels> [accessed 23 August], who opines of Akerman's iconic film, 'It was authoritarian, brutal and painful'.
55. By centering alternative motifs such as pleasure, nomadism, ritual, and gestures of queer sexuality, my discussion distances itself from more traditional Akerman scholarship investigating questions of displacement, exile, trauma, and ambivalent maternity in the late filmmaker's work.
56. See Nora Cottille-Foley, 'L'Usage de la photographie chez Annie Ernaux', *French Studies*, 62.4 (October 2008), 442–54.
57. Annie Ernaux, *Regarde les lumières mon amour* (Paris: Broché, 2014); *L'Événement* (Paris: Folio, 2000); and *Je ne suis pas sortie de ma nuit* (Paris: Folio, 2007).

58. Annie Ernaux, 'Vers un je "transpersonnel"', *RITM*, 6 (1993), 219–22.
59. Annie Ernaux, *Passion simple* (Paris: Folio, 1992), p. 1.
60. Tom Paulin, 'Writing to the Moment', *Writing to the Moment: Selected Critical Essays, 1980–1986* (London: Faber & Faber, 1996), pp. 215–39 (p. 220).
61. For a reading of Bourgeois's work in psychoanalytic terms, see particularly Mignon Nixon, *Fantastic Reality: Louise Bourgeois and a Story of Modern Art* (Cambridge, MA: MIT Press, 2005), and Rosalind Krauss, *Bachelors* (Cambridge, MA: MIT Press, 2000).
62. Yves-Alain Bois and Rosalind Krauss argue for Bourgeois's indulgent melancholy in *Formless: A User's Guide* (New York: Zone, 1997).
63. For a reading of Sophie Calle's art in terms of an 'art relationnel', see Nicolas Bourriaud, *Esthétique relationnelle* (Paris: Le Réel, 2001), p. 31.
64. See Michel Foucault, *Histoire de la sexualité, tome 3: Le Souci de soi* [1984] (Paris: Gallimard, 1994).
65. Saidiya Hartman, *Wayward Lives, Beautiful Experiments: Intimate Histories of Riotous Black Girls, Troublesome Women and Queer Radicals* (New York: Serpent's Tail, 2019), p. 33.
66. See Mark Fisher, *Capitalist Realism: Is There No Alternative?* (London: Zero Books, 2009).
67. I borrow the phrase 'conceptual sensation' from Lisa Robertson, *Cinema of the Present* (Toronto: Coach House Books, 2014) p. 32. My argument takes further inspiration from Laura Mulvey's *Death 24x a Second: Stillness and the Moving Image* (London: Reaktion Books, 2006), which suggests that in changing a spectator's apprehension of cinematic and narrative time, digital technology reveals the stillness and repose at the heart of the traditional film experience.

CHAPTER 1

Chantal Akerman: An Experience of Immersion and Duration

> I want the spectator to have a physical experience, for him or her to feel time. Films are generally made to literally and metaphorically pass the time. But I want you to experience the time of a character. I don't want you to just go through an emotional experience, but also another kind of experience, like with music, that is unique because it is purely physical. — CHANTAL AKERMAN[I]

The films of Chantal Akerman embed lush explorations of solitude, space, silence, and desire within coolly geometric frameworks. Eager to immerse and situate the spectator in the real-time cadences and rhythms of lived experience, yet disclosing at the same time influence from formally astute, minimalist filmmakers such as Andy Warhol and Michael Snow, they measure an aesthetics of affect, visceral materiality, expenditure, and yielding against highly rigorous, consciously enforced, structural constraints. This balancing act, as Ivone Margulies has observed, both aligns Akerman's cinema with a 'hyperrealist' practice of the everyday and encourages escape from it.[2] In Akerman's work, both an immanent film praxis of immersion and duration, and a more transcendent interest in the singular moments which, born of excessive violence, instinct, or sexual revolt, fissure the surface of daily existence, are insistently affirmed.[3]

In this chapter, I annotate two of Akerman's earliest and most enduring works — *Je, tu, il, elle* of 1974 and *Jeanne Dielman, 23 quai du commerce, 1080 Bruxelles* (hereafter *Jeanne Dielman*) of 1975 — to encounter luxury as a phenomenological experience of immersion and duration afforded by the medium of cinema. I argue that, whilst haunted by motifs of distance, displacement, and indelible personal and historical trauma, Akerman's luminously spacious films — composed of unencumbered, elongated long takes, decadently static fixed frontal framing, and the non-hierarchical recording of quotidian detail — invite a sensual, haptic, and indeed 'luxurious' re-engagement with the body in an era of acute physical remoteness and virtual reality.[4] Her films' thick, intimate attention to everyday life and exploration of novel economies of desire and pleasure prompt, I suggest, a deeper inhabitation of the spectatorial body in space and time and unfold modes of luxurious contemplation, attentiveness, but also, in the absence of montage, jump-cuts, and almost all forms of what Patricia Patterson and Manny Farber call 'filmic spicing', a voluptuous capacity for reverie and drift.[5] Shrewd focus on Akerman's production from the 1970s specifically (which also encompasses the Manhattan shorts *La Chambre* (1972) and *Hotel Monterey* (1973), plus *Les Rendez-vous d'Anna* (1978) and urban epistolary drama, *News from Home* of 1977) acknowledges the period as one of, in Akerman's own terminology, particular 'openness' and intellectual 'freedom' while also showing how its formal inventiveness set the stage for more expanded forms of cinema practised by the filmmaker later on in her career.[6] Departing from a more thematic focus, in this chapter, then, luxury becomes a formal possibility and a felt sensation in the body;[7] a co-production on the part of the spectator and the filmmaker in forefronting the surfaces and the materiality of the cinematic image; and a process, as Deleuze writes on Akerman in his book *Cinéma 2: L'Image-temps*, of 'showing gestures in their fullness', or of giving space to existential amplitude and aesthetic plenitude.[8]

While the chapter argues that *Jeanne Dielman*'s and *Je, tu, il, elle*'s exercises in temporal endurance invite forms of intricate attention to the pro-filmic object and to spaces of projection which feel absorbing and secluded,[9] it is careful to affirm that they do not endorse a model of uncomplicated cinephilia, nor any straightforward rehabilitation of 'visual pleasure' as corrosively critiqued by Laura Mulvey in her landmark essay from 1975, 'Visual Pleasure and Narrative Cinema'.[10] In distinction, a Deleuzian commitment to allowing gestures and modes of embodied life to burgeon and become on their terms on screen harbours, both from a formal and political perspective, an acute feminist import, liberated both from the possessive gaze of mere absorption (and from limited ideas of luxury as mere passive consumption) and the objectifying contours of the famed 'male gaze'.[11] In refusing to cut 'into a hundred pieces', the predominantly feminine bodies that her camera traces on screen, Akerman, as expressed in a 1977 interview in *Camera Obscura*,[12] not only marshals against objectification but lavishes women's daily, routinised, and corporeally inhabited experiences with a sense of dignified integrity.[13] In positioning the mundane markers of everyday life (feeding oneself and dependents, waking, sleeping, cleaning) and less urgently 'essential' tasks such as sex, drinking coffee, smoking, and writing letters on the same diegetic 'plane of immanence', to quote Gilles Deleuze and Félix Guattari, she affords the grinding repetitions of women's domestic, emotional, but also sexual labour space and time, a luxury with which such work is rarely bestowed.[14]

In her inventive phototext *Autoportrait en cinéaste*, published on the occasion of her career retrospective at the Centre Pompidou in 2004, Akerman cites Georges Bataille in relation to her cinema, specifically his observation from *L'Érotisme* that 'tout problème en un certain sens est un problème du temps' [every problem in a certain sense is a problem of time].[15] Throughout the chapter, taking cue from Akerman's direct citation of Bataille's work, I employ observations from Bataille's texts *L'Érotisme* and occasionally *La Part maudite* in order to position my reading of luxury here as primarily a temporal category, as, mediated through the filmic encounter, the phenomenological opportunity to 'feel time', as Akerman herself describes, as a visceral experience enriched with sensuous potential.[16] In *Jeanne Dielman*, which I discuss in the first half of the chapter, Akerman affords us the presentation of three different temporal modes. In the first third of the film, I argue, Akerman unfolds a time of full, uninterrupted duration or what Adam Roberts calls 'unmodulated continuity'; in the second, as Jeanne's painstaking routine begins to splinter and she experiences orgasm against her will and commits murder, a time of epiphanic irruption is explored; and in the final, yet essential, seven-minute coda of the feature, a temporality of what I term 'post-evential languor' where both Jeanne and the spectator 'come back to their senses' and steep in sensory impressions and texture memories, is installed.[17] All three chronologies, I suggest, can be encountered as luxurious in their dislocation of ordinary rhythms and subsequent exposure of regimes of exception and novelty. In the second half of the chapter, I suggest that Akerman's earlier and structurally looser film *Je, tu, il, elle* engages broadly with a multisensory presentation of unproductive time, unhinged from gendered and societal expectations. *Je, tu, il, elle*, I show, in depicting 'immaterial' states of voluntary isolation, secluded creative retreat and unscheduled nomadism breaks obstinately from the fabric of the capitalised working day to stage instead a bacchanalia of non-production. In both films, a feminist resonance accrues not only from the time granted to invisible regimes of women's labour but from the protagonists', in both features gradual emancipation from pernicious cycles of sexual debt and exchange. Confronted with, as Elena Gorfinkel observes, the 'cruelties of subsisting in the exhaustion of just being, in facing, time and again, the circumscribed terms of [a woman's] value, a value defined by men, by capitalism, by law', both Jeanne Dielman and Julie, the protagonist of *Je, tu, il, elle*, refuse such circumscription, becoming 'luxurious outlaws'.[18] They embrace their marginality and the new tempos of time, longing, and sensation that living on the fringes of commodified existence disclose.

Voluptuous Rupture, Luxurious Reprieve: *Jeanne Dielman, 23 quai du Commerce, 1080 Bruxelles*

Chantal Akerman's 1975 film, *Jeanne Dielman, 23 quai du commerce, 1080 Bruxelles*, commonly affirmed as both her breakthrough work and timeless masterpiece, follows the domestic rituals and rhythms of a Brussels woman in her forties, played by Delphine Seyrig, and her leading of a double life as a housewife and a prostitute.[19] Such an existence — stringently choreographed and compartmentalised, suspicious of contagion from the outside world or any granular infraction of routine — is given full expression via Akerman's aesthetic praxis of extended takes, and a policy, via an affected, yet strictly adhered to, 'real time' chronology, of full duration and an attentive *être-avec* (being-with), or luxuriating in, the filmic image.[20] Though the diegesis of the film mounts an exhaustively maintained resistance to luxury and pleasure in the sense of sexual release and erotic *jouissance* — Jeanne so wary of conflating domestic and erotic labour that she lives her life with antiseptic strictness — my reading here suggests that formally, the film stages a voluptuous production of surfaces, a capacious framing, and an expanded sense of temporality.[21] That the camera is allowed to so radically linger over the full scope of Jeanne Dielman's life, or that it is painstakingly permitted to 'take its time', invests the screen, I argue, alongside readers of Akerman's work such as Ivone Margulies and Maria Walsh, with a particular surfeit of details and visual extravagance.[22] Its deliberate stagnation in the cadences of cinematic temporality furthermore inflates and rehabilitates the viewer's own relationship to their embodiment. Emancipated from distraction or from other escapist mechanisms of narrative, we are brought back to ourselves. As Akerman herself has noted, 'Attendre le plan suivant, c'est aussi et déjà se sentir vivre, se sentir exister' [Waiting for the next shot is also and already to feel oneself alive, to feel oneself exist].[23]

The film begins, somewhat in tension with its title's direct address or intense convocation of its subject, with a shot of the eponymous Jeanne Dielman with her back to the camera, refusing correspondence, putting some potatoes on to boil. The sequence is meticulously sketched, fully prone to its conceit. Yet, other than the ambient noises of the task at hand, there is no dialogue, or no voice-over to lend the salve of further context. All language has been rinsed clean from the scene as the spectator is abandoned to the full duration of the chore: immersed, without the habitual anchors of narrative cinema, in gesture, repetition, ritual, and the particular modalities of this one specific action.

Against the backdrop of this seeming 'visual chastity',[24] or what Deleuze appoints the 'austere theatricalisation' of Akerman's aesthetics, unfolds, however, the subtler phenomenological luxuries of the film's approach.[25] In refusing to grant the spectator a face-to-face encounter with its key protagonist or to affix closely to her body, her expression, or the sphinx-like landscape of her features, the film clearly puts checks on the audience's unfiltered consumption of Jeanne's image;[26] refuses any facile rapture or uncritical absorption in its diegesis, what Laura Mulvey has described as the limiting 'visual pleasure' of fascination.[27] At the same time, Akerman's defending against psychological depth, signalled by the camera distance she maintains from Jeanne, and reportedly, the strictly minimal and gestural way in which she directed Delphine Seyrig, declining to provide her with any 'psychological motivation' for her character's obsessive choreographies, liberates the film from hermeneutic wrangling and forefronts a more sensual preoccupation with materiality and surfaces.[28] The retreat from semiotics and keen tropism towards a more corporeal and gestural economy further spotlights presence, pose, the loving precision of ritual, and the luxury of witnessing corporeality present and alive before us. Mulvey writes in 'Visual Pleasure and Narrative Cinema' how:

> The first blow against the monolithic accumulation of traditional film conventions (already undertaken by radical film-makers) is to free the look of the camera into its materiality in time and space and the look of the audience into dialectics, passionate detachment.[29]

Already in the opening two minutes of the scene, Akerman's detachment from the conventional anchors of cinematic representation — character, backstory, voice — passionately steeps us in alternative sensory regimes of the body, extends us the gift of, as Deleuze has written of her cinema, 'a new exploration of the body'.[30]

In the middle of *Jeanne Dielman*'s initial sequence, the audience, gradually attuning to the film's abundant symphony of sounds — the roiling gas of the stove cooker, the running water as Jeanne thoroughly cleanses her hands, the evocative click of Delphine Seyrig's patent heels as she glides ceremoniously across the kitchen tiles, all of which affirm the film as a turn away from scopic bias — hears a shrill ring which approximates the 'ding' of a functional egg-timer but is in fact the front door.[31] The sound in no way fazes Jeanne; rather, she is perfectly, exactingly prepared for it. Suggesting that this is an integrated part of her routine, she languorously takes off her blue-checked housecoat, checks again on the stove and turns off the light as she, unhurried, exits the kitchen to greet the caller. It is a client, one of whom she receives every afternoon and sexually services in the precise fifteen-minute window that it takes for that evening meal's potatoes to cook.

In contrast to the full, meticulous choreography afforded to the kitchen chores, as soon as Jeanne answers the front door from the downstairs corridor and takes her client's coat, hat, and scarf, Akerman conspicuously starts to cut away from the proceedings. Applying strategies of radical ellipsis and omission, she curtails the audience's voyeurism and refuses to indulge what Roland Barthes identifies as 'l'espoir de voir le sexe' [the desire to see the sex] at play in mechanisms of narrative desire.[32] Instead, we see the john only from behind as Jeanne, with the halting choreography of a formal waltz, strictly escorts him to the room she has assigned for such activities, his face and hands deliberately out of frame as he commences to disrobe for the encounter. The carnal luxury of coital rapture or, in conventionally pornographic terms, the 'money shot', is obscured as the interior of such a boudoir remains rigorously out of bounds.[33] Instead, the only sign registered by Akerman that the event has taken place is a change to the quality of daylight in the corridor which, by the time Jeanne and the john re-emerge, has drained down from the honeyed waves of dusk into the dark, bruising blue of early evening.[34]

In reference to her 1978 feature *Hotel Monterey*, a devoutly formal film replete with shots of corridors and rooms and heavily inflected by the structural devices of 1970s experimental cinema, Akerman has reported how upon re-watching the piece, she felt it to be — despite its lack of traditional portrayals of sexuality — a highly 'erotic' film. In her words, 'When I saw *Hotel Monterey* again this morning, I really thought it was an erotic film. I felt that way — *la jouissance du voir*'.[35]

A similar sensation permeates the first third of *Jeanne Dielman*, which derives its luxury, its *jouissance*, in looking, not from the austere automation of the diegesis — which acutely chronicles the rhythms of what David Harvey calls 'the body as accumulation strategy', burdened by the pressures of financialized life — but from the friction of diverse sensual and formal registers being brought into vibrating co-existence.[36] Such friction conjures a form of *jouissance* for the spectator, more intricate and multi-layered than the blunter regime of mere 'visual pleasure'. One source of visual overflow bestowed upon us by the film comes from the sheer length of the frontal shots, whose elongated, even extravagant duration produces a luxurious 'surplus' of information, what Margulies beautifully terms 'the excess of detail that results from a fixed stare'.[37] The space given in *Jeanne Dielman* to what Margulies further appoints 'the images between the images' permits a floating away from action and the sporadic move towards abstraction: the luxury of 'drawing away', as the etymology of abstraction emphasises, from narrative progress or events to embrace a more aesthetic realm of beauty and order, of colours, images, and atmosphere.[38] In further reference to *Hotel Monterey*, Akerman has articulated this process at work in her films, the erotic oscillation between visual drift and embodied presence, departure and return:

> When you look at a picture, if you look just one second, you get the information, That's a corridor. But after a while, you forget it's a corridor, you just see that it's yellow, red, that it's lines, and then again it comes back as a corridor.[39]

As Jeanne finalises this transaction with the john, the corridor comes back as a corridor. The formal decadence of the domestic space, 'ornate with the written vestiges of silence', impresses on the audience as Jeanne methodically returns him his coat and he, wordlessly and awkwardly, fumbles in a pocket to locate her some cash.[40] 'A la semaine prochaine alors' [Until next week then], he eventually stutters. To this statement of habitual arrangement Jeanne makes no indication of assent or even minor acknowledgment. Still pristinely coiffed, she says nothing, takes the money, and as she shuts the front door briskly switches the hall light back off. After a beat, the respectful distance of Akerman's camera proceeds to track Jeanne as she moves into the dining room, a shrine to bourgeois ornaments and fussy post-war trinkets, where she quickly folds the bills into a china soup tureen which stands upon a centrally placed dark wooden table.[41] With automatic crispness, Jeanne is then seen to return to the kitchen, where she readies the potatoes, now cooked, to be drained.

Despite the sensory lushness of the film's opening few minutes, the closed circuit of this first sexual transaction, or the explicitness with which Akerman indexes the exchange of erotic services for money, in addition to the way Jeanne carefully conserves the funds within the soup tureen immediately afterwards, aligns Jeanne Dielman's lifestyle in the first third of the film with Bataille's concept of a 'restricted economy'. In contrast to a 'general economy' of freedom, contingency, and the sovereign abandonment to luxury in the sense of an emancipation from debt or conventional propriety, for Bataille a 'restricted economy' is marked by ascesis, 'servile' conservation, laborious *travail*, and disciplined restraint.[42] In counterpoint to luxury's qualities of festiveness, consumption, and lavish wasting, in *L'Érotisme* Bataille writes that a restricted economy 'exige une conduite où le calcul de l'effort, rapporté à l'efficacité productive, est constant. Il exige une conduite raisonnable, où les mouvements tumultueux qui se délivrent dans la fête et généralement, dans le feu, ne sont pas de mise' [demands a conduct where the calculation of effort, conducive to productive efficiency, is constant. It demands reasonable conduct, where the tumultuous movements which take place during parties and generally within festivity, are not admitted].[43]

Consistent with its opening temporal regimen of elongated continuity and uninterrupted duration, no tumultuous movements infringe upon the first third of Akerman's film. The first day of the film's tri-diurnal structure is indeed balletic, unhurried, placid in its serenity. Following the client meeting, Jeanne glides into the room reserved for such encounters and begins to strip the protective towel from the bed, to place it in the laundry basket, and to smooth down the only slightly ruffled linen. Marion Schmid, in her monograph on Akerman, has read such practiced movements as the advent of a 'complex purification ritual' whose objective is to cancel out the prior sexual exchange by means of sanitising, efficacious gestures.[44] Yet though Jeanne Dielman's motions are brisk, they are seamlessly performed, mesmerisingly enacted, and incur no pinch of worry upon Delphine Seyrig's enigmatic and hypnotic countenance.

A subsequent protracted shot of Jeanne taking a bath illustrates what Michelle Orange has called the 'fruitful ambivalence' at the core of Akerman's portrait, its oscillation between sensory envelopment and luxury, and a protocol of austere hygiene.[45] The scene, accented by seafoam-green porcelain tiles and pastel-hued pink walls is sumptuously framed; imbued with cinematographer Babette Mangolte's radiant attention to colour, texture, plushness, and fabric. At odds with this exquisite tableau, nonetheless, intra-diegetically Jeanne embarks on feverishly scouring down her body and the bath around her. Wearing an abrasive exfoliating mitt, she 'scrubs away', as Carol Mavor writes, at her own capacity for comfort and at the image's potential for erotic contemplation.[46] Though it is a scene which offers glimpses of Seyrig's bare breasts, Dielman's reticence to horizontally surrender to the bath's warm waters, her kinetic hyper-vigilance, refuses to re-circulate the images for explicit, pornographic purposes. Akerman, again, refrains from homing in on isolated body parts or from penetrating Dielman's psychic undercurrents. The effect, by virtue of the hazy, soporific pinks and greens, is lulling, soothing, and stilling, as opposed to titillating or exciting.[47]

The scene's fastidious formal attention to symmetry, outline, and a Baudelairean sense of balance, in concert with Jeanne's avid policing of the boundaries of her body after she has sold it for sex, at the same time can be mapped more soberly onto the backdrop of the Holocaust, which freights the entirety of Akerman's production.[48] The luxury of 'staying on the surface of things', or of keeping up appearances, which Jeanne so carefully invests in, becomes not only an aesthetic but an ethical and even political stance when it is a matter of preventing an onslaught of horrific memories and disorienting residues, or a fracturing 'return of the repressed'.[49] Natalia, or 'Nelly', Akerman's mother, tragically lost her sister to the inhumanities of Auschwitz, where, as a young woman, she was also imprisoned. In numerous interviews and reported essays on *Jeanne Dielman*, Akerman has confirmed inklings that the specificities of her protagonist are grafted from her mother's own, post-traumatic aversion to the *horror vacui*, or the gaping void of the unknown. In an interview with Élisabeth Lebovici for *Mousse* magazine, she is even more explicit, underscoring how 'my fixation with borders comes from the camps'.[50]

The phobia of touching on the depths of the Holocaust's splintering trauma motors the first third of the film's ornamental exteriority;[51] its commitment to luxury, at first, as a 'restricted economy' of propriety, cleanliness, conservation, and containment.[52] As the film shifts into the second of its three successive days in Jeanne Dielman's life, Akerman gradually reveals this stance as flawed; exposes it as vulnerable to fragmentation, nonetheless. As cracks begin appearing in Jeanne's routinised existence, a new concept of luxury as voluptuous abandon and what Bataille would term the 'sovereignty' of an unprecedented 'acte gratuit' starts, enticingly, to glimmer.[53]

The film's vulnerable undercurrents sputter to the surface following an incident with a client on Day 2, which, consistent with the film's shrouding of Jeanne's sex work, the spectator does not see. Yet, breaking with the patterns which until now have postscripted such encounters, on her way out of the downstairs bedroom, Jeanne, the expression on her face a shade less glacial than usual, visibly forgets to turn off the hall light as she leads the man to the front door. This minute disruption sets off a whole chain of subsequent ancillary diversions, opening the film's aesthetics of rehearsal, seriality, and repetition to excess and the uncanny.[54] As a result of the delayed sign-off with the client, the lid of the soup tureen is not replaced, the potatoes for that evening's dinner are burnt, and Jeanne's hair and impeccable outfit jolted conspicuously out of place. Such visual disruptions, enacting an aesthetic surplus in excess of normative functioning, carry over into the third day, too. A quest for a button in various haberdashery shops across Brussels embarrassingly fails; a baby that a friend has entrusted Jeanne to look after for a few short minutes rejects her over-eager embrace; and her habitual spot in her local café — perhaps the one moment of pleasure Jeanne permits herself in the context of her otherwise punishing schedule — has been taken over by another woman. A subsequent attempt, at home, to make herself a pot of coffee and to sit and drink it is parodically inflated into a painful, almost touching performance as Jeanne, deciding that her efforts are inadequate and taste strange, repeats the process until an end point of unsatisfied exhaustion. The next morning she wakes up too early, flopping with resigned defeat into a green armchair in the living room with no outstanding chores to execute. Daniele Dubroux diagnoses how at this point of the film Akerman confronts her protagonist with 'dead time', or with the blank surplus of an extra hour which threatens to encroach and engulf by virtue of its emptiness.[55]

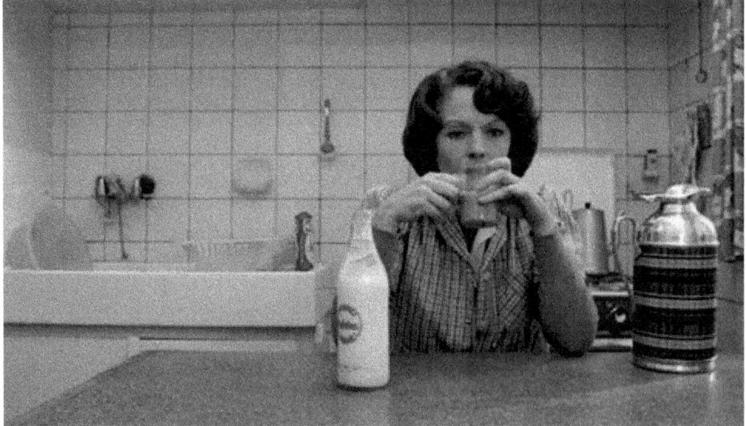

Fig. 1.1. Chantal Akerman, *Jeanne Dielman, 23 quai du Commerce, 1080 Bruxelles* (1975)

Though clearly sources of acute anxiety for Jeanne, these wrinkles in the film's hitherto unruffled, placid surface — what Deleuze calls the 'smooth' space 'unstriated' by societal impingements — on a formal level reveal time as malleable and labile, or as harbouring potential for sensory stretching.[56] They prepare the spectator for the imminent revelation of temporality as elastic and ecstatic exposed by the film's climax, where a luxury of prolongation and of 'taking time' is over-written by the radiance of the incisive instant or the exceptional 'event' so lavishly imagined by Bataille. This shift in temporal logic, though perhaps abruptly registered by the spectator, is consistent with the dialectical swing between order and abandon, wildness and inertia which inflects all of Akerman's wide-ranging corpus. It irradiates her multivalent brilliance, which reaches to encompass multiple modalities, idioms, and genres.

The Ecstatic Rupture of the Instant

Foregrounding its exceptionality within the film's structure, and alignment with a temporality of novelty and the unforeseen, the murder is prefaced by an unexpected parcel sent to Jeanne's front door. Moving with conspicuous surprise into the bedroom where she usually receives clients to open it, the packaging proves cumbersome, unwieldy. In order to unwrap it, Jeanne is inspired to fetch a pair of sewing scissors from her dresser, which cut away to reveal, delicately wrapped in layers of tissue, a pink silk nightgown. The object's frivolity, its' sumptuous luxury in both colour and fabric, momentarily dazzles Jeanne, lifting her out of her mundane existence. In a passage resonant with how this surprise offering sets off a process of disturbance and dislocation in the film's diegesis, Derrida, in the work *Given Time, Counterfeit Money*, theorises how the figure of the gift is able to suspend hermetic circles of economy and transactional exchange.[57] He writes:

> On ne peut pas traiter du don sans traiter de ce rapport à l'économie [...]. Mais le don, s'il y en a, n'est-ce pas aussi cela même qui interrompt l'économie ? Cela même qui, suspendant le calcul économique, ne donne plus lieu à échange? Cela même qui ouvre le circle pour défier la réciprocité ou la symétrie, la commune mesure, et pour détourner le retour en vue du sans-retour?
>
> [One cannot treat the gift, this goes without saying, without treating the relation to economy, even to the money economy. But is not the gift, if there is any, also that which interrupts economy? That which, in suspending economic calculation, no longer gives rise to exchange? That which opens the circle so as to defy reciprocity and symmetry, the common measure, and so as to turn aside the return in view of the no-return?][58]

Though Jeanne's rapture in the moment points towards a similar opening, a shrill ring of the doorbell lands to interrupt this defiance of exchange. Introducing the materiality of the outside world, the sound signals that her client for the afternoon has arrived. Hastily, she stuffs the nightgown and its adjacent packaging underneath the bed.

The sequence that ensues, in which the usually coolly disaffected Jeanne appears to sexually climax against her will, an acute sense of struggle and dismayed resistance visibly contorting her features, forfeits Akerman's elongated and balletic plateaus of domestic repetition to expose a different rhythmics of sensation, affect, and embodied pose.[59] That this is an unprecedented moment in both Jeanne's life and the film's unfolding continues to be emphasised by Akerman as the audience is led to understand that, for the first time, we will be allowed to 'see the sex'. At the same time drawing attention to the tableau's mediation, its complex bonds to the experience of framing, witnessing, and being seen, Akerman somewhat loosens the rigid chastity of her fixed frontal position as Jeanne is perceived taking off her blouse via the reflection of her dresser's mirror. The irruptive sound of a man's cough at the margins of the image is, at first, the only signal that her client is also in the scene.

Further thwarting the established tempo to which the spectator of *Jeanne Dielman* has grown accustomed, the murder is the sole event within the film's 'real-time' unfolding not to be showcased in full duration; to be uniquely subject to staccato moves and jumps in editing. A praxis of immersion and luxurious distention of the image is,[60] indeed, replaced with quick cuts, abrupt truncation, and a punctuated camera movement which curtails our leisurely absorption of the scene.[61] The sequence's initial invitation to intimacy is revised by the camera's incisive guillotining, which indexes the presence of this very present moment, its trenchant singularity.[62] Abandoning the film's prior languor, what Rob Nixon calls slowness's 'attritional lethality', after unintentionally orgasming Jeanne indeed lies only very briefly in appalled repose, before extricating herself from the client's pinned embrace and repairing to her dressing table to locate her clothes.[63] Visibly disturbed as she buttons up her blouse, on a downbeat she grabs the sewing scissors stacked by her perfumes and definitively, without the barest wisp of hesitation, stabs the john, who is still luxuriating in post-coital stillness. The action is abruptly searing: jolting the spectator out of indolent passivity and mesmeric drift.[64] At the same time, the act's authoring by a pair of sewing scissors — possibly enacting the double fold or 'hinge' of the feminine, after Luce Irigaray — as opposed to a more obviously phallic knife, invites associative links with feminine *jouissance*;[65] with waves of ambivalent affect, friction, and desire.[66] In their co-authored volume on the application of Bataille's thinking about entropy and dissolution to contemporary art and art history, Rosalind Krauss and Yves-Alain Bois speak about the former's concept of pulsation as 'an endless beat that punctures the disembodied self-closure of pure visuality and incites an irruption of the carnal'.[67] This echoes the murder scene's deliberate pivot away from its earlier, more optical preoccupation with façades and with surfaces towards a more anarchic, multi-sensory embrace of gesture, sound, tonality, and rhythmic displacements.

In both *L'Érotisme* and *La Part maudite*, Bataille speaks of an intransitive expenditure ('dépense') which inevitably follows periods of diligent work or accumulation, and which catapults 'servile' subjects out of the allotted forms of a restricted economy.[68] Such a 'mouvement violent', made of 'brusque surprise qui [...] bascule et retire à l'esprit le repos [brusque surprise which [...] shake the mind out of rest], have as motoring principle a desire to 'déborder [la] pensée rationnelle, que le travail implique' [overcome the regimes of rational thought implied by work].[69] The ultimate manifestation of such an overcoming is, Bataille suggests, the *crime passionnel*, which represents 'la plus grande satisfaction voluptueuse, à l'assouvissement du désir le plus fort' [the most voluptuous satisfaction; the satiation of the strongest form of desire].[70] Underscoring the 'impersonal' abandonment of such an act, resonating with Deleuze and Guattari's depersonalised currencies of affect and desire, Bataille further emphasises how, 'dans la violence de ce mouvement, la jouissance personnelle ne compte plus, seul compte le crime et il n'importe pas d'en être la victime: il importe seulement que le crime atteignit le sommet de crime' [in the violence of this movement, personal *jouissance* no longer counts; what counts is solely the crime, of which it is unimportant to be the victim: all that matters is that the crime reaches peak crime state].[71]

In the preface to a novel appearing in the same year as *L'Érotisme*, *Le Bleu du ciel*, this 'violent movement' is glossed in more explicitly temporal terms as an unforeseen 'moment' or 'sursaut de rage' [sudden spurt of rage] able to make contact, in its sacrificial and unobligated nature, with novel modes of living otherwise.[72] In a passage applicable to *Jeanne Dielman*, and to Akerman's forfeiting of audience expectations in order to touch upon different regimes of sensation it is ventured by Bataille that 'le récit qui révèle les possibilités de la vie [...] appelle un moment de rage, sans lequel son auteur serait aveugle à ces possibilités' [the narrative which reveals the possibilities of life [...] calls forth a moment of rage, without which its author would be blind to life's possibilities].[73]

Rooted in a lexicon of insight and exposure, such a statement poses luxury as the elucidation of potentiality, as, attentive to the 'lux' embedded in its syntax, a radiant disclosure of alternative perspectives, telegraphed by the abundance of mirrors, frames, and *mise en abyme* devices indulged by Akerman in this brief scene. Even more critically, in its allusion to revealed terrains of further vision and discernment, Bataille's thinking in *Le Bleu du ciel* opens space for a reading of Jeanne's violent act as less a reactive 'breakdown' than an incisive breakthrough, making contact with the singular and new.[74] In such a context, indeed, the murder becomes an opening, able to dissolve and lift the pressures of duration and sequential, rehearsed, fictional time in order to inhabit the more open-ended landscape of real time. It abandons, in Bataille's terms, the 'servitude' of a general economy characterised by 'la pesanteur paralysante des routines et exactitudes superficielles' [paralysing weight of routine and superficial exactitude] in favour of the unknown of a future in which lawful and secure positions have been sacrificed.[75] In so doing, it accesses what Bataille appoints the domain of 'ecstatic time' aglow with the shimmer of irruptively accessed, mysteriously enigmatic worlds.[76]

Luxurious Reprieve

> My mother had started to slightly
> glow, turning into an ecstatic, without
> air, it was like those clearings, as if something
> was there though her spirit was no longer confined
> there. She was free of her life. — SHARON OLDS[77]

In a 2012 article exploring the dialectics of agitation and gratification in narrative cinema, Adrian Martin pinpoints a tendency within slow film towards ending abruptly on explosive, unforeseen events: towards replacing the cumulated, platitudinal time of *chronos* with the fissuring chronology of *kairos*, and towards the detonation of established temporal continuums in order to make space for singularity, dynamism, and exuberant encounters with the new.[78]

Such a trope can logically be traced in Akerman's short, debut feature *Saute ma ville*, where the laying of her head upon a still-lit stove during the film's final sequence by the young female protagonist, played by Akerman herself, ends the work on a decisive bang, abandons the work's slow, languorous build-up of gestural tension to outright explosion.[79] In her *Autoportrait en cinéaste*, Akerman suggests that her attachment to explosive modes of being and creating is embedded and deep-rooted: 'j'explose de temps en temps' [I explode from time to time], she muses. 'Après l'explosion, je rentre à nouveau en moi et je reste là pendant des mois comme hébétée' [After the explosion, I retreat once again within myself and I stay there, dumb-founded, for months].[80]

Following her spontaneous, self-funded apprenticeship in Manhattan, where she established contact with *Jeanne Dielman*'s cinematographer, Babette Mangotte, and devoured intricate, formalist masterworks by Jonas Mekas and Michael Snow, Akerman discovered other modes of temporality beyond the fissuring and the explosive. In his monograph on Akerman, Jérôme Momcilovic indeed notes how Snow's 1971 experimental documentary piece, *La Région centrale*, composed of slowly intensifying circular pans and entirely pre-programmed movements, were instructive, showing Akerman

> ce que peut le cinéma après l'explosion, quand la caméra balance sans plus personne à regarder et ramène dans son mouvement seul tout le drame, tout le suspense qu'on avait d'un mensonge réservé au récit et à la figure humaine.[81]
>
> [what cinema can do after an explosion, when the camera evens out without anyone to look at and recuperates within its movement all the drama and suspense we prior attributed towards a human figure.]

The result was the enigmatically abstract, deliberately depopulated *Hotel Monterey*, and the shorter, sphinx-like excavation of a single-room, *La Chambre*, made up, in homage to Snow, of exacting 360-degree mechanical tours of the four walls of a New York living space.

In an interview with Nicole Brenez, Akerman recounts how, simultaneously on the festival circuit for her film *India Song* also starring Delphine Seyrig, Marguerite Duras questioned Akerman's inclusion of the murder in *Jeanne Dielman* following its premiere at Cannes. 'She said that she wouldn't have filmed the murder, she

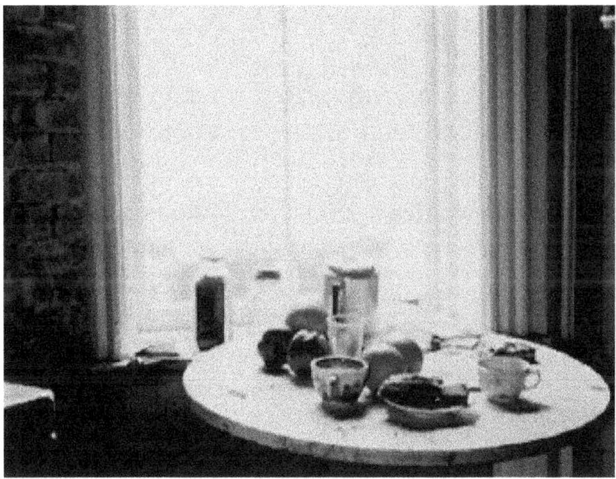

FIG. 1.2. Chantal Akerman, *La Chambre* (1977)

would have made a 'chronicle,' Akerman states.[82] Such a view was also echoed by Jonas Mekas, who saw the film's sensationalist apex,[83] indexing a moment of pure visual spectacle antithetical to its prior carefully composed 'cinema of care', as a concession to nakedly commercialism which deflected from the film's impressive cerebrality and structural devotion.[84] With trademark insouciance and sovereign defiance, nonetheless, Akerman, in a different interview, disputed readings of her film as 'selling out' to violence and high drama, reminding viewers of the fact that *Jeanne Dielman* does not terminate with its protagonist's incisive act but continues to unfurl an extended, stretched-out, and lushly indexed shot of seven minutes: 'There are seven really very strong minutes after [the murder],' Akerman quips.[85]

With minimal narrative or indeed commercial 'value', the scene, registering Jeanne sitting in repose at her downstairs dining-room table, daubed with blood and steeping in the aftermath of her exceptional abandonment to violence, luxuriates in stasis, release, and the rapture that postscripts moments of considerable tension. Replete with the exacting symmetry that furnishes a Dutch still life or *vanitas*, post-coital languor is replaced with post-murderous voluptuousness, in a feminist reversal of habitual chronologies that allows Jeanne to reclaim some time and space of her own.[86] Extra-diegetically, the *tableau vivant* further introduces space within the film's momentum for absorption, contemplation, reverie, and drift, disrupts the film's hitherto grid-like aesthetics of insistent verticality, and opens a more spherical economy of stillness, waiting.[87] From an audience perspective, it allows us a degree of pause following the jolting and abrasive stabbing, and re-imagines 'visual pleasure' as a haptic engagement with texture, light, and the material presence of a body vibrantly alive in space. Forfeiting the instant gratification of a legible conclusion, it extends an offer of a pleasure that is more sustained: an invitation to immerse oneself within a co-productive and embodied mode of spectatorship closely resonating with Deleuze's concept of an 'affection-image'.

Writing in *Cinéma 1: L'Image-mouvement*, Deleuze defines the affection-image as an image making possible the manifestation and absorption of 'pure qualities', and an image 'in between' action and perception, concerned less with the unfolding of a plot per se than with the creation of spaces and atmospheres.[88] Such spaces and atmospheres are, in his terms, 'unstriated' or uninterpellated by subject-object definitions — defined instead as temporally and anomically labile.[89] As he suggests:

> Il s'agit de dépasser le subjectif et l'objectif vers une forme pure qui s'érige en vision autonome du contenu. Nous ne sommes plus devant des images subjectives ou objectives. Nous sommes pris dans une corrélation entre une image-perception et une conscience caméra qui la transforme.[90]
>
> [It's a question of overcoming the subjective and objective and embracing a pure form which establishes itself as a vision independent from 'content'. We are no longer in front of subjective or objective images. We are taken into a correlation between a perception of the image and a camera consciousness which transforms it.]

Emphasising the fecundity of the affection-image, its abundance of 'virtual' potentiality unhooked from typical spatiotemporal co-ordinates,[91] Deleuze continues:

> L'espace [de l'image-affection] garde une seule et même nature: il n'a plus de coordonnés, c'est un pur potentiel: il expose seulement des Puissances et des Qualités pures, indépendamment des états de choses ou des milieux qui les actualisent. Ce sont donc les ombres, les blancs, les couleurs qui sont aptes à susciter et constituer des espaces quelconques, espaces déconnectés ou vides.[92]
>
> [[The space of the affection-image] retains one sole, consistent quality: it has no co-ordinates, it represents potential in its purest form: it exposes only Powers and pure Qualities, independent from the state of things or the spaces which actualise it. It's therefore shadows, whites and colours which are apt to provoke or constitute its space, disconnected and emptied.]

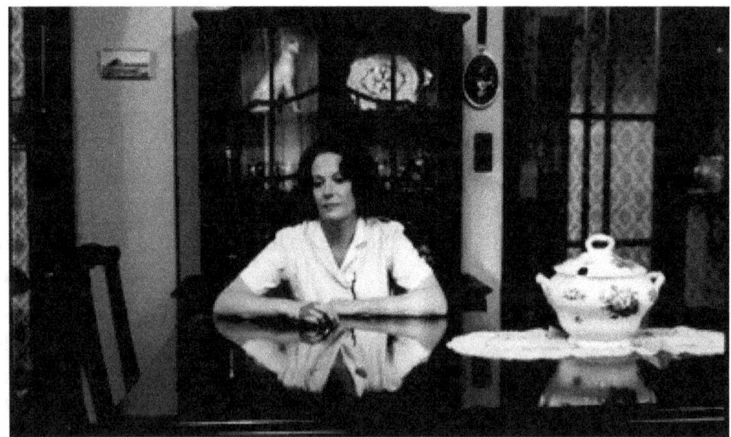

FIG. 1.3. Chantal Akerman, *Jeanne Dielman, 23 quai du Commerce, 1080 Bruxelles* (1975)

In the final, seven-minute coda of *Jeanne Dielman*, Deleuze's evocation is fleshed out by the thirdness of the dining-room space, caught between the domestic hub of the kitchen and the fraught transactions of the bedroom, by the stillness and immersive quality of the scene's rich framing, and by Akerman's non-judgmental, patient filtering of the post-evential scene. It is made manifest by the dense textural attention to the dark tint of the table's wood, the white starch of Jeanne's dress, and the tannic stain of the client's blood, which indent the space with a fragile form of intimacy. Jeanne, indeed, simply sits while the camera, in contrast to its earlier exhaustive and excessive display of detail, glosses over her half-smiling, visibly palliated face, calmly registering the aftermath of the incisive act.[93] Having catapulted herself out of the petty cycle of sexual debt and exchange, Akerman's protagonist, humming quietly under her breath, indeed, visibly exudes serenity — no longer a consumable or marketable object, but, having made such a radical and uncalculated sacrifice, no longer a servile subject, either. For Bataille, such exoneration from fixed pronominal positions in order to return to a kind of elemental form, the 'calme du repos' or 'l'immanence profonde de tout ce qui est' [the profound immanence of all that is] is the precise definition of sovereignty,[94] re-conceived not as power over but as emancipation from and immersion in: 'liberté *dans* l'instant, indépendante d'une tâche devant être accomplie' [freedom *in* the moment, independent of a sense of a task having to be completed].[95]

In contrast to the murder's temporality of exception and aesthetics of irruption, the effect of this shot, for both Jeanne and the spectator, is of calm absorption, glossed by Lauren Berlant as 'a sense of being held in a scene, of having reciprocity, and being unanxious somewhere'. The sense is of a somnolent floating in the present, what Akerman calls a 'senti flottant' [floating feeling] rather than entrapment in a constant, fraught *ressassement* [rumination] of the past.[96] Though the film begins by compiling an exhaustive portrait of a woman who is so resistant to the blank state of an hour, to the daunting temporal and spatial vacancies of the *horreur vacui*, that she is committed to 'killing time' by whatever means necessary, it ends with a killing which makes time irrelevant; with what Bataille calls the luxury of total annihilation accessed by the sovereign subject, whose privilege is never having to explain themselves, 'ne devant de comptes à personne' [owing no account to anybody].[97] Indeed, the scene is conspicuous in its refusal to explain, contextualize, or further gloss the gory murder, sourcing its potency purely from textural and haptic — as opposed to hermeneutic — details. Here, Akerman's protagonist has exactly realised Annie Ernaux's fervently expressed desire to 'aller jusqu'au bout' or to push against the very limit-points of visceral experience.[98] In this serenity of absolute annihilation and exhaustion of a scene, both Jeanne and the spectator, Akerman suggests, can enter into the receptive state of the affection-image, steer closer to sensation than signification. With no higher place for the diegesis to formally or logically 'go', for the spectator there remains no further interpretative labour to be done, other than the act of receiving the sequence of images, of learning to be prostrate and receptive.

Despite the scene's appeal to the ecstasy of sovereignty and entropy, its summoning of, to borrow words of Slavoj Žižek in response to Jacques Lacan's account of *jouissance*, a 'mystical beatitude beyond speech, exempted from the symbolic order', certain anchors and indices of productive time and the external world do in fact persist, calling into question how far a complete escape from the confines of a 'restricted economy' is being signalled here by Akerman.[99] Even as Jeanne appears to retreat totally into the relief afforded by the breaking of the cycle of interminable and transactional sexual encounters, a light from the open window flickers — possibly an emergency vehicle judging by its jerky, on-off movements.[100] It projects patterns onto her daydreaming face, suggesting the inscrutable beam of the outside, as well as the numerous legal consequences imminently on the horizon. Its blueish tint further threads portents of emergency through the otherwise serene classical balance of the tableau. In addition, the soup tureen — the financial centre of the household in which Jeanne secretly stashes her fees — sits unmoved, ominously on the table, and remains in shot throughout the duration of the coda.[101] The sustained verticality of its presence disrupts the otherwise soft sphericality and languor of Jeanne's abandonment. The character's slumped posture, her slight incline towards it, registers a kind of deference towards the humble object, a resigned acknowledgment that while she may have momentarily suspended the mechanics of the sexual marketplace, its shadow still looms large.

Such affective remainders presented by Akerman challenge a philosophy of absolute expenditure, sacrifice, and non-relational, radically solitary sovereignty. They also question how far we might ultimately engage with an experience of immersion, exposure, and escape from the numbing templates of routine whilst the props of capital are, so to speak, still on the table. Continuing a dialogue with an ethics of suspension rather than with one of total fracture and abandon, it is tempting to read Jeanne's half-smile, in the final seconds of the feature, as a knowing one: as knowing that this respite from lawful and accounted-for being can only be temporary.[102] By such means the feature's 'luxury' becomes ephemeral, elusive, a momentary flicker of the light. By such means Akerman's cinema would, in keeping with her manifesto to explore 'the images between the images', become one of intervals, born, in Kathleen Stewart's words, 'of a momentary suspension of narrative [...] a quivering in the stability of a category or trajectory, a glitch in the projects we call things like the self, agency, home, a life'.[103]

In *Cinéma 2*, Deleuze writes that sometimes, 'Il faut faire des trous, introduire des vides et des espaces blancs, raréfier l'image, en supprimant beaucoup de choses qu'on avait ajoutées pour nous faire croire qu'on voyait tout. Il faut diviser ou faire le vide pour retrouver l'entier' [It is necessary to make holes, to introduce voids and white spaces to rarify the image, so it doesn't become cliché, it is necessary to make a division or make emptiness in order to find the whole again].[104]

To invite a void, a space for sensory absorption, spreading out, rapture, and contemplation is, for both Jeanne and her audience, the function of Akerman's expansive, lavish seven-minute coda, where the residual pleasures of immersion and duration are re-installed. Though the murder incisively exposes Akerman's spectator to contingency, violence, and the ecstatic novelty of the event, and the feature as a whole semaphores an abject phobia of falling into the 'black holes' of history and of the psyche, *Jeanne Dielman* affords us space, in its final composition, to take shelter, find reprieve.[105] This, perhaps, is the gift of its luxury and offering: a quick sketching of potentiality before the light spills out, definitively fades. A dreaming scene, a pause from the pressures of the market, if only for a minute. A hiatus. A glitch, before the reel rolls on.

Je, tu, il, elle: Languorous Unproductivity

> Il y a sexe là où il n'y a pas production, résultat, position d'un terme quelconque.
>
> [There is sex where there is no production, result, position of any term.] — Jean-Luc Nancy[106]

Je, tu, il, elle, filmed in Belgium in 1973, begins, like *Jeanne Dielman*, with its back to the spectator. It shows a young woman, played by Akerman herself, sitting on a hard-backed chair in the middle of a room otherwise abundant with plush furnishings, in the wake of the departure of a girlfriend.[107] In ways further familiar to Akerman's most famous feature, *Je, tu, il, elle* richly re-imagines tropes of rote 'visual pleasure' and mobilises a detachment from fatigued tropes of commercialised female sexuality on screen.

Unlike *Jeanne Dielman*, however, whose ambition is to fill time and space with the repletion of ritual, *Je, tu, il, elle* aspires to a radical evacuation of the landmarks which consolidate 'productive' experience and stages an embrace of stasis, indolence, indulgence, and peripatetic purposelessness (or 'nomadism') in contrast to *Jeanne Dielman*'s initial policy of hyperkinesis and surface surveillance.[108] *Je, tu, il, elle*, indeed, bears witness to a period of mourning and permissive contemplation in which, Akerman's voiceover recounts, the protagonist Julie remains 'immobile, attentive... accouchée sur mon matelas' [immobile, attentive... lying on my mattress], aimlessly lounging and voluptuously loitering in her apartment in order to avoid a hostile outside world. This sheltering is often diagnosed by viewers of the film as a strategy resisting the eviscerating force of loss, yet also, I intend to argue in this section of the chapter, subtends an active form of sensual enjoyment, of pleasure taken in deliberately staged inertia.[109] In coalition with Bataille's model of the *informe*, or spiral, which lavishly uncurls as opposed to ecstatically 'exploding', I will subsequently read the movement of the feature as entropic, or, in Bataille's terms, 'une luxueuse dilapidation d'énergie' [luxurious dilapidation of energy] which extends *Jeanne Dielman*'s irruptions of affect into dissipations, and replaces the precision of direct address with, as performed by the film's title, a decadent displacement of identity.[110] Such diversions and detours from prescribed routes of cinematic pleasure and gratification cultivate, as in *Jeanne Dielman*, the luxury of intuiting alternative temporalities of affect and desire, into which the spectator can embed and embody themselves.[111]

For Gilles Deleuze, writing specifically on *Je, tu, il, elle* in *Cinéma 2*, the film's deemed 'feminine' aesthetics of slow sensuality, ritualised gestures, and a gradual absorption of and by the image, becomes more than a stylistic choice, but an ethics and a politics. It becomes a means of overcoming entrenched histories, of carving refuge from chaos.[112] In a passage resonating with his controversial concept, coined together with Félix Guattari, of *devenir-femme* or 'becoming-woman', broadly translatable as a dialoguing with life on the level of vibrations, affects, and intensities

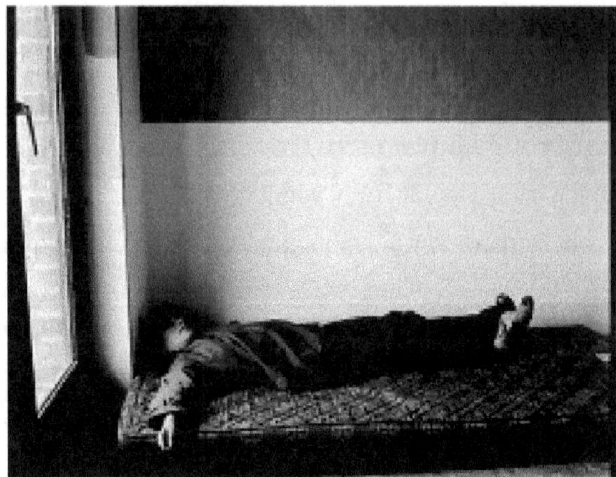

FIG. 1.4. Chantal Akerman, *Je, tu, il, elle* (1974)

rather than of institutions,[113] yet often fiercely interpreted as a literal appropriation of feminized bodily properties, Deleuze notes indeed how in Akerman's films, 'Les états du corps sécrètent la lente cérémonie qui relie les attitudes correspondantes, et développent un gestus féminin qui capte l'histoire des hommes et la crise du monde' [The states of the body secrete the slow ceremony which joins together the corresponding attitudes, and develop a female gest which overcomes the history of men and the crisis of the world].[114]

Yet, in its evocation of withdrawal and appeal to new, embodied modes of perceiving, Deleuze's reading of the film also tessellates with Maurizio Lazzarato's broader meditation on Marcel Duchamp's 'refusal of work', and the latter's encouragement of a 'renunciation, a non-movement, a radical *désœuvrement*, an unworking or inaction, and a suspension of production' in order to 'carry out a reconversion of subjectivity, to invent new techniques of existence and new ways of living time'.[115] As I will go on to show, *Je, tu, il, elle*, in excess of its perceived feminist ambitions, invests in generative 'reconversions of subjectivity' from the hazing of its titular pronouns to the framing shot of its opening few minutes to indeed expose new paradigms of living differently.[116] The film moves between three discrete explorations of incalculable temporality and non-penetrative, radically anorgasmic sexuality: firstly, what I call 'voluntary captivity', where Julie, the protagonist, experiments with creativity and autoeroticism in confinement; secondly, nomadism and itinerancy as she hitchhikes with a lorry driver; and thirdly an itinerantly non-romantic, indeed arguably 'queer' form of sexuality as she calls upon her former girlfriend and they make love in a sensuously non-teleological fashion.[117] It echoes *Jeanne Dielman* in its assertion of luxury as the pleasure of suspended duration and refusal to insert oneself within certain symbolic economies, yet approaches such an exploration in distinctly different temporal and spatial modes.

Voluntary Captivity

Motivated to refine a specifically feminine gestural economy thick with the materialities of visceral experience, *Je, tu, il, elle*, like *Jeanne Dielman*, wilfully resists the forwards march of narrative and instant visual gratification and ventures, as Deleuze notes, a haptic 'cinéma du corps' as balm against a cinema of capital and calculation.[118] In the latter film, in order to eject the viewer from passive cinematic norms of straightforward consumption, Akerman cast Delphine Seyrig in the title role, an actress so renowned for her queenly, feminine demeanour and untouchable, regal beauty that she was generally unimaginable as a housewife. In *Je, tu, il, elle* Akerman, inserts her own corporeality into the frame, a strategy aimed not at defamiliarising but at bringing the audience into closer and more intimate proximity with their own spectating bodies, in concert and collaboration with the feature. An insistence on participation, yet also upon subjectivity itself as an imaginative space fertile with erotic and creative possibility, determines the first section of *Je, tu, il, elle.* Toggling between desire for shelter and desire for indefinite adventure, its' 'Je' cultivates a feminist politics of unapologetic self-citation, yet also, by means of retreating from productive society, the luxury of self-evasion, or the 'extra-vagance' of wandering beyond how a woman should ideally look and behave.[119]

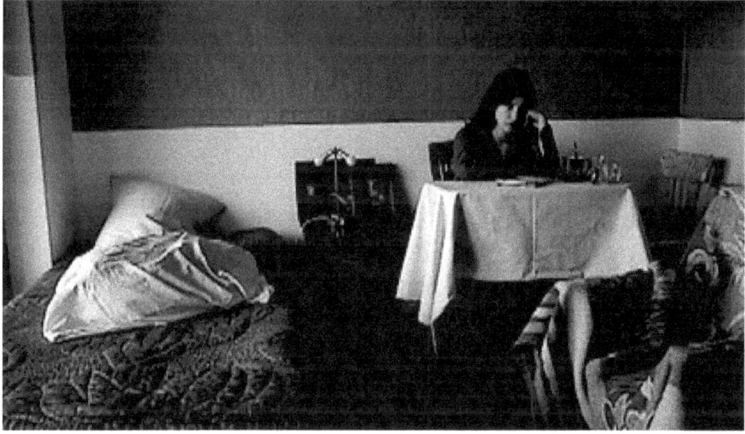

FIG. 1.5. Chantal Akerman, *Je, tu, il, elle* (1974)

In *Je, tu, il, elle*'s initial thirty minutes, the desire for dwelling and for authoring an insulating 'room of one's own' in the grip of devastating heartbreak is arrived at, somewhat perversely, through a process of divestment.[120] The initial note of resolute paralysis lent by the first shot — of the young woman at the piece's centre slumped inertly in a chair — transmutes into a burst of manic energy as the voiceover narrates her decision to repaint the furniture in her apartment uniformly blue, then green, and then to radically remove such furniture, so that only an uncovered mattress, visibly dismantled from its frame, remains.[121] The sudden excavation is in tandem expressed by the disjointed progression of Akerman's filmed tableaux: moving jerkily to show us the young woman first sitting on a hard-backed chair, then at a desk, with her head in her hands, in a different room, and finally stretched out on a sofa, staring unabashedly at the camera in echo of *La Chambre*'s deliberately staged 'female gaze'.[122] Concluding the sequence, the camera then proceeds to register the protagonist pushing a wooden chair, with manifest effort, across the apartment floor: replacing unapologetic leisure with obvious exertion.

Whilst such actions may seem punitive — gesturing towards ascesis and towards a bid for simplification and refinement in the wake of emotional devastation — they also tangibly make space for Julie's retreat from productive society and accommodate a full, expansive expression of her grief unencumbered by the gaze of the outside. Following the exportation of the furniture, the room feels bigger, she tells us ('Vide, la chambre est plus grande, je trouve'). A sense of stifled-ness and of the protagonist being encroached upon by her domestic items, or the feeling, as Rita Felski notes, that we can feel 'owned by what we own', opens out onto a ventilated sense of reprieve from the commodity's obligated usefulness, and establishes a space as yet undented by societal and market demands.[123] Having pushed the furniture out of the bedroom, Akerman as the young woman throws herself without reserve onto the mattress. The scene is in thrall to solitude, to the pleasures of aloneness and autoerotic contact, resonating with Akerman's observation made in her later documentary *Là-bas* that when left to her own devices, 'Je me replie sur moi-même' [I fold in upon myself].[124] In line with this general ambiance of permissiveness and accommodation, the camera no longer performs quick, jumpy cuts but full, uninterrupted surveys of the space: probes and excavates, takes care.

Further writing on *Je, tu, il, elle* in *Cinéma 2*, Deleuze argues that, 'Cloitrée dans la chambre, l'heroine de *Je, tu, il, elle* enchaîne les postures asilaires et enfantines, involutives, sur un mode qui est celui de l'attente, en comptant les jours: une cérémonie de l'anorexie' [Cloistered in a room, the heroine of *Je, tu, il, elle* links involutive refuge and infantile postures in a mode which is that of waiting, counting the days, a ceremony of anorexia].[125]

Such an observation helps to align Akerman's work with the concept of the time-image, and its immanent relation to duration. While the movement-image is defined by the relentless advancement of plot and action, the time-image, in contrast, immerses the spectator in a slow cumulus of gestures and attitudes. Deleuze's reading of the film as a 'ceremony of anorexia' further telegraphs how *Je, tu, il, elle* extracts pleasure from withdrawal, from a certain obstinate refusal to absorb, or partake of, the habitual consumptions of productive society.[126] His diagnosis of a certain atmosphere of 'involutive refuge' or playful *attente* distills the first part of the feature's preference for a burlesque, irreverent regression into the self, or for the luxury of solace, retreat, indulgence, and seclusion over a connection to the outside world.[127]

Initially the feature's temporality, as in *Jeanne Dielman*, is assiduously mapped and tautly circumscribed. Akerman's voice, in droning, litany-like fashion, mediates the narrative of her romantic catatonia in quasi-biblical fashion as she recounts how, in response to her grief, 'J'ai peint les meubles en bleu le premier jour. Je les ai repeint en vert le deuxième jour' [On the first day, I painted the room's furniture blue.

On the second, I repainted it green]. In total, she will stay sequestered in the flat for twenty-eight days, a number dense with ritualistic and religious resonance (and typically the stretch of time assigned to purifying fasts, or cleanses). Her quantitative rationing, or in Deleuze's words 'counting of the days', appears pre-meditated and ascetic, undergirded by the impulse of what Anne-Lise François terms 'the poetics of the count'.[128] The sense indeed is of killing, rather than of lavishly wasting time, of transitively 'getting through' the hours.

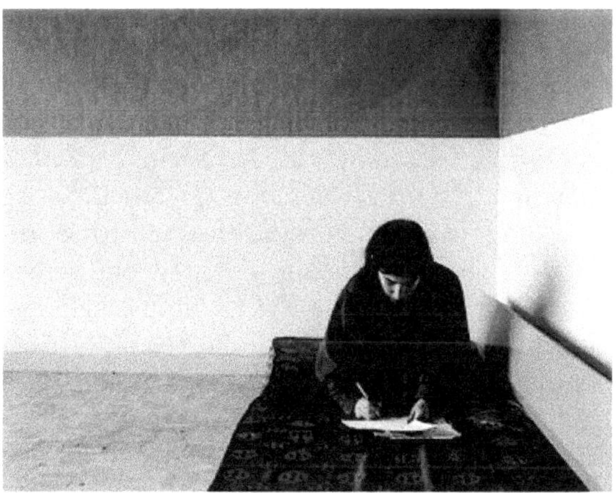

Fig. 1.6. Chantal Akerman, *Je, tu, il, elle* (1974)

Somewhat challenging Deleuze's reading, as Julie starts to feel more comfortable within the space, her 'countdown' conceit is less strictly adhered to, and eventually forgotten altogether. At first listless and cerebrally anaemic, indulging in gratuitous and futile exercises such as using her mattress to block the light from a window before moving it back to the floor again, on the sixth day she decides to start writing a letter to the ex who jilted her, becoming incrementally absorbed in, and enraptured by, the act. Faithful to her filming policy of painstaking respect for the women's bodies that she registers on screen, Akerman tracks this process of absorption silently, and from a fixed, set distance, refusing to intrude upon the intimacies of her character's creative process. We are not made privy to the contents of the letter, which remain opaque, withheld from our consumption. That the letters end up never getting sent iterates their intransitivity, the futility of their luxury.[129]

In the film, writing's estrangement from the sphere of productivity and 'work' is clearly signalled by Julie's composition of the letter in a slackened, horizontal position. She writes supine, spread out on her mattress, arranging recently completed pages on the floor around her like a cocooning structure, a provisional *habitus*, or nest.[130] Eschewing the typical props or postures of the writer, this voluptuous, luxurious approach to the demands of *l'écriture* is further underscored by Julie's desultory eating of sugar from a bag while drafting a second letter to her ex. 'J'ai recommencé la même lettre et mangé beaucoup de sucre en poudre' [I re-started the same letter and ate a lot of granulated sugar], Akerman's lilting voiceover attests.

The effect appears less 'anorexic' than unrestrained, excessive, indulgent.[131] Julie eats with abandon, suggesting a desire for self-dilapidation and an urge to — in line with Bataille's account of luxury in *La Part maudite* — expend resources, fritter, and pointedly stop 'taking care'. Highlighting this instinct, Akerman makes a point of showing her protagonist, on repeated occasions, tipping the sugar she has previously been subsisting on languorously out onto the floor (at one point, telling us non-committally, 'J'ai renversé tout le sucre' [I spilled all the sugar]) and thereby abandoning sensible impulses towards storing, hoarding, or accumulation to a more extravagant economy of squandering. Such a policy not only seems to sanction a defiant mode of consumption for consumption's sake but appears symbolically, historically loaded.[132] To waste an item that was so rarefied, fetishised and rationed in the straitened days of the Second World War seems indeed, as Akerman boldly recounts in her *Autoportrait*, a perverse mode of 'rebellion' against her family's history, a way of keeping some autoerotic pleasure back for herself.[133] Extra-diegetically, the sound of the sugar being scattered out across the floor further extricates the sequence from a purely optical economy, helping to insert it within more diffuse, multi-sensory contexts of the auditory and tactile.

Mirrored by the stilled, protracted nature of the section's lush, panoramic shots which frame and lend attention but never perform commodifying close-ups of the female body, such a process of abandonment to interior space, and to deliberate, intransitive expenditure feels unscarred by the constraints of need. It semaphores the 'in-itselfness' of pleasure rather than the restless forwards motion of desire. In such a context, luxury, as well the ability to sink immanently into a space, becomes a kind of surrender to unknowingness, an embraced state of voluntary passivity, a freedom from time or intricate chronology performed by woozy statements such as, 'Je me demandais ce qui m'arrivait' [I asked myself what had happened to me] and 'J'ai encore attendu que ça passe ou qu'il arrive quelque chose' [I kept waiting for it to pass or for something to happen]. With striking relevance to *Je, tu, il, elle*, Saidiya Hartman writes of how withdrawal from oppressive measures of productive time conjures a 'looking otherwise, by retreating within, by a radical withholding that makes visible and palpable all that is held in reserve — all that power, love, brilliance, labor, and care'.[134]

At the same time, such radical passivity, Akerman suggests, also accesses a state of letting oneself be traversed by incremental differences and possibilities, and a certain openness to the exterior. Increasingly, as Julie's sojourn in the flat continues, signs of life from the external world interrupt the sense of dense seclusion: footsteps from passers-by, rain lashing the windows. Briefly, the reflection of a visibly male stranger appears at the flat's back patio doors, fracturing the sense of haptic 'involution' into the self and feminine autoeroticism and introducing a desire to be looked at and appraised by others ('Je suis restée immobile et nue pour que d'autres qui passent puissent me regarder' [I remained naked and motionless, so that others could come and look at me], the voice-over notes). The sighting prompts Julie out of her torpor, motivating her to get dressed and ultimately to leave the house to begin the second, more nomadic part of her journey. At the same time, her sudden gravitation to the outside world does not draw any decisive lines under her depression, but, as Akerman's film continues, initiates a dialectics between a desire to collapse into the self and to extend out towards others: what Gilles Deleuze, in his work on Francis Bacon, calls an undulating movement of the 'fold' that reaches out as much as it regresses.[135] In contrast to *Jeanne Dielman*'s cumulative build towards explosion, then, *Je, tu, il, elle*, as the pronominal itinerancy of its title signals, cultivates the luxury of being able to shift back and forth between several subject positions; both the full, sensual enclosure of a *je* or self, and, as the next section of the feature demonstrates, a more 'masculine' economy, or *il* of a life adrift, unhooked from the domestic and motored by the brutal and indifferent tempos of the road.

Nomadic Ambling

In his work from 1988, *Le Pli*, translated into English as *The Fold*, Deleuze puts emphasis on 'la tendance de la matière à déborder l'espace, à se concilier avec le fluide' [the tendency of matter to overflow space, to be reconciled with fluidity].[136] In so doing, he underlines the excessive quality of sensuous materialism, and the ever-present opportunity for stasis to dissolve into free-flowing currents of life and becoming.[137] In *Je, tu, il, elle* such a process finds expression in the film's undulant unfolding, which swaps, as it segues into the second section of its third-part structure, a celebration of stagnancy and willed, sensual torpor for nomadic peregrination. In this segment of the film, the protagonist Julie exits the flat she has sheltered herself in for twenty-eight days and embarks on a spontaneous journey with an unnamed trucker who has picked her up after she has hitch-hiked at the side of the road.[138]

Lacking any pre-disclosed destination or explicit purpose, such a trip dialogues with the feature's hymn to Margulies's 'radical liminality' and unproductiveness, or to what Bataille has termed 'l'oisévété contemplative' [contemplative idleness].[139] Departing from what McFadden calls the screening of a 'confined domestic body' in the first half of the film, in *Je, tu, il, elle*'s second chapter this contemplation is kinetic, crucially inhabited by a *corps en mouvement* or a body in motion.[140] In Akerman's own words offered in her *Autoportrait*, Julie evolves from stagnancy into someone who wanders, loiters. A figure of the voluptuous depressive is replaced by what Akerman appoints, in French, the 'célibataire' or single person, who 'n'a rien devant lui, et de ce fait rien non plus derrière' [has nothing in front of them, and from this fact nothing behind them either].[141] A luxuriantly melancholic clinging to the past is abandoned to devotion to the present moment as time narrows to the strip of road ahead. This shift in temporality is echoed by the motions of the camerawork, which forfeit an impression of profound inhabitation for a hazier 'skimming' of the surface of the screen.[142] The lighter, less profoundly haptic attachment to the image attunes to what Steven Shaviro, in his writings on the concept of 'post-cinematic affect', describes as 'a thin sliver of pure present, without any thickness of duration'.[143]

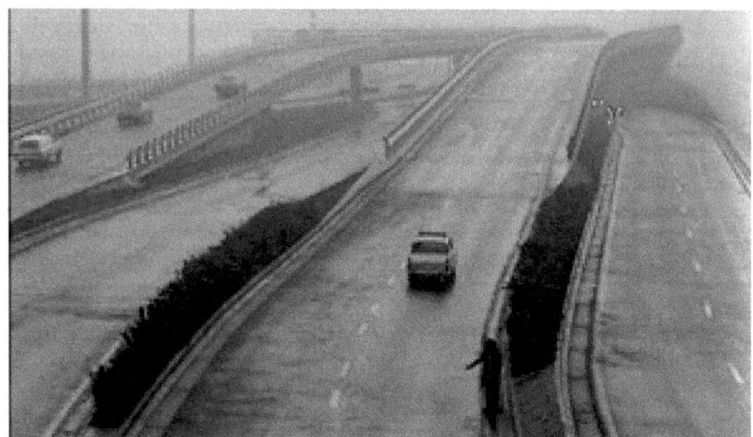

Fig. 1.7. Chantal Akerman, *Je, tu, il, elle* (1974)

The first shot of the section scrutinises Julie from a remote, fixed distance, standing at the edge of a busy *autoroute* and attempting to secure a ride. In contrast to the first third's lingering, respectfully caressing captures which glossed the character's sensuality, here she is a speck in a wide, impersonal vista, a figure unmoored in a post-industrial world. The tableau's emphasis on dissolution and effacement as Julie almost disappears into the dense motorway surroundings maps onto Deleuze and Guattari's concept of *devenir-imperceptible*, ('becoming-imperceptible'), or with the pleasures of surrendering the blinkers of 'identity' to the emancipating anonymity of the crowd.[144] In his theoretical account of road-tripping across America, Jean Baudrillard observed in a related fashion how 'Driving is a spectacular form of amnesia. Everything is to be discovered, everything is to be obliterated'.[145]

In *Mille plateaux*, Deleuze and Guattari link the process of becoming-imperceptible, or of freeing oneself from the strictures of 'majoritarian' identity, politics, and family, with the related process of *devenir-femme*, or 'becoming-woman'. As well as re-conceptualising 'Woman' as an energetic, as opposed to essential or biological, state, *devenir-femme* claimed femininity as an 'in-between', 'intermedial' affect, open to being crossed, accessed, and traversed by altering regimes of sensation.[146] In such a context Deleuze makes the assertion, in his reading of Akerman's films in *Cinéma 2*, that, attuned to subtler, more 'molecular' refinements of time and space, 'le corps d'une femme conquiert un étrange nomadisme qui lui fait traverser les âges, les situations, les lieux' [a woman's body achieves a strange nomadism which makes it cross ages, situations, and places].[147] This 'strange nomadism' does not however telegraph destructive desires for pure escape; or what Momcilovic, reading *Je, tu, il, elle*, calls an uncompromising 'fugue de soi-même' [fugue of the self].[148] Rather, as Braidotti, making a case for the 'nomadic subject' as a viable avatar for feminism, writes, 'The nomad does not stand for homelessness, or compulsive displacement; it is rather a fixation for the kind of subject who has relinquished all idea, desire or nostalgia for fixity'.[149]

The circumstances under which Julie flags down the unnamed 'il' of the feature's title — hereafter referred to only as 'le camionneur' or 'the truck driver' — are almost ecstatically devoid of all nostalgia, enthrallment, or affect, seeking only what Gorfinkel calls the rudimentary gratifications of 'bare attachment'.[150] The aura of emotional anaemia contrasts sharply to the prior section's richly fervent sense of heartbreak as Julie's droning voiceover recounts: 'J'ai arrêté un camion. Je suis entrée. Le camionneur est devenu silent' [I stopped a lorry. I got in. The truck driver grew silent]. Refusing to enshrine the encounter in saccharine romanticism, this exact moment of their meeting is withheld from the spectator. We hear briskly how the driver encourages Julie to lie down on the vehicle's backseat, intuiting how she must be tired, before the next grainy shot of him at the steering-wheel, his face half-entombed in darkness, occurs.

Initially, the makeshift partnership is not sexually explicit. There are echoes of the chaste banality on display in Sophie Calle and Greg Shephard's performance art film *No Sex Last Night* that chronicles a sexless drive across America to San Francisco; as Julie and the trucker tour prosaic roadside destinations such as dingy diners and café-bars in mutual, unerotic silence.[151] Emphasising their estrangement from each other, Akerman films these sequences from a prescribed vantage point that is even more outlying than her usual fixed distance (the impression, underlining the chapter's motifs of surveillance and nomadic lawlessness, is one of a CCTV camera tracking a moment of intimacy) and choreographs the characters sitting side by side rather than across from one another, frustrating the potential rapture of a face-to-face encounter.[152]

When the sexual component of their haphazard relation does begin to blossom, it is introduced with a certain element of agency by Akerman: 'Je me suis rendu compte que je voulais embrasser le camionneur' [I realised that I wanted to kiss the trucker], Julie announces, in her lilting, sing-song cadence. Yet, signalling the emotionally frigid quality of the dynamic, the film refuses to indulge the trope of 'the kiss' as cornerstone of conventional visual pleasure. The affective ornaments of heartbreak and sustained romantic attachment are replaced by the brute mechanics of climax as the scene cuts to the trucker, back in the enclosed dimensions of his lorry, being masturbated by Julie.[153] In a searing image of asymmetry, as his body takes up the entirety of the screen space, as he writhes with pleasure and dispatches terse instructions to Julie — 'Plus vite, ne bouge pas' [Faster, don't move] — she remains silent, and totally off-screen.

Extending his sustained meditation on the distinct phenomenological and affective luxuries of driving, Baudrillard observes how cruising for great distances in the American West produces 'a kind of invisibility, transparency, or transversality in things, simply by emptying them out'.[154] Anticipating the luxurious annihilations of the ego courted in the later work of Sophie Calle and Annie Ernaux, the pleasures of what Wilson calls self-absenting, of emptying oneself out, are at work here for Julie in the masturbation scene with the trucker.[155] Underscoring the crystalline singularity of the encounter, Julie observes, musingly, post-climax (which, furthering the film's interest in the dialectics of desire rather than the emphatic moment of orgasm, we do not see) how 'Il n'y a pas de futur. Uniquement le présent' [There is no future. Only the present], echoing Akerman's hymn to the *célibataire* in her *Autoportrait*, her ode to the 'continuous present' that being a person unyoked to long-term partnership can sponsor.

Keeping close to its commitment to spontaneous unfoldings and peripheral, haphazard intimacies, the second chapter of *Je, tu, il, elle* ends unexpectedly with a scene in a bathroom. The trucker shaves his beard with an electric pair of clippers as Julie, this time visible at the edges of the shot, slumps against the mirror and observes him, both boredom and devotion flickering across her face. This digression, as well as offering extra-diegetical relief to the spectator, offers the protagonists a moment of diversion from the onslaught of the road, introduces curvature and contingency where before there was only a straight line. The scene's suspension of conventional narrative progress echoes the stilling pause of *Jeanne Dielman*'s coda, inviting the spectator to absorb sensory details, to extract themselves from crude transactions. Writing on an aesthetics and an ethos of 'endurance' in post-economic-crisis, global cinema, Elena Gorfinkel appoints the typical 'road film' a 'genre of mythic, masculinist American mobility and individualist adventure', yet *Je, tu, il, elle*'s infinitely more meandering, circuitous, and indeed undulating and unfolding dialectics of desire summons something more expansive and, in a non-essentializing sense, 'feminine' in its 'unproductive' temporal vacillations.[156] Though seeming to afford inordinate amounts of cinematic space and time to male desire and the rapacious appetites of masculine Eros, this section of Akerman's film closes in a celebration of the feminine nomad who has freed herself of her attachments and embraced the shape-shifting pleasures of self-transformation.[157] In such a context, Julie's upcoming 'reunion' with her ex-girlfriend in *Je, tu, il, elle*'s final section will not be read as a regression nor collapse back into the 'dyad' of the couple but as a further extension of boundless, sensual desire; specifically, the desire to expand the self into an insatiable, objectless lusting which cannot be fixed or defined.[158]

Desire Unlimited

> Isn't it interesting that a male orgasm has a DNA imprint that will replicate itself over and over again [...], but the female orgasm has no use, no mark, no locatability? [...] I want to think how that can be the model for a new gesture.
> — Laura Owens[159]

In the final sequence of its three-part structure, *Je, tu, il, elle* stages itself as a film against orgasm and a film against climax. Tracing a visit made by the protagonist to her ex-girlfriend's flat, where they proceed to embark on an erotic 'reunion' of sorts, it declines to punctuate, over-index, or explicitly conclude its presentation of sexual activity. Eschewing the irruptive, cataclysmic force of *la petite mort*, it substitutes an ideology of orgasm for deferred eroticism, and models an 'unreproductive' sensing of queer desire.[160]

In contrast to the sovereign release of violence and self-dissolution brought about by the climax in *Jeanne Dielman*, its predecessor *Je, tu, il elle* re-imagines luxury's voluptuous *luxuria* or active lusting as a willed protraction of desiring forces, as a languishing upon the charged *plateaux* of erotic pleasure rather than the 'servile' submission to its peaks and troughs. In her monograph *Le Regard féminin*, Brey locates the film's non-objectifying, feminist erotic potency in its framing of a labile, horizontal form of sexuality: one able to pivot pleasurably between ossifying categories but also decidedly egalitarian in its embrace of the Other independent of vertical power dynamics. The two lovers 'diffuse' towards each other, she writes.[161] In its sensual indifference to orgasm or relational objectives (before the two women even undress it is agreed that Julie will leave promptly the next morning) the section dove-tails with Bataille's articulation of sexuality as a 'luxurious detour' from more essential expenditures.[162] Yet, in its blurring of the bodies of its two central actors it also resonates with Deleuze's free-floating, non-subject and non-object anchored vision of sexuality, understood as an uninterrupted 'flow' of energy and erotic charge, indifferent to repressive oedipal configurations. In *Mille plateaux*, together with Guattari, Deleuze, indeed, ventures the idea of the erotic plateau as 'une région continue d'intensités, vibrant sur elle-même, et qui se développe en évitant toute orientation sur un point culminant ou vers une fin extérieure' [a continuous, self-vibrating region of intensities whose development avoids any orientation toward a culmination point or external end].[163]

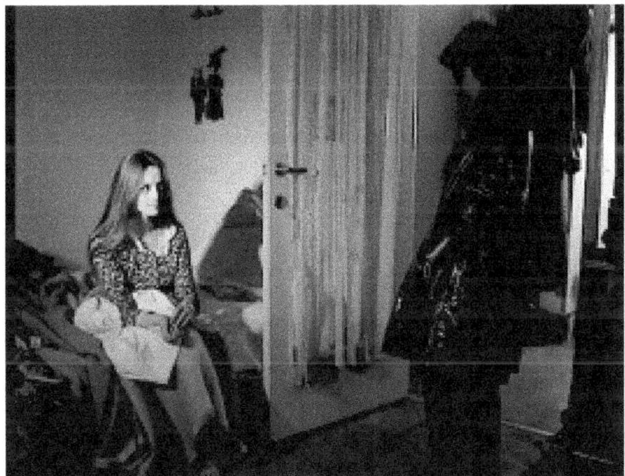

FIG. 1.8. Chantal Akerman, *Je, tu, il, elle* (1974)

The section opens with a chain of shots redolent of *Saute ma ville*'s initial overtures: Akerman's avatar, dressed in a glossy PVC jacket, rings the doorbell to the apartment of 'elle' and, declaring 'C'est moi' over the intercom, takes the lift to her door, checking her appearance over in the mirror as she does. Further echoing the former film's manic bursts of comic energy, as soon as Julie enters the space, she trips over her shoelaces and stumbles to the floor. She removes her jacket and then, in a gesture of ambivalence and indecision, puts it back on again. Further estranging the audience from the conventions of erotic foreplay or titillating cinema, her lover stifles laughter before announcing soberly, 'Je ne veux pas que tu restes, tu sais' [I don't want you to stay, you know].

Despite these strictly voiced conditions, the atmosphere is tender and close. After the abrasions of her precarious road-side existence with the trucker the sense is one

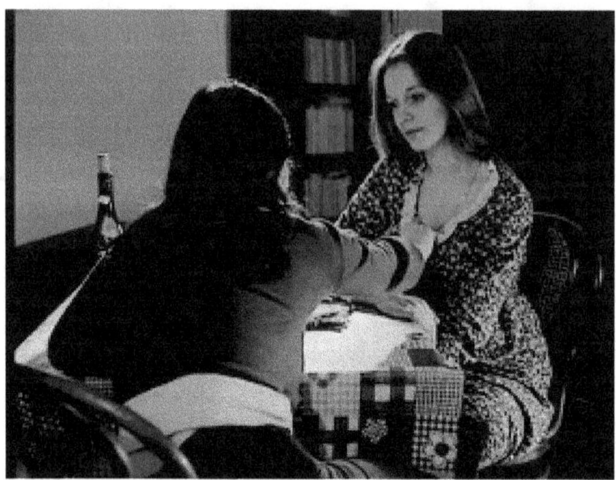

Fig. 1.9. Chantal Akerman, *Je, tu, il, elle* (1974)

of respite, of familiarity and warmth.[164] The lovers hug affectionately, taking time to take in and digest one another's presence, before Julie announces fittingly that she is hungry. The simple luxury of shelter, or of being cared and provided for, is summoned by the humble meal that 'elle' assembles for Julie of Nutella sandwiches and a tumbler of red wine. By means of this affective choreography of nurturance, this section of the film could be seen as a reference back to maternal concerns and childhood yearnings, yet the relation on display is more nuanced, less fusional and unilaterally devotional than the mother-daughter dyad.[165] 'Encore!' Julie announces, after she has devoured her first course, indicating greater appetites, yet eating in such a way that transcends straightforward hunger. In further accordance with Bataille's notion of eroticism as that which persists in excess of need, it is only after she has sated both her thirst and hunger that Julie reaches towards the buttons of her lover's dress.

In *Nothing Happens*, Margulies reads *Je, tu, il, elle*'s coda and its adjacent eleven-minute love-making scene as an assertion of 'literalness and concreteness' and even 'over-visibility' as the static framing of the tableau 'insists to the point of excess on the body's materiality'.[166] Yet, while the scene's haptic proximity is a stark departure from the alienating *anomie* of the earlier encounter with the trucker, the fact that Akerman elects to register it in monochrome rather than colour maintains a level of opacity and inconclusiveness faithful to the film's dialectical, enigmatic presentation of desire. After Julie seduces her ex-girlfriend at the kitchen table, the minimalist palette of the bed and surrounding bedroom as they recline sumptuously naked together lends the scene a quality of timelessness, a certain artfulness and monumentalism which transcends the obscenity of conventional pornography. In their stony pallor, the two bodies entwined in one another evoke, rather than visceral flesh and blood women, the clasped, marble figures of Rodin.[167] The starkness of the palette telegraphs the radicality of the desire at play — confirmed by the kinetic, fevered way the women reach for one another — and yet anatomical explicitness is avoided as Akerman frustrates the easy fetish of the breasts or genitals.

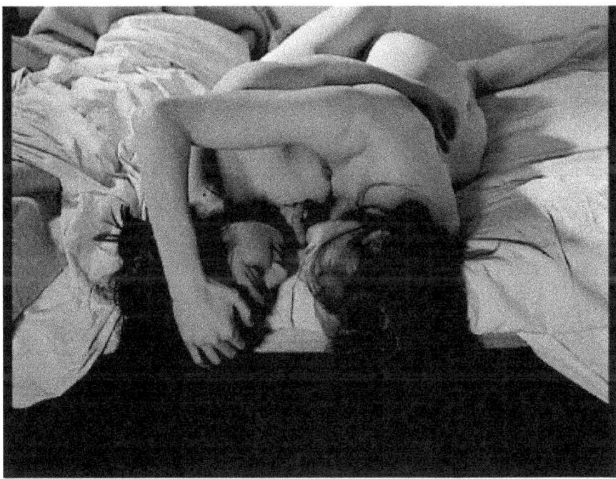

Fig. 1.10. Chantal Akerman, *Je, tu, il, elle* (1974)

The impression of the gestures is less urgently carnal than inquisitive and playful as the lovers tumble in and out of intimate disarray and stroke each other's hair.

Though towards the end of the take the character of 'elle' delicately opens Julie's legs and begins performing cunnilingus, the tableau depicts neither of the women being brought to climax. In an interview with B. Ruby Rich, Akerman expressed the sentiment that 'I don't consider that to have an orgasm is always the best thing. That's why so many women don't have pleasure, because they protect some space unconsciously', aligning feminine *jouissance* with a certain sanctity, an aneconomy of exceptionality.[168] In *Mille plateaux* Deleuze and Guattari elevate the protean, always-becoming force of desire over the blunt finitude of pleasure, arguing that the latter narrowly returns sexuality to being the domain or 'affection of a subject' when the objective, following Bataille, is to dissolve into an fluid, formless sovereignty.[169] Frida Beckman, in her work on 'Deleuze and Sex' explores further how pleasure is a mode of reterritorialisation that Deleuze and Guattari strive to circumvent. As long as the pursuit of pleasure is related to the 'deplorable' fact of orgasm, and pleasure is thus a norm, desire remains in a relation with lack. Pleasure thus has an intimate connection with lack and subjectification. If instead we untie pleasure from desire, the latter can be allowed to exist in a constructive positivity in its own right.[170]

In proximate terms, Bataille praises forms of sexual activity 'détournée de la finalité génitale' [undirected towards genital finality] or emancipated from orgasm's sense of telos. Freed from expectations of orgasmic climax, sexuality 'entre du moins en ébullition: sans exploser, son extrême exubérance s'écoule en un mouvement toujours à la limite de l'explosion' [at least enters into ebullition: without exploding, its extreme exuberance pours out in a movement always bordering on explosion].[171] Evading linearity or firm conclusions, *Je, tu, il, elle*, in contrast to *Jeanne Dielman*'s pyrotechnic irruptions, favours more entropic modes of dissolution and a slow burn of desire which fizzles with sensation yet does not adhere to resolution. According to such patterns, the last line of *Je, tu, il, elle*, 'Elle m'a dit de partir' [She told me to leave], when folded up against the first, 'Et je suis partie' [And I left], resists habitual narrative maps, reverses the logic of loving and leaving in an erotic *détournement* which resists attachment to one outcome or intent. Instead, faithful to the film's luxury of multiple perspectives and identities in constant transport and fluidity, Julie, after sleeping next to 'elle', hastily departs from the apartment in the early, half-light hours of morning.[172] The sex has not marked a regression, nor a blissful return to the heteronormative unit of 'the couple'. Without uttering a further word — the film's aesthetic definitively more gestural than verbal — Julie, as she closes the front door and the light of the film drains, is clearly shown as returning to her solitude; as embarking towards a future horizon of possibility that hasn't yet been sketched.[173]

Writing generally on Akerman's 'politics of anti-messianism' and 'suspended image', Chrysanthi Nigianni calls the Belgian filmmaker's 2006 feature *Là-bas*, shot in an apartment in Tel-Aviv, 'a film that sees but does not grasp or seize, a film that has learned to see as pure and unintended *contact*'.[174] Such an epithet might ultimately also be affixed to *Je, tu, il, elle*, which cultivates a non-rapacious, non-possessive gaze (and sexuality) in order to make space for new relations — and new desiring configurations — to blossom, take root. Whilst situating itself in a hazy, pointillistic context of radical unproductivity and non-exchange, the film, indeed, being far from materially flimsy or insubstantial, suggests that touch is possible when not transactional, and that the conflicted, fractious textures of desire are preferable to the world-effacing force of overwhelming pleasure. Although richly evocative of a horizontal 'female gaze', Deleuze's fold, and Bataille's spiral of lavish wastefulness and squandering, its imprint, in conclusion, is unique. Its goal, as its very title signifies, is to dissolve all fixed pronouns and positions into a sinuous haze of impressions, leaving its captive audience suspended in a present richly overlaid with sensuous stimuli. This luxurious abstraction from the grinding tedium of 'real', capitalist time furnishes a template for the audience to, like Julie, burgeon and become on their own terms, to enter, as Robertson writes, a 'supple kaleidoscope of different thinking'.[175] On both an internal and an extra-diegetic level, then, *Je, tu, il, elle* makes manifest the power of artistic production to positively alter restrictive conditions of embodiment, a privilege and luxury also shared and revelled in by Calle, Ernaux, and Bourgeois.[176] Both similar yet uniquely distinct from *Jeanne Dielman*, it is a work which makes us intimate with immanence and negotiates escape from the entrenchments of the everyday.

Conclusion: *l'éclosion du regard*

In a day-long retrospective dedicated to her work held in London in October 2014, Chantal Akerman spoke of her determination to avoid image-idolatry within her *œuvre*.[177] The statement, echoing those made in interviews throughout her tragically abbreviated life, might illuminate her tendency towards, in her final installation pieces, presenting various screens and visual images in shreds and in tatters, and towards subjecting the intactness of the filmed and filmic object both to refraction and expansion beyond the frame.[178]

The ephemeral, open-ended aesthetic of Akerman's late phase — vulnerable to contact and interruption by the engaged spectator — might, in the final instance, offer an idea of luxury within her work as less unadulterated plenitude or total absorption in filmed materials than as the opportunity, however brief, to experience a moment of communion with the artwork, to meet the stimulus in question eye to eye. It might, departing from the paradigm of easeful, leisurely consumption of film matter and materiality, encourage a new mode of spectatorship requiring us, as Giuliana Bruno writes in relation to Akerman's cinema, to become active witnesses to images and involved producers in our own distinctive right.[179] It might encourage us to source cinephilic 'pleasure' not only in modes of reception to visual spectacle and display but in the ongoing braiding together of heterogeneous visual and haptic elements.

For Nancy, writing on and with Abbas Kiarostami in the work *L'Évidence du film*, the ideal is to cultivate 'l'éclosion d'un regard au milieu de la turbulence ordinaire' [a blossoming of the gaze in the midst of ordinary turbulence]. Such quiet flowering, such careful blossoming — when everything outside is chaos — is cinema's unique contribution, staging it, he writes, as 'un lieu de la méditation [...] comme l'avoir-lieu d'un rapport au sens du monde' [a place of meditation [...] like the taking-place of a relation to the sense of the world].[180]

What Chantal Akerman's films uniquely offer, I have argued in this chapter, is a new relationship to time, sexuality, and the necessary expenditures which rhythm our lives. Questioning the sense of how we frame and look at the world, they cast meticulous and detailed attention on varying temporal and material positions which have subsequent and visceral effects on our own spatialised relation to embodied life. This relationship, in sync with the prodigious range of Akerman's work, contracts and expands, can encompass both the weight of duration and the flighty striking of an instant.

In a chapter about finding precious moments of expansion and release in the folds between filmed images, or in the interstices often glossed over by plot-centric, commercial cinema, the luxurious experience of time granted by Akerman's earliest works is, in conclusion, fittingly two-fold. An envelopment in durational, immersive filmic practices is balanced by the frequent extrication from, and suspension of, normative, representational visual economies: flight and staying still, stasis and escape. Like the sinuous, terminology-defying experience of luxury itself, the films of Chantal Akerman worry the fault-line between lofty transcendence and comfortable immanence, thickening the texture of the ordinary as well as crafting moments of distinct, luxurious exception from that paradigm.

Notes to Chapter 1

1. Chris Dercon, 'An Interview with Chantal Akerman About Too Much and Not Enough Cinema', *Contour* (2005) <http://www.contour2005.be/UK/ca.htm> [accessed 15 October 2015].
2. Margulies, *Nothing Happens*, p. 20.
3. I use 'immanent' in the Deleuzian sense of a vitalist, material commitment to the thick potential of the present moment. For an account of Akerman's 'flat image of a "here and now" that does not seduce' and politics/aesthetics of an 'immanent image as inward flexion' which 'initiates a new thinking of time' as 'emptied time' (see Chrysanthi Nigianni, 'Chantal Akerman's *Là-bas:* The Suspended Image and the Politics of Anti-Messianism', in *Senses of Cinema*, 67 (July 2013) <http://sensesofcinema.com/2013/feature-articles/chantal-akermans-la-bas-the-suspended-image-and-the-politics-of-anti-messianism/> [accessed 25 September 2015]).
4. For an account of Akerman's cinema as a study of 'existential difficulty', see, amongst others, Boris Lehman, 'Non-éloge (aujourd'hui je dirais)', *Sabzian* (September 2019) <https://sabzian.be/text/non-%C3%A9loge-aujourd%E2%80%99hui-je-dirais> [accessed 24 August 2020]. Griselda Pollock, in an article on the 'long maternal journey' in regards to Akerman's filmmaking, calls this her camera's 'agnostic attention' ('The Long Journey: Maternal Trauma, Tears and Kisses in a Work by Chantal Akerman', *Studies in the Maternal*, 2.1 (2010), 1–32 (p. 5). See again Preciado, 'Learning from the Virus', for a detailed look at our time of confined 'immaterial production' and 'pharmacopornographic consumption'.
5. Patricia Patterson and Manny Farber, 'Kitchen without Kitsch', *Film Comment* (November-December 1977) <https://akephale.com/2016/06/20/kitchen-without-kitsch/> [accessed 20 March 2020].
6. See Chantal Akerman, *Entretien avec ma mère, Natalia Akerman* (2007: 28 minutes). I borrow the term 'expanded cinema' from Elena Gorfinkel, who uses it in her article 'At the End of Cinema, this Thing Called Film', *Lola Journal*, 1 (January 2011) <http://www.lolajournal.com/1/end_of_cinema.html> [accessed 13 November 2015]. The term is also usefully employed in *Expanded Cinema: Art, Performance, Film*, ed. by Steven Ball and others (London: Tate Publishing, 2011).
7. As Dirk Lauwaert has noted of *Jeanne Dielman*, 'the adventure is not that of content, but that of form. The lesson is not that of argument, but that of process and the power with which it is conducted' (Lauwaert, '23, quai de Commerce, Brussels').
8. See Gilles Deleuze, *Cinéma 2: L'Image-temps* (Paris: Minuit, 1985); *Cinema II: The Time Image*, trans. by Hugh Tomlinson and Robert Galeta (London: Bloomsbury, 2013): 'Starting with Jeanne Dielman, Chantal Akerman wants to show gestures in their fullness' (p. 202).
9. See for example Mulvey, *Afterimages*, p. 103, who writes of *Jeanne Dielman*'s titular character, 'an intricate tapestry is made up of her daily rituals'.
10. See Giuliana Bruno's essay 'Projection: On Chantal Akerman's Screens, from Cinema to the Art Gallery', in *Chantal Akerman: Too Far, too Close*, exhibition catalogue (Antwerp: Ludion, 2012), pp. 15–26 (p. 19).
11. This approach is echoed by Patterson and Farber, 'Kitchen Without Kitsch', who suggest *Jeanne Dielman* as filmic work portrays 'the integrity of things as they already stand.'
12. See Chantal Akerman, 'Chantal Akerman on *Jeanne Dielman, 23 quai du Commerce, 1080 Bruxelles*', *Camera Obscura*, 2 (Fall 1977), 115–21 (p. 119), where the aim is stated 'to avoid cutting the woman in a hundred pieces, to look carefully and be respectful'.
13. A similar ethos is expressed in Jean-Luc Nancy and Abbas Kiarostami's account, in *L'Évidence du film* (Brussels: Yves Gevaert, 2011), of the *juste regard* or 'fair gaze', defined as 'un respect pour le réel regardé, c'est à dire une attention et une ouverture à la force propre de ce réel et à son extériorité absolue; le regard ne captera pas cette force, il la laissera se communiquer à lui ou il communiquera avec elle' [a respect for the regarded real; which is to say an attention and an opening to the proper force of this reality and its absolute exteriority: the gaze would not *capture* this force, it would communicate with it] (p. 39).
14. Gilles Deleuze and Félix Guattari, *Mille plateaux* (Paris: Minuit, 1980). For a beautiful reading of *Jeanne Dielman* as 'an insistence on women's labour as art' see Carol Mavor, *Reading Boyishly: Roland Barthes, J. M. Barrie, Jacques Henri Lartigue, Marcel Proust, and D. W. Winnicott* (Durham, NC: Duke University Press, 2008), p. 399.

15. Georges Bataille, cited in Chantal Akerman, *Autoportrait en cinéaste* (Paris: Cahiers du Cinéma, 2004), p. 11.
16. Dercon, 'An Interview with Chantal Akerman about too Much and not Enough Cinema'. For an account of the 'vivid, visceral reception experience' endemic to Akerman's cinema, see Barbara McBane, 'Walking, Talking, Singing, Exploding... and Silence: Chantal Akerman's Soundtracks', *Film Quarterly*, 70.1 (<https://filmquarterly.org/2016/09/16/walking-talking-singing-exploding/> [accessed 24 August 2020].
17. Adam Roberts, 'Preparing to See *Jeanne Dielman*', *ICA Bulletin* <https://archive.ica.art/bulletin/preparing-see-jeanne-dielman> [accessed 24 August 2020].
18. Elena Gorfinkel, 'Wanda, Loden, Lodestone' (London: Institute for Contemporary Art London, May 2018) <https://kclpure.kcl.ac.uk/portal/files/96107025/ICA_Wanda_Loden_lodestone_v2.pdf> [accessed 24 August 2020].
19. See for example, Joanna Hogg and Adam Roberts, 'Chantal Akerman: Extraordinary Artist of the Everyday', *Guardian*, 8 October 2015 <http://www.theguardian.com/film/2015/oct/08/chantal-akerman-feminist-film-maker-died-retrospective> [accessed 15 October 2015].
20. This idea of 'being-with' or *être-avec* is partially inspired by Jean-Luc Nancy's work in *La Communauté désœvrée* (1986) where *être-avec* is articulated as a shared yet non-fusional exposure to finitude and the material 'sense' of existence.
21. In a podcast interview on Akerman's life's work, Daniella Shreir persuasively suggests that the excessive length of *Jeanne Dielman* can be read as an actively, deliberately expansive act of feminist 'arrogance', insisting upon taking up space in a heteropatriarchal cinematic sphere ('Another Gaze: Feminist Filmmaking and the Work of Chantal Akerman', *Suite 212* podcast <https://podcasts.apple.com/ie/podcast/another-gaze-feminist-filmmaking-work-chantal-akerman/id1366889715?i=1000436833971> [accessed 24 August 2020]).
22. See Margulies, *Nothing Happens*, p. 23, where it is noted that Akerman's cinema expresses interest in 'images between images', and Maria Walsh, 'News from Home the Redux Version: Amodal Perception and 'la jouissance du voir', *The Moving Image Review & Art Journal*, 8.1–2 (1 September 2019), 28–38.
23. See Akerman, *Autoportrait en cinéaste*, p. 2.
24. See Mateus Araujo, 'Chantal Akerman, between the Mother and the World', trans. by Mark Cohen, *Film Quarterly*, 70.1 (Fall 2016), 32–38 (p. 36).
25. Deleuze, *Cinema II*, p. 202.
26. For accounts of such strategies of formal distance as granting and affording pro-feminist space both to Akerman's protagonists and audiences, see the readings of *Jeanne Dielman* offered by Teresa De Lauretis, 'Aesthetics and Feminist Theory: Rethinking Women's Cinema', in *Female Spectators: Looking at Film and Television*, ed. by E. Deirdre Pribam (London: Verso, 1988), pp. 178–79, and B. Ruby Rich, 'Designing Desire: Chantal Akerman (1983)', in *Chick Flicks: Theories and Memories of the Feminist Film Movement* (Durham, NC: Duke University Press, 1998), pp. 169–207.
27. This avoids both objectification but also forms of idolatry, in conflict with Akerman's Jewish faith. In the self-authored documentary *Chantal Akerman par Chantal Akerman* (1996: 64 minutes) she explains, 'Dans un milieu réligieux on n'a pas le droit de représenter' [In a religious context one doesn't have the right to represent].
28. In a chapter on *Je, tu, il, elle* and *Jeanne Dielman* in *Le Regard féminin*, Iris Brey calls this strategy specific to Akerman's filmmaking 'une mise à distance viscerale' [a visceral distancing] to nuance how, while held at firm remove, her camera is still intimate with Jeanne's existence, 'ni trop près ni trop loin' [neither too close nor too far] (*Le Regard féminin* (Paris: L'Olivier, 2020), p. 163). Sandy Flitterman-Lewis argues in her essay 'What's behind her Smile?' that in refusing interiority, Akerman conceived of an entirely new expression of female subjectivity ('What's behind her Smile? Subjectivity and Desire in Germaine Dulac's *The Smiling Madame Beudet* and Chantal Akerman's *Jeanne Dielman, 23 quai du Commerce, 1080 Bruxelles*', in *Identity and Memory: The Films of Chantal Akerman*, ed. by Gwendolyn Audrey (Carbondale: Southern Illinois University Press, 2003), pp. 27–40, and Patterson and Farber, in 'Kitchen Without Kitsch', affirm that in Akerman's work 'there is a definite respect for surfaces'.

29. Mulvey, 'Visual Pleasure and Narrative Cinema', p. 18.
30. Deleuze, *Cinema II*, p. 203.
31. In her essay 'Minimalism's Radical Quiet: Chantal Akerman's *Jeanne Dielman*', *Four by Three Magazine* (2016) <http://www.fourbythreemagazine.com/issue/silence/chantal-akermans-jeanne-dielman> [accessed 24 August 2020], Emilija Talijan argues persuasively how in the film 'everything is made to sound'. In reference to *News from Home*, Chantal Akerman herself once said, 'Je pense que ce film est une sorte de film voluptueux, à cause du bruit, à cause des images, à cause de la couleur. On est assis et cela donne l'impression de rentrer en soi' [I think this film is a kind of voluptuous film, because of the sound, because of its images, its colour. One is sitting down and that gives the impression of retreating inside] (cited in Jérôme Momcilovic, *Chantal Akerman: Dieu se reposa, mais pas nous* (Paris: Capricci, 2018), p. 63).
32. Roland Barthes, *Le Plaisir du texte* (Paris: Seuil, 1973), p. 18.
33. The redistribution of visual value which takes place in this film, or the decision that the sex is less worthy of being shown than the minute act of making meatloaf or preparing coffee, is in line with Jeanne's remark to her son in the first hour of the feature as she is putting him to bed that making love, in the wider context of life, isn't so important ('Faire l'amour... C'est un détail').
34. For a reading of turning lights off and on in *Jeanne Dielman* as a gesture of feminist agency, see Frances Morgan, 'Afterword', in Chantal Akerman, *My Mother Laughs*, trans. by Daniella Shreir (London: Silver Press, 2019), pp. 191–203. For a reading of light in Akerman's cinema more broadly, see Cyril Béghin, 'Light out of Joint', in *Chantal Akerman*, ed. by Schmid and Wilson, pp. 139–49. For a delicate account of the blueness in the film, see again Mavor, *Reading Boyishly*.
35. See again Akerman, 'Chantal Akerman on *Jeanne Dielman, 23 quai du Commerce, 1080 Bruxelles*', p. 121.
36. David Harvey, 'The Body as an Accumulation Strategy', *Society and Space*, 16 (1998), 401–21.
37. See Rhodes, 'Art Cinema's Immaterial Labors', which chronicles '*Jeanne Dielman*'s extravagant, excessive visualization of the most mundane details of everyday domestic life' (p. 114). Margulies, *Nothing Happens*, p. 46.
38. Margulies, *Nothing Happens*, p. 23.
39. Chantal Akerman, cited in Margulies, *Nothing Happens*, p. 43.
40. Lisa Robertson, *The Baudelaire Fractal* (Toronto: Coach House Books, 2020), p. 140.
41. Despite the intricate attention to interiors in *Jeanne Dielman*, Steven Jacobs notes how the dwelling in domestic space in Akerman's work proves tricky: 'Despite the fact that domestic rooms are predominant in Akerman's *œuvre*, the dwelling in them is often problematic. Only rarely do Akerman's characters feel at home in the household spaces that her camera so extensively and meticulously records. Benjamin's thesis that the nineteenth century interior, like a cocoon or womb, offers a sense of security, is one that Akerman only rarely seems to illustrate' ('Semiotics of the Living Room: Domestic Interiors in Chantal Akerman's Cinema', in *Chantal Akerman: Too Far, Too Close*, pp. 73–87 (p. 82)).
42. See also Jacques Derrida's essay on Bataille, 'De l'économie restreinte à l'économie générale: un hégélianisme sans réserve', in *L'Écriture et la différence* (Paris: Seuil, 1967), pp. 369–407 (p. 390), for a useful distinction between these terms.
43. Bataille, *L'Érotisme*, p. 44.
44. Marion Schmid, *Chantal Akerman* (Manchester: Manchester University Press, 2010), p. 36.
45. Michelle Orange, 'Femme vérité: The Films of Chantal Akerman', *Virginia Quarterly Review* (Spring 2016) <https://www.vqronline.org/tv-film-criticism/2016/03/femme-verit%C3%A9> [accessed 24 August 2020].
46. Mavor, *Reading Boyishly*, p. 431.
47. See again Talijan, 'Minimalism's Radical Quiet', for whom 'the initial rhythm of Jeanne's daily existence lulls us into a low state of attention that for the (inevitably at times) bored spectator provokes a drift into daydream, it relaxes us and allows our bodies to fall into a state of response that is not to do with semantic content'.
48. A reading of *Jeanne Dielman* via Baudelaire might be supported by a scene included in the film in which Jeanne's son, Sylvain, practices memorising Baudelaire's short poem 'L'Ennemi', to his mother.

49. Zain Jamshaid argues that Akerman's cinema 'avoids the "politics of emotion" by being constantly fixated on the visible reality, the surface of things' ('"Invested in Expression or in Its Destruction?" The Politics of Space and Representation in Chantal Akerman's Cinema', *Senses of Cinema*, 64 (September 2012) <https://www.sensesofcinema.com/2012/feature-articles/invested-in-expression-or-in-its-destruction-the-politics-of-space-and-representation-in-chantal-akermans-cinema/> [accessed 24 August 2020]). The importance of keeping up appearances to Chantal's mother Natalia is glossed by Eileen Myles in her introduction to the English translation of *My Mother Laughs*. Myles discusses Akerman's reluctance to 'duplicate the spectacle of the mother's own much vaunted spectacle of being the beautiful woman, the tight, spiffy, eloquent female being' ('Introduction', in Akerman, *My Mother Laughs*, pp. I–VI (p. III)).
50. Akerman, in Lebovici, 'No Idolatry and Losing Everything that Made You a Slave'.
51. For a fascinating account of the use of ornament and boundaries in Akerman's cinema as strategies against memories of the Holocaust, see Shelley Hornstein, 'Ornament, Boundaries and Mourning After Auschwitz', in *Reading Charlotte Saloman*, ed. by Michael P. Steinberg and Monica Bohm-Duchen (Ithaca, NY: Cornell University Press, 2006), pp. 126–40. For a reading of Akerman's filmography as 'intimately bound up with the horrors of the Holocaust', see also Schmid, *Chantal Akerman*, p. 2.
52. For a reading of 'the manner in which Jeanne scrupulously eschews waste of any kind', in Akerman's film, see Jenny Chamarette, '*Jeanne Dielman, 23, Quai du Commerce, 1080 Bruxelles*', *Senses of Cinema*, 67 (May 2013) <http://sensesofcinema.com/2013/cteq/jeanne-dielman-23-quai-du-commerce-1080-bruxelles/#5> [accessed 25 September 2015].
53. See Georges Bataille, *La Part maudite* [1949] (Paris: Minuit, 2011), p. 31.
54. For a reading of *Jeanne Dielman* in terms of a category of Freud's *unheimlich*, see Daniele Dubroux, 'Le Familier inquietant', *Cahiers du Cinéma*, 265 (March-April 1976), 17–20.
55. Daniele Dubroux, 'Il n'y aurait plus qu'une seule image', *Cahiers du Cinéma*, 278–79 (Autumn 1977), cited in Akerman and Martin, 'Chantal Akerman's Films', p. 44.
56. See Gilles Deleuze, *Cinéma 1: L'Image-mouvement* (Paris: Minuit 1983), p. 171.
57. This is faithful to luxury's etymological roots in the Latin term *luctari*, meaning 'dislocation', 'strain'. See <https://www.etymonline.com/word/luxury> [accessed 23 August 2020].
58. Jacques Derrida, *Donner le temps: la fausse monnaie* (Paris: Galilée, 1991), p. 18; *Given Time, I, Counterfeit Money*, trans. by Peggy Kamuf (Chicago: University of Chicago Press, 1992), p. 7.
59. For Ros Murray, *Jeanne Dielman* is 'a film that focuses on repeated gestures, whilst inserting one gesture that cannot be repeated (the murder)' ('Revisiting Jeanne Dielman: *Autour de Jeanne Dielman* (2004), *Woman Sitting After Killing* (2001) and Akerman's "cinéma de ressassement"', *The Moving Image Review & Art Journal*, 8.1–2 (1 September 2019), 54–66 (p. 60).
60. For Lucy Lippard, such motions are central to establishing eroticism in art ('Eros Presumptive', *The Hudson Review*, 20.1 (Spring 1967), 91–99.
61. My reading here is shared by Marsha Kinder, who ventures the violence and the sex on display as 'highly disruptive' to the platitudinal rhythms of the film at large ('Reflections on "Jeanne Dielman"', *Film Quarterly*, 30.4 (Summer 1977), 2–8 (p. 8). In contrast, Schmid and R. Patrick Kinsman ('She's Come Undone: Chantal Akerman's *Jeanne Dielman, 23 quai du Commerce, 1080 Bruxelles* (1975) and Countercinema', *Quarterly Review of Film and Video*, 24 (2007), 217–24) read the scene as unspectacular and banal. As the former writes, 'the gliding movement from skirt to scissors and the unspectacular depiction of the murder fuse the act into a homogenous depiction of a life where the singular and habitual, banality and drama, share the same status' (Schmid, *Chantal Akerman*, p. 45).
62. Margulies in *Nothing Happens* argues that the murder 'constitutes an expenditure without exchange within the economy set up by the film text' (p. 94). Whilst however Margulies reads the act as an 'eruption of the semiotic' (p. 94), I am interested to move beyond psychoanalytic terms and to insert the violence into a context of embodied and affective discharge and release. Closer to my reading's underscoring of the murder's exceptionality, Brey writes how Jeanne 'ne peut pas la réguler comme ses autres taches domestiques' [cannot regulate it like her other domestic tasks] (*Le Regard féminin*, p. 145).
63. See Rob Nixon, *Slow Violence and the Environmentalism of the Poor* (Cambridge, MA: Harvard University Press, 2011).

64. Anti-feminist readings of the film deserve also to be taken under consideration. Jayne Loader, in 'Jeanne Dielman: Death in Installments', *Jump Cut*, 16 (1977), 10–12, for example, argues that the film displays a 'male' narrative structure of 'tension, climax, release' (p. 11)
65. See Luce Irigaray, *Ce sexe qui n'en est pas un* (Paris: Minuit, 1977).
66. See again Flitterman-Lewis, 'What's Behind her Smile?'; Peggy Phelan, 'Survey', in *Art and Feminism*, ed. by Helena Rickett (London & New York: Phaidon, 2006), pp. 14–49, who argues that 'the violent pleasure of fatally shattering orgasm' jolts the film out of 'fatal stillness' (p. 22); and Chamarette, '*Jeanne Dielman*' who writes that within Jeanne Dielman's 'meticulous ethnography of feminine domestic labour, a phenomenology of affect unfolds'.
67. Bois and Krauss, *Formless*, p. 27.
68. See Bataille, *L'Érotisme*, p. 102.
69. Ibid., pp. 43, 49.
70. Ibid., p. 180.
71. Ibid., p. 186.
72. Georges Bataille, *Le Bleu du Ciel* (Paris: Fayard Pauvert, 1985), p. 11.
73. Ibid.
74. Both Kinder, 'Reflections on "Jeanne Dielman"', and Loader, 'Jeanne Dielman', make reference to Jeanne's violent act in these terms.
75. Bataille, *L'Érotisme*, p. 237.
76. Cited in Akerman, *Autoportrait en cinéaste*, Babette Mangolte describes the film in terms of 'the repressed and unspeakable passion of Jeanne who embodies the immobility of the world and the sudden transformation of this world into mystery' (p. 176).
77. Sharon Olds, 'Sacred', in *Arias* (London: Jonathan Cape, 2019), p. 194.
78. See Adrian Martin, 'A Theory of Agitation, or, Getting Off in the Cinema', *Continuum: Journal of Media & Cultural Studies*, 26.4 (2012), 519–28.
79. Chantal Akerman, *Saute ma ville* (1968: 13 minutes).
80. Akerman, *Autoportrait en cinéaste*, p. 65.
81. Momcilovic, *Chantal Akerman*, p. 10.
82. Cited in Nicole Brenez, 'Chantal Akerman: The Pajama Interview', *Devils*, *LOLA Journal*, 2 (2011) <http://www.lolajournal.com/2/pajama.html> [accessed 12 November 2015].
83. Cited in Margulies, *Nothing Happens*, p. 241. See also Loader, 'Jeanne Dielman', who criticises this scene for its deemed unnecessary compliance with sensationalist demands for a 'bang-up ending'.
84. I use this term inspired by Nancy and Kiarostami in *L'Évidence du film*.
85. Chantal Akerman, cited in Margulies, *Nothing Happens*, p. 96.
86. The scene is infused with what Lippard terms a 'post-dynamic sensuousness characteristic of provocation, fore or after play, rather than of climax' ('Eros Presumptive', p. 96). Brey has argued that the fact the film does not end on the client's murder (and therefore the telos of penetration) should be viewed as a feminist gesture (*Le Regard féminin*, p. 144.) Mulvey (*Afterimages*) understands the sequence, following Julia Kristeva, as an opening to 'woman's time', which is to say a temporality that is 'interiorized, multiple, cyclical, monumental and eternal' (see 'Women's Time', in *The Kristeva Reader*, ed. by Toril Moi (New York: Columbia University Press, 1986), pp. 187–213) and both Laura McMahon ('Animal Worlds: Film, Philosophy and Time', talk given at the University of Cambridge, 30 October 2019) and Ros Murray index the scene as a withdrawal of feminized labour, or in the latter's case, a disruption of 'chrononomative' narratives ('Revisiting Jeanne Dielman', p. 7).
87. Rather than allowing for a moment of extended affect and prolonged reflection, Mulvey reads the scene as a continuation of the film's interest in novelty and in exceptionality: '*Jeanne Dielman*'s seven-minute shot of Jeanne, after she has murdered her client, stands as an image outside the rationale of the narrative. The shot floats in its own temporal dimension, defying structure and pattern' (*Afterimages*, p. 95).A more horizontal viewing pattern is affirmed by Babette Mangolte (Bryony Gillard and Louis Hartnoll, 'Seeing Horizontally: Babette Mangolte Interviewed by Bryony Gillard and Louis Hartnoll', *The Moving Image Review & Art Journal*, 8.1–2 (1 September 2019), 138–47.

88. Deleuze, *Cinéma 1*, p. 169.
89. Ibid., p. 171.
90. Ibid., p. 107
91. For an account of the virtual in Deleuze as an 'affirmative ethics' and, close to the positivity of luxury I am augmenting throughout this book, a source of 'generative life', see Rosi Braidotti, 'Affirmative Ethics and Generative Life', *Deleuze and Guattari Studies*, 13.4, (2019), 463–81.
92. Deleuze, *Cinéma 1*, p. 169.
93. Such was Akerman's interest in the aftermath of Jeanne's violent act that she subsequently went on to recycle the footage in a separate exhibition shown at the 2001 Venice Biennale, under the title *Woman Sitting after Killing*. For a painstaking reading of the value of this work within Akerman's wider *œuvre*, see Murray, 'Revisiting Jeanne Dielman'.
94. See Georges Bataille, *Théorie de la religion* (Paris: Gallimard, 1973), p. 60.
95. Bataille, *La Part maudite*, p. 181.
96. Lauren Berlant, 'Nearly Utopian, Nearly Normal: Post-Fordist Affect in La Promesse and Rosetta,' *Public Culture*, 19.2 (April 2007), 273–301 (p. 277). Akerman, *Autoportrait en cinéaste*, p. 130. For a rich discussion of the highly charged and complicated term *ressassement* in Akerman's filmography, see Kate Rennebohm, 'La Ressasseuse: Chantal Akerman, 1950–2015', *Cinema Scope*, 64 (2015) <https://cinema-scope.com/columns/deaths-of-cinema/> [accessed 24 August 2020].
97. Bataille, *L'Érotisme*, p. 189.
98. This concept of Ernaux's will be fully glossed in Chapter 2.
99. Slavoj Žižek, *The Fragile Absolute: Or, Why Is the Christian Legacy Worth Fighting For?* (London: Verso, 2009), pp. 144–45.
100. A reading of the scene as proffering relief and as fulfilling Akerman's protagonist's 'desire for stasis' is given in Ivone Margulies, 'A Matter of Time: *Jeanne Dielman, 23, quai du Commerce, 1080 Bruxelles*', *Current: The Criterion Collection* blog (August 2009) <https://www.criterion.com/current/posts/1215-a-matter-of-time-jeanne-dielman-23-quai-du-commerce-1080-bruxelles> [accessed 6 November 2015].
101. As Murray has observed, a humble table is resonant with 'the feminist recuperations of the family dinner table. It is a surface on which to perform illegal abortions, for example' ('Revisiting Jeanne Dielman', p. 13).
102. See again Flitterman-Lewis, 'What's Behind Her Smile?'.
103. See Kathleen Stewart, *Ordinary Affects* (Durham, NC: Duke University Press, 2007), p. 19.
104. Deleuze, *Cinéma 2*, p. 33; *Cinema II: The Time Image*, trans. by Tomlinson and Galeta, p. 21.
105. See Akerman, *Autoportrait en cinéaste*, p. 30: 'Mon enfance était plein de trous' [My childhood was full of holes].
106. Jean-Luc Nancy, 'Il y a du rapport sexuel — et après', *Littérature*, 142.2 (2006), 30–40 (p. 35).
107. For an account of the question of self-portraiture in Akerman, see Cybelle McFadden, *Gendered Frames, Embodied Cameras: Varda, Akerman, Cabrera, Calle, and Maïwenn* (Lanham, MD: Rowman & Littlefield, 2014), p. 85.
108. See Margulies, *Nothing Happens*, p. 162, and also McBane, 'Walking, Talking, Singing, Exploding'.
109. See Mayne, who reads the shape of the film as 'regressive' and in terms of a 'desire to fuse with the maternal object' (*The Woman at the Keyhole*, p. 133), and Margulies, who sees the feature's 'radical liminality' as enacting a 'demise of subjectivity' (*Nothing Happens*, p. 116).
110. Bataille, *La Part maudite*, p. 49. See Keifer Taylor, '*Jeanne Dielman*: A Soundtrack of the Everyday', *A Nos Amours* blog (2014) <https://anosamoursblog.weebly.com/blog/category/jeanne-dielman> [accessed 25 August 2020].
111. This is partly argued by Brey in her reading of the film in *Le Regard féminin*.
112. See Deleuze, *Cinéma 2*, p. 255.
113. See Deleuze and Guattari, *Mille plateaux*, pp. 339, 338.
114. Deleuze, *Cinéma 2*, p. 255 *Cinema II: The Time Image*, trans. by Tomlinson and Galeta, p. 196. For feminist critiques of becoming-woman see amongst others Rosi Braidotti, *Nomadic Subjects* (New York: Columbia University Press, 1994), p. 122; Alice Jardine, 'Woman in Limbo:

Deleuze and his Br(others)', *SubStance*, 13.3–4 (1984), 46–60; and Claire Colebrook, 'Modernism without Women: The Refusal of Becoming-woman and Post-feminism', *Deleuze Studies*, 7.4 (November 2013), 427–55.

115. See Lazzarato, *The Making of the Indebted Man*, p. 7.
116. Akerman herself, eager to distance the work from the narrower focus of Second Wave lesbian-separatist groups, infamously barred the film from being shown at lesbian and gay film festivals (details given in Raymond Murray, *Images in the Dark: An Encyclopedia of Gay and Lesbian Film and Video* (New York: Titan Books, 1998), p. 2). Further distancing her cinema from the trap of sex-essentialism, this withdrawal prompted her notorious assertion that 'I'm not making women's films... I'm making Chantal Akerman's films' (Akerman and Martin, *Chantal Akerman's Films*, p. 24)
117. In arguing for a non-penetrative, radically anorgasmic sexuality as elaborated in the film, I draw partly upon Deleuze and Guattari's notion of a 'molecular' sexuality composed of a '*n* sexes' as opposed to genital essentialism (see Gilles Deleuze and Félix Guattari, *L'Anti-Œdipe* (Paris: Minuit 1972), p. 352). Lippard alternatively calls this a mode of 'languorous sensuality' ('Eros Presumptive', p. 96) motivated to remain in a state of 'controlled voluptuousness' as opposed to outright climax. For a reading of *Je, tu, il, elle* as an enactment of a 'queer phenomenology' and 'queer existentialism', see Ros Murray, 'The Radical Politics of Possibility: Towards a Queer Existential Phenomenology through Chantal Akerman's *Je, tu, il, elle*', *feral feminisms*, 5 (Spring 2016) <https://feralfeminisms.com/radical-politics-of-possibility/> [accessed 17 September 2020].
118. Deleuze, *Cinema II*, p. 255.
119. For a discussion of self-evasion as feminist politics of refusal in relation to Barbara Loden's 1970 film *Wanda*, see Gorfinkel, 'Wanda, Loden, Lodestone'.
120. This desire for the full inhabitation of a space, and the practicing of a profound and unmitigated dwelling, contrasts with *Jeanne Dielman*'s wariness of domestic enclosure and claustrophobia, and more superficial interest in ornaments and surfaces.
121. Momcilovic, for example, has read this as a significantly empowering act of agency (*Chantal Akerman*, p. 15).
122. This beseeching stare appears to seal the film's ethos of participation and proximity. In contrast, *Jeanne Dielman* might be read as a study in avoiding eye contact.
123. See Rita Felski, 'Object Relations', *Contemporary Women's Writing*, 1.1–2 (December 2007), 185–91 (p. 186).
124. Chantal Akerman, *Là-bas* (2006: 79 minutes).
125. Deleuze, *Cinéma 2*, p. 255 *Cinema II: The Time Image*, trans. by Tomlinson and Galeta, p. 202.
126. For a more expanded, albeit slightly problematic account of anorexia as 'body politics', or political refusal of capitalism's unchecked productions and consumptions, see Gilles Deleuze and Claire Parnet, *Dialogues* (Paris: Flammarion, 1977), p. 123; and also Chris Kraus, *Aliens and Anorexia* (Los Angeles: Semiotext(e), 2000).
127. See Jenny Chamarette, *Phenomenology and the Future of Film*, (London: Palgrave, 2012), p. 143.
128. François, *Open Secrets*, p. 11.
129. Akerman's valorisation of a 'non-ends' directed writing echoes the form of writing without intended address that Deleuze and Guattari champion in *Mille plateaux* (p. 2).
130. For a sinuous discussion of the supine as a decadently unproductive mode see Emma Wilson, *The Reclining Nude* (Liverpool: University of Liverpool Press, 2019). The affiliation of the horizontal with abandonment, release, and rapture is also iterated by Louise Bourgeois, to be discussed in Chapter 3.
131. It is nonetheless worth nuancing that in *Dialogues*, Gilles Deleuze and Claire Parnet appoint anorexia as a pleasurable 'bingeing' on illicit, low-calorie foods — 'fizzy drinks, diet yoghurts', which constitute 'anorexic feasts' — as opposed to a total refusal of food (*Dialogues*, trans. by Hugh Tomlinson and Barbara Habberjam (New York: Columbia University Press, 1987), p. 110).
132. For an account of the first half of *Je, tu, il, elle* as an exhibition of 'orality and consumption', see Schmid, *Chantal Akerman*, p. 30.

133. Akerman, *Autoportrait en cinéaste*, p. 55: 'ne pas manger, c'était une façon de se révolter contre la génération sacrifiée. Une révolte que je retournais contre moi'.
134. See Saidiya Hartman, 'Extended Notes on the Riot', *e-flux*, 105 (December 2019) <https://www.e-flux.com/journal/105/302565/extended-notes-on-the-riot/> [accessed 25 August 2020].
135. I borrow this conceptual emblem from Gilles Deleuze, *Le Pli* (Paris: Minuit, 1988).
136. Ibid., p. 5.
137. Such a quality is also emphasised by Lippard, 'Eros Presumptive'.
138. Tamara Tracz has read this segment of the film conversely as 'the movement of the infant into the world, into self-dom' ('Je tu il elle', *Senses of Cinema*, 67 (May 2013) <http://sensesofcinema.com/2013/cteq/je-tu-il-elle/> [accessed 25 August 2020]).
139. Margulies, *Nothing Happens*, p. 119. Bataille, *La Part maudite*, p. 117.
140. McFadden, *Gendered Frames, Embodied Cameras*, p. 103. See Brey, *Le Regard féminin*, p. 187.
141. Akerman, *Autoportrait en cinéaste*, pp. 81, 80.
142. Such a view is also partially endorsed by Jamshaid, who argues that the film 'keeps returning to a kind of material, photographic surface' and 'lingers on the surface of things, on matter and physical existence and does not seem interested in penetrating that material surface' ('"Invested in Expression or in Its Destruction?"').
143. Steven Shaviro, *Post-Cinematic Affect* (London: Zero Books, 2010), p. 112.
144. Deleuze and Guattari, *Mille plateaux*, p. 342. Such pleasures find echoes in the work of Sophie Calle and Annie Ernaux, to be explored later in the book.
145. Jean Baudrillard, *America* (London: Verso, 1989), p. 9.
146. See Deleuze and Guattari, *Mille plateaux*, pp. 339, 255–26.
147. Deleuze, *Cinéma 2*, pp. 255–56 *Cinema II: The Time Image*, trans. by Tomlinson and Galeta, p. 256.
148. Momcilovic, *Chantal Akerman*, p. 58. Any unilateral endorsement of nomadism in Akerman's work must remain alive to context and nuance. As Alisa Lebow has implied, the Jewish faith is often associated with painful, traumatic experiences of exile and transience, as opposed to pleasurable nomadism ('Identity Slips: The Autobiographical Register in the Work of Chantal Akerman', *Film Quarterly*, 70.1 (Fall 2016), 54–60 (p. 54.). See Deleuze and Guattari, *Mille plateaux*, p. 199, for a warning against going to the point of suicidal destruction.
149. Braidotti, *Nomadic Subjects*, p. 22.
150. See Gorfinkel, '*Wanda*'s Slowness', p. 27.
151. See Elena Gorfinkel, 'Attachment Road: No Sex Last Night and American Honey', in *America: Films from Elsewhere*, ed. by Shanay Jhaveri (Mumbai: Shoestring Press, 2019), pp. 467–93, for a discussion of *No Sex Last Night*.
152. In her interview with Nicole Brenez, Akerman, a lifetime student of Emmanuel Levinas, expresses her care taken with the face-to-face encounter, suggesting, 'It's from this crucial face-to-face that your sense of responsibility begins' (Brenez, 'Chantal Akerman').
153. I employ this phrase from Lisa Robertson's *Nilling: On Noise, Pornography, The Codex, Melancholy, Lucretius, Folds, Cities, and Related Aporias* (Toronto: Bookthug Press, 2012), p. 51.
154. Baudrillard, *America*, p. 7.
155. Wilson, *The Reclining Nude*, p. 70. Mercedes McGrath has seen in Julie's retreat from the shot less a numbing of her agency than 'the potential desirability of invisibility'. Julie's figurative, as opposed to literal, contribution to the sex act, she further argues, can be linked to Jack Halberstam's understanding of a 'female gaze' as 'a willingness to see what is not there' (Mercedes MacGrath, 'Lesbian Gestures in the Cinema of Chantal Akerman' (unpublished MPhil thesis, University of Cambridge, June 2019); and Jack Halberstam, *In a Queer Time and Place: Transgender Bodies, Subcultural Lives* (New York & London: New York University Press, 2005), p. 87).
156. See Elena Gorfinkel, 'Weariness, Waiting: Enduration and Art Cinema's Tired Bodies', *Discourse*, 34.2–3 (Spring-Fall 2012), 311–47 (p. 334). The film's novel circuitries of feminine temporality might again relate to Kristeva's (1986) concept of 'women's time'.
157. For an account of this section of the film as a pointed feminist critique of the crude itineraries

of male pleasure, see Schmid, *Chantal Akerman*, p. 30. Margulies qualifies the film's nomadism in terms of 'the drama of the shifter' (*Nothing Happens*, p. 127).

158. See for example Mayne, *The Woman at the Keyhole*, p. 133.

159. Laura Owens, in Sarah Lehrer-Graiwer, 'Optical Drive: Sarah Lehrer-Graiwer talks with Laura Owens', *Artforum* (March 2013), 231–39.

160. Given that Akerman herself took distance from identifying categories, I am using the term 'queer' in relation to this section in less overtly ontological than aesthetic terms: indeed, to convey a sense of *Je, tu, il, elle*'s sinuosity, its sensuous traversal of ossified positions. For a pertinent account of lesbian desire as 'unproductive' and non-futurist through the specific lens of Deleuzian philosophy, see Chrysanthi Nigianni, 'Butterfly Kiss: The Contagious Kiss of Becoming-Lesbian', in *Deleuze and Queer Theory*, ed. by Chrysanthi Nigianni and Merl Storr (Edinburgh: Edinburgh University Press, 2012), pp. 168–83. For a further reading of *Je, tu, il, elle* as enacting a mercurial 'queer existentialism' as opposed to an explicit form of lesbian visibility, see Murray, 'The Radical Politics of Possibility'.

161. Brey, *Le Regard féminin*, p. 155.

162. Georges Bataille, *The Accursed Share: An Essay on General Economy. Volume I: Consumption*, trans. by Robert Hurley (New York: Zone Books, 1988), p. 181.

163. Deleuze and Guattari, *Mille plateaux*, p. 32; *A Thousand Plateaus: Capitalism and Schizophrenia*, trans. by Brian Massumi (London: Continuum, 2004), p. 24.

164. For Schmid, in *Chantal Akerman*, the interchanging between first, second, and third person indicated in the film's title underscores the affective dissonance or self-estrangement weighing down on women in male-oriented temporalities and space. Here, as in *Jeanne Dielman*, it is tempting to assign to the cocooning enclosure of the (female) lover's embrace a more feminine temporal and spatial logic, an architecture of reprieve from techno-capitalist patriarchy.

165. Such is Longfellow's reading of this section of the film ('Love Letters to the Mother').

166. Margulies, *Nothing Happens*, p. 123. Andrea Weiss, *Vampires and Violets: Lesbians in the Cinema*. (London: Jonathan Cape, 1992), p. 114, and Tracz, 'Je tu il elle', go quite the other way in declaring this scene 'absolutely uneroticized' and 'not erotic' respectively, neither of which are readings I subscribe to here.

167. This is more the approach of the 'New Extremist' filmmaking practiced by directors such as Catherine Breillat. For an expansive discussion of Breillat in relation to affect, pose and sensuality, see Wilson, *The Reclining Nude*.

168. See B. Ruby Rich, 'Chantal Akerman Interview, Chicago: 1976/2016', *Film Quarterly*, 70.1 (Fall 2016), 16–24 (p. 19).

169. See Deleuze and Guattari, *Mille plateaux*, p. 173.

170. Frida Beckman, 'Introduction', in *Deleuze and Sex*, ed. by Frida Beckman (Edinburgh: Edinburgh University Press, 2011), pp. 1–29 (p. 12).

171. Bataille, *La Part maudite*, pp. 26, 37; *The Accursed Share*, trans. by Hurley, p. 29.

172. Margulies has termed such shape-shifting as *Je, tu, il, elle*'s 'utter impossibility of "pure" indexicality' (*Nothing Happens*, p. 127).

173. See Blackhurst, 'The Defiant Muse', p. 49.

174. See Nigianni, 'Chantal Akerman's *La-bàs*'.

175. Robertson, *The Baudelaire Fractal*.

176. McFadden also makes this point in relation to the power of creative agency in *Je, tu, il, elle* (*Gendered Frames, Embodied Cameras*, p. 105).

177. Chantal Akerman, *A Nos Amours: Chantal Akerman Day*, JW3, London, 12 October 2014.

178. See solo exhibitions such as *Maniac Shadows*, The Kitchen, New York, 2013, and *BOZAR*, Palais des Beaux Arts, Brussels, 2013, as well as *Moving through Time and Space*, MIT List Visual Arts Centre, Cambridge, MA, 2008, and *A Spiral Autobiography*, Tel-Aviv Museum of Art, Tel Aviv, 2006.

179. See Bruno, 'Projection'. Laura Marks similarly argues for the forging of a form of 'dynamic subjectivity between looker and image' (*The Skin of the Film: Intercultural Cinema, Embodiment, and the Senses* (Durham, NC: Duke University Press, 1999), p. 64).

180. Nancy and Kiarostami, *L'Évidence du film*, pp. 23, 45.

CHAPTER 2

Annie Ernaux: l'écriture, un luxe

> Qu'est-ce que je cherche à faire? Comment je suis devenue écrivain? Pourquoi j'ai aimé ainsi? D'où cela vient? Cette passion, ce luxe?
>
> [What am I looking to do? How did I become a writer? Why did I love it so much? Where does it come from? This passion, this luxury?] — ANNIE ERNAUX[1]

In the closing paragraphs of *Passion simple*, a brief, best-selling work from 1992, Annie Ernaux's narrator considers how:

> Quand j'étais enfant, le luxe c'était pour moi les manteaux de fourrure, les robes longues et les villas au bord de la mer. Plus tard, j'ai cru que c'était de mener une vie d'intellectuel. Il me semble maintenant c'est aussi de pouvoir vivre une passion pour un homme ou pour une femme.[2]
>
> [When I was a child, luxury for me was fur coats, long dresses and villas next to the sea. Later, I believed luxury was leading the life of an intellectual. It seems to me now that it is also being able to live a passion for a man or for a woman.]

Tracing popular, iconic cinematic tropes of luxury, before evoking the more immaterial 'luxe de l'esprit' of an intellectual, writerly life, Ernaux's reflections form the focus of this chapter.[3] Oscillating between a bald hunger for commodities, the more ascetic pleasures of the bookish, scholarly vocation, and finally the sensual excess of what Jacques Derrida has called 'la vie la plus intense possible' [the most intense life possible], the passage opens questions of permission, possibility, fulfilment, and desire.[4] Emphasising *Passion simple*'s trajectory from what I term 'attachment to the object' to a willed immersion in embodied sensuality, it further corresponds to the book's aim at large to emancipate ideas of luxury from processes of 'conspicuous consumption' and to affirm alternative accounts of the luxurious as an affective and experiential register. In the discussion to follow, I subsequently privilege the lived, visceral textures of Ernaux's writing, and showcase its intentions, often cited by the author, to probe the limits of language.[5] In so doing, I expose luxury's 'aceconomies' of exposure, immoderation, abandonment, and passionately lived intensity.

Given Ernaux's expressed fondness and respect for the work of sociologist Pierre Bourdieu,[6] it is tempting to directly map her thinking about luxury onto Bourdieu's model of class ascension, in 'Le Champ littéraire' and *La Distinction*, as a progression from a model of conspicuous consumption to one of aristocratic production, or 'pretension'.[7] More than the capacity to consume culture and commodities, for Bourdieu, aristocratic pretension names the ability to assume an active role in their making, and to evolve beyond the status of passive spectator in thrall to mainstream culture. Since the publication of *La Place* Ernaux has described extensively her exit from the straitened Normandy milieu of her childhood and her entry, via education, into the rarefied realms of academia, teaching and writing for a living.[8] In the process she has underlined how Bourdieu's thinking has proved central to her own; specifically, to her ability to articulate 'la réalité objective des rapports sociaux' [the objective reality of social relations].[9] Yet, to read luxury as straightforward intellectual acquisition — as a mode of 'distinguishing' oneself as a member of the aristocratic intelligentsia — overlooks the polyvalent nature of this concept in Ernaux's *œuvre* at large, and posits the author as a docile disciple of a sociological school. As she writes in *Le Vrai Lieu*, a collection of interviews conducted and published by Michelle Porte, 'Je dois à la sociologie de Bourdieu beaucoup de choses, mais je ne "fais" pas de Bourdieu' [I owe to Bourdieu's sociology many things, but I am not 'doing' Bourdieu].[10] In the coda to *Passion simple*, Ernaux's additional reflection that 'c'est aussi pouvoir vivre une passion' [It's also the ability to live a passion] extends the concept of luxury beyond the acquisition of intellectual knowledge into the immersive pleasures of physical and experiential rapture.[11] Countering Bourdieu's model of luxury as sociological 'distinction', in *Passion simple*, Ernaux writes searingly of how both 'the time of passion' and 'the time of writing' move her closer to the thrilling limits of life. The imbricated realms of writing and eroticism permit her to 'lose herself' in the absolute obsession and 'perfection' of a process which momentarily dissolves, rather than affirms, rigid social and economic demarcations.[12]

Stylistically, since the publication of *La Place*, and taking inspiration from Barthes's *neutre* and Camus's 'écriture blanche',[13] Ernaux has honed an infamously austere 'écriture plate' which she has explicitly anatomized as being 'sans luxe' [without luxury].[14] She has attributed this rigorously spartan prose, excised of all embellishment, to a desire to pay tribute to the unaffected Normandy vernacular of her parents and relatives, for whom the florid cadences of literary composition would be deemed an alienating act of violence.[15] Allergic to excessive metaphors and fiercely shorn of sentimentality Ernaux's prose is not unsensuous, however.[16] Instead, it brims with potent scenes, impressions, and sensations which bespeak both the pleasures and the material anguishes of being gendered as a woman in twentieth- and twenty-first-century France.[17] In addition, the idea of writing as luxurious *procedure*, both in the material sense of privileged activity removed from manual labour and as an economically unnecessary supplement to Ernaux's decades-long employment as a teacher at a *collège*, recurs with frequency throughout her *œuvre*.[18] That writing further grants Ernaux a pleasurable opportunity to catapult herself beyond the usual parameters of her everyday identity is signalled in various interviews and metatextual discussions where she describes relishing both writing as if she were 'absent' from the publication of a text and abandoning attachments to personal propriety in order to write 'sans prix', or 'at whatever cost'.[19] Avoiding a quasi-Romantic or sublime fetishisation of writing, however, in the same exchanges Ernaux registers her anxiety that writing has definitively squandered, wasted, or exhausted the resources of her life.[20]Such accounts resonate with Georges Bataille's thinking about luxury, resonant throughout this study, as a 'dépense improductive', or as an intransitive, entropic lavishing of energy, and with Maurice Blanchot's concept of *l'écriture* as an act of radical and wilful separation from the world.[21] And yet, my intention is to show that while Ernaux might be situated within such lineages, her work also goes beyond them. If, in her conception, writing implies the 'refus d'un monde pour en créer un autre' [refusal of a world to create another] then this emphasis on creation resists ideas of luxury as mere decadent destruction, or consumptive passivity.[22] In Ernaux's case, to give oneself wholly to limitless abandonment via writing is, while exhausting already-existing modes of living and being, also to imagine radical alternatives for life, and more broadly, for the life of others.[23]

In post-1968 French thought and conceptual production, a desire to conceive of a form of writing that would not be subject to mercantile society and the reductive purchase of what Jacques Derrida, Jean-Luc Nancy, and others term an economy of 'general equivalence' was insistent.[24] Out of this intention to overturn fixed ideas of *écriture* as transactional and perpetually in deference to capitalism's dominant regimes of oppression sprung accounts such as Nancy's notion of 'exscription', or a writing that would always exceed the prescribed limits of rational calculation, Derrida's *écriture de la difference* which, countering 'self-presence', 'produces the trace as trace', Blanchot's writing of disaster, and Hélène Cixous's striking formulation that 'écrire, c'est toujours en cassant la valeur d'échange qui maintient la parole sur son rail, faire à la surabondance, à l'inutile, leur part sauvage' [To write is always to break the value of exchange [...] to appeal to superabundance; to uselessness; to writing's savage share].[25] Here, Cixous's call to re-sensitize writing to its 'savage share' resonates with Bataille's formulation of luxury as a 'potlatch', or an overspill of energy inevitably magnetised towards wasteful ends.[26] And yet, despite such novel re-conceptualisations, the post-68 intelligentsia's eagerness to affirm the act of writing as separate from the mechanistic forces of the market risked rarefying it as an activity impervious to the rhythms of everyday life. A desire to foreground writing's exceptional status, but also its quotidian materiality, is instilled in Ernaux's project to 'seize' or render the fraught residues and traces of everyday existence, to record the imprints made by mundane life, and to, in the author's own words, 'atteindre la réalité d'une époque' [arrive at the reality of an era].[27]

In my reading of *Passion simple* which opens the chapter, I suggest that the luxury of pausing time and space occasioned by enthralment to a major passion (or what Blanchot more emphatically calls the 'destruction of society' enabled by the private world of a 'community of lovers') and later, the ability to refine and 'perfect' the account of that acute eroticism via writing, is, by the text's end, exposed to the contingencies or the 'extravagance' of the wider outside world.[28] While initially dedicated, as its arresting final sentences make clear, to the narrator's total immersion and luxuriation in, the 'limit experience' of her erotic obsession, as Ernaux progresses in her reconstructive project of *écriture*, the universality, and indeed, collective structures that subtend a feminised experience of love and loss are exposed.[29] Ultimately, the ability to share the common features of this passion — to use the story of the I to enable what Jean-Luc Nancy terms a 'partage des voix' [sharing of voices] or an exultant 'being-in-common' — becomes the greater gift; the greater luxury.[30] As Madeleine Schwartz has noted in relation to her work, Ernaux reads the personal as always already structural, her ambition never solely to excavate individual memories, but to show the subtle ways in which they interact with the historical, collective experience.[31]

In the second half of the chapter, I examine the later text *Se perdre*, a voluminous *journal intime* published in 2001.[32] Kept during the living out and later composition of *Passion simple*, the book offers a digressive wildness and breadth of literary sensibilities largely pruned from the more famous work. Without making facile conclusions about the diary's 'formlessness' in distinction to the more crafted and canonical literary text, as warned against by Anna Jackson, I argue that *Se perdre*'s unique luxury is situated in the space the diary genre affords Ernaux as a writer to indulge in more experimental literary practices, or in her own words, 'jouir de la plus grande liberté d'écriture' [take pleasure in the greatest freedom of writing].[33] I suggest, following Tom Paulin, who has argued that the diary form embodies an 'idea of expressive motion' singular within literary culture, that *Se perdre* permits a more continuous, mobile, and indeed kinetic prose style which embraces a more cinematic register than *Passion simple*'s snapshot, starkly graphic cadences.[34] Though Ernaux's writing has, since her earliest publications, been steeped in visual modalities, I show throughout the chapter how the immanence and alluring process of *l'écriture* itself remains her most enduring form of luxury, which, far from being hoarded solely for the self, is made magnanimously available for public view.[35]

From the 'Community of Lovers' to the Exposure of Community: *Passion simple*

In a section titled 'The Community of Lovers' in his monograph *La Communauté inavouable*, Maurice Blanchot analyses Georges Bataille's fictional text *Madame Edouarda* and the author's evocation of 'le monde vrai des amants' or the 'true world of lovers'.[36] For Blanchot, the exclusionary community of two that Bataille's enraptured lovers form instigates a luxurious 'loosening' of the social bond and an aristocratic 'abolition', or 'suspension', of the world in favour of the primary amorous relation. He suggests indeed that 'le relâchement sournois du lien social que suppose un tel monde précisément est l'oubli du monde' [the sly loosening of the social bond that such a world presumes is in fact the forgetting of the world].[37] Furthering this reading of Bataille, Blanchot writes, 'La relation qui ici est en jeu n'est pas *mondaine*, supposant même la disparition, voire l'effondrement du monde' [The relation at play here isn't *worldly,* but sets its sights on the disappearance or collapse of the world], and 'La communauté des amants, que ceux-ci le veuillent ou non, qu'ils soient liés par le hasard, "l'amour fou", la passion de la mort (Kleist), a pour fin essentielle *la destruction de la société*' [The community of lovers, whether they like it or not, and whether they are linked by chance, 'l'amour fou', or the passion of death (Kleist), has as its essential objective *the destruction of society*].[38] In his 1989 book *La Communauté désœuvrée*, published partially as a response to Blanchot's text, Jean-Luc Nancy further takes Bataille to task, accusing him of dispensing with all forms of community other than 'un isolement maudit des amants et de l'artiste' [a cursed isolation of lovers and artists] and of offering 'l'amour en guise de refuge ou de substitut pour la communauté perdue' [love in the guise of refuge or substitute for lost community].[39] For Nancy, Bataille reifies 'la rupture de la passion' [the rupture of passion] as a form of sacred separation and conceives it as a symptom of an antiquated 'société de la fête, de la dépense, du sacrifice et de la gloire' [society of festiveness, of expenditure, of sacrifice, and of glory].[40] In Bataille's own terms, expressed in an essay on the history of eroticism, 'L'amour n'unit les amants que pour dépenser, que pour aller de plaisirs en plaisirs, de réjouissances en réjouissances: leur société en est une de consummation, à l'inverse de l'État, qui en est une de l'acquisition' [Love only unites lovers so that they can squander and go from pleasure to pleasure, from enjoyment to enjoyment: their society is one of consumption, in opposition to the State's, which is one of acquisition].[41] In *Passion simple*, Ernaux reconstructs the intensity of a transgressive lived experience — an ephemeral affair she once conducted with a married Russian diplomat — by exhibiting the material and visual traces such a relationship deposited in her day-to-day experience.[42] Resonating with Bataillean notions of *l'écriture* as a reckoning with waste and expenditure, the text brims with detritus: used ashtrays, drinking glasses, stained items of underwear. In showcasing the extant products of a passion, or what Naomi Schor terms the 'bad objects' usually consigned to the sentimental, 'feminine' literary genre, Ernaux soils the conventionally polished, indeed luxuriant, surfaces of bourgeois textual production.[43] In surrendering herself, for the best part of a year, to the entropic bent of a relationship that will never assume the contours of a more conventional life path (monogamy, marriage, children) her narrator, further, undercuts the propriety of heteronormative conceits. Rather than conserving her energy for a more outwardly respectable arrangement, Ernaux's 'je' lavishes her time, money, and other material resources on an affair that, in her words, will go nowhere, seamed with the textures of its own destruction.[44]

Ernaux's account of cyclically waiting, anticipating, and eventually being abandoned by her lover approaches Roland Barthes's account, in *Fragments d'un discours amoureux*, of luxury as an 'économie noire' [black economy] and an 'intolerable' state, or, to employ a more Bataillean register, a spiral into pure abjection.[45] Yet to immerse and enclose oneself in this suffering is also, for Ernaux's narrator, to experience a heightened, almost ecstatic, sense of sensitivity towards the world, an extreme distillation of experience in which 'tout allait dans le même sens' [everything was concentrated in the same direction].[46] In Blanchot's reading of Bataille, the affective state of passion is classified as a 'sentiment ravageur, à la verité au-délà de tout sentiment, ignorant le pathos, débordant la conscience, *rompant avec le souci de moi-même*' [ravaging sentiment, in truth beyond all sentiment, ignorant of pathos, exceeding conscience; breaking with a sense of care for the self].[47] This corresponds to Ernaux's generally expressed desire when writing to 'fuir toute cohérence; toute identité fixe [...] me tenir à une telle distance de moi-même que je me considérais une autre femme' [flee all coherence; all fixed identity... to keep myself at such a distance from myself that I would even consider myself another woman].[48] The extreme level of attention demanded by erotic obsession enables, in *Passion simple*, a luxurious suspension of habitual and transactional social bonds, installing an economy in which the sole metric is the other person ('L'unique qui éclipse tous les autres' [the unique being who eclipses all the others]), or a regime whereby, in Ernaux's own insistent phrasing, 'seul compte le désir' [the only thing that counts is desire].[49]

Further resonating with Blanchot's account of Bataille's obsessive lovers 'forgetting' the tumult of the outside world, *Passion simple* opens with a scene of absolute absorption: Ernaux's first exposure to a pornographic film: 'Cet été, j'ai regardé pour la première fois un film classé X à la television, sur Canal +' [This summer, I watched for the first time an X-rated film on television, on Canal +].[50] In its cinematic visuality, the tableau appears to substitute the objective distance of writing for the moving image's haptic proximity, or to install, as Sam Ferguson has noted, 'a photographic ideal of language that sacrifices all possibility of interpretation in favour of complete presence'.[51] At the same time, the narrator's lack of a decoder to correctly process the sequence renders the dialogue inaudible, and the images slack and gauzy: 'L'histoire était incompréhensible et on ne pouvait prévoir quoi que ce soit, des gestes ou des actions' [The story was incomprehensible and one could not make out barely anything, whether gestures or actions], she recalls.[52] With contextualising qualifiers — narrative, plot, and psychological intent — sanded away, all that remains is the coarse act of penetration which Ernaux registers as less shocking in itself than the fact that she has never seen the process so explicitly displayed before. The effect is avowed as 'bouleversante' [shocking], the cloudy reception giving rise, both intra and extra-diegetically, to a heady state of sensuous libidinous multiplicity where bodies and desires are indistinct from one another and entwined.[53] Unmoored from all social, decorous conventions, sex in this instance is permitted to become a purely carnal act, delivered from romantic prerequisites or lyrical footnoting. Unencumbered by what the narrator later will disparage as a 'luxe de détails' [luxury of details] inherent to normative modes of literary presentation, passion is related in strikingly pared back, 'simple' terms — presented as material fact, exposed as clinical testimony.[54]

In a signature metatextual gesture, in which she deliberately focuses attention on the writing process *in medias res*, Ernaux draws a line under this initial scene by offering the observation that 'il m'a semblé que l'écriture devrait tendre à cela, cette impression que provoque la scène de l'acte sexuel, cette angoisse et cette stupeur, une suspension du jugement moral' [It seems to me that writing should aim towards this, to the impression provoked by the scene of the sexual act, that anguish and that stupor, a suspension of moral judgment].[55] In so doing, she ventures an economy of writing as one able to detach from sanitized codes of moralistic judgment, and outlines her conception of *l'écriture* as a sensory process able to suspend the schedules and regimens of 'calculable' or 'productive' time.

A further sense of the effects the affair has wrought upon Ernaux's habitual mode of being and conducting herself in the world is introduced in the ensuing section of the text where the narrator plainly states, 'A partir du mois de septembre l'année dernière, je n'ai plus rien fait d'autre qu'attendre un homme: qu'il me téléphone et qu'il vienne chez moi' [Starting from the month of September of last year, I did nothing except wait for a man: for him to call me and come over to my place].[56] She continues to suggest provocatively that 'les seules actions où j'engageais ma volonté, mon désir et quelque chose qui doit être l'intelligence humaine (prévoir, évaluer le pour et contre, les conséquences) avaient toutes un lien avec cet homme' [the only activities where I engaged my willpower, my desire, and something of the order of human intelligence (predicting, evaluating pros and cons, consequences) were ones which had a link with this man] (p. 14). Yet, far from 'intolérable', or a source of predictable self-reproach, this suspension of ordinary time is consistently invoked by Ernaux's persona as generative, as unfurling a sort of perfection (p. 23), or in Nancy's apposite terms expressed in *La Communauté désœuvrée*, 'Une vie exemplaire d'où rien ne se retire, où rien ne demeure en deçà d'une limite singulière, où tout se communique' [An exemplary life in which nothing retreats, in which nothing remains below a singular limit, in which everything communicates].[57] In the totality of focus it requires, it unfolds a pleasurable 'perte de soi', or loss of the self, a phrase which Ernaux will continue to employ in regards to the relationship. It also instills a liberating sense of existential simplicity. The narrator's erotic obsession, which she observes with near-religious devotion, indeed allows her to consign sundry other administrative tasks and duties of her life to unimportance, to a displaced mode of ecstatic forgetting. Her world contracts to:

> Un espace de temps délimité par deux bruits de voiture, sa R25 freinant, redémarrant, où j'étais sure qu'il n'y avait jamais rien eu de plus important dans ma vie, ni avoir des enfants, ni réussir des concours, ni voyager loin, que cela, être au lit avec cet homme au milieu de l'après-midi.[58]
>
> [A time frame bordered by two car engine noises, his R25 braking, re-starting, in which I was certain that there had never been anything more important in my life, not having children, nor succeeding in exams, nor travelling to far-far-flung places, nothing but that, being in bed with this man in the middle of the afternoon.]

Such 'constraints' are vaunted as expansive and volitional: 'sources d'attente et de désir' [sources of expectation and desire] (p. 38). Querying somewhat the absolutism of Bataille's lovers' radical withdrawal from the world, at the same time, Ernaux sagely checks the material co-ordinates enabling her to undergo this experience, citing 'le temps et la liberté dont j'ai pu disposer pour vivre cela' [the time and the freedom which I had at my disposal to live this experience] (p. 32).

The deliverance in *Passion simple* from what Roland Barthes repudiates as 'la gestion', and Emily Apter translates as the 'managed life', also triggers the release of instrumental cognition, or the pausing of the cerebral existence upon which the author's livelihood, reputation, and precarious class status is normally upheld.[59] During 'le temps de la passion' [the time of passion] Ernaux's usual intellectual endeavors of reading, cinema visits, and conversations with friends are seen as superfluous diversions: 'J'évitais les occasions qui pouvaient m'arracher à mon obsession: lectures, sorties, et toute activité dont j'avais goût avant' [I avoided occasions which could snap me out of my obsession: readings, excursions, and all activities I had a taste for before].[60] Even television proves too mentally depleting: 'Je ne pouvais pas regarder la télévision ni feuilleter les magazines, toutes les publicités ne montrent que ceci: une femme attend un homme' [I couldn't watch television or flick through magazines; all the adverts showed only this: a woman waits for a man] (p. 13). In the same, extended passage, Ernaux will explicitly describe this phenomenon in terms of a 'désœuvrement', suggesting a desire to, through the prism of her passion, thoroughly dismantle the protective carapace of intellectual culture, and, evoking Blanchot, forget, abolish, or suspend the menial transactions of mundane society (p. 41).

In his essay 'Una fama da bue', Giorgio Agamben understands *désœuvrement* or 'inoperativity' not as a complete annihilation or obliteration of the world (which would more closely approximate Blanchot's and Bataille's model) but rather as a making-sacred, an adornment of life by means of festive ritual. He writes that inoperativity 'is not mere inertia or abstention; it is, rather, a sanctification, that is to say, a particular modality of acting, and living' and maintains that 'what is essential here is a dimension of praxis in which simple, quotidian human activities are neither negated nor abolished but suspended and rendered inoperative in order to be exhibited, as such, in a festive manner.'[61]

In the most ardent phase of the affair, before her lover returns home to Russia and largely falls out of contact, Ernaux exhibits the insatiability of her desire by means of consumerist exuberance. Attending to the overlaps that can occur between commodity acquisition and erotic expenditure, whilst refusing to fall into gendered tropes of women who buy cosmetic articles before sexual encounters with men, she documents her own frantic purchasing of branded goods such as make-up, items of clothing, and perfumes. She declares how, in between sporadic rendezvous with the diplomat, 'les seuls moments heureux en dehors de sa présence étaient ceux où j'achetais de nouvelles robes, des boucles d'oreilles, des bas et les essayais chez moi devant la glace' [the only happy moments outside his presence were those in which I bought new dresses, earrings, tights, and tried them on at home in front of the mirror].[62] Such expenditures appear precisely to indulge a form of conspicuous consumption, or a kind of luxury materialism that seems to bolster, rather than suspend, the economic world. Yet, in anticipating and prolonging the acute pleasure of physical encounters, these acquired items also come to embody the ritualistic exhibition of erotic love and become portals of connection to her lover, who, it is observed, 'aimait les costumes Saint-Laurent, les cravates Cerruti et les grosses voitures' [loved Saint-Laurent suits, Cerruti ties and massive cars] (p. 32). His rather vulgar appetite for consumer culture resuscitates the 'adolescente avide de robes, de disques et de voyages' [adolescent desperate for dresses, CDs and trips] that Ernaux once was but has learnt to suppress behind the more discreet signals of wealth and status demanded by the middle classes (p. 33). In an essay on the scope of Bourdieu's legacy for the edited volume *Pierre Bourdieu: l'insoumission en héritage*, Ernaux observes these counter-intuitive demands of haute-bourgeois refinement, noting, 'Les professeurs, les artistes, tous ceux qui ont un capital culturel plus important qu'un capital économique — se caractérisent par l'aristocratisme ascétique, qui consiste à choisir les loisirs culturels moins *coûteux* et plus rares, à préférer la sobriété au luxe' [Professors, artists, all those who have cultural capital in excess of economic capital — are characterised by an aristocratic asceticism, which consists of choosing less *costly* and more rare, cultural pursuits, of preferring sobriety to luxury].[63] In an astute observation, Ernaux further argues that 'le luxe et l'ascèse sont tous deux, cependant, des manières de nier la nature, et tous les dominants se retrouvent dans le souci des formes, une *rupture avec la vie*' [luxury and asceticism are both, however, ways of denying nature, and all members of the dominant class can identify themselves in their concern for forms, their *rupture with life*].[64] In other words, 'aristocratic asceticism' is still a mode of calculated class display, as deliberate and as exclusive in its intentions as more conventional stagings of luxury, which Ernaux, in *Passion simple*, underscores as an ambivalent, though ultimately generative experience.

As the narrative of *Passion simple* progresses and the tenor of the sexual affair heightens, the narrator's amorous expenditures become increasingly immaterial. Evolving beyond fetishistic attachments to the consumer object they form part of what Ernaux's persona terms a broader ambiance of 'dépense générale, nécessaire... inséparable de ma passion pour A' [General, necessary expenditure... inseparable from my passion for A].

Handing out money to beggars in the tunnels of the metro and making elaborate donations to charitable organizations Ernaux reflects, 'Contrairement à ma façon habituelle de vivre, je jetais facilement l'argent par les fenêtres' [Contrary to my usual way of living, I effortlessly threw money out the windows]. Such profligacy extends to the temporal realm, with Ernaux noting, in the midst of the affair, the time 'que je perdais en rêveries et en attente' [that I lost to daydreams and whilst waiting] for her lover to emerge.[65]

Again resonating with a Bataillean register of 'dépense' or general expenditure, Ernaux's narrator positions herself here as willingly abstracted from the circuits of economized existence and from any impulse towards self-conservation. Instead, eager to kill time in 'rêveries' and 'attentes' and gravitating towards waiting-rooms and train stations, or Marc Augé's 'non-lieux' unhooked from the unblinking grids of a 24/7 capitalist culture, Ernaux expends herself without reserve, overwriting expected feminine modesty and decorum with volitional self-dereliction and exhaustion.[66] And yet, again troubling the absolute hermeticism of Bataille's lovers' 'society of two', the intended objects of her frenzied donations — the homeless, the charity Secours populaire français — belie a certain attunement towards the inequalities of hierarchized society, sketching ambitions to compensate for this sexually, materially, and emotionally decadent experience.

In the second half of *Passion simple*, as the married diplomat returns to Russia and blocks Ernaux's continued efforts to remain in touch, a desire to postpone the mechanisms of productive society is performed less by external rituals and gestures than by the act of *écriture* itself. At this stage in the text, writing indeed becomes increasingly sacred to Ernaux's narrator, cathected as a mode of access to the 'absolute presence' she experienced in sex. While during this period ordinary life has a fracturing, dissociative effect on Ernaux, writing, in contrast, enables access to 'une durée que je ne voulais pas finie, celui de "en ce temps-là la vie était plus belle," d'une repetition éternelle' [A duration which I didn't want finished, one of 'at that time life was more beautiful', one of an eternal repetition].[67]

The writing of this passion, which Ernaux initially registers as a mere 'notation', begins to accrue material resonance for the narrator (p. 18). Ejecting her from the solipsistic circuits of romantic bereavement, it begins to connect her to an imagined community of readers. This is recognised in a passage comparing the comforts of a dressing-gown once belonging to her lover with the ongoing composition of the text we now hold in our hands. For the narrator, re-reading the pages she has written is as 'painful' as touching the dressing-gown, emphasising the material, sensuous nature of her writing enterprise. Yet she notes in contrast that her writing will always retain 'meaning' for her, whereas the charge of the dressing-gown will fade, will evoke nothing for her one day (p. 62).

This projection installs something of a turning point in *Passion simple*'s narrative, expanding Bataille's exclusionary community and its desire only to instate an 'ecstasy of the instant' into a desire to affect and interact with others. Having exhausted — 'gone to the ends of', in Ernaux's own words — the affective and corporeal co-ordinates of a singular affair, what remains for the author is the opportunity to extend its template out to readers, to offer what the narrator calls a 'inverted gift'. The unlimited abandonment with which she gave herself to the relation will now be transposed into a desire to make something universal and enduring out of this exceptional experience: 'J'ai seulement rendu en mots — qu'il ne lira sans doute pas, qui ne lui sont pas destinés — ce que son existence, par elle seule, m'a apporté. Une sorte de don reversé' [I only rendered into words — which he'll no doubt not read, and which are not destined for him — what his existence, by itself alone, brought to me. A sort of inverted gift] (p. 77). This gift — inviting comparison with Marcel Mauss's and Jacques Derrida's understandings of the gift as an intransitive concept, or as the gesture of an unlimited giving without expectation of return — has no intention, the narrator states, of influencing or even reaching her estranged Russian lover.[68] The question of whether he deserves such consecration in textual form is, she argues, senseless: 'Qu'il ait mérité ou non n'a évidemment aucun sens' [whether he deserved it or not obviously has no sense at all].[69] The point is rather that the thrilling existential latitudes made possible by passion have expanded the narrator's understanding of the world, have unfurled a new, luxurious in the sense of extraordinary, conception of space and time: 'J'ai mesuré le temps autrement, de tout mon corps' [I measured time differently, with my whole body] (p. 76). The usual formulaic prescriptions of an 'exchange economy' have been re-imagined.

By the end of *Passion simple*, the luxury of having 'lived a passion', or of having reached the summit of erotic, passionate obsession, illuminates new thresholds of quotidian existence, troubles the economy of a separate self, existing only to preserve itself and live by its own means. 'Grâce à lui, je me suis approché de la limite qui me sépare de l'autre' [Thanks to him, I approached the limit that separates me from the Other], the narrator declares (p. 76). The text's earlier kinetic lust for objects and commodities is overlapped by the quietude of aesthetic contemplation when Ernaux's persona further observes: 'J'ai découvert de quoi on peut être capable, autant dire de tout' [I discovered what we are capable of, which is to say everything] (p. 76). This expanded sense of capability resists definitive narrative closure; and indeed, near the text's end, each time Ernaux tries to conclude and draw a line under the story it reconfigures itself sinuously just outside her grasp. She notes, in another admission which creates the impression she is composing the text in 'real' time, how 'l'ensemble des signes qui constituent le roman non écrit d'une passion commence à se défaire' [the entirety of signs which constitute the non-written novel of a passion are starting to undo themselves] (p. 69) before landing on the thought that 'l'écriture est toujours ouverte' [writing is always open] (p. 71).

In *L'Entretien infini,* Blanchot uses the word *extravagance* to name the 'unworldliness' of love and literature, which resist containment by the limits of the ordinary world .[70] For his part, Nancy coins the concept of 'exscription' to name a kind of *écriture* which always exceeds permanent inscription, whose 'sense' drifts out beyond terminal comprehension.[71] Both concepts resonate with the mercurial, resistant end of *Passion simple*, illuminating how the open-ended process of *l'écriture* evolves the text beyond its initial immersion in a 'society of lovers' or hermetic structure of the couple to embrace more outwards-facing, ephemeral emotions and experiences.

In an essay on the movement of the sublime in art, which he titles 'L'Offrande sublime', Nancy writes that 'à la limite de l'art il y a le geste de l'offrande: le geste qui offre l'art, et le geste par lequel l'art lui-même touche à sa limite' [at the limit of art there is a gesture of offering: the gesture which art offers, and the gesture through which art itself touches on its limit].[72] For there to be this offering there has to be an 'abandon', a total giving of oneself over to experience, or an 'abandon à l'extension totale, illimitée, et donc à la limite. Ce qui se passe à la limite, c'est l'offrande' [abandonment to a total, unlimited extension, and therefore to the limit. What happens at the limit is an offering].[73] In *Passion simple*, Ernaux might be understood as having 'touched' upon the finitude of sensory experience, at which point, Nancy maintains, an inevitable and primary exposure to community in the form of an offering occurs. Without his knowing, the narrator acknowledges of her lover, 'il m'a reliée davantage au monde' [he connected me even more to the world].[74] Luxury reveals itself, in the text's final expository paragraph, as the ability to transmute an intense fugue state into a sublime textual object, but also to transition from the *huis clos* of an affair between two people to a more contingent, communal sensorium.

In *Se perdre*, I argue in the section to follow, a sense of contingency and porousness is amplified by the uninterrupted consciousness and propulsive motion of the diary genre, whose deferral of closure and radically 'open form' allows for further immersion in the experience, and counterpoint analysis, of passion.[75] Departing from *Passion simple*'s need to control, perfect, and simplify the telling of the relation in favour of a more voluptuous, capacious textual container, *Se perdre*, I suggest, offers 'different ways of playing with the passionate moment, different ways of spilling its contents', to borrow the poet Anne Carson's terms.[76] And yet unifying both texts, I suggest, is a commitment to *l'écriture* over the emotional ephemera of sexual and romantic love, and a desire to stay in the present tense of writing independent of events of the past.[77] Such a process, I argue, ultimately counters the compulsions of shame, guilt, and feelings of betrayal frequently attributed to Ernaux's *œuvre* with luxurious attention to the rhythms of a life lived and shared.[78]

Se perdre: vivre une histoire

> La souveraineté [...] doit se dépenser sans réserve, se perdre, perdre connaissance, perdre la mémoire de soi, l'intériorité à soi [...] elle doit pratiquer l'oubli. — Jacques Derrida[79]
>
> [Sovereignty [...] must expend itself without reserve, lose itself, lose consciousness, lose all memory of itself and all the interiority of itself [...] it must practise forgetting.]

In January 2000, Annie Ernaux decided to re-read her diaries kept during the affair taken as the subject of the 1992 work *Passion simple*. Having been out of access to her for a while, their rediscovery is intoxicating, generative, to the author. Upon their reconsideration, Ernaux writes, 'Je me suis aperçue qu'il y avait dans ces pages une "vérité" autre que celle contenue dans *Passion simple*' [I realised that in these pages there was another 'truth' than the one contained in *Passion simple*].[80]

This realisation and exposure to a different kind of sensibility — 'Quelque chose de cru et de noir, sans salut, quelque chose de l'*oblation*' [Something raw and dark, without redemption, something of the order of *oblation*] — and sense that 'cela aussi devait être porté au jour' [it too should be brought to light] — occasions, in 2001, the publication of these urgent, extensively notated fragments and notes, under the broad title of *Se perdre*.[81] In contrast to *Passion simple*'s meticulously crafted, refined style, and its luxury of being able to 'perfect' a passion in the act of writing, this work, without the privilege of hindsight or detached distance, immerses us in an account of an affair in the midst of its unfolding, gratifies an *écriture immédiate* predicated on 'peu de pensée, ou plus exactement, la pensée sans issue: le présent, la peau, l'Autre' [little thought, or more precisely, thought without origin: the present tense, the texture of skin, the Other].[82]

Exempt from the pressures of potential publication, and free to surrender to what Nancy calls an abandonment to language, an account of *Se perdre* as a space of permission and authorial allowance, and as an unpoliced 'spillage' of meaning, will be offered in this section as a counterpoint to *Passion simple*'s writerly self-consciousness, and, before the moment of its scintillating final coda, its internal logic of narrative restraint, checks, and interventions.[83] Emphasising the enriched space that *Se perdre* occupies, I claim that, rather than a mere expanse of narcissistic self-inscription, the collection can be read as a site of creative play and experimentalism to invite readings of luxury as a form of sensual exploration through writing, and specifically, as the ability to 'lose oneself' in a particular context and *histoire*.[84]

Elaborating further on her decision to make *Se perdre*'s excerpts public, in an interview exchange with Fréderic-Yves Jeannet, Ernaux comments that 'une des raisons qui m'a fait publier *Se perdre,* c'est de montrer le "jeu" — au sens d'espace qui sépare — entre le journal intime et le texte de *Passion simple*' [one of the things that made me publish *Se perdre* was the desire to reveal the 'game' — in the sense of the separating space — between the *journal intime* and the text of *Passion simple*].[85] Reading *Passion simple* and *Se perdre* side by side, I argue, accentuates such playfulness, illuminates the luxury of being able to expand on a prior publication, and to, by different means, give a different, enhanced account of the same story.[86] Raising further questions about luxury as embellishment, adornment, extension, and elaboration, it makes space for other readings and opens up the possibility that, in Ernaux's own terms, 'une histoire n'est jamais finie' [a story is never over].[87]

Effusion and Allowing

Explicitly foregrounding its subtexts of desire and longing from the outset, *Se perdre* opens with an assertion of will, or the epigraph, rendered in Italian and translated into French, 'Voglio vivere una favola: Je veux vivre une histoire'.[88] Taken from a tangle of graffiti engraved on a flight of stairs leading to the church of Santa Croce in Florence, and read by chance during a trip to the city by Ernaux, such an inscription forms immediate and striking counterpoint to *Passion simple*'s experience of having 'lived a passion', exhibiting the differences in outlook and intent between the two, superficially very similar, projects.[89]

In contrast to the latter work's sated temporality of having lived, and of having been exposed to an experience of an incisive affect, *Se perdre*'s opening pronouncement — 'je veux vivre une histoire' — envelops those who read the text in the immediacy of a passion in the present tense, in the pleasurable haze of a libidinal relationship that has yet to be entirely exhausted or indulged. Given over to the immersive flux of happenings as they occur, and delivered from retrospective self-reproach or rumination, here writing is not wielded 'like a knife' (in the words of Ernaux and Jeannet) but encountered as a gesture of Nancean 'unburdening'. This is in echo of Maurice Blanchot's evaluation of the *journal intime* as a space of permission and inclusion, or a site in which 'pensées, rêves, fictions, commentaires de soi-même, événements importants, insignifiants, tout y convient, dans l'ordre et le désordre qu'on veut' [thoughts, dreams, fictions, self-commentaries, important and insignificant events — all fits there, in the order or disorder that one wishes].[90]

This climate of uninterrupted consciousness is corroborated by Ernaux's observation in the preface to *Se perdre* that, contrary to *Passion simple*'s austere writing economy of edits and re-workings, no amendments were made to the gathered entries prior to their publication.[91] A sense of permissive letting-be is communicated by Ernaux's declaration in her introduction that 'je n'ai rien modifié ni retranché du texte initial en le saisissant sur ordinateur' [I didn't modify anything or cut down the initial text while typing it up on the computer].[92] This impression of the diary form as offering reprieve from craft and from anguished authorial interference is further offered by the testimony, also in the preface, that, at the time of its writing, the project was immune to any 'soucis de forme' [worries about form] or 'astreintes de régularité' [penalties of regularity], free to function instead as an open forum for the vibrant dissemination and offloading of ideas.[93] A sense of ease and of a certain leisure of production in relation to the diary form is figured even more explicitly in Ernaux's interview with Jeannet, where the *journal intime* in general is ventured as a 'lieu de *jouissance*' permitting flight away from the strenuous constructions demanded by the *œuvre totale*.[94] In *Se perdre*, the realisation of a kind of pleasurable losing of authorial intention and of 'self-decomposure', to rehearse a term of Robyn Wiegman, competes with simultaneous desires to 'redoubler la jouissance des rencontres en consignant les paroles et les gestes érotiques' [double the *jouissance* of encounters by depositing erotic words and gestures].[95] Such exercises elevate *Se perdre*'s diary form beyond mere transcription or indexation, and expand upon *Passion simple*'s exercise in 'simple' exposition, by fleshing out the latter text's refined anatomy of an affair. Subsequently, in this taut two-page account which precedes the dense mass of diary entries to follow, we learn, amongst other things, that Ernaux first met A, later transposed to become 'S', following a writers' trip to Moscow, Tbilisi, and St Petersburg (p. 700), a fact omitted from *Passion Simple*, the prior text.

In her reading of the work, Emmanuelle Lacore-Martin notes that the objective of *Se perdre* 'is certainly a question of offering', arguing that Ernaux's 'bonuses' of insight granted to the reader should be principally viewed as means of trying to compensate for the narcissistic 'luxury', indulged in *Passion simple*, of being able to fulfil a passion without monetary, professional, or other similar material concerns.[96] Whilst this account is compelling, and bolstered perhaps, by the preface's attempts to 'justify' the swell and surfeit of observations to come, the overall language of 'oblation' entered into by the *avant-propos* seems less interested in making up for past capriciousness than eager to subject the who's, what's and why's of the initial passionate relationship to what Nancy in 'L'Excrit' terms a 'dissolution éclatante' [shattering dissolution] of reasoning.[97] Although *Se perdre* can enrich interpretations of *Passion simple*, it also arguably suspends the former polished and perfected text in a flotsam of impressionistic memories and even threatens to undo its seamless, luminous narrative logic by revealing in explicit and uncensored fashion the visceral and affective 'mess' of the affair before it is repackaged into a more digestible literary form. In such a way, *Se perdre* might be said to both reify and sacrifice its antecedent. In particular, the latter reading of the work as a risky exercise in self-exposure corresponds to Ernaux's broader aims to 'create dangerously' and to write as if she were completely absent from the context of her publications' readings.[98]

A sense of the audaciousness of *Se perdre*'s ambitions is communicated by the wealth of rawly confessional, at times 'crude', statements exposed by the text, which trespass on the decorum of both gendered and professional expectations.[99] Such statements revisit and expand upon questions raised by *Passion simple* of erotic performance, display, and exhibition, and further figure Ernaux's wish to 'aller jusqu'au bout' [go to the limit] in her life and written projects. In an account of a literary cocktail party attended in Paris, Ernaux writes, for example, 'J'aurais mieux fait de travailler la conférence pour le Barbican College, au lieu d'aller au cocktail. Nul. Parisien. Plus de journalistes que d'écrivains' [I would have been better off working on the lecture for Barbican College, instead of going to the cocktail party. Rubbish. Parisian. More journalists than writers], dispensing with habitual practice in diary publication of obscuring names.[100] Dispensing too, with the more nuanced reification of sexual difference admitted by *Passion simple*, Ernaux further courts controversy by choosing here to publish quickly jotted-down assertions, observing, after a long period of frustrated idleness whilst waiting for her lover to come back after trips abroad, for example, that 'les lesbiennes choisissent la facilité' [lesbians choose facility] (p. 788), or, at odds with her more explicitly feminist politics expressed elsewhere, 'Mère et pute, je suis les deux. J'ai toujours aimé tous les rôles' [Mother and whore, I'm both. I've always loved all the roles] (p. 767). An impression that this is a festival of unselfconsciousness, given free reign of expression at the time of both writing and ensuing publication, is supported by the frank accounts of carnal lust and post-coital rituals which thicken the import of *Passion simple*'s at times slightly clinical, abstract presentations. Ernaux expresses 'la faim absolue' [the absolute hunger] (p. 707) that she has for her lover, catalogues sexual acts and positions, and tells of finding a used condom stuck to one of her contact lenses (p. 767). Such fragments of naked sentiment and avowal, unvarnished by the gloss of retrospection and revision, enrich readings of *Passion simple*, amplify and heighten the first text's already provocative premise. Whilst incurring at times clichéd tropes and modes of expression, they also register the pleasure of disseminating or emitting thoughts and sensory impressions at free will without subjecting such impressions to a process of censorship or manipulation.

Throughout *Se perdre*, Ernaux emphasises the desire to 'lose herself' not only in the twists and turns of her affair but also in the act of *écriture* itself, furthering a case for the project as an exercise in abdication and offloading. Midway through the text, she renders this impulse perhaps most explicit when she notes, 'Il est évident que cette perte du sentiment de soi, comme dans l'alcool ou dans la drogue, est ce qu'il y a de plus désirable et de plus dangereux, de moins pour moi' [It's evident that this loss of a feeling of the self, like when drinking alcohol or taking drugs, is what is most desirable, and most dangerous, at least for me] (p. 799), and in her interview with Jeannet identifies a broader 'desire for dissolution' as a consistent motive across her *œuvre*.[101] For Bataille, as we have seen, this ability to dissolve subjectivity and lose oneself in transgressive acts is a sovereign, luxurious position. In *L'Érotisme* he observes:

> Dans le mesure où ils peuvent, les hommes recherchent les plus grandes pertes et les plus grands dangers [...]. Que la force leur échoie, ils veulent aussitôt se dépenser et s'exposer au danger. Quiconque en a la force et les moyens se livre à des continuelles dépenses et s'expose incessamment au danger.[102]
>
> [Insofar as they are able, men risk the greatest losses and go to meet the

> most serious threats [...]. If we generally believe the contrary, this is because they generally have little strength; but within their personal limits they have nonetheless been willing to spend and to expose themselves to danger. In any event, whoever has the strength and of course the means for it indulges in continual spending and repeatedly exposes himself to danger.]

In *Se perdre* there is a shift from *Passion simple*'s positive conception of luxury as the ability to 'live a passion' towards a celebration of self-dereliction and self-loss. The work's sinuous, labyrinthine passages of text which proceed without teleological fixing or intent appear a means (which Ernaux confirms) of stupefaction, or of wasting and squandering time between sexual encounters. In contrast to *Passion simple*'s distilled atoms of truth, long passages in which the writing 'I' is displaced and exceeded by digressive sequences or involved and convoluted ruminations abound, textually reproducing Nancy's evaluation that 'writing is an act of self-desertion, of wandering off course'.[103] The dissolution of boundaries and willed writerly *flânerie* occasionally entertained by the text finds expression in the following passage from *Se perdre*, where Ernaux segues into the third person, anticipating the experiment in dispossessed, transpersonal life-writing that would be brought to fruition by her later work *Les Années*:

> Elle va s'arrêter, la belle histoire, la folie, la tendresse, tout va devenir blanc comme le temps quand il ne se passe rien. Sur l'écran, l'après-midi, Dorothée, Les rues de San Francisco, La cause est entendue, ou quelque chose comme cela, *Le journal de la Revolution*, toujours les mêmes émissions, et nous faisons l'amour, nous mangeons, la sueur, les bouches liées, inséparables, pendant les caresses. Oui, quelle belle histoire. Hier, les limites du plaisir reculaient encore pour moi.[104]

> [She is going to stop herself, the *belle histoire*, the madness, the tenderness, everything is going to become white like time does when nothing happens. On the screen, in the afternoon, Dorothée, The Streets of San Francisco, The Cause is Heard, or something like that, *The Diary of the Revolution*, always the same programmes, and we make love, we eat, sweat, mouths enjoined, inseparable, during the caresses. Yes, what a beautiful story. Yesterday the limits of pleasure were pushed back even further for me.]

Although eventually drawn back to the lure of the writing 'I', such a passage, for the majority of its unfolding, suspends subject-object relations. It immerses us, recalling Paulin's assessment of the diary, in a kinetic and indeed cinematic rush of images and textually creates an atmosphere where the limits of pleasure are continually being melted down and redrawn. Departing from the all-consuming self-awareness and continually modifying voice of *Passion simple*, it makes space for a stream of consciousness and impulse of creative play often absent from the latter work, toggling indiscriminately between 'elle' and 'nous' and subjecting all movements and observed minutiae to a general, as opposed to a more restricted, economy. This loss of referential parameters and abandonment to a flow of sensory impressions as they are experienced challenges Blanchot's reading of the diary as a mode of overt self-attachment in distinction to the 'espèce d'égarement' [type of loss] entered into by the novel or more 'literary' work.[105] In *Se perdre*, the diary is less placeholder for a sense of self than embraced as a space where that self — via experimentation, and the trying on of different literary *personnages* — can be playfully dissolved.[106]

If frequently abandoning itself to long streams of confession without *telos* or external measure, in its latter stages *Se perdre* transcends solipsism and sovereign desires for dissolution in debating how it might relate to others. Despite claiming in its preface that 'le monde extérieur est presque totalement absent de ces pages' [the outside world is almost totally absent from these pages], a sense of the outside world, as in *Passion simple* as the affair wanes and the diplomat returns to Russia, increasingly impresses on the entries.[107] Ernaux, less 'lost' to the 'stupefaction' of her passion, transitions from a squandering or waste economy to consider the use value of her lived experience: 'et si, au moins, cela pouvait *servir* à quelque chose' [What if, at least, this could *serve* towards something] (p. 735). Yet, unlike *Passion simple*'s serene sense of gratitude for simply 'having lived' a passionate relation and almost passive exposure to the dispossession of that singularity, a sense of urgency and a need for action is signalled as Ernaux situates herself within a broader genealogy, investigates a possible 'return to origins'.[108] Swapping a commitment to writerly intransitivity for a more Sartrean paradigm of writerly *engagement*, resonating with the utilitarian work ethic of her childhood, Ernaux writes:

> Je songe à la fébrilité de ma mère, a son désir de travail continuel, à mon propre besoin de *faire,* mais rien que des choses utiles, et surtout utiles au monde. Écriture politique, action sociale, d'où me vient cette volonté d'engagement (et même dans l'amour, je m'engage à mort) de nécessité de praxis, de donner aux autres.[109]
>
> [I think of the fervour of my mother, of her desire to work continuously, of my own need to *do something*, but only useful things, especially things useful to the world. Political writing, social action, where do I get this will for engagement from (even in love, I engage to the point of death), this need for praxis, to give to others.]

The consideration of a plural, non-identifiable multiplicity of others here is striking, contrasting with implicitly expressed desires in *Passion simple* that the 'don reversé' which Ernaux intends to conjure from her experiences be, for the most part, addressed to her ex-lover, that it compensate for what '*son* existence, par elle seule, m'a apporté' [*his* existence, in itself, brought to me].[110] In *Se perdre*, a desire to pay homage to an individual and fetishised object of desire, to choose one other above all other others recedes before more politicised incentives to investigate how 'le livre peut fonctionner comme moyen de liberté pour les autres' [books might function as a method of freedom for others]. The text broadens its premise to consider a plurality of readers who are weighed judiciously against self-motivated longings 'pour la perte de moi-même, l'expérience du vide comblé' [for the loss of myself, for the experience of a fleshed-out emptiness].[111]

This transition, as the account of the affair reaches its conclusion, into a decided 'gift economy' suspends *Se perdre*'s endless stretch of solipsistic perambulations, which, deprived of *Passion simple*'s punctuating force of self-reflexiveness, risks, even more than in the latter text, entangling the reader in an 'incessant round' of living and writing, or what the author herself terms '*vivre-écrire*'.[112] If it is tempting to interpret such a gesture as an attempt by the narrator at compensation, or as a means of 'making up' for the indulgences of her affair, Ernaux herself skewers such a reading by continuing to affirm the 'risk' and 'danger' of her project which extricates the offering from a straightforward system of exchange. For Bataille, a sense of risk is crucial in order to access the pleasurable nothingness of sovereign existence, which is not attached to anyone or anything and is concerned only to activate different possibilities of movement and life. Derrida, writing on Bataille's theory of a general economy, glosses this abandonment of mastery as, resonating with *Se perdre*'s emphasis on playfulness and experimentation, 'une mise en jeu de la vie' [a subjecting life to play].[113] At the same time, this giving oneself over to contingency must starkly confront the possibility of failure: 'La maîtrise devient souveraine lorsqu'elle cesse de redouter l'échec et se perd comme la victime absolue de son sacrifice' [Mastery becomes sovereign when it stops fearing failure and loses itself like the absolute victim of its sacrifice].[114] A sense of *Se perdre*'s defiance before risk and dangerous exposure is communicated by the final entry of the work, in which Ernaux refers explicitly to 'ce besoin que j'ai d'écrire quelque chose de dangereux pour moi, comme une porte qui s'ouvre, où il faut entrer coûte que coûte' [this need I have to write something personally dangerous, like a door which opens up, through which I have to enter, at whatever cost].[115]

Despite stating in the preface that no edits were inflicted on the entries before publication, such a fragment seems an apt note on which to conclude the collection, leaving us to question whether the journals did indeed trail off at this point, or whether Ernaux herself intervened on this occasion to synthesise the project on her own aesthetic terms. This fitting closure is, indeed, in conflict with the evocation of a liberating space opened by a policy of self-dissemination and explicit risk, and bespeaks more sovereign impulses to re-author a potentially demeaning affair on revised feminist, and textually sophisticated, terms. In her grand photo-textual autobiography, *Autoportrait d'une cinéaste*, Chantal Akerman recalls the solace taken by her grandmother, who lost her life in Auschwitz, in the keeping of a diary, which became a repository for unspeakable artistic ambitions for a woman of her class at the time, as well as for private thoughts.[116] In writing about Frida Kahlo's diary, Sarah M. Lowe describes the artist's journal similarly as a 'private record written by a woman for herself'.[117] The emphatic ending of *Se perdre* complicates questions around diaries, privacy, and deliberate performance, however, hosting a confusion which the inherent ambivalence of the French term *journal*, which connotes both the public record of factual events (i.e. in newspapers) and a personal space for recording intimate ephemera, might confirm. Thomas Mallon, for his part, sees both meanings as being rooted in the core idea of 'dailiness', an ambidextrousness which *Se perdre*'s breadth of reflections constantly return to in their weave of the poetic and mundane.[118]

Again in his essay 'L'Offrande sublime', Nancy writes that for an offering to be 'sublime', 'Ce qui est offert est offert — adressé, destiné, abandonné, à l'avenir éventuel d'une présentation, mais il est laissé à cet à-venir, il n'impose pas ni le détermine' [What is offered is offered — addressed, destined, abandoned to the eventual future of a presentation, but it is left to this 'à-venir', which is not imposed or determined].[119] Such a statement sums up *Se perdre*'s non-appropriating, non-possessive stance: its decadent desires to leave alone and let things evolve in the present, but also its keen eye towards the future, to the exercises in exposure and in *écriture* to come. Delivered from the burden of 'perfection' and partaking of the luxury of space without concern for publication, the text invites accounts of writing as 'spillage' and unfettered expenditure whilst enriching, at the same time, readings of its textual double, *Passion simple*, in an ongoing, extensive process of writing, reading, and creative (re-)interpretation. In keeping with Ernaux's desires expressed in the text's preface to bear witness to something 'cruder and darker' in publishing the work, such statements read less as refined distillations of a passionate affair than as immediate and visceral 'deposits' left upon the page in 'real time', to make space for an 'aesthetics of the unfinished', to cite Kate Zambreno, which defies the status of the monumental text and its demands to be 'worked over, finished, cultivated'.[120] As such, *Se perdre* might be seen as a gesture of appreciation for 'minor' modes of literary production, which fall outside habitual criteria of value and esteem, further positioning the text as a shrine to surplus affects and to the incalculable.

In my 'close-up' and zoomed-in-on viewings of *Se perdre* and *Passion simple*, I have tried to showcase two modes of writing: both the employment of *écriture* as a form of excessive transgression and — via an aesthetics of perfection, refinement, and revision — a mode of control. Such a discussion has been informed by Nancy's, Bataille's, and Derrida's philosophies of writing as a channel of dispossession rather than a means of subjective purchase. At the same time, I have argued that Ernaux's extreme attention to the specificities and material co-ordinates of the writing act, both in *Passion simple* and *Se perdre*, avoids a kind of neo-sacralisation of writing as a displaced portal to transcendence. Whilst, then, writing in *Se perdre* and *Passion simple* gives shape to desires to subject the self to a willed giving away and offering to others, it comes back to the intention to seize, render, or make sensible material and affective residues. This conflict positions the activity of writing as both inscribing and, in Nancy's terms, 'exscripting'. In such a way, Ernaux's project in both texts both invites sensory immersion in the singularities of a fully lived and full-blooded affair whilst also withdrawing to allow the reader space for their own conclusions. In both works luxury emerges as a deep concern for literary textures which resists, at the same time, an apolitical, vainly aesthetic culture of mere ornamentation.

Conclusion: Vast Collective Sensation

> Je ne veux pas faire rêver, évader, etc. Faire sentir l'épaisseur du réel.
>
> [I do not want to make people dream, escape, etc. But to make them feel the thickness of the real.] — Annie Ernaux[121]

On 30 March 2020, Annie Ernaux published an open letter to the President of the French Republic, Emmanuel Macron, which was later read out loud on the radio channel France Inter. Powerfully stating her opposition to the president's response to the quickly-evolving crisis of Covid-19, and his use of war-like rhetoric to mobilise the country, the document was potent, searing, and profoundly engaged. Appealing to the desire for 'un nouveau monde', Ernaux expressed how:

> Nous sommes nombreux à ne plus vouloir d'un monde dont l'épidémie révèle les inégalités criantes. Nombreux à vouloir au contraire un monde où les besoins essentiels, se nourrir sainement, se soigner, se loger, s'éduquer, se cultiver, soient garantis à tous, un monde dont les solidarités actuelles montrent, justement, la possibilité.[122]
>
> [There are many of us who no longer want a world in which an epidemic reveals shocking inequalities. There are many of us who on the contrary want a world in which essential needs such as eating healthily, taking care of oneself, shelter, education, self-cultivation are guaranteed for all, a world in which solidarity allows for possibility.]

In this chapter, I have tried to show, through readings of *Passion simple* and *Se perdre*, that luxury in Annie Ernaux's work is first and foremost an affective state of expanded possibility, a 'pouvoir-vivre' that enables the living of life more laterally, more intensely, and more acutely, which has little to do with swimming pools, holiday villas, or indeed fur coats. While invested in sensations, textures, and what the author infamously calls the 'épaisseur du réel' [thickness of the real] and, resonating with the cinematic work of Chantal Akerman, 'the pure immanence of a moment' accessed via the immersive state of *écriture*, her literary enterprise is embedded in the real substance of other people's lives, and in questions of 'essential needs'.[123] In her magisterial work of 2008, *Les Années*, an impressionistic literary history of twentieth- and early twenty-first-century France by means of the third person, bewilderment is frequently expressed at the escalating ubiquitousness of consumer culture. Yet, on recalling the tumultuous protests which definitively changed the country in May 1968, the narrator is emphatically more decisive: palpably revelling in the memory of 'le sentiment exaltant de s'ouvrir à la diversité du monde' [the exultant feeling of opening up to the diversity of the world].[124]

In an essay on the concept of the beautiful in art, Jean-Luc Nancy ventures a 'withdrawal' from literary surface effects as an attempt to remain in the realm of the 'sensible', i.e. the material, and to avoid resignation to the realm of signifying meanings. Resonating with Ernaux's concentrated efforts to commit to an *écriture* 'sans luxe' he ventures the possibility of 'une littérature qui s'interdit d'être littéraire, qui se retire des prestiges et des voluptés littéraires' [a literature which bans itself from being literary, and which retreats from literary privilege and voluptuousness].[125] At the same time, he suggests, there is something voluptuous itself in this refusal. In echo of the dance between labour and lassitude, abandon and restraint, and efforts to write the self both from the inside and outside in Ernaux's work, he suggests, ultimately, that the effort with which this withdrawal is enacted is itself sublime. What indeed remains constant in this dialectics between self-presentation and self-withdrawal is the space made for the hosting of other subjectivities. It is a commitment to 'vast collective sensation' that makes Annie Ernaux's literature a project which exceeds transactional economies and sits at the threshold of a longer, more inclusive view.[126]

Notes to Chapter 2

1. Annie Ernaux. *L'Atelier noir* (Paris: Busclat, 2011), pp. 87–88.
2. Ernaux, *Passion simple*, p. 77.
3. See Aurélie Adler, 'Annie Ernaux: émiettement et consolidation du sujet auctorial', in *Éclats des vies muettes* (Paris: Presses Sorbonne Nouvelle, 2012) <http://books.openedition.org/psn/2174> [accessed 11 August 2020].
4. Jacques Derrida, *La Vie la mort: Séminaire (1975–1976)*, ed. by Pascale-Anne Brault and Peggy Kamuf (Paris: Seuil, 2019).
5. The expression 'aller jusqu'au bout' [to go towards the very end of things] recurs with frequency across Ernaux's *œuvre*. See Ernaux, *Passion simple*, p. 69, but also *L'Événement* (Paris: Folio, 2000), p. 9, where the author debates whether memory 'ne consiste pas à regarder les choses jusqu'au bout' (p. 9), and *L'Occupation* (Paris: Folio, 2002), where the experience of abortion is narrated as 'une expérience vécue d'un bout à l'autre à travers du corps' (p. 124) and where the narrator reaffirms this recurring desire to probe 'au bout de la relation de cette expérience' (p. 58). In Annie Ernaux, *L'Écriture comme un couteau: entretien avec Frédéric-Yves Jeannet* (Paris: Folio, 2003), p. 39, a desire for loss and dissolution through the writing act is explicitly noted.
6. Annie Ernaux, 'Bourdieu: le chagrin', *Le Monde*, 5 May 2002.
7. See Pierre Bourdieu, 'Le Champ littéraire', *Actes de la recherche en sciences sociales*, 89 (September 1991), 3–46, and *La Distinction*.
8. In Annie Ernaux, *La Place* (Paris: Gallimard, 1982), p. 20, this childhood is described as 'une vie soumise à la nécessité' [a life subjected to necessity]. Such a life trajectory has led Isabelle Charpentier to describe Ernaux as an 'intellectuelle déplacée' ('Une intellectuelle déplacée: enjeux et usages sociaux et politiques de l'œuvre d'Annie Ernaux (1974–1998)' (unpublished PhD thesis, Université d'Amiens, 1999).
9. Ernaux, 'Bourdieu'.
10. Annie Ernaux, *Le Vrai Lieu: entretiens avec Michelle Porte* (Paris: Gallimard, 2014), p. 77.
11. Ernaux, *Passion simple*, p. 77.
12. In the writing of *Passion simple*, Ernaux admits to wanting to embark 'vers une sorte de perfection' [towards a sort of perfection] (p. 23).
13. See Roland Barthes, *Le Neutre: cours et séminaires au Collège de France (1977–1978)* (Paris: Seuil, 2002).
14. Ernaux, *Le Vrai Lieu*, p. 71.
15. Ernaux, *L'Écriture comme un couteau*, p. 68. Such a register further distances Ernaux's work from the lyric cadences of Second Wave feminism's notorious *écriture féminine* (see Alice Blackhurst, 'Is the Future of French Feminism Female?', *n+1* <https://nplusonemag.com/online-only/online-only/is-the-future-of-french-feminism-female/> [accessed 13 August 2020].
16. In *La Honte*, Ernaux suggests, 'Je ne connaîtrai jamais l'enchantement des métaphores, la jubilation du style' [I will never know the enchantment of metaphors, the jubilation of style] (*La Honte* (Paris: Gallimard, 1997), p. 74). Elsewhere Ernaux has identified her writing as 'dépourvue de marques affectives' [deprived of emotional markers] ('Raisons d'écrire', in *Le Symbolique et le social: la réception internationale de Pierre Bourdieu*, ed. by J. Dubois, P. Durand and Y. Winkin (Liège: Presses universitaires de Liège, 2005), p. 345.
17. In an interview with Isabelle Charpentier, Ernaux suggests, 'Lorsque j'écris [...] ce qui me vient, ce sont des scènes, ce sont des sensations' [When I write [...] what comes to me are scenes, are sensations] (Isabelle Charpentier, 'La Littérature est une arme de combat', interview with Annie Ernaux, in *Rencontres avec Pierre Bourdieu*, ed. by Gérard Mauger (Paris: Le Croquant, 2005), p. 169.
18. Ernaux, *Le Vrai Lieu*, p. 95; *L'Écriture comme un couteau*, p. 59.
19. Ernaux, *L'Occupation*, p. 11: 'J'ai toujours voulu écrire comme si je devais être absente à la parution du texte. Écrire comme si je devais mourir, qu'il n'y ait plus de juges' [I've always wanted to write as if I were absent from the publication of a text. To write as if I were already dead, as if there were no longer any judgment]. See also, Annie Ernaux, *Se perdre* [2001], in *Ecrire la vie* (Paris: Gallimard/Quarto, 2011), pp. 697–876 (p. 875): 'coûte que coûte'.

20. Ernaux, *Le Vrai Lieu*, p. 90.
21. See Maurice Blanchot, *La Communauté inavouable* (Paris: Minuit, 1983), p. 72.
22. Ernaux, *Le Vrai Lieu*, p. 94.
23. A concern to be a 'porteuse de la vie des autres' [vector for the life of others] and to make her life a 'transpersonal' template able ultimately to be of service to other people inflects the whole of Ernaux's ethically-oriented *œuvre* (see Annie Ernaux, *Journal du dehors* (Paris: Folio, 1993), p. 69).
24. See Jean-Luc Nancy, 'La Politique doit montrer ce qui la dépasse', *Le Monde*, 12 April 2012 <http://purl.oclc.org/mls/05–2/sohmlear.htm> [accessed 2 November 2015], and Jacques Derrida, *Glas* (Paris: Galilée, 1974), p. 7.
25. Jean-Luc Nancy, 'L'Excrit', in *Une pensée finie* (Paris: Galilee, 1990), pp. 55–64. Derrida, *L'Écriture de la différance*, p. 390. Hélène Cixous, *La Jeune Née* (Paris: Union générale d'Éditions, 1975), p. 171.
26. Bataille, *La Part maudite*, p. 30.
27. Ernaux, *Le Vrai Lieu*, p. 18; Ernaux, *Journal du dehors* (Paris: Folio, 1993), p. 8.
28. Blanchot, *La Communauté inavouable*, p. 58. In his essay 'Extravagance', William Flesch recounts how Blanchot uses the term 'extravagance' to denote a 'wandering beyond the limits of the world' (William Flesch, 'Extravagance', *Oxford Literary Review*, 42.1 (2020), 52–75 <https://doi-org.ezp. lib.cam.ac.uk/10.3366/olr.2020.0293> [accessed 13 August 2020].
29. I ultimately take this expression from Blanchot, whose 1962 essay 'L'Expérience-limite' was later republished in *L'Entretien infini* (Paris: Gallimard, 1969), pp. 119–418.
30. Jean-Luc Nancy, *Le Partage des voix* (Paris: Galilée, 1982).
31. Madeleine Schwartz, 'A Memoirist who Mistrusts her Own Memories', *New Yorker*, 20 April 2020.
32. *Se perdre* is unusual in the context of Ernaux's preference for rigorously impersonal *journaux extimes* (a phrase originating from Michel Tournier) such as *Journal du dehors*, *La Vie extérieure: (1993–1999)* (Paris: Folio, 2000) or her chronicles of her local Auchan hypermarket in *Regarde les lumières mon amour*.
33. Anna Jackson, *Diary Poetics: Form and Style in Writers' Diaries, 1915–1962* (London: Routledge, 2010), p. 1. Ernaux, 'Vers un je "transpersonnel"', p. 220.
34. Paulin, 'Writing to the Moment', p. 220.
35. For an excellent discussion of Ernaux's photographic strategies, see Akane Kawakami, *Photobiography: Photographic Self-writing in Proust, Guibert, Ernaux and Mace* (Oxford: Legenda, 2013). See also Natalie Edwards's chapter on *L'Usage de la photo*'s innovative use of photography as ekphrastic motif ('The Absent Body: Photography and Autobiography in Hélène Cixous's *Photos des racines* and Annie Ernaux and Marc Marie's *L'Usage de la photo*', in *Textual and Visual Selves: Photography, Film, and Comic Art in French Autobiography*, ed. by Natalie Edwards, Amy L. Hubbell and Ann Miller (Lincoln & London: University of Nebraska Press, 2011), pp. 79–99).
36. Blanchot, *La Communauté inavouable*, p. 58.
37. Ibid., my emphasis.
38. Ibid., pp. 72, 80, my emphasis.
39. Jean-Luc Nancy, *La Communauté désoeuvrée* (Paris: Christian Bourgeois, 1986), pp. 63, 92.
40. Ibid., pp. 80, 92.
41. Bataille, *Œuvres complètes*, VIII, 140.
42. Later in the text Ernaux indeed will assert, 'Je ne veux pas expliquer ma passion — cela reviendrait à la considérer comme une erreur ou un désordre dont il faut se justifier — mais simplement l'exposer' [I do not want to explain my passion — that would resort to considering it as an error or a disorder to be justified — but simply to expose it] (*Passion simple*, p. 32).
43. See Naomi Schor, *Reading in Detail: Aesthetics and the Feminine* (London: Routledge, 2013), and *Bad Objects: Essays Popular and Unpopular* (Durham, NC: Duke University Press, 1989).
44. Ernaux, *Passion simple*, p. 55.
45. Roland Barthes, *Fragments d'un discours amoureux* (Paris: Seuil, 1977), p. 101.
46. Ernaux, *Passion simple*, p. 61.
47. Blanchot, *La Communauté inavouable*, p. 59, my emphasis.

48. Ernaux, *Journal du dehors*, p. 65.
49. Blanchot, *La Communauté inavouable*, p. 76. Ernaux, *Se perdre*, p. 806.
50. Ernaux, *Passion simple*, p. 11.
51. Sam Ferguson, *Diaries Real and Fictional in Twentieth-century French Writing* (Oxford: Oxford University Press, 2018), p. 200.
52. Ernaux, *Passion simple*, p. 11.
53. Ibid.
54. Ibid., p. 15.
55. Ernaux, *Passion simple*, p. 12. For Simon Kemp, Ernaux frequently subscribes to intratextual interruptions and metadiscursive reflections *in medias res* as a form of 'policing' the reader's interpretation and saving the text on display from a kind of unselfconscious and uncritical absorption ('Contamination Anxiety in Annie Ernaux's Twenty-first-century Texts', in *Women's Writing in Twenty-first-century France: Life as Literature*, ed. by Amaleena Damlé and Gill Rye (Cardiff: University of Wales Press, 2013), pp. 168–79). Taking distance from this reading, I am interested to venture Ernaux's intratextual reflections and contemplations as an embellishment of the surface of her prose, and an enhancement of the reader's textual experience, however.
56. Ernaux, *Passion simple*, p. 13.
57. Nancy, *La Communauté désœuvrée*, p. 193.
58. Ernaux, *Passion simple*, p. 19.
59. Roland Barthes, *La Préparation du roman: cours au Collège de France (1978–1979 et 1979–1980)* (Paris: Seuil, 2019), p. 27. Emily Apter, *Unexceptional Politics* (London: Verso, 2018), p. 213.
60. Ernaux, *Passion simple*, pp. 66, 41.
61. See Giorgio Agamben, 'Hunger of an Ox: Considerations on the Sabbath, the Feast, and Inoperativity', in *Nudities*, trans. by David Kishik and Stefan Pedatella (Stanford, CA: Stanford University Press, 2011) pp. 104–12, (pp. 111, 112).
62. Ernaux, *Passion simple*, p. 22.
63. See Annie Ernaux, '*La Distinction*: œuvre totale et révolutionnaire', in *Pierre Bourdieu: l'insoumission au heritage*, ed. by Édouard Louis (Paris: PuF, 2016), pp. 27–54 (p. 45).
64. Ibid., p. 46, my emphasis.
65. Ernaux, *Passion simple*, p. 28.
66. Marc Augé, *Non-lieux* (Paris: Seuil, 1992).
67. Ernaux, *Passion simple*, p. 61.
68. See Marcel Mauss, *Essai sur le don* (Paris: Seuil, 1925), and Derrida, *Donner le temps*.
69. Ernaux, *Passion simple*, p. 76.
70. See Blanchot, *L'Entretien infini*, p. 568: 'Tout récit, sous la citation du neutre, est déjà un lieu d'extravagance [...] parce que, se fiant [...] au seul mouvement de raconter, il se livre à l'"extravagance" [Every *récit*, under summons of the neutral or in citing it, is already a site of extravagance [...] because trusting [...] in the sole movement of recounting, it gives itself over to 'extravagance'].
71. Nancy, 'L'Exscription', p. 61.
72. Jean-Luc Nancy, 'L'Offrande sublime', in *Du sublime*, ed. by Jean-François Courtine (Paris: Belin, 2009), pp. 62–95 (p. 94).
73. Ibid., p. 85.
74. Ernaux, *Passion simple*, p. 76.
75. On 'open form', see Jackson, *Diary Poetics*, p. 1.
76. See Anne Carson, 'Foam (Essay with Rhapsody) On the Sublime in Longinus and Antonioni', *Conjunctions*, 37 (2001), 96–104 (p. 99).
77. In making such an argument I implicitly draw upon Vivian Gornick's *The End of the Novel of Love* [1998] (New York: Picador, 2020).
78. See, for instance, readings offered in Jennifer Willging, 'Annie Ernaux's Shameful Narration', *French Forum*, 26.1 (2001), 83–103; Barbara Havercroft, 'Dire l'indicible: trauma et honte chez Annie Ernaux', *Roman 20–50*, 40 (December 2005), 119–31; and Loraine Day, *Writing Shame and Desire: The Work of Annie Ernaux* (Oxford: Peter Lang, 2007).
79. Derrida, 'De l'économie restreinte à l'économie générale', p. 389.

80. Ernaux, *Se perdre*, pp. 700–01.
81. Ibid., p. 701.
82. Ernaux, *Se perdre*, p. 712. Ernaux uses the term 'écriture immédiate' in *Se perdre* to qualify her project (p. 785). In *Je ne suis pas sortie de ma nuit*, the author's diaristic account of her mother's deterioration from Alzheimer's, Ernaux characterises diary-writing as a form of not knowing what will follow ('inconscience de la suite', p. 11).
83. Nancy 'L'Exscrit,' p. 60.
84. Adler, for her part, notes how the desire for 'une dissolution du sujet' reverberates across the breadth of Ernaux's *œuvre* ('Annie Ernaux').
85. See Ernaux, *L'Écriture comme un couteau*, p. 46.
86. While not dwelling on the arguable pleasures of expansion and textural overlay, Kawakami has similarly argued that 'by offering the "raw material" alongside the récits, [Ernaux's] readers are privileged to see how the snapshots are transformed into the literary portraits, how the ordered narratives are built on fleeting impressions or illegible traumas' ('Annie Ernaux: Photography and the Real', in *Photobiography*, p. 99).
87. Ernaux, *Se perdre*, p. 719.
88. Ibid., p. 698.
89. The desire to surrender to a narrative conceit expressed early in *Se perdre*'s unfolding has resonant parallels with Sophie Calle's conceptual piece *Suite vénitienne*, to be discussed later in the book.
90. Nancy, 'L'Exscrit,' p. 62. Maurice Blanchot, *Le Livre à venir* [1959] (Paris: Folio, 1986), p. 252.
91. At the same time, Jackson, for her part, is eager to show how the literary diary genre is always a 'negotiation between experience and form' (*Diary Poetics*, p. 1), and Kathryn Scanlan how it inhabits the 'frictional edge of accident and intention' ('There is the Sound, too, of a Ticking Clock: A Time-based Reading of Anne Charlotte Robertson's "Five Year Diary" ', *Another Gaze* (10 August 2020) <https://www.anothergaze.com/sound-ticking-clock-time-based-reading-anne-charlotte-robertsons-five-year-diary/> [accessed 15 August 2020]).
92. Ernaux, *Se perdre*, p. 701.
93. Ibid.
94. See Ernaux, *L'Écriture comme un couteau*, p. 25.
95. Robyn Wiegman, 'Sex and Negativity; or, What Queer Theory Has for You', *Cultural Critique*, 95 (Winter 2017), 219–43 (p. 219). Ernaux, *Se perdre*, p. 701.
96. See Emmanuelle Lacore-Martin, 'Le Cerceau de papier: mémoire, écriture et circularité dans *Passion simple* et *Se perdre* d'Annie Ernaux', *French Forum*, 33.1–2 (Winter-Spring 2008), 179–93 (p. 190): 'l'expérience de la passion sexuelle est un "luxe" que l'indépendance financière de l'écrivain lui permet de vivre pleinement, sans qu'aucune obligation professionnelle ne vienne jamais menacer la vacance nécessaire de tout son être dans le désir et dans l'attente'.
97. Nancy, 'L'Excrit', p. 59.
98. Echoing comments made in *La Honte*, Ernaux writes in *Se perdre* how 'j'ai toujours écrit comme si je devais mourir après' [I've always written as if I should die afterwards] (p. 804).
99. In the context of the book at large, I see these deliberate transgressions as having a distinct feminist purchase, voluptuously rebelling against gendered expectations put on women in the throes of extreme affective and embodied states.
100. Ernaux, *Se perdre*, p. 743.
101. Ernaux, *L'Écriture comme un couteau*, p. 39.
102. Bataille, *L'Érotisme*, p. 92.
103. Nancy, 'Exscription', trans. by Lydon, p. 64 (not in original French version).
104. Ernaux, *Se perdre*, p. 806.
105. Blanchot, *Le Livre à venir*, p. 229.
106. This counters Adler's reading, who suggests in 'Annie Ernaux' that the *journal intime* 'c'est le lieu où s'affirme une subjectivité' [is the place where a subjectivity is affirmed].
107. Ernaux, *Se perdre*, p. 701.
108. See Siobhan McIlvanney, *Annie Ernaux: The Return to Origins* (Liverpool: Liverpool University Press, 2001).

109. Ernaux, *Se perdre*, p. 805.
110. Ernaux, *Passion simple*, p. 77, my emphasis.
111. Ernaux, *Se perdre*, p. 873.
112. Ibid., p. 823. This dialectic patterns the entirety of Ernaux's work. In *La Place* she cites Jean-Paul Sartre's aphorism from *La Nausée* that 'vivre ou raconter — il faut choisir' [living or storytelling — one has to choose] (*La Place*, p. 55).
113. Derrida, 'De l'économie restreinte à l'économie générale', p. 388.
114. Ibid., p. 389.
115. Ernaux, *Se perdre*, p. 875.
116. Akerman, *Autoportrait en cinéaste*, p. 71.
117. Sarah M. Lowe, *The Diary of Frida Kahlo: An Intimate Self-portrait* (New York: Abrams, 2006).
118. See Thomas Mallon, *A Book of Their Own: People and Their Diaries* (London: Picador Books, 1984), p. 1.
119. Nancy, 'L'Offrande sublime', p. 85.
120. See Kate Zambreno, *Heroines* (Los Angeles: Semiotext(e), 2012), p. 136.
121. Ernaux, *L'Atelier noir*, p. 17.
122. Annie Ernaux, 'Sachez, Monsieur le Président, que nous ne laisserons plus nous voler notre vie...' <https://www.franceinter.fr/emissions/lettres-d-interieur/lettres-d-interieur-30-mars-2020un nouveau monde> [accessed 15 August 2020].
123. Ernaux, *L'Atelier noir*, p. 17. Schwartz, 'A Memoirist who Mistrusts her Own Memories'.
124. Annie Ernaux, *Les Années* (Paris: Gallimard, 2008), pp. 115, 135.
125. See Nancy, 'L'Offrande sublime', p. 91.
126. Ernaux, *Les Années*, p. 250.

CHAPTER 3

Louise Bourgeois: Sensuous Matter

> To create is an act of liberation and every day this need for liberation comes back to me.
>
> Life is made of experiences and emotions. The objects I have created make them tangible. — LOUISE BOURGEOIS[1]

The sculptures, drawings, and multi-dimensional installations of the late Franco-American artist Louise Bourgeois are frequently read as complicit with a culture of redemption and therapeutics, as co-extensive with a larger project of repair and restoration, or as corroborating an idea of art as a cathartic means of 'doing over' or extinguishing past trauma.[2] Such readings, heavily invested in biographical detail, risk reducing Bourgeois's prolific and far-ranging *œuvre*, consistent in output right until her death in 2010, to a repeated and compulsive need to sublimate negative effects, or to a form of cathartic penury removed from luxury's more sensuous phenomenologies.[3] In addition to her work's concerns to render visceral and difficult emotions tangible, however, Bourgeois was an artist interested in the erotic textures of embodied life, in the haptic quality of lush, organic forms, in the material fecundity of both the exterior and more contemplative interior worlds, and in the nascent possibilities of creativity. In this chapter, then, I depart from readings of her work in terms of melancholy, pain, and cyclical neurosis, and venture it in terms of sensual enjoyment, material presence, and creative exuberance.[4] Such an interpretation, unhinging from persistent psychoanalytic investments in the fetish or part-object in relation to Bourgeois, re-imagines luxury in tandem as an opening to touch and sensitivity and an immersion in the rhythms and materialities of art-making.[5] It refashions it, to borrow Maggie Nelson's terms, as a celebration of 'sculptural play', oscillating between abstraction and figuration, ardour and repose.[6]

The chapter's shift in seeing luxury not only in terms of the sexual but in terms of the creative and aesthetic finds echo in Jean-Luc Nancy's philosophy and his work on an 'erotics of art' in monographs such as *Le Plaisir au dessin*.[7] With 'pleasure' often taken as shorthand for what Nancy disparages elsewhere, in *La Naissance des seins*, as 'une métaphysique de la réplétion' [a metaphysics of repletion] or a brand of narrowly self-interested satiation, Nancy's care to extricate the term from these associations to re-cast it as a fervent movement of artistic impulse, and his understanding of eroticism not in terms of satisfaction and completion, but in terms of tension and mobility, will be crucial to my reading.[8] A focus on kinesis, and on an idea of art — rather than terminal product, object, or commodity — as an insatiable gesture, ever eager to initiate new projects and to 'start again', will insure against interpretations of Bourgeois's work as unilaterally reparative or transactional. In *La Naissance des seins*, a focus on a thought of opening, or what I will refer to as the non-linear 'plenitude of possibility' accessed by the figure of the breast, will encounter Bourgeois's production through a spherical and generative lens, taking distance from pervasive mappings of her work onto tired templates of entropy, depression, and decay.[9] A reading of Bourgeois through Nancy, informed in part by Maurice-Merleau Ponty's work,[10] highlights in particular Bourgeois's endeavour to create a defiantly material, finite interpersonal ecology that affirms an 'optimistic continuity' between subjects and the world.[11]

A focus on touch, embodiment, matter, and eroticism in Bourgeois re-calibrates her art as an expression of material contingency, bodily exposure, and the labile slippage between fixed embodied states. While she is not conventionally read as an artist or practitioner of the moving image, her art calls out to what Vera Dika has described as the 'cinematized body', given its insatiable investment in tenderness, in flesh, and in particular the 'tension between presence and absence, kinesis and stasis' in her sculptures.[12] Resisting an overtly architectural, geometric, or canonical account of the artist's large-scale, 'macro' sculptures I therefore argue — following Lucy Lippard and Rachel May Walker — that Bourgeois's art reserves a defiant interest in the 'sensuous matter' of the everyday.[13] At the same time, avoiding the pitfalls of obvious humanism or sexual difference, and moving beyond Nancy's at times heteronormative account of sexuality and the female body,[14] I suggest that Bourgeois's plural, ambiguous, and at times alienating bodily morphologies burgeon out beyond the grammars of the human and the heterosexual to encourage a 'luxuriant' aesthetics of embodied mutability and multiplicity.[15]

Enjoying a career of over eight decades, Bourgeois was a mistress of self-re-invention, adapting and transforming her art to respond to both the volcanic richness of her inner life and the resonance of the specific period. In the 1960s, having launched her career in the previous decade with a series of rectilinear and pointed *Personnages* sculptures (see Fig. 12, below), she revised her focus to embrace an abundance of softer, spherical and indeed breast-like formulations to reflect the expansive possibilities of the era.[16] For Nancy, the figure of the breast opens to unpredictability, to 'ce qui abonde et fleurit, la luxuriance des plantes, la vie florissante' [what abounds and blossoms, the luxuriance of plants, flourishing life], yet also to vulnerability, withdrawal, and concealment — a contact-displacement or 'double-movement' to which, I argue in the first section of this chapter, Bourgeois's work appeals.[17] Nancy's dialectics also shapes the second focus of the chapter: Bourgeois's self-appointed *Insomnia Drawings* which I argue, via Nancy's shorter texts *Le Plaisir au dessin* and *Tombe de sommeil*, engage the expansive temporality of the middle of the night in excess of the capitalist obligations of the '24/7' working day.[18] Though created in the thrall of a distressing state, the *Insomnia Drawings* are luxurious, I suggest, in their pursuit of wild, gestural 'unruliness' and the textures of the 'minor work', in their embrace of contingency and experimentation, and in their holding space for ambivalent emotions which suspend, as in Sophie Calle's work, the performative labour of 'consistent' subjectivity. In these suspensions the spectator of Bourgeois's work finds sensory richness, direct material engagement, and imaginative shapes for different worlds, which work together to produce an assured art of plenitude, as opposed to one of deprivation. The artist's own animated words serve as the rationale behind this chapter:

> I do not have to live in an empty world
> world of vacuum (Marie Bonaparte)
> I can create my own, artist world of omnipotence and fantasy.[19]

Hers is a fantasy which meets us halfway and incites us to engage.

Mid-career Soft Sculptures: The Birth of Breasts

> Le sein n'attend rien, ne promet rien, n'échange rien.
> [The breast waits for nothing, promises nothing, exchanges nothing.]
> — Jean-Luc Nancy

> There's not only the breast. There's what's underneath it. Breathing.
> — Marguerite Duras[20]

In the early 1960s, Louise Bourgeois moved away from the stacked, totem-like, and rigidly upright figures making up the substance of her early exhibitions and began showing work of a notably more pliable and visceral nature.[21] Featuring rubber and latex configurations subject to decaying, molten surfaces, or distorted landscapes studded with flesh-like protuberances, such pieces bore close resemblance to the textures and erotic zones of the sexed body,[22] privileging soft, orb-like shapes, or in Bourgeois's own evocative description, 'clusters of breasts like clouds'.[23]

Bourgeois's gravitation towards breast-like structures and motifs in this period were often taken literally as evidence of the artist's growing fascination with abjection, or of her developing interest in attachment theory and child psychology.[24] Following Nancy in *La Naissance des seins*, it is my intention in this section to avoid reducing the figure of the breast to a fetishised 'part-object' compensating for artistic castration, depression, or loss, however.[25] Instead, I suggest *les seins* can operate as openings to volume, abundance, and creativity within Bourgeois's *œuvre*, or, in Nancy's terms, as indicators of 'la naissance incessante du monde' [the incessant birth of the world].[26]

Nancy's reading of the breast as an opening, reaching, offering, or movement,[27] rather than an instrumental object or organ, avoids tired tropes of luxury as either grasping object fetishism or 'surrender to entropy'.[28] Simultaneously, it sidesteps the pervasive Kleinian grooves into which Bourgeois's production of this period is too often neatly slotted.[29] Such association with Melanie Klein indeed reads the breast, and its seemingly insistent appearance in Bourgeois's mid-career sculptures, as a 'part-object' compensating for the 'whole' presence of the mother, or as a metonymic fragment deployed to insure artificially against the dread of loss.[30] Countering this logic, in *La Naissance des seins* Nancy appoints a thinking of the part-object as 'une pauvre pensée, une pensée du manque' [an impoverished thinking, a thinking of lack] which operates in terms of substitution and replacement to obscure the incalculable realm of sense and nascent possibility.[31] 'La pensée de l'objet partiel suppose un morceau qui vient à la place de ce qui serait perdu, ou inaccessible' [The thought of the part-object assumes a piece replacing that which would be lost, or inaccessible], he writes, reducing the idea and concept of the breast to:

> Un sein abstrait, un fétiche équivalent à d'autres nombreux fétiches aussi castrés que lui, pénis, scybale ou petit animal en peluche, objets partiels, transitionnels disent-ils, objets de transit, oui, merchandises circulant pour combler — disent-ils — un vide menaçant.[32]
>
> [An abstract breast, a fetish equivalent to numerous other castrated fetishes such as the penis, scybala, or a little stuffed animal; traditional transitional part-objects, let's say: objects of transit, circulating merchandise to fill a threatening void.]

In contrast, Nancy's project is to extricate the breast from exchange economies and to reinstate its 'promising' and 'elevated' curvature as a template for thinking differently, and for allowing new conceptual encounters to be birthed.[33]

Avoiding any notion of *les seins* as conferrers of unmediated contact, or, in Julia Kristeva's terms, as 'fantasy of untouchable fullness', Nancy's monograph is careful to articulate the breast's syncopated logic to which Bourgeois's mid-career soft sculptures similarly correspond.[34] In the same way that touch, within Nancy's thought, remains always a contact-separation, the breast, he writes, both rises and falls, both invites palpation and withdrawal, exposes and presents but also crucially conceals, bringing to a point both 'l'élévation exorbitante du corps humain' [the exorbitant elevation of the human body] but also 'le secret, l'intimité, le retrait au creux de la vallée' [its secret, its intimacy, the retreat at the depth of the valley].[35] Poised between sustaining functionality and sensual eroticism, the breast portrays the flesh at both its most sensitive and extroverted, its most exuberant and vulnerable. Both as fleshy mass of tissue and as concept it enacts, he maintains, an experience of exposed interiority in accordance with the homophonic meaning of the French *sein*, which refers both to the outwards protrusion of the nipple and the inner chamber of the womb.[36]

This logic of a double-bind or 'mutual doubling' which Nancy seeks to articulate in *La Naissance des seins* also pertains to the assumptions of gender that the breast provokes. Whilst easy to read Bourgeois's burgeoning of bulbous, tumescent forms from the 1960s onwards as a calculated move from masculine to feminine morphologies, and as a displacement of the phallic linearity of her early pole-like sculptures, for Nancy and Bourgeois alike the breast less articulates than troubles the abrupt *punctum* of sexual difference, exposing, in its oscillation between mechanisms of compulsion and retraction, the 'acte de l'entre-deux qui n'est ni l'un, ni l'autre' [act of the in-between which is neither one, nor the other].[37]

In a self-authored piece treating the recurrent 'merging' of traditionally male/female templates within her work, Bourgeois similarly writes how this 'between-two' approach avoids any essentialisation of sculpted material, giving rise to a sumptuous creative practice in which harsh binaries are permissively, luxuriously dissolved: 'Sometimes I am totally concerned with female shapes [...] but often I merge the imagery — phallic breasts, male and female, active and passive'.[38] Encompassing identifiable breast-like clusters but also clouds, eggs, sacs, and menacing abscesses, and often producing half-animalistic, half-mythical sculptures with multiple fleshy swells or teats, Bourgeois's baroque profusions crucially displace not only the rigid grammars of sexual difference but also the privileged dialectics of the gaze to encourage openings beyond visuality, and towards sensations of haptic tactility.[39] Her multi-dimensional and polysemic 'breasts' explore both viscous, liquid forms of sculpture and also a fascination with processes of hanging or 'suspended' art works. In both cases, furthering a shift away from readings of Bourgeois in terms of Bois and Kraus's 'formlessness', her luxurious experimenting with materials traces ambiguities of embodied utterance and bears witness to what Nancy terms an irrepressible 'amour des formes' overlapping negative desires or drives to subject the flesh to decay or disintegration.[40]

Fecundity and Vulnerability

> Of course the warm palm which is a mother can be a bad one. An inadequate or degenerate mother. — Louise Bourgeois[41]

In Bourgeois's black marbled sculpture *The She-Fox* of 1985 (see Fig. 1), a work typically read, in its dually tender and defiant posturing, as ode to Bourgeois's deceased mother,[42] the concurrent vulnerability and what Nancy terms the 'fécondité surabondante' [overabundant fecundity] of breasts is articulated by the work's ambiguous positioning between hardness and softness, crouched precariousness and steely aggression.[43] Composed of a headless, quasi-animalistic figure with multiple teats kneeling on a rough stone block which Bourgeois elevates, pulpit-style, on a smoother square of black marble, the sculpture appears both steeped in an act of sacred prostration and offering, whilst at the same time furtively shielding itself from intrusive view. Such sheltering of fertile corporeality and *The She-Fox*'s hunched, defensive stance might draw comparisons with Bourgeois's later, infamous *Spider* creations, which nest sacs of fragile insect 'eggs' underneath titanic, sturdy 'legs' of metal and steel. Both enveloping but also, by means of their gigantic architecture, engulfing, such massive configurations speak to Bourgeois's fascination with devising installations at once cocooning and comforting but also immersive and ensnaring. For Ann Coxon, these paradoxes illustrate the maternal subject as one divided, enmeshed in oppressive webs of duty.[44] Furthering this line of argument, such a reading — informed by psychoanalysis and the couching of Bourgeois's work in discourses of the 'good enough' or bad mother[45] — incites Coxon to interpret *The She-Fox*'s involuted and recessive posture, almost seeking to 'fold in' upon itself, as indicative of the weighty burden of maternal consciousness, and of the immanence of the female subject caught up in and reduced to her own reproductive materiality.[46]

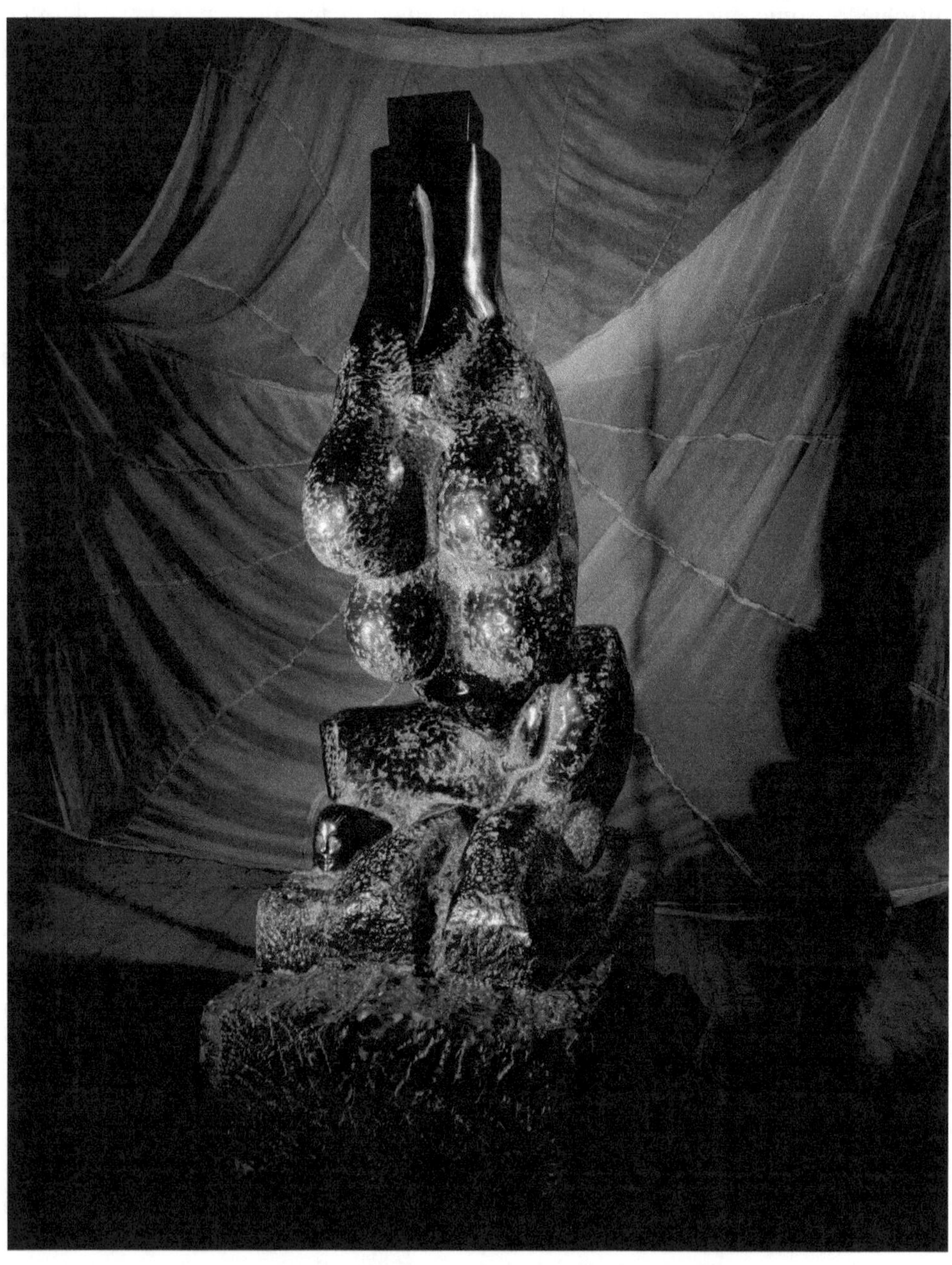

Fig. 3.1. Louise Bourgeois, *The She-Fox*, 1985, marble and steel, 179.1 × 68.6 × 81.3 cm. Collection Museum of Contemporary Art, Chicago Photo: Peter Bellamy, © The Easton Foundation/ Licensed by DACS, UK and VAGA at ARS, NY

Taking distance from this interpretation, one might note the way in which the breast-like clusters on display in *The She-Fox* are conspicuously figured without nipples, voiding their productive function so that they appear as flaccid, unsexed sacs of flesh without obvious, utilitarian use-value. Despite the anthropomorphic presence of multiple teats, the opportunity for suckling, nursing, or material dependency has been notably excised so that the spectator-viewer is indeed confronted only with the cool, varnished patina of marble standing in conspicuous textural contrast to the rough chunk of granite on which it is balanced. In regards to *The She-Fox*'s dual composition, Bourgeois herself ventured in a diary from her archives how 'the mound is the passive self holding to the ground with the maximum gripping surface'.[47] Challenging a reading of the work in terms of 'holding on', or of anxious gripping, Emma Wilson views the sculpture's downwards trajectory as enacting a sensual 'fall of the body' and a 'lowering to horizontality'.[48] Through Nancy, it is further possible to read *The She-Fox* dialectically, as both a shielding and surrender of the body and the proud exhibition of its qualities. In *La Naissance des seins*, for example, he sees the simultaneous gesture of elevation and holding back as encompassing the very 'sense' of breasts which stage a 'double-movement' of presentation and withdrawal in their very existence. In a passage speaking to *The She-Fox*'s dual invitation to exposure and obstruction from spectator view, Bourgeois's notes sharpen her account of the making of the sculpture as follows:

> Yesterday in my sculpting I made drawings of
> breasts pressed against each other; there was a double
> attitude to be like a mother and liked by a mother.
> the emphasis was on the
> nipple. Pursing of the lips
> and all the body thrust to
> give a
> pursing of the lips kiss like
> sucking all the
> person
> becomes a breast that
> thrusts itself to give This
> was an identification of all
> day with a part
> of the body.[49]

This elusive 'double attitude' and thrusting motion which is both dangled before yet retracted from spectator purchase is reflected in the slippery or glossy surface of *The She-Fox*'s marble which both attracts the viewer's attention and, as per Nancy's understanding of *le toucher*, resists ultimate purchase.[50] Whilst the hunched, effortful stance of the ambiguous figure may for many viewers of the piece evoke the visceral, messy materiality of childbirth, Nancy's thinking in *La Naissance des seins* — in broad keeping with his larger project to affirm bodily existence less in terms of assimilable 'presence' than in terms of evanescence and exteriority — might be useful given its conception of birth both as a positive opening and ecstatic pushing back of the boundaries of the world as well as a vanishing, a 'dissipation dans sa propre énumération' [dissipation in its own enumeration] or a becoming-coextensive with multiplicity and incommensurability.[51]

Resonating with the Bataillean idea of a luxurious or 'sovereign' existence as one able to dissolve fixed attachments and identifications, Bourgeois herself on numerous occasions has termed *The She-Fox* a 'self portrait' in its testimony to the possibilities of identity mutation through art, or in its ode to the ability, indeed, to disperse subjectivity through unlikely kinship with alternatively amoeba and animal-like forms.[52] Such impulses towards self-estrangement and the auto-decapitation of artistic consciousness are made material by the headless structure of the piece, and ultimately safeguard *The She-Fox*'s fleshy, fecund forms from capture or possession. Instead, the piece registers as multi-directional and inassimilable. In making space for various divergent readings, the piece ultimately celebrates the luxury of mutability and metamorphosis, refusing to encase the maternal artist — and templates of aesthetic contemplation — into one restrictive mould.

Multiplicity and Exposition

In distinction to *The She-Fox*'s ambiguous and vulnerable morphology, the rubber wall relief *Mamelles* of 1991 seems to openly elicit engagement, eschewing the former work's recessive posture in order to expose what Nancy understands as the breast's primary expression as a surging forth or elevated presentation.[53] Envisaged as a horizontal frieze or series of erect, udder-like bulges with visible nipple-like tips protruding from the wall into the viewer's space, the effect is striking and explicit. It probes and prompts us, by means of its pointed and invasive conception, to respond.[54] Building on the legacy of works such as Marcel Duchamp's infamous *Prière de toucher*, the dynamics of the spectator-artwork exchange are fore-fronted, cleverly exploited. In the highly specific context of the installation space, the three-dimensional protrusion of the nipple is remoulded as a haptic point of contact, a seductive nodule onto which to 'fasten' our interpretations.

The rubber casting of the piece, reminding us of the breast's malleability and fundamental plasticity, seems to warn against such interpretations becoming overly fixed, nonetheless. At various turns the breasts on display in *Mamelles* seem indeed to blur into one other, to cluster together so that the points of separation between one 'pair' and another are conflated, blurred. Such a presentation underscores relationality, the community, as Nancy writes, of appearing 'à la face des autres, dans le simple ordinaire côtoiement d'être-les-uns-avec-les-autres' [in front of others, in the simple ordinary communion of being one with others]. It avoids the 'pauvre représentation' [poor representation] of 'la poitrine parfaitement dupliquée' [the perfectly duplicated chest] and by extension, the isolated zoning of a fetishised approach to the breast, its employment as mere prop to a narcissistic staging of desire.[55]

Always able to be melted down, to be remoulded, or reshaped, rubber — as medium and message — in *Mamelles* articulates the mutability of breasts, their 'abandon,' Nancy writes, to what is always moving, reaching, yearning.[56] Viewing and encountering *Mamelles* in person at the Tate Gallery in Liverpool, where it

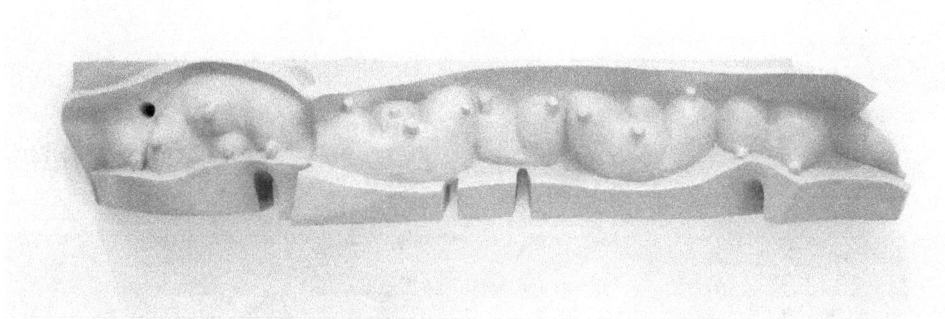

Fig. 3.2. Louise Bourgeois, *Mamelles*, 1991, Pigmented urethane rubber, wall relief, 48.3 × 304.8 × 48.3 cm. Collection Tate Modern, London
Photo: Lee Stalsworth, © The Easton Foundation/
Licensed by DACS, UK and VAGA at ARS, NY

is currently on display, taking into account its rubber casting, its flexibility, its suppleness mimics this fecund swelling of sense. The piece encompasses a wealth of possible templates and readings: able to be cast as ironic commentary on the seriality of reproduction, and the weighty history of women's labour therein, or alternatively viewed as an erotic, multi-layered gathering of vital, fleshy points of tumescence and emergence. Eschewing what Lana Lin has called 'the tyranny of symmetry' pertaining to most anatomical interpretations, the sculpture instead creatively re-distributes the symbol of the breast into a novel allegory, while simultaneously touching on the body's delicate plasticity.[57]

This emphasis on a coming-into-presence that is both audaciously erotic and tentatively fragile is, for Nancy, crucial. Continuing in *La Naissance des seins*, he reminds us how, in its figuration as a 'blossoming' rather than a definitive punctum of sense, 'le bouton est d'abord un bourgeon, une fleur non épanouie' [the nipple is above all a bud, a flower not fully realized] (p. 14), and that further, 'la pointe du sein sera toujours promise à l'impossible' [the point of the breast will be forever promised to the impossible] (p. 23) or to the birth that hasn't happened yet, to the birth that might still be. Such a birth is not punctual, he writes, in the sense of a 'punctuation' in time or space but occurs '*entre* le point d'origine et la courbe pleine d'une présence advenue jusqu'à l'autre point, le point de la plénitude' [*between* the point of origin and the full curve of a presence reaching to the other side, the point of plenitude] (p. 15). By extension, it is between and besides themselves that the breasts hold 'leur secret, leur gorge, leur évasement, leur recueillement' [their secret, their cleavage, their evasion, their welcoming] (p. 47).

Making a distinctive feature of the singular, raised tip of the nipple, whilst, at the same time, melding multiple breast-like configurations together to obscure their difference, *Mamelles* stages an aesthetics of the 'between and the besides' by both reifying punctuation and effacing it, by both plotting precise co-ordinates whilst simultaneously following a tangential logic of the drift and the *dérive*. Providing a template to think through the seriality of artistic production yet,

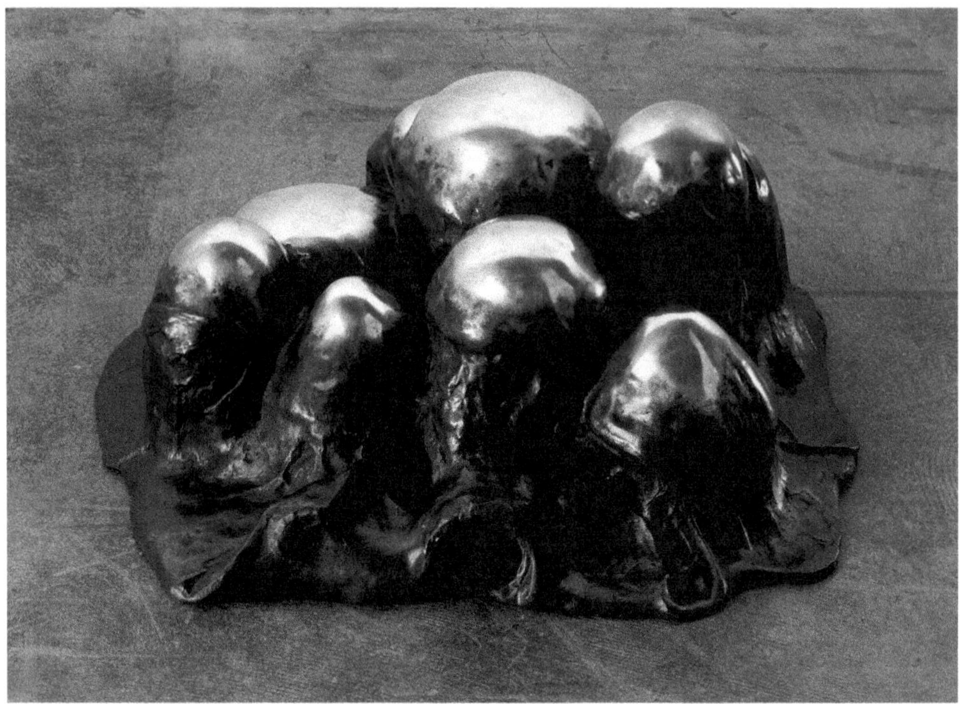

FIG. 3.3. Louise Bourgeois, *Unconscious Landscape*, 1968, Bronze, black and polished patina, 30.5 × 55.9 × 61 cm. Photo: Christopher Burke, © The Easton Foundation/ Licensed by DACS, UK and VAGA at ARS, NY

by means of its rubber casing, showing such a 'line' of aesthetic expression to be subject to re-meldings and re-modellings it both articulates exposed multiplicity and amorphous plurality whilst remaining encased in a fixed form. Consistent with the dialectic I have traced throughout the book thus far, then, *Mamelles* speaks to the double-bind of luxury as both the desire for order and containment and the urge to spill out of sedimented functions, stances, and positions, subscribing both to conceptual and aesthetic plasticity but also to the more rigid, 'linear' aesthetics of the 1950s represented by early Bourgeois works such as the wooden, pole-like figures created as part of the series *Personnages*.

Abandon, Entropy

In works such as *Unconscious Landscape* of 1968 or *Double Negative* of 1963, overt identification or bodily empathy with the breast-like clusters on display is troubled by Bourgeois's ludic disregard for any sharp distinction between 'hard' and 'soft' matter. In the first of these two works, simultaneously compelling and repugnant, the typically burnished, static patina of bronze takes on a viscous, molten quality so that the fleshy shapes appear to well up out of themselves, breaking out of ossified qualities and moulds. In the second work, on the other hand, traditionally pliable materials such as latex and plastic are set in erect mounds troubling the difference

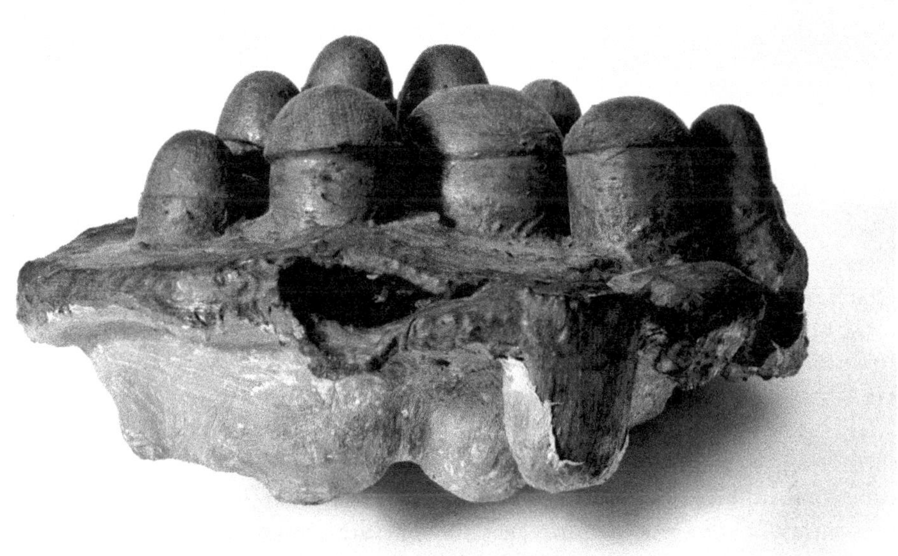

Fig. 3.4. Louise Bourgeois, *Double Negative*, 1963. Latex over plaster, 49.2 × 95.3 × 79.7 cm. Collection Kröller-Muller Museum, Otterlo Photo: Peter Bellamy, © The Easton Foundation/ Licensed by DACS, UK and VAGA at ARS, NY

between the recognisably phallic and pectoral.[58] This imbrication of the properties of hardness and softness echoes, in *La Naissance des seins*, Nancy's insistence on the breast's oscillation between turgid potency and fragile vulnerability, and on its promise of luxurious access that always threatens, nonetheless, to be withdrawn.

Resonating with Nancy's emphasis in *La Naissance des seins* on the body as an ephemeral, vulnerable container, both *Unconscious Landscape* and *Double Negative* are pieces partially made up of materials (specifically, plastic and latex) which, when exposed to light and heat, decay over time, pointing to a certain independence of the work of art beyond artist intentions.[59] Pre-empting desires expressed by Bourgeois in relation to *The She-Fox* to dissolve the presence of authorial self-identity into an inchoate whirl of shapes and half-animalistic forms, both works indeed, by means of their vulnerable and soluble appearance, articulate a willed exposure of the sculpting process to surrender and contingency.[60] This echoes the move by the period at large 'away from a hard edge aesthetic towards a materials and process-based sculpture where gravity, viscosity etc. become the actual subject of the work', as Ann Coxon has observed.[61] Further resonating with desires staged in Sophie Calle's work of drowning out the loud din of the ego, or, to borrow an expression from the writer Hervé Guibert, the luxury or 'delight of feeling myself becoming aquatic again', Bourgeois wrote in a diary-entry of 1957 how 'I would like to be like water or rather like milk — completely pourable'.[62] Transcending individual desires for self-dilution, though, this blend of process and artistic product loosens rigid binaries between artist and artwork to affirm more communal, indeed Nancean, models of material connection and sharing. As Nelson writes of Bourgeois's work, 'mould and work are conjoined in a primary unity of inside and outside, positive and negative', to convey a sense of surfaces in contact or in 'touch' with one another.[63]

In interviews, Bourgeois gives enthusiastic testimony to the new possibilities of form afforded by the use of such novel materials, and to the experimenting with new processes — such as pouring, stretching, and melting — able to 'delegate' the labour of the making of the work of art to properties beyond her own control.[64] An interpretation of these sculptures in terms of a thrilling letting-loose of authorial attachment is not common, with the most persistent readings of her works coalescing most recurrently around Bataille's ideas of the *informe*, the entropic, and the abject. In such accounts, *Unconscious Landscape*'s and *Double Negative*'s soft, cursory forms are either seen as — with their production in the wake of Bourgeois's father's death affirmed as evidence of such analyses — melancholic statements on the inevitable subjection of the body to decay and degradation, or, countering the full, reparative function of the breast as 'good' part object, as figures of Klein's 'bad breast', which, in contrast to the 'good' part object which the subject strives to internalize, the infant seeks to expel as abjected faecal matter.[65]

Reading Bourgeois with Nancy, and specifically in coalition with the understanding of the breast offered in *La Naissance des seins* as dialectical and conceptually ambivalent, offers new perspectives on such sculptures. In *Double Negative*, fleshy, organ-like growths are shown to project both above and below the plaster ground or base of the piece, suggesting — rather than a formless 'spiral' into negativity — a 'double' process of tumescence and flaccidity and a certain rootedness in productive cycles of ferment and renewal. In *Unconscious Landscape*, the unruly liquid traces of the flow of the latex which spill out from and exceed the perimeters of the piece's base preserve reminders of a certain mode of formal exuberance and process which imprint an otherwise seemingly sombre statement on the shadow-side of the unconscious with technical effusion and a new idea of art as malleable action rather than fixed meaning.[66] Such traces again emphasise the sensuality of art-making, articulate an irrepressible 'love of forms' which encounter luxury as the decadent embrace of creative range. Against the fetish's dominant logic of a 'détachement fantasmatique' [phantasmatic detachment], to borrow a term from Nancy, they encourage close attention to the work of art and material engagement, inciting us to locate marks of tactile contact with the shapes on display.[67] In an essay titled 'Le Corps du plaisir', Nancy emphasises how 'sites of an effusion, a spurt, a flowing of humor, liquor' mobilise a 'solution/dissolution of form in which an incessantly *new* possibility of form is sketched'.[68] This theorisation of dissolution as expansive rather than entropic envisages both *Double Negative* and *Unconscious Landscape* less as exercises in the deprivation or effacement of formal templates than as experiments in the pleasurable loosening of old models. In the process, 'given' grounds of the body, the breasts, and the unconscious might be understood and re-fashioned anew.

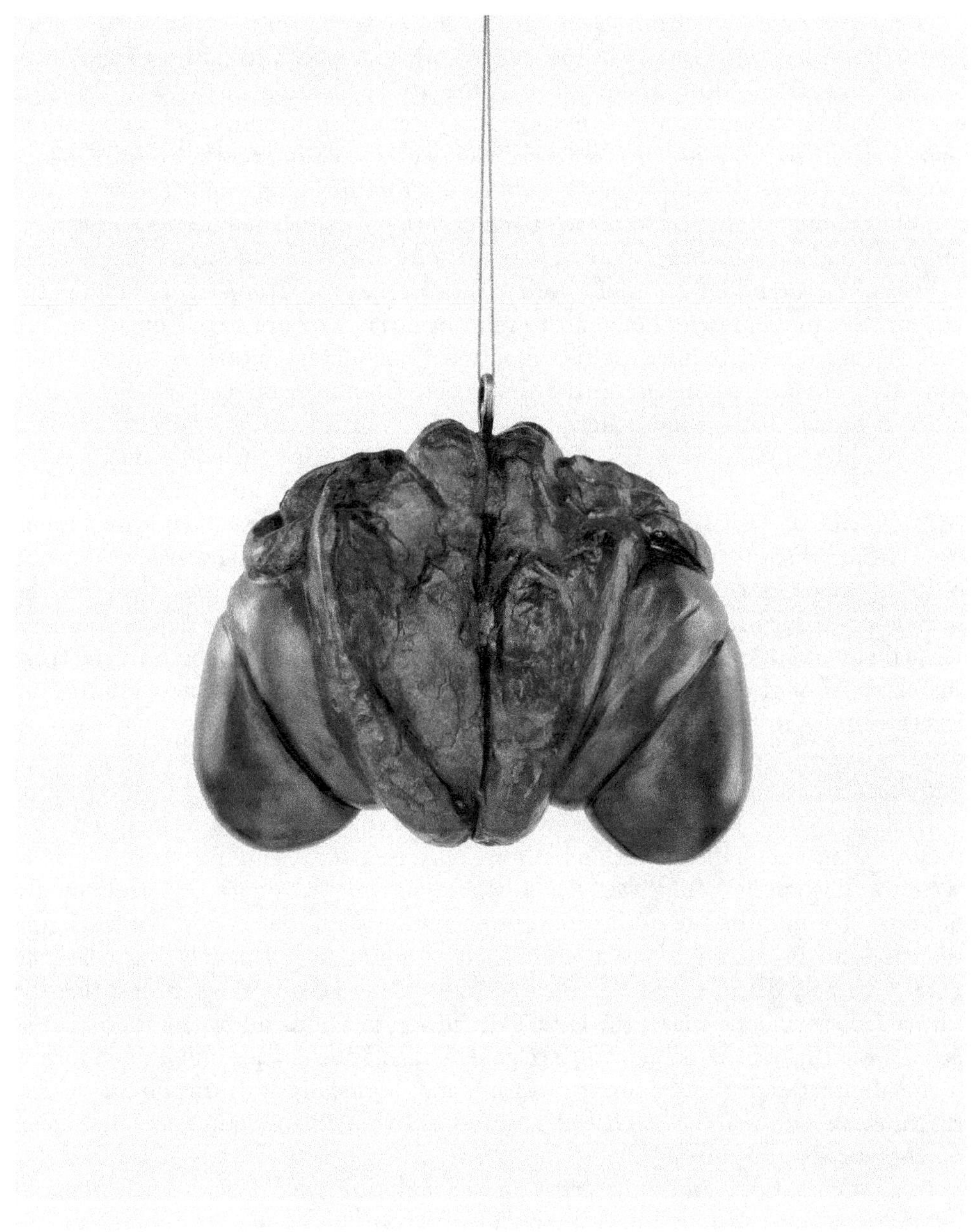

Fig. 3.5. Louise Bourgeois, *Janus Fleuri*, 1968,
Bronze, gold patina, hanging piece, 25.7 × 31.8 × 21.3 cm,
Photo: Christopher Burke, © The Easton Foundation/
Licensed by DACS, UK and VAGA at ARS, NY

Hanging

In a passage excerpted from *Destruction of the Father /Reconstruction of the Father*, Louise Bourgeois suggests that 'my early work is the fear of falling. Later on it became the art of falling. Later on it is the art of hanging in there'.[69] Building on the logic of abandon and extension that I traced in the previous sub-section, such a statement counters the potential density of breasts and fleshy immanence assigned to Bourgeois's mid-career embodied sculptures with explicitly articulated impulses to take flight and to detach from traditional wall-based modes of aesthetic presentation. Giving shape to such articulations, the hanging, aerial pieces *Janus Fleuri* and *Fillette*, both from 1968, work to subvert the ground and figure of mimetic, voyeuristic, and representational art to transform the spectator's confrontation with the artwork into a mobile, multi-dimensional encounter, luxurious in its diffuse spread of mutating signifiers. In the first work, an indeterminately phallic, vulvic mass in bronze patina, alternately glossy and rough in texture, subverts classical ideas about symmetry and balance to menace and disturb in equal measure. In the second, what initially appears to unobtrusively resemble an 'oversize cock and balls' is divested of priapic power by means of its precarious dependency on a metal hook from which it pendulously hangs.[70] In both, the emphasis seems less on the outright liquidation of masculine/feminine, hard/soft distinctions than on the suspension of such signifying circuits. This suspension enables the aeration of new sensual potentialities. A detachment of such sculptures both from the wall and from the platform or plinth facilitates a freeing of perspective, space for new affects, and interpretations to come into being, ensures that the 'abandon' of the fleshy parts on display, to cite Nancy, remains mobile, 'continue de naître' [continues to be born] but also preserves something of their original morphologies.[71]

In their volume *Formless*, Krauss and Bois read the constant movement or what they appoint the 'pulsion' or 'pulsation' of suspended, hanging works such as Alberto Giacometti's *Suspended Ball (*1930) as having the effect of introducing a libidinal elan into the site of the viewer's encounter with the artwork, of 'engaging the spectator in a kind of visual equivalent of coitus' to ultimately 'sexualise the gaze'.[72] Closely liaising with Bataille's account of the *informe*, they suggest that the suspended work both enacts the latter's definition of the formless as a kind of *sein-lassen*, or letting matter be, permitting 'genéralement que chaque chose dit sa forme' [generally that each thing express its form], and, by means of its throbbing, restless rhythms, an agitation of established postures to 'irremediably puncture' the screen of aesthetic formalism.[73]

In a public talk given by the artist on her sculpture *Janus Fleuri*, where mutant, hybrid flesh-like forms appear turned inside out to expose the simultaneous interiority/exteriority of corporeality, Bourgeois generally agrees that hanging as artistic praxis equates to a form of 'rebellion': changing the 'hierarchy of the work' so that 'the base disappears' and subjecting the erectness of most modern art to languid horizontality and dissolution.[74] Diverging somewhat from Krauss and Bois's emphasis on hanging's possibilities for interruption, however, she suggests that her suspended sculptures, often slung low to the ground and heavy in weight, express, as well as flight and mobility, 'resistance and duration'.[75]

Such a statement instigates a change of pace away from the repetitive propulsions of sexuality but also, crucially avoids the entropic giving way or inevitable degradation of Bataille's (and by extension, Krauss and Bois's) account. For Coxon, the effect of Bourgeois's hanging works is to indeed perform a reluctance to letting go, staging a voluptuous resistance both to the expectation for evolution, movement, and progress but also to the expectation that things always decay, must forcibly be lost to the ground.[76] This performance, Bourgeois attests, is provisional and intricate, requiring a suspension of usual beliefs about life and art. 'All my pieces are subject to a "precarious balance,"' she writes.[77] This testimony to her work's status as consistently pulled in multiple directions, as suspended in a field of conflicting, rather than one-way, forces and intensities evokes, rather than the downwards spiral of the formless, Nancy's polysemic reading of the breast, and the emergence of pleasure as an expansion of ideas and forms which opens out onto a terrain of thrilling differences. Echoing the double movement which Nancy reads in the breast of exposed exteriority but also of retraction and withdrawal, such hanging works ultimately show that any act of letting go is subtended by a downwards pull of gravity to, rather than dissolve fixed bodily morphologies completely, subject recognisable forms and templates of the body to momentary suspensions which imbue the static art object with kinetic charge. Integrating the recto-linear, phallically inflected origins of Bourgeois's earliest sculptures with the new softness and sensuality of the works of the 1960s, then, both *Janus Fleuri* and *Fillette* confuse anatomical parameters to replace rigid grammars of sexual difference with an open-ended libidinal amorphousness which takes pleasure in refusing to conform.

Fillette: Lateral Expansions

In this section I argue that Bourgeois's 1960s sculptures trouble the divide of normalised sexual difference and the substitutive logic of the part-object to embrace instead a luxurious profusion of diffuse bodily perspectives and practices. I argue that such sculptures forgo the telos and implicit linear bias of high Modernist art but also the downwards spiral, seen as indissociable from the reign of the *informe*, to trace soft, expansive shapes granting holding spaces for continuously circulating affects and impressions.[78] Such a reading is perhaps challenged by one of Bourgeois's most iconic works, the bold — and seemingly explicitly phallic — hanging sculpture *Fillette*, often cited as evidence of the artist's obsession with male genitalia and the threat and violence of castration. Despite initial impressions, I argue here that *Fillette* can be read in conjunction with the breast's alignment with softness, surrender, and abandon, and transcends obvious accounts of sexual anatomy.

Dangled from a menacing, sharp metal hook, *Fillette* constructs at its base two bulbous, orb-like shapes which compete with an erect, half plastic, half latex roughly surfaced 'shaft' overlaid with an ambiguous, or what Hannah Westley appoints a 'yonic', sheath of smoother, thinner-seeming material.[79] Such amendments to what on first glance, or from a distance, seems an immediately recognisable and graphic depiction of a penis, suspends normative anatomical demarcations, leaves our

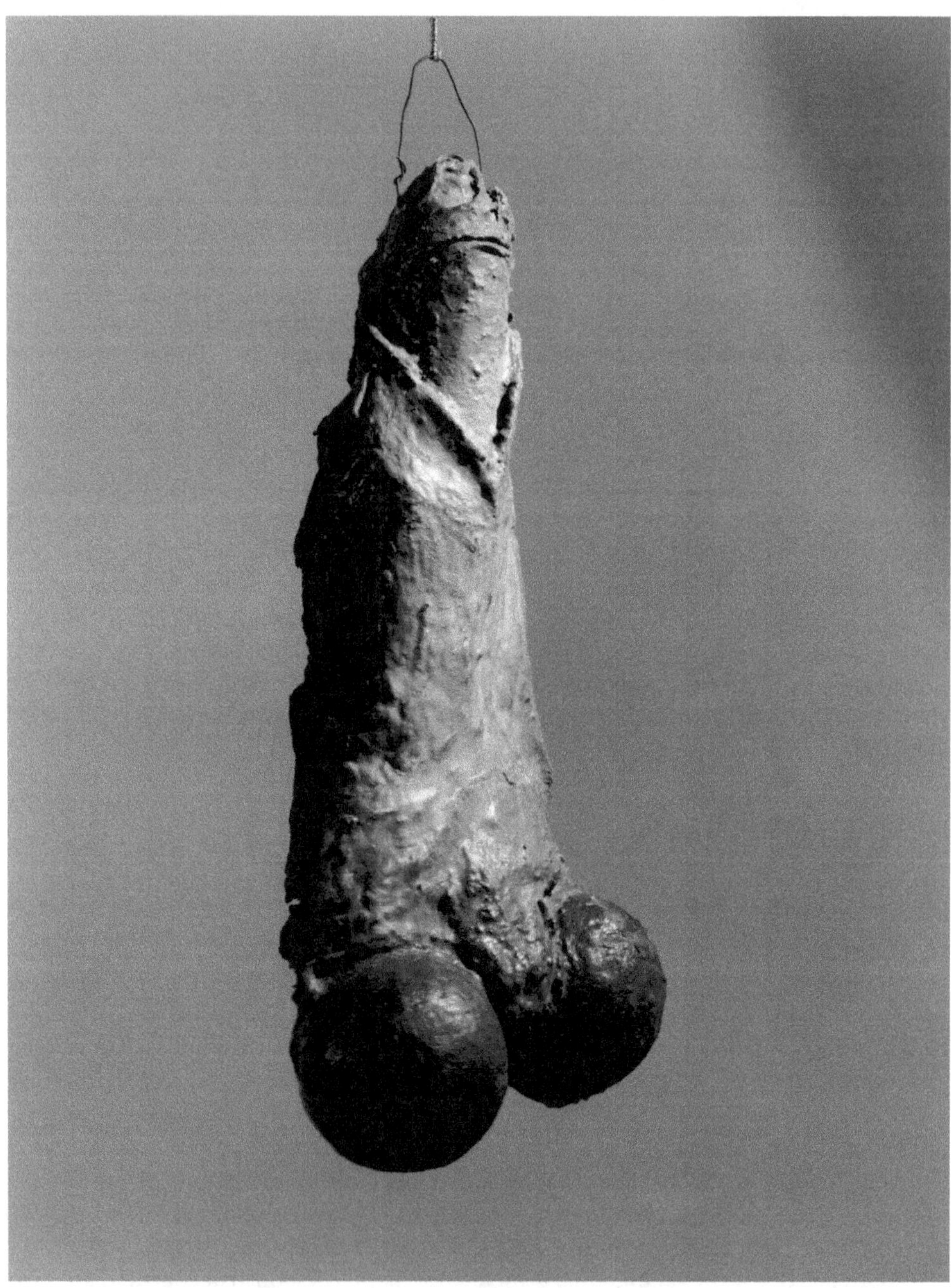

FIG. 3.6. Louise Bourgeois, *Fillette*, 1968, Latex over plaster, hanging piece, 59.7 × 27.9 × 19.1 cm. Collection of the Museum of Modern Art, New York. Photo: Allan Finkelman, © The Easton Foundation/ Licensed by DACS, UK and VAGA at ARS, NY

expectations as to how these organs should be represented hanging in the balance. The primary disjunction between the work's title — *fillette* meaning 'little girl' — and its subsequent ludic re-signification of a masculine outline preps us for this disarming, this removal of the solid ground of artistic interpretation from beneath the viewer's feet. On closer inspection, the cloak of supplementary 'foreskin' or sexually amorphous folds gathered around the shaft seems indeed, a protective, almost nurturing addition, exposing what could otherwise be viewed as a totem of priapic mastery as vulnerable, in need of care. Avoiding the part-object's coalition with the fetish, and with processes of over-attachment and regressive reparation, then, *Fillette* precisely asks us to detach from what we think we see in it, to surrender our received ideas in order to re-engage with the material, tactile, haptic features of the artwork which elude classification.

At stake, subsequently, is not only an exuberant overlapping of sexed bodily morphologies but a re-drawing of the conditions of, and possibilities for, absorption in the artwork. Favouring close engagement, double takes, and second examinations, *Fillette* shows us, in line with Nancy's dialectical movement of the breast which reaches out as much as it withdraws, that what we think is being starkly rendered has, the closer we implicate ourselves in its vulnerable architecture, the potential to change shape or fade away. The game of hide-and-seek *Fillette* plays with the viewer — the means by which Bourgeois hangs it 'like a piece of meat in an old fashioned butcher's shop' (to quote Alex Potts) simultaneously willing a carnal consumption and an almost visceral disgust — resonates with Nancy's understanding of the breast as that which is offered and presented but which also, always, risks being usurped or displaced, 'abandonnée' [abandoned] as he writes, 'pour une paume ou pour une bouche' [for a hand or a mouth].[80]

After a fourteen-year hiatus Bourgeois would revisit *Fillette*, employing it as prop in a portrait photograph taken by Robert Mapplethorpe on the occasion of her retrospective exhibition at New York's Museum of Modern Art. Taken off its hook and turned on its side, its original hanging display arrested, Bourgeois nestles it beneath the crook of one arm, grinning knowingly, dressed in a hirsute coat of monkey fur. Looking at the photograph, one senses — despite the portrait's dominant interpretation as an exercise in symbolic one-upmanship or obvious fetishism — Bourgeois's revelry in both pieces 'textural and material interest: in the immediate, audacious and stark contrast between the leathery, crude surface of the rubber-latex sculpture and the slick gloss of the fur'.[81] Wrenched out of its usual context, pulled down from its prior elevated suspension, *Fillette* is given an entirely different reading by the portrait: one in which its 'breasts' or balls burgeon triumphantly beyond Bourgeois's elbow to suspend phallocentric economies of pleasure and desire.

To emancipate the concept of the breast from fixing voyeurism or unmediated *jouissance*, and to liberate restrictive categories so that something new might be created from the cleavage between terms, is Nancy's project in *La Naissance des seins*, where *les seins* are — more than fleshy masses — understood as movements, impulses, or, as he writes, emblems of 'l'exubérance de la vie même' [the exuberance of life itself].[82] This revision of the breast as an ecstatic, overflowing, and dynamic, dialectical movement which exceeds its own containment troubles the request, made by Lucy Lippard, to 'call a breast a breast' in relation to Bourgeois's work.[83] As soon as a breast is termed a breast, Nancy suggests, it becomes something else, to leave behind only the possibility of its affirmation, only the fragrance of its being here.[84] Towards the close of *La Naissance des seins*, Nancy frames such a process less in terms of active/passive objects than in terms of the possibility itself of availability:

> Lui, renforcé. Lui, insistant. Se désistant en même temps, retenu, retombé, pesant vers le sol, mais toujours élevant doucement l'affirmation de la douceur même: je suis là, je ne suis rien d'autre que l'être de ce 'là', sa possibilité, sa disponibilité. Ni l'activité, ni la passivité: la disponibilité.[85]
>
> [Reinforced. Insistent. Stopping itself at the same time, held back, retained, weighted towards the ground, but always sweetly elevating the affirmation of sweetness itself: I am here; I am nothing other than this being 'here', its possibility, its availability. Neither activity nor passivity: availability.]

This pleasure of availability which does not equate to any notion of pure 'access' or self-identical presence but which traces the possibility of softness and touch might here venture luxury as latency, or as a promise of contact and of plenitude which is endlessly deferred, rarified. Swelling out beyond human heteronormativity (and sexual difference) to encompass the maternal, the animalistic, the mythical, and the mystical, Bourgeois's breasts, I have argued in this section, therefore disclose more than a new bodily materiality or fleshy erotics of art. They replace the teleology, evolution, or 'infinite line' of modern art — and the gaze-based optics of the history of moving imagery — with tactile, overlapping and imaginative curves which trace volume and dimensionality and the mutability of form.[86] They install new circuits of spectator involvement, or a novel model of attending to and being with the artwork. In the process, they beseech us not to call 'a breast a breast', but to see *les seins* as expansive conceptual templates which incubate creative possibility and luxurious world-making via art.

The *Insomnia Drawings*: Pleasure in Drawing

> You lose track of time. You follow the pleasure of the activity of drawing. You do not care what the result is going to be. All the connections are unconscious. You do not know where you are going to end. It is a journey without an aim.
> — LOUISE BOURGEOIS

> as if dreams would be a
> limited resource, as if keeping my
> dreams for myself would be some
> form of luxury.
> — ANNA ZETT[87]

An aspect of Louise Bourgeois's work that is often overshadowed by the artist's infamous arachnid structures and amorphous casts of body parts is her investment, over the long arc of her career, in the act of drawing. Bourgeois's collected diaries and notebooks, currently held by the Easton Foundation in Manhattan, reveal drawing to have been a consistent form of creative germination for the artist since her schooldays. In later life, the practice attained a more important, even urgent, status, becoming both a mode of aesthetic experimentation and a means of holding space for the artist's affective fluctuations and embrace of multiple aesthetic forms. An ongoing sufferer of insomnia, Bourgeois in her seventies developed a practice of drawing late at night on disarrayed sheets of paper which she would let fall over the bannister of her Manhattan home, to be collected in the morning by her long-standing assistant, Jerry Gorovoy. Such works would eventually be curated under the title *Insomnia Drawings*, yet have been under-theorised by Bourgeois scholars. Incorporating small-scale media such as paper, pencils, and pens, and giving free reign to ideas, thoughts, and latencies of creative impulses independent of the scrutiny and finitude of more polished works, such pieces, in their ephemeral itinerancy, unfurl a different chapter in Bourgeois's production, one more aligned with Situationist-inspired models of *dérive* and drift than with graphic literality.[88]

In his 2009 monograph *Le Plaisir au dessin*, Nancy ventures drawing as a 'vulnerable' medium, due to the sensitivity of the drawn line — often etched in pencil — to *effacement*, erasure, or abrupt withdrawal. And yet, as the short work's title signals, Nancy's thinking about drawing seeks primarily to understand it as a medium of pleasure, which 'erotically' conjoins frictional aesthetic references and sensibilities. For Nancy, in art, 'ce n'est pas la forme, mais le mouvement retiré d'une formation d'un plaisir de laquelle il faut être sensible' [it isn't form, but the retreating movement of a pleasure to which one must be sensitive].[89] Drawing, in its tracing of a fragile line always under threat of being rubbed out, embodies such a 'retreating movement', whose evanescent, flickering sensuality flees the monumental. In accordance with such qualities Nancy defines the 'pleasure of drawing' as:

> Par essence plaisir du commencement, de l'ouverture. Plaisir, donc, d'un désir moins tendu vers un objet à atteindre que vers cette ouverture même, vers son élan, vers sa propre possibilité — encore que, précisément, celle-ci ne se présente pas en termes de possibles représentables, calculables et réalisables, mais comme la possibilité indéterminée du possible en tant que tel.[90]
>
> [In essence the pleasure of beginning, of opening. Pleasure, then, of a desire less aimed towards an object to acquire than towards this very opening, towards its impulse, towards its own possibility. This possibility materialises not in terms of representable, calculable, or realizable 'possibles', but in terms of the indeterminate possibility of the possibility as such.]

In this section, I once again bring together Nancy and Bourgeois in conversation to foreground a rhetoric of spontaneity, risk, and pleasure taken in contingency which is under-emphasised within the artist's work. With support from Nancy's thinking, I suggest that Bourgeois's improvisational nocturnal etchings re-conceive insomnia as a space of creative plentitude and indeed, aesthetic luxury, rich in novel possibilities of genre, texture, shape, and colour, or what Wayne Koestenbaum evocatively terms a 'dreamworld of enlarged thought'.[91] Such an argument will be less invested in 'reclaiming' the nocturnal landscape as a quantifiably 'productive' space than in re-imagining insomnia in terms of what it can enhance and enrich (as opposed to what it may annul or deprive). As the art critic Marina Benjamin has written in an auto-theoretical account of insomniac conditions, 'in sleeplessness I have come to understand that there is a taxonomy of darkness to uncover, and with it, a nocturnal literacy we can acquire'.[92] In indulging an abundant range of materials and media, and embracing new prolific possibilities not only for insomnia but also for visual and concrete poetry and abstract expressionism, Bourgeois's drawings, I suggest here, prompt the spectator to revel in these uncovered acquisitions, and to step into the lines sketched by a mind vulnerably exposed, liberated from wakeful restraints.

Efflorescence and Insatiability

Louise Bourgeois's *Insomnia Drawings,* a collection of 220 etchings made on loose-leaf sheets during nights when the artist was unable to sleep from 1994–95, unfold multiple inchoate dreamscapes whose itinerant, delicate digressions sketch an artist willing to explore tangents and diverge from strictly linear configurations. Composed of fleshy, tumescent, and proximately uterine figures and shapes, and often annotated with aphoristic fragments of language and half-ludic lists and series of instructions, they evade efforts to construct a 'habitat', shelter, or what Mieke Bal, in relation to Bourgeois's work, has termed the search for an 'autotopography', to trace instead a labile space of shifting structures and conflated subject/object positions.[93] Privileging a morphology of the contingent and unfinished, they advance a model of luxurious art-making embedded in pleasurable gesturality, unencumbered creativity, or in Nancy's terms, 'une sensibilité se communiquant pour elle-même' [a sensuality valid in itself].[94] In the latter's understanding of aesthetics:

> L'art est voué à la communication de la sensibilité, ou plus précisément, à une sensibilité se communiquant pour elle-même, pour sa valeur ou pour son *sens* propre, et non pour ses valeurs d'information sensorielle, soit pour ce qu'ici nous avons nommé sensualité.

Art is devoted to the communication of sensibility, or more exactly, a sensibility communicating itself for itself, for its value or its own sense, and not for its sensory, informational values — that is, for what we have here called sensuality.[95]

This resonates with the drawings' haptic, proximate quality and Bourgeois's 'belief in the primacy of the material body' as the bedrock of artistic life.[96]

A sense of urgency, contingency and of the drawings' formation *en media res* is evinced by the non-hierarchy of materials upon which Bourgeois etched these works: most predominantly on thick sketchbook paper, but occasionally on music manuscript paper and fragile slips of old postcards or receipts.[97] Such circumstantial canvases imply that the artist did not envisage these individual wisps of pencil works to form part of a larger *œuvre,* though they were later collected as one (and have been, since the artist's death in 2007, variously exhibited at the Whitney Museum,

FIG. 3.7. Louise Bourgeois, *The Insomnia Drawings 1994–95* [no. 46], 220 mixed media works on paper, various dimensions
Photo: Christopher Burke, © The Easton Foundation/
Licensed by DACS, UK and VAGA at ARS, NY

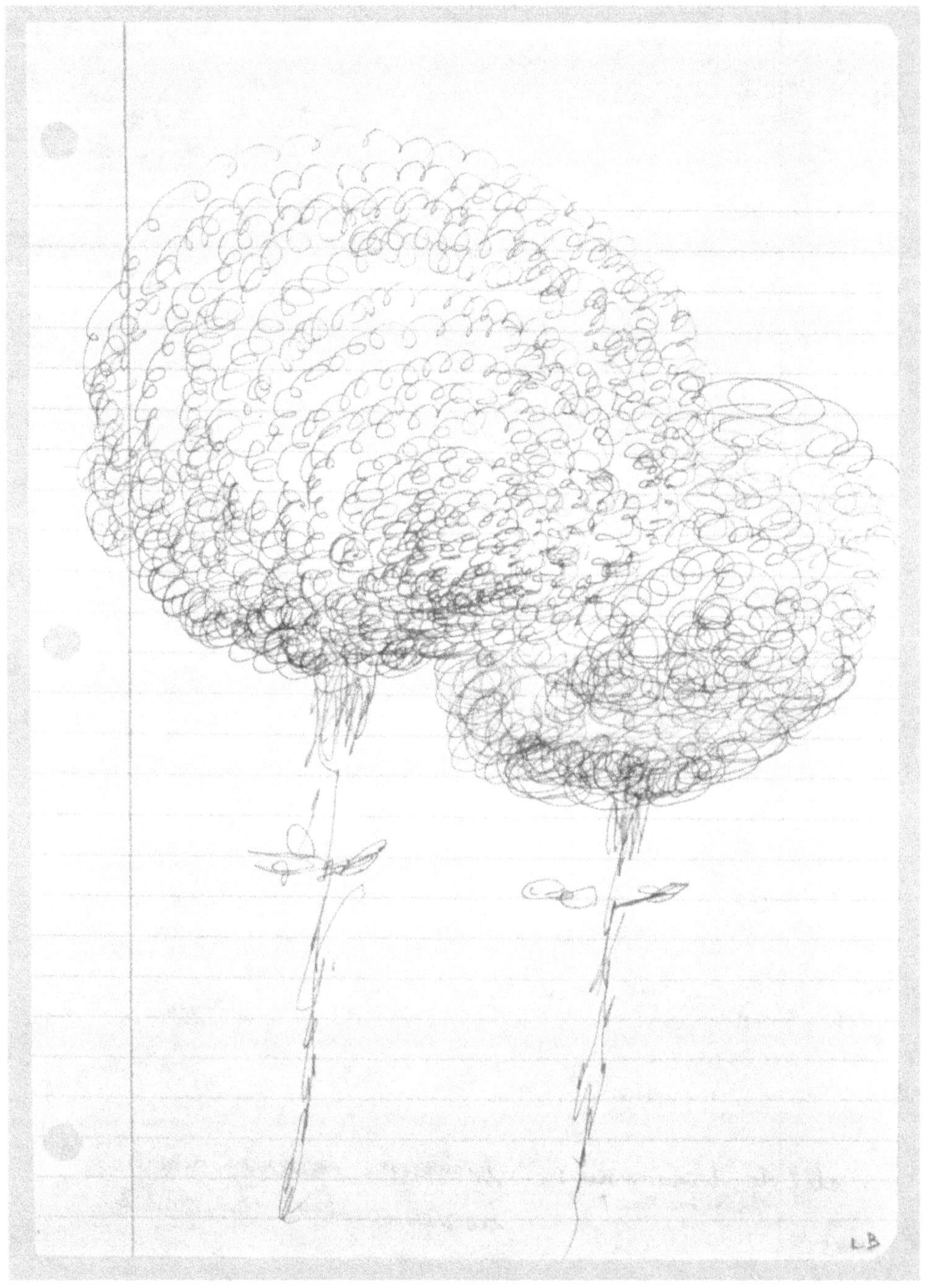

FIG. 3.8. Louise Bourgeois, *The Insomnia Drawings 1994–95* [no. 27], 220 mixed media works on paper, various dimensions
Photo: Christopher Burke, © The Easton Foundation/
Licensed by DACS, UK and VAGA at ARS, NY

MoMA, Tate Modern, and the Fruitmarket Gallery in Edinburgh, amongst other venues). Rather, the conditional backdrop of the drawings points towards an instinct for immediate transcription and the desire to register feelings, emotions, and sensory impressions as they arise. In this vein, the *Insomnia Drawings* emanate, as do some of Sophie Calle's and Annie Ernaux's works, a diaristic quality, each page a private portal for the witnessing and sketching out of sentiments and thoughts.[98]

Though the drawings reveal resonances with the *journal intime* and re-iterate motifs traceable throughout Bourgeois's production (houses, rivers, hair, plants, distended and engorged sex organs) they also project their own distinct sensibility. 'There are lots of things that appear in drawings that are never explored further,' the artist herself once confirmed in an interview with the director of Tate Modern, Frances Morris, underscoring the opacity of their containment, their exemption from the pressures of the major work.[99] Throughout the series itself, Bourgeois often interrupts her stream of nocturnal illustrations with meta-discursive annotations which foreground the specificity of drawing as aesthetic mode. On the verso of one of the collection's many sheets, she muses on the difference between drawing and the more pre-meditated, conscious medium of sculpture. Whilst the latter, she writes, gives expression to a certain 'souci de direction' [concern for direction] drawing is distinguished in contrast as a mode of 'syncopation', able, in its stuttered and offbeat articulation, to trace and open out onto 'the shapelessness of the night'.[100] Accompanied by a finely-grained etching of several long-stalked dandelion flowers, which evoke free-flowing transport and ephemerality, such an account challenges persistent readings of these sketches as conciliatory means of ordering chaotic or nocturnal emotions. As Bourgeois attests in scrawling hand on the back of another sheet, 'the work does not illustrate it/it confuses it'.[101] Moreover, she suggests that there is pleasure in these oscillating interruptions and meanderings, in what Amy Sillman has appointed the frequently imperfect 'phenomenology of making':[102] 'I am stumbling, I am tripping over but I like that, I am ready, out of breath'.[103]

Evoking the enjoyment to be found in a certain abandonment to process, or in an embodied synchronisation with poesis, here Bourgeois's purposeful self-estrangement extracts drawing from a merely therapeutic or cathartic function. Likened to a proto-organic, auto-reproducing process, here the act of *le dessin*, as in her experiments with latex and other perishable substances, directs the artist, as opposed to the other way round. Emphasising the non-voluntary, volatile, and pre-conscious act of putting pencil to paper, in an interview with Marie-Louise Bernadec Bourgeois likens the series of sketches to 'thought-feathers' or 'ideas that I seize mid flight and put down on paper'.[104] In another interview they would be conjugated as 'secretions' or 'threads in a spider's web'.[105]Both sets of imagery bespeak the initiation of a process rather than the need to put an end to anxious and insomniac conditions. Both re-imagine the blank slate of the *nuit blanche*, or sleepless night, as brimming with exuberance and creative potential.[106]

The scriptophilic content of the series, which gives rise to a range of written forms, such as aphorisms, snatched lines from poems, and personal to-do lists,

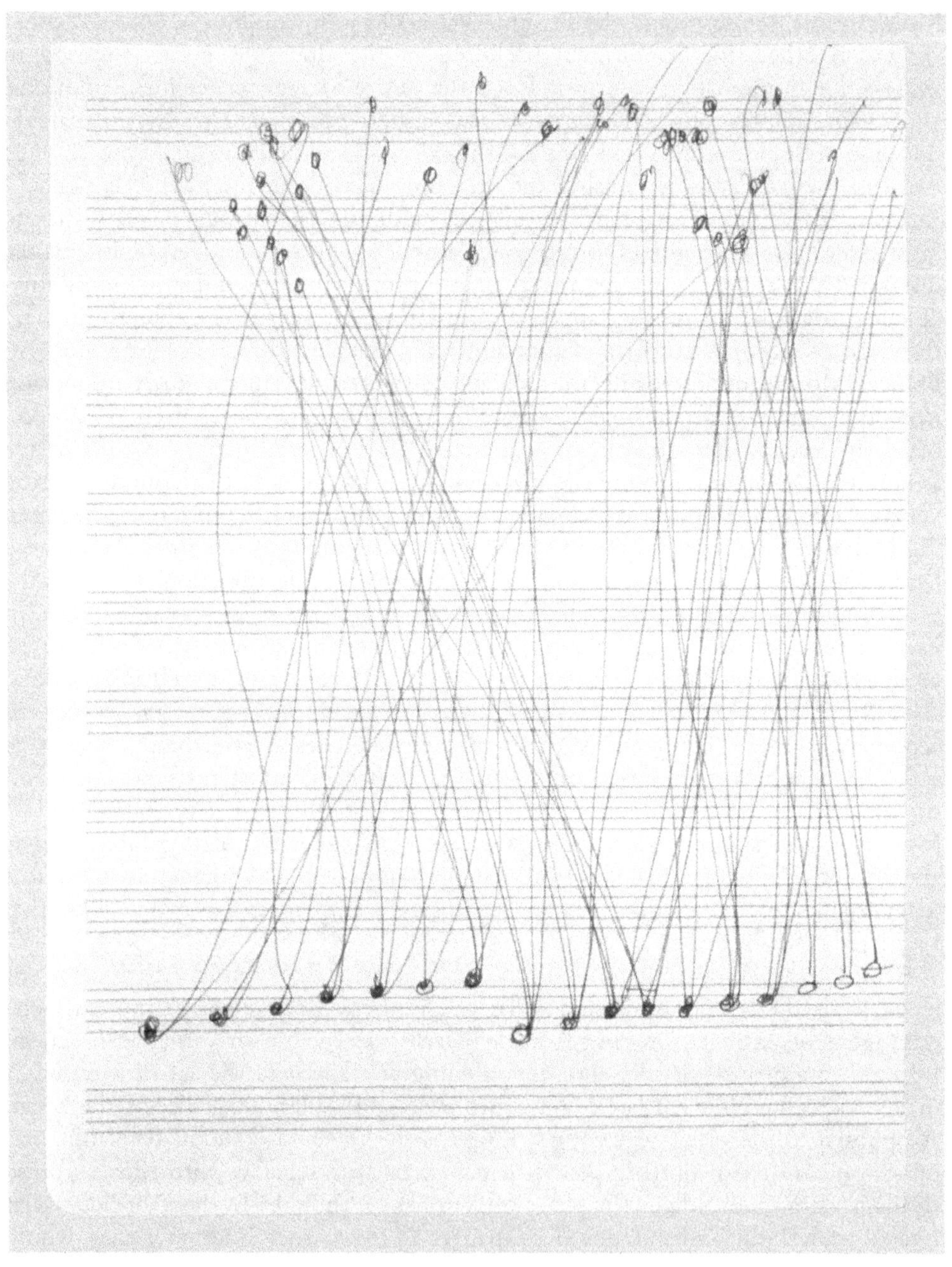

FIG. 3.9. Louise Bourgeois, *The Insomnia Drawings 1994–95* [no. 50, verso], 220 mixed media works on paper, various dimensions
Photo: Christopher Burke, © The Easton Foundation/
Licensed by DACS, UK and VAGA at ARS, NY

testifies to the imaginative capacities — both textural and literary — on display within the *Insomnia Drawings*. The curator Ann Coxon, who oversaw the first major Bourgeois exhibition which took place at Tate Modern in 2010, evokes the baroque sweep of textual experimentation engaged in by the artist when she writes: 'One finds cautionary tales, puns, nursery rhymes, graphic descriptions of bodily functions, conjugations and declensions, poetic aphorisms, catechismal questions and answers'.[107]

This broad range of verbal sources overlaps with the account of art as an 'amour des formes' [love of forms] or indiscriminate embrace of different genres emphasised by Nancy in *Le Plaisir au dessin*, which diagnoses the creative act as an insatiable, continuous desire to 'touch' different modes of aesthetic expression (p. 97). For Nancy, drawing is particularly apt at exposing the inherent multiplicity of art in its tracing of 'la possibilité d'une ligne' [the possibility of a line] which can always be extended to meet others (p. 89). There are 'lignes mélodiques, lines architecturales, filmiques' [melodic lines, architectural lines, filmic lines], he writes (p. 52). Drawing therefore should not be thought of as a graphic notation but as 'une pluralité irreducible' [an irreducible plurality] (p. 52). Its very singularity allows it to encompass other, more diverse forms of expression, in a microcosm of Nancy's post-metaphysical ontology of 'being singular plural' where each human being's unassimilable irreducibility is the basis of connection and communities with others.[108] In a different, yet related context, Bourgeois emphasises the fragility of the spider's web, whose silken and diaphanous threads break easily under concentrated pressure. The image of the 'thought feather' similarly is connotative of impermanence and evanescence, and an interest in viscera and vulnerability abounds across the suite of *Insomnia Drawings*. Resonating with the soft structures of the 1960s but also the later fabric works of the 1990s and 2000s such as *Ode à l'Oubli* of 2004, several round, organ-like sketches evocative of fascia or interior corporeality persist as a motif, rendered in furtive, shadowy strokes.[109] In one etching from the series, breast-like mounds or 'cumuls' blossom out across a page, so faint as to be almost co-extensive with the lines of the music manuscript paper on which they are drawn (see Fig. 5.7). Other pages bear witness to gossamer-thin spoolings of notation, like locks of hair or skeins of wool (see Fig. 5.8). Such motifs, as well as summoning tactility and haptic engagement, testify to what Alain Badiou calls the fundamental 'fragility' of drawing, its delicacy, rarity, and permanent subjection to disappearance.[110] This vulnerability to effacement prevents the act of drawing's calcification into strategy or tool. Rather, the fragile nature of drawing is inseparable, Nancy writes, from the pleasure taken in its atmosphere of transience or flight, its process of 'passage'.[111]

Echoing Bourgeois's sceptical relationship to resolution and her tendency across her art to present opposing forces in a dialectical rather than synthesised movement, the drawings' vulnerability remains throughout the series in dialogue with their simultaneous deep grounding in materiality. Ethereal pastel hues are often interspersed with fierce, incisive reds suggestive of emboldened affect but also visceral (and vegetative) forms of organic life and growth.[112] Coxon has

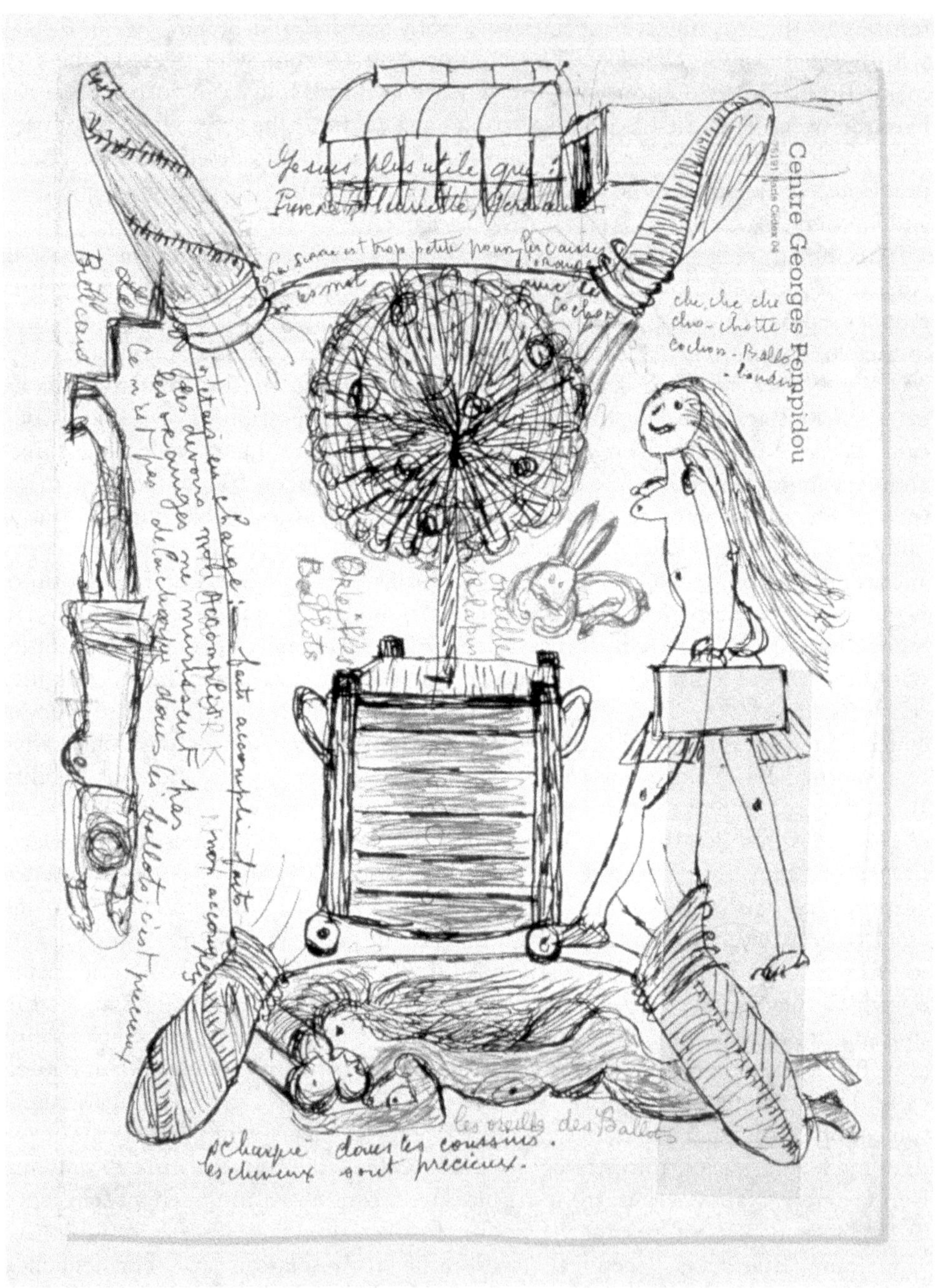

Fig. 3.9. Louise Bourgeois, *The Insomnia Drawings 1994–95* [no. 72, verso], 220 mixed media works on paper, various dimensions
Photo: Christopher Burke, © The Easton Foundation/ Licensed by DACS, UK and VAGA at ARS, NY

observed how many of the sheets in the series host illustrations of flowering, botanic forms which 'grow across the page, like plants' suggesting a luxuriant, contagious movement proliferating in excess of design and control.[113] Other pages are colonised by multiple illustrations which overlap and intrude upon each other, speaking simultaneously to the lush sensorium of the insomniac, suspended between consciousness and hazy reverie, and a continual discharge of creative movement unconcerned by the restraints of space. This exultance of artistic impulse independent of aesthetic ordering or uniformity brings the *Insomnia Drawings* close to Nancy's account of the diffuse 'tas' [stack] of sensory materials which contiguously touch upon each other 'sans principle de coordination' [without principle of coordination], or to his understanding of the artistic *œuvre* as that which precisely 'opens out' to embrace an 'infinity' of elements and presentations.[114] This again corresponds to the drawings' dominant aesthetics of insatiability and profusion, and to Bourgeois's commitment to an ongoing expansion of expression, to a pleasurable movement of sense that resists calculation. As the artist herself has commented:

> You lose track of time. You follow the pleasure of the activity of drawing. You do not care what the result is going to be. All the connections are unconscious. You do not know where you are going to end. It is a journey without an aim.[115]

Such a statement speaks to the experience of being steeped in the thrill of improvised creation. It also resonates with Nancy's diagnosis of writing, in his essay 'L'Exscrit,' as a 'dissolution' of sense as opposed to a fixing down of meaning, and, in *Le Plaisir au dessin*, his account of *le dessin* as an auto-determining creative practice concerned to instigate a sensibility and value-system categorically its own.[116] While the *Insomnia Drawings*' borrowing from the templates of visual poetry and frequent diaristic formulations enter into pleasurable communion with the rhythms and spacings of more traditional prose forms, they should not, at the same time, be approached as a form of *écriture* or, indeed, 'scriptothérapie' *tout court*. The immediate and urgent nature with which they are jotted down on paper side-steps the transactions of catharsis to embrace instead the constant flux of a shared, sensory world. A dizzying late sheet from the collection which bears witness to sketches of human, animal, aqueous, architectural, poetic, and vegetative forms, all playfully scrawled over a sheet of notepaper stamped with the credentials of the Centre Pompidou in Paris (see fig. 5.9), testifies to their accumulative, analogical aesthetics at considerable remove from the geometric *tableaux* of the *Cells* series, or the cool encroachments of the internationally acclaimed *Spider* sculptures. The *Insomnia Drawings*' accommodation of detritus, and their willingness to host the unshapely surpluses of everyday life, remodels luxury, again, as both sustained material praxis and a certain privileged ability to veer off course.[117] The devotion with which Bourgeois gave herself each night to this practice — in the artist's own terms, 'I Give Everything Away' — also re-invigorates insomnia as a space able to be mined for further exploration and enchantment, rather than a symptom to be painfully endured.[118] As I will discuss in the sub-section to follow, insomnia takes on a more pleasurable charge and even latent feminist politics when it is considered, via Bourgeois, as an arena vibrantly exempted from the obligations of the working day, and as an expanse of time set adrift from the duties of domestic life.

Blood and Water

Louise Bourgeois's *Insomnia Drawings* trace the voluptuous unfolding of a gesture independent of manipulation, fabricating, or explicit ordering.[119] Sketched out over a long period of sleepless nights, with no project other than to trace what Bourgeois calls the 'shapelessness' of the night-time hour, they resist an exchange economy's prescription of use-value, or a psychoanalytic investment in remedy to instead embrace a sensual *désœuvrement* and alternative artistic and affective registers.[120] Their interest in rhythm, multi-sensuality, and textural variety evades, moreover, the traditional fixed postures of the gallery space and allies them closely with the haptic and kinetic qualities of the moving image.

In her notes which figure intermittently as annotations to the series, Bourgeois's emphasis on engulfment and amorphousness and on the experience of being 'carried away' by the flux of an aesthetic act resonates with the sketches' abundant representations of water, blood, and other secretions. These in turn evoke Nancy's account, in *Le Plaisir au dessin*, of drawing's uninhibited protrusion of artistic sensibility which exceeds and overcomes fixed categories. Such representations of organic and corporeal fluids, going beyond Nancy's at times abstract philosophy, see the aesthetic experience as subject to the residues and products of the external world and material body. Conceiving pleasure in terms of a 'stream of consciousness', these representations stage the drawings as both formally creative but also as sensate and sensual, to align with notions of luxury as embodied and expressly material. As Mary Hamel Schwulst has noted of the series, 'a variety of subjects — including people, architecture, and flowers — intertwine in a seemingly endless flow'.[121]

Departing from Bourgeois's predilection elsewhere for cocooning, architectural, geometric, and enclosing shapes, images of waves and floods deluge the viewer of the *Insomnia Drawings*, corresponding, in *Le Plaisir au dessin*, to Nancy's privileging of *le dessin* as a mode of artistic expression able, in its status as an unrestrained 'premier jet' [first jet] of thought or creativity, to expose 'l'inimitable surgissement de l'être en général' [the inimitable surging forth of being in general].[122] Illustrations of rivers, lakes, and oceans which give rise to exaggerated, triangulated crests of waves, ripples, rising waves, and floods all feature. Frequent word association games conjure river names and different modes of inorganic and organic flow: 'Seine, Bièvre, Creuse, Hudson, Eastern Reservoir, fausse bièvre; deep well, rain, water, eau, water tap, kettle, moss. Splash, waddle, puddle, mudpies, muddle, drip, leek' are on multiple occasions played, revealing water's status as an infinite and ludic source of creative flux.[123]

For the most part, the *Insomnia Drawings*' illustrations of water depart indeed from perspectives offered by Freud and Julia Kristeva, where the oceanic figures as a threatening, malevolent force in its potential to dissolve the foundations of the ego.[124] In her essay 'Oceanic Feeling and Communist Affect', Jackie Wang ventures the experience of ego loss engendered by the oceanic as swelling with political potential, enabling 'one to commune with the substance of existence in a way that radically alters one orientation to the world'.[125] Bourgeois goes one step further in affirming this dissolution as for the most part pleasurable, resonating with desires to become aquatic, amniotic, to slough off the obligations of the 'optimized', productive self, and to enter into flux with the subtler attunements of the subterranean organic world.[126] In one sketch, crests and troughs of waves concertina in intensity across the page, the line of their rendering growing thicker and more filled in as the eye descends, suggestive of the cumulative, infinitely multiplying force of water and of Nancy's definition of exuberance in *La Naissance des seins* as 'le jaillissement d'un flot qui passe la mesure' [the gushing of waves which bypasses measure].[127] These accounts of water as an infinite creative source further echo Nancy's testimonies to the fecund 'élan' of pleasure which strives to never cease creating. Celebrating a liquid as opposed to architectural aesthetics, the *Insomnia Drawings* situate the *informe* from within the formal and pursue their praxis in the fluid, boundless circulation of materials.

On a scrawled note on the back of one of the drawings in the series, Bourgeois makes the link between drawing, sleeplessness, and water explicit, writing, 'the drawings of night | They all emerge from the water'.[128] Such a statement — close to earlier accounts of her drawings as 'secretions' or as 'threads' in a spider's web spinning out from the fibres, sinews, and rhythms of the lived body rather than the conscious mind — emphasises latency, a gradual process of coming-into-presence, and slow modes of production. This understanding diverges from accounts of drawing as a mere preliminary outline of a future model of thought. It privileges, instead, a steady, almost imperceptible, tracing of a line from an underlying reservoir of image and memories. This evolution illustrates Bourgeois's (and to varying degrees, Nancy's) often dialectical account of water as a both positively differentiating force but also one of stupor, languor, stillness. On another sheet Bourgeois indeed suggests that water in her work becomes a 'metaphor for uncontrollable [*sic*]' but also testifies to the process of 'stagnating', and in another annotation she suggests that she derives solace and a form of comfort in such quietude, writing, in a column headed by the underlined handwritten title 'Eau', the words, 'le travail', 'la beauté', 'le silence'.[129] This sense of rapture before the calm voluptuousness of water which dissolves everything within a continuous, unceasing mass is compounded by the recurring motif, within the *Insomnia Drawings*, of series of images of concentric circles, reminiscent of ripples, which appear to have the function of palpating for Bourgeois a new mode of temporality and spatiality in which the linear divisions between night and day are overlapped by the more cyclical and circadian rhythms of the natural world.

In distinction to this sense of serenity, elsewhere the aggression of water and its 'dangers' are forefronted, underscoring the ambivalence of water's function in the drawings. One sketch in the collection indeed registers the outlines of a drowning girl, speaking to Bourgeois's conflictual accounts of 'l'eau' as both nurturing and enveloping but also as invasive and contaminating, as that which both irrigates creative life but also threatens to submerge it completely. Complicit with this undercurrent of aggression, the dominant tonality and colour of the series is red: many of the drawings, indeed, rendered in a dark vermilion ink or even suspended in a haze of crimson gouache paint. Such a tonal backdrop challenges the drawings' soothing intention, speaking rather to the viscerality of affects on display and the profound instability of the material body, evoking even what Nancy, in an essay on Claire Denis's film *Trouble Every Day* calls 'la splendeur du sang' [the splendour of blood].[130] Playing off the homonymic proximity between *sang*, *sens*, and *sans*, Nancy sees blood not as bodily excretion or sign of the body's surplus expenditure but as an expression of the 'sans limite' or 'sans réserve': an inscription, he writes, of 'the assured extreme of extra partes'.[131] Blood in his world view figures as an opening of sense and of the body rather than a mark of what one rejects as excremental. It registers as an opening of the sanguine and an interest in the body in extremis.[132] Such a reading, corresponding to my broader project at large, helps to distance luxury from accounts of wasting and wastefulness, and further to align Bourgeois's work with charged, urgent expressions of the finite material body that are nonetheless anti-essentialist in their leanings.

Other critical accounts of the *Insomnia Drawings* have attempted to read the presence of water as autobiographical homage to the Bièvre river which ran alongside Bourgeois's childhood home and in which Bourgeois as young assistant to her parents' trade in restoring antique tapestries used to dip selected fabric works to loose them of old dyes.[133] Such a detail, as well as to water's re-vitalizing and rejuvenating force, speaks to the river as a sort of anti-archive, where certain marks and inscriptions are erased and forgotten. Speaking to the pull of water as obliterating force, and to pleasure as a form of voluptuous forgetting and erasure, in an interview with Lawrence Rinder Bourgeois would evoke how 'all the houses I have lived in were next to a river: the Bièvre, which appears all the time — Creuse and the Hudson. This water, and its dangers, appears, disappears, and reappears'.[134] Here Bourgeois adds a third element to the surging forth and then subsequent retraction which pertains to the movement of the current or the wave: the inextinguishable cycle of water's re-appearance, which resonates with Nancy's account of *le dessin* as that which proves insatiable in its perpetual taking up again of the 'demand' to create and sketch anew, or as that which is always subject to the re-emergence of aesthetic desire.[135] For Bourgeois, 'the wave repeats itself and falls back again' in echo of the peaks and plateaus, the exuberant extroversions but also counterpart recessions, of creative life.[136] In this vein, water (and drawing) becomes a function, like luxury, of both 'too much and not-enough', rather than an unchecked 'oceanic gushing' or 'entropic surfeit' which, Nancy cautions, risks eradicating difference.[137] In such a context, Bourgeois's practice of drawing at night becomes, as the artist herself observes, 'une question d'intensité' [a question of intensity], or a *syncopated,* both exuberant and cautious movement that derives pleasure not exclusively within the obliterative rush of *jouissance* but in the folding or 'waving' together of asymmetric entities.[138] This frictional and undulating motion of creativity of which Nancy writes distances the *Insomnia Drawings* from the total unconsciousness necessitated by the process of Surrealist 'automatic writing', and allows for a degree of sensual autonomy to be executed by the artist. Such autonomy allows for the experience of insomnia not only to be re-imagined as a bountiful creative space but one textured with complexities, and a broad relay of sensibilities, which make use of the secretions of the natural and embodied world while also illuminating different formal possibilities.

Boundless Night

Emphasis in the *Insomnia Drawings* on the inexhaustible currents of artistic impulse, or on the abundant 'flow' of sense which impels she or he who makes art to forever start again, re-imagines the *nuit blanche* — typically seen as a non-space of inertia and ennui — as a fecund creative arena, or an alternative aesthetic landscape which, exempted of the vigilance and intensity pertaining to the capitalist unit of the working day, becomes free to host new modes and energies of artistic praxis. This re-imagining of sleeplessness as a rich, artistic space for sensory exploration distances Bourgeois's drawing practice from capitalism's pathologising of insomnia as a potential threat to the labouring body's continual efficiency.[139] A recasting of insomnia in positive terms as a space of pleasurable amnesia and as the letting-go of obligations towards productivity and the replenishing of material labour-power sees the *Insomnia Drawings* less as means to an agonistic end than as modes in their own right. It envisages them as movements towards evanescence, which, like the breast sculptures, harness transient materials to explore dialectical desires to both dissolve the artistic ego and affirm it via generative and exploratory traces.[140]

In his short monograph *Tombe de sommeil*, Nancy likens sleep to a process of abandon to a realm in which 'rien n'est à prendre ni à gagner' [nothing is to be gained or won] or to an act of 'laisser-aller' [letting-go] where 'une acuité s'émousse, une vigilance s'endort' [a sharpness softens and a vigilance slumbers].[141] He or she who sleeps, he writes, 'entre dans la déliaison des projets et des visées, des anticipations et des calculs' [enters into the undoing of projects and aims, anticipations and calculations] (p. 14), subtracted from and unperturbed by 'la conscience vigile, de la surveillance et du contrôle, de la projection et de la différentiation' [the domain of vigilant consciousness, of surveillance and control, projectivity and differentiation] (p. 15). Such emancipation from 'les requêtes de la vigilance' [the demands of vigilance] (p. 15) is envisaged not as a withdrawal from the world, nor as the creation of a new utopic space but as the forging of a new intimate relation with consciousness. Granted leave from goals and functions, thoughts 'viennent se jouer librement, indistinctement distinctes' [come into free play, indistinctly distinct] (p. 14). The sleeper is therefore neither 'repoussé ni refoulé dans une stupéfaction' [repressed or buried into stupefaction] (pp. 50–51) but, on the contrary, 'disposé dans une adoration du monde où il ouvre son étrange paix' [disposed to an adoration of the world which opens its strange peace] (p. 34).

This account of *le sommeil* as a loosening of intentionality and obligation and as a suspension of 'vigilance' in order to aerate new affects and sensibilities corresponds to Nancy's larger project to recuperate sleep from its persistent evocation in philosophy as an intransitive negativity ('négativité sans emploi', p. 60) and to reinstate it as a positive site of starting again, as a source of infinite abundance, and as a space where a constant renewal, or a sense of 'confiance dans le retour du jour' [trust in the return of the day] (p. 67) is, on a nightly basis, re-articulated. 'Pour qu'il y ait nuit,' he writes, 'il faut qu'il y ait jour' [In order for there to be night, there must also be day] (p. 40). Similarly, the descent or fall of night-time necessarily pre-empts the return of the light, the two mutually imbricated in a double rhythm (p. 40). Sleep therefore becomes an act of faith, a quotidian investment in the promise of re-birth, or in the certainty that 'sense' will be re-found. Sleep becomes a site of active creation — of confidence, of *sens*, of new ways of being and perceiving — as opposed to a vacuum in which the body feeds off or consumes its own resources. Sleep becomes the site of an infinite expansion rather than a closing-down or pausing of potentiality.

On a late sheet in the series, Bourgeois conjures the sensation of insomnia as a dislocation or a turning-upside-down of time, evoking an alternative, little-known etymology of luxury as a dislocation relating to the Latin verb *luctari* (to wrestle, strain).[142] In a hallucinating blend of French and English, she writes:

L'art
ou est
la vie,
toi et vous
inspire
unafraid: Art
est le
contraire
du acting. Les paysages de nuit ont envahi les jours.[143]

This statement, however fugitive, distills both the drawings' and insomnia's quality of in-betweenness, their cross-pollination and indeed 'contamination' of presumed polar states (wakefulness and sleep). What remains as motif, not unlike in the work of Ernaux, is the ongoing present tense of composition, the immersion in poesis out of which commercial art may or may not emerge. Elizabeth Bronfen, in an essay forming part of the original publication of the *Insomnia Drawings*, summons up Bourgeois's uniquely liminal praxis when she observes, 'Because her insomnia brings states of ambivalence to the fore, she keeps returning to the question of being suspended between two emotions — between plenitude and lack, proximity and absence, inundation and deprivation, agreement and contradiction'.[144]

Yet this foundational ambivalence, and the sensory suspensions of insomnia, are not suffered by Bourgeois as paralysing or immobile states. Rather, they inspire what the artist appoints 'the joy of creation'.[145] The 'landscapes of the night time hour' and their attendant velvet textures may have taken over the more quantifiable and profitable expanse of the capitalised working day, but this invasion proves for the most part inspiring and enlivening. Night and day remain in sensual relation, or in a state of dialectical friction, constantly igniting novel sensibilities.

In *Tombe de sommeil*, Nancy is clear that, in distinction to the 9-to-5's algorithms of efficiency, what we call *la nuit* cannot be quantified, nor 'n'admet aucune mesure autre qu'elle-même' [admits no measure other than itself].[146] This testimony to the inassimilable and incalculable value of the night-time hours — their exceptionality, and deviation from use-value — aptly tessellates with the account of drawing in *Le Plaisir au dessin* as an act which only comes into being in the process of its own configuration, or as that which proceeds by caution, in the dark, without pre-established motive or design.[147] Nancy offers an explicit link between sleep and drawing when he writes in *Tombe de sommeil* that the night gives expression to an amniotic, enigmatic realm 'toute figure vient se figurer, toute couleur chatoyer' [where all figures come to figure themselves, all colours shimmer].[148] In this iridescence is permitted an unpressurised 'trying on' of thought prior to its scrutiny before the light of day. In the *Insomnia Drawings*, too, the lability and latitude of the first draft takes singular precedence over the impenetrable sheen of finished works for purchase.

Despite this commitment to contingency, in *Le Plaisir au dessin* Nancy remains eager to put emphasis on the material, corporeal origins of the activity of drawing, evoking it in terms of a 'configuration rythmée du réel naissant du rythme même du corps' [rhythmic configuration of the real born out of the rhythm itself of the body].[149] Bourgeois in an interview with Marie-Laure Bernadec echoes such impressions of material tactility, likening her nocturnal sketches to a mode of embodied attunement to, or meditation on, the breath and pulse and to a 'kind of rocking or stroking' which sounds out the subtler inflections of the half-conscious sensorium. 'I want to bring my whole body into the process of drawing,' she continues, 'the lines are like knitting. They are like a heartbeat'.[150] Such statements conceive drawing less as sedative or tranquillising tool than a means of abundant awareness, of feeling a life 'turn on', as the novelist Samantha Harvey has recently described.[151] In many verses captured by the series, there is evidence of a prosaic, yet profound witnessing to the simple act of being alive, or what Harvey, citing Philip Larkin, calls 'the million-petalled flower of being here'.[152]

In the conclusion to *Tombe de sommeil*, Nancy, in striking parallel to Crary, casts doubt over a world which has annulled the *espacements* [spacings] between night and day and which, in order to maximise profit, has induced a generalized conscription into an experiential regime of duration without breaks, rest, or renewal. 'Comment dormir dans un monde sans berceuse, sans refrain apaisé, sans capacité d'oubli?' [How to sleep in a world without a rhythm, without peaceful refrain, without capacity for forgetting?], he asks.[153]

In this section, I have argued that Bourgeois's *Insomnia Drawings* develop a compelling, multi-sensual and rhythmic relationship to time and effect that is not purely visual. Up against what Nancy calls the 'non-differentiation' of contemporary life, the drawings re-instate texture and striation, and affirm nascent and emergent modes of artistic production unavailable for capture, possession, or quantifiable analysis.[154] Moving luxury away from lethargy, passivity, and stillness, the drawings effervesce with life and invention, celebrating, like the breast sculptures, the pure potential of creativity unencumbered by object attachments. By association, the experience and cultural entrenchment of insomnia is transformed, takes on a different patina and hue. In Bourgeois's hands, sleeplessness becomes less a 'deprivation' or a categorical 'abuse of time' than an occasion for an alternative creative practice, in which art transcends everyday parameters, and displays infinite desires for variation and extension.[155] In Bourgeois's playfully perverse configuration (anticipating discussions of the artist Sophie Calle's work in the chapter to come), wakefulness, sustained vigil, and an unbroken commitment to artistic praxis are a choice. Both the expectations of the market and the strict partitions of 'clock' time are dismantled as Bourgeois secludes herself in the private chamber of her bedroom and devotes herself to the abundant, haptic power of form.

Conclusion: Metamorphosis and Mutability

In this chapter I have argued that Bourgeois's art reveals understandings about luxury as a form of material re-modelling, corporeal lability, and a certain feminist ability to engage powerfully with formal properties.[156] In aligning Bourgeois with the post-metaphysical, finite, and embodied philosophy of Jean-Luc Nancy, my interpretation has departed from consistent readings of the artist's *œuvre* as a cathartic, compensational exercise, rooted in the 'negative affects' of apology and suffering. Taking two recurrent motifs from two major periods within Bourgeois's work — the *Insomnia Drawings* of the 1990s and the gravitation towards breast-like shapes in the soft, visceral sculptures of the 1960s — I have shown that independent of the artist's volatile personal struggles, her work bespeaks sensuality, *jouissance*, and an immersive joy in the pleasures of creation. Through Bourgeois, a re-vivified idea of luxury as the participation in a multiplicity of different rhythms, moulds, and axioms of making art, beyond the sexual and carnal declination of the term, therefore becomes possible.

In an extract from 'Ode à ma mère', of 1995, Bourgeois would herself write that 'this endless analysis is exhausting, and visually it can be reductive. It makes me want to rush out onto the street and fill my lungs with air'.[157]

Resisting the belaboured strategies of psychoanalysis in particular, this chapter has augmented the arena of interpretations of Bourgeois's work by emphasising what drawings and sculpture might open out to, or gesture towards, rather than explain away. Whilst not undermining the ambivalence, anger, and depression latent in Bourgeois's process, I have argued that the furtive outlines accessed by the trace of drawing and the outline of the breast enable new conceptual paradigms to take shape and emerge. Such paradigms — disabling abilities to fetishise or commodify Bourgeois's work — insist on shifting, morphing, fluctuating, like the artist did herself throughout her life.[158] A dream of luxury as eternal and immobile is challenged as Bourgeois's sculptures and drawings fail to correspond to major tropes or consistencies, eschewing final comprehension or critical consensus.

To conclude I want to consider that there is, however, pleasure in such critical unknowing and *désœuvrement*. In *Tombe de sommeil*, Nancy writes of the phenomenon of daybreak that 'l'initiale lux n'est toujours rien d'autre que la différence même, la partage et l'indistinction primitive d'un chaos, d'un khora, d'un magma, d'une profusion sourcière' [the initial light is still nothing other than difference itself, the sharing and the primitive indistinctiveness of chaos, of *khora*, of magma, of a foundational profusion].[159] Immersed in an art of emergence and indulging in the vibrant possibility of form prior to its moulding into fixed, definite terms, Bourgeois's sculptures and drawings, in contrast to the larger-scale, architectural constructs which would make her name, bear witness to these primitive beginnings of creativity. Actively revelling in the unfiltered outbursts of initial insight or ideation, they revise ideas of luxury in espousing a different kind of *art engagé* and in producing utterly original, material residues from a life fully experienced and lived. Such residues eschew definitive interpretation. Echoing Bourgeois's own tendency to change her mind in relation to her artworks, her pieces resist easy consumption and persist as surpluses, defiant traces, and new templates that shrink back from a repressive gaze.

Notes to Chapter 3

1. Louise Bourgeois, in Paulo Herkenhoff, 'Interview: Paulo Herkenhoff in conversation with Louise Bourgeois, transcribed and edited by Thyrza Nichols Goodeve', in *Louise Bourgeois*, ed. by Robert Storr, Paulo Herkenhoff and Allan Schwartzman (London: Phaidon, 2003), pp. 6–25 (p. 19). Louise Bourgeois, 'Passage dangereux', cited in *Louise Bourgeois*, ed. by Frances Morris (London: Tate Publishing, 2007), p. 201.
2. See, variously: Joan Acocella, 'The Spider's Web: Louise Bourgeois and her Art', *The New Yorker*, 4 February 2003; Rosalind E. Krauss, *Bachelors* (Cambridge, MA: MIT Press (October Books), 2000); Nixon, *Fantastic Reality*; Robert Storr, 'A Sketch for a Portrait: Louise Bourgeois', in *Louise Bourgeois*, ed. by Storr, Herkenhoff and Schwartzman, pp. 28–93; and Donald Kuspit, *Louise Bourgeois* (New York: Random House, 1988).
3. In the accompanying wall-text to a recent exhibition (16 June 2014–12 April 2015) of Bourgeois's works on paper at the Tate Modern in London, curated by Ann Coxon, it was noted that 'for [Bourgeois], the repetitive, rhythmic act of drawing had a soothing effect' <http://www.tate.org.uk/whats-on/tate-modern/display/louise-bourgeois-works-on-paper/wall-text-0> [accessed 26 August 2015]. For further readings of Bourgeois's work in terms of therapeutics and palliation, see Griselda Pollock, 'Seduction, Mourning and Invocation: The Geometry of Absence in Works by Louise Bourgeois', in *After-affects/ After-images: Trauma and Aesthetic Transformation in the Virtual Feminist Museum* (Manchester: Manchester University Press, 2013).
4. See for example Emily Wei Rales, *Louise Bourgeois: To Unravel a Torment*, ed. by Emily Wei Rales (Potomac, MD: Glenstone Museum, 2018) and Britt-Marie Schiller, who argues that 'an emotion that runs like a thread through Louise Bourgeois's art, diaries, and dreams is the anxiety of being alone, disconnected, and abandoned' ('Hair, Threads, and Umbilical Cords: Louise Bourgeois's Dream of Connection', *Psychoanalytic Review*, 105.6 (December 2018), 657–73 (p. 657)).
5. For an extensive analysis of a theory of part-objects in relation to Bourgeois's work, see particularly Nixon, *Fantastic Reality*.
6. Maggie Nelson, *The Art of Cruelty: A Reckoning* (New York & London: W. W. Norton, 2011), p. 174.
7. Jean-Luc Nancy, *Le Plaisir au dessin* (Paris: Galilee, 2009), p. 43.
8. Jean-Luc Nancy, *La Naissance des seins*, p. 61; *Le Plaisir au dessin*, p. 37. See also Derrida, who in *Donner le temps* makes a distinction between 'the pure auto-affective pleasure' of pure consumption, and the more syncopated, aporetic pleasure of giving without expecting a return (p. 134).
9. Via Adriana Caravero, it might be generative to think Bourgeois less in terms of entropy than through a lens of 'inclination', understood in broad terms as a 'disposition towards affect' (*Inclinations: A Critique of Rectitude* (Stanford, CA: Stanford University Press, 2016), p. 1). Nancy's work adds further layers to Caravero's assertion, in seeing the movement art makes towards the

viewer as a 'double-movement' (*La Naissance des seins*) of contact and withdrawal. Such templates are particularly prominent in Bois and Krauss, *Formless*, and Pollock, *After-affects/ After-images*.

10. Merleau-Ponty's suggestion that 'I cannot understand the function of the living body except by enacting it myself, and except in so far as *I am a body which rises toward the world*' (*The Phenomenology of Perception*, trans. by Colin Smith (London: Routledge, 1962), p. 75, my emphasis) will be useful, for example, in my discussion of Bourgeois's fecund, anticipatory aesthetics.
11. See Saul F. Nelson, 'I Was not a Surrealist. I Was an Existentialist': Louise Bourgeois Reconsidered', *Oxford Art Journal*, 40.3 (December 2017), 469–90 (p. 490).
12. See Vera Dika, *The (Moving) Pictures Generation: The Cinematic Impulse in Downtown New York Art and Film* (New York: Palgrave Macmillan, 2012), p. 107.
13. For an attentive reading of the architectural impulse in Bourgeois's work, see particularly John Ashbery, 'Anxious Architecture', *New York Magazine*, 16 October 1978, or Mieke Bal, 'Narrative Inside Out: Louise Bourgeois's Spider as Theoretical Object', *Louise Bourgeois*, special issue of *Oxford Art Journal*, 22.2 (1999), 103–26. See Lippard, 'Eros Presumptive', and 'Louise Bourgeois: From the Inside Out', *Artforum*, 13 (March 1975), 26–33.
14. For a critique of the 'disproportionate number' of male thinkers referred to in *La Naissance des seins,* for example, see Andy Campbell, 'Straight Sense', *Reviews in Cultural Theory,* Volume 5, Issue 2, (1 August 2014), <http://www.reviewsinculture.com/?r=139> [accessed 8 November 2015].
15. This line of my argument resonates with Michel Foucault's reading of Werner Schroeter's *Der Tod der Maria Malibran* (1972), in which, Foucault argues, 'it's a question of the multiplying and burgeoning of the body, an exaltation, in some way autonomous, of its least parts, of the least possibilities of a body fragment. There is an anarchizing of the body, in which hierarchies, localizations and designations, organicity if you like, is being undone' ('Sade: Sergeant of Sex', in *Foucault Live: Collected Interviews, 1961–1984*, ed. by Sylvère Lottringer, trans. by Lysa Hochroth and John Johnston (Los Angeles: Semiotext(e) 1996), pp. 186–87). Such a reading also displays obvious resonance with Deleuze and Guattari's idea in *Mille plateaux* of a body without organs.
16. Phillip Larratt-Smith has read this evolution in terms of a shift from the harshness of the father to 'the figure of the nurturing mother', a reading more aligned to a psychoanalytical approach than my own ('Petite maman', in *Petite maman*, ed. by Phillip Larratt-Smith (Mexico City: Instituto Nacional de Bellas Artes, 2014), pp. 40–50 (p. 40)).
17. Nancy, *La Naissance des seins*, p. 84.
18. See Jonathan Crary, *24/7: Late Capitalism and the Ends of Sleep* (London: Verso, 2012).
19. Louise Bourgeois, 29 January 1958, cited in Courtney Fiske, 'Louise Bourgeois: The Return of the Repressed', *Brooklyn Rail* (September 2012) <https://brooklynrail.org/2012/09/art_books/louise-bourgeois-the-return-of-the-repressed> [accessed 26 August 2020].
20. Nancy, *La Naissance des seins*, p. 65. Marguerite Duras, cited in Wilson, *The Reclining Nude*, p. 200.
21. I refer particularly here to Bourgeois's early *Personnages* series, made between 1945 and 1950. As Phillip Larratt-Smith has noted, this effervescence of new work followed several inert years (approximately 1952–66) of deep depression following the death of Bourgeois's father. 'In this period of deep depression and withdrawal', he records, '[Bourgeois's] artistic production slowed and at times seems to have ceased altogether, with the work of analysis taking the place of art making' ('The Volcanic Unconsciousness: Ten Dreams of Louise Bourgeois', *Psychoanalytic Review*, 105.6 (December 2018), 639–56 (p. 640))
22. Bryony Fer makes this comparison in her piece 'Objects beyond Objecthood', *Louise Bourgeois*, special issue of *Oxford Art Journal*, 22.2 (1999), 27–36.
23. Louise Bourgeois, 'A Merging of Male and Female 1974', in *Louise Bourgeois*, ed. by Storr, Herkenhoff and Schwartzman, p. 120.
24. See Bois and Krauss, *Formless*, and Lippard, 'Louise Bourgeois'.
25. Bourgeois herself was keen to distance readings of her work from object fetishism; writing at one stage in her extensive diaries (dated Sunday, 27 July 1995), 'Louise is anti-fetishist' (cited in Larratt-Smith, *Petite maman*, p. 42).

26. See Nancy, *La Naissance des seins*, p. 12. Donald Winnicott, foreshadowing Nancy's conceptual alignment of the breast with creativity, wrote in 1971 how 'the breast is created by the infant over and over again out of the infant's capacity to love' (*Playing and Reality* (Harmondsworth: Penguin Books, 1971), p. 13). While not focusing on infant psychodramas, it is this recursive, iterative, generative potential of the breast as holding space for the voluptuous unfurling of impressions and sense-memories that I wish to advance in this section.
27. Nancy, *La Naissance des seins*, p. 23.
28. I borrow this phrase from Joshua Cohen, *Not Working: Why We Have to Stop* (London: Granta, 2019), where it is used in relation to Tracy Emin's 1998 work *My Bed*.
29. For the most extensively Kleinian reading of Bourgeois, see Nixon, *Fantastic Reality*.
30. See again Larratt-Smith, *Petite maman*, p. 40.
31. Nancy, *La Naissance des seins*, p. 28.
32. Ibid.
33. Bourgeois thought extensively about the links between birth and the act of artistic creation. At the legendary 1950 'Artists Sessions' moderated by Robert Motherwell and Alfred H. Barr Jr., she submitted the following questions as a suggestion for a discussion topic: '*The Genesis of a Work of Art;* or in what circumstances is a work of art born: *Definition* of the term "genesis" = process of creation. Is it the process of being born or the process of giving birth?' (cited in *Louise Bourgeois & Pablo Picasso: Anatomies of Desire*, ed. by Marie-Laure Bernadec (New York: Hauser & Wirth, 2019), p. 78).
34. Julia Kristeva, *Black Sun: Depression and Melancholia* (New York: Columbia University Press, 1989), p. 7.
35. Nancy, *La Naissance des seins*, pp. 12, 66.
36. Ibid., p. 15.
37. See Nancy, 'Il y a du rapport sexuel — et après', p. 31.
38. Bourgeois, 'A Merging of Male and Female 1974', p. 120.
39. For a study of baroque vision as that which resists the separation between mind/body, form/matter, line and colour separation, see Mieke Bal, *Quoting Caravaggio: Contemporary Art, Preposterous History* (Chicago: University of Chicago Press, 2001). On the return of the baroque in contemporary visual culture, see also *Resurgences baroques: les trajectoires d'un parcours transculturel*, ed. by Nicolas Goyer and Walter Moser (Brussels: La Lettre volée, 2001).
40. See B. K. Fischer, 'Shake Forth a Nest: Feminist Ekphrasis and the Example of Louise Bourgeois', *Los Angeles Review of Books*, 9 August 2014 <https://lareviewofbooks.org/essay/feminist-ekphrasis-example-louise-bourgeois> [accessed 8 November 2015], who argues that Bourgeois's work gives shape to 'the ambiguity of embodied utterance, of the body and mind in pain and the impossible, ongoing effort to represent it'. Nancy, *Le Plaisir au dessin*, p. 97.
41. This quotation comes from a loose sheet I accessed while in residency at the Easton Foundation in July 2019 (Louise Bourgeois (1957, September 16). The Easton Foundation. LB-0141, verso).
42. Nixon, *Fantastic Reality*, p. 270, makes this point.
43. Nancy, *La Naissance des seins*, p. 63.
44. See Ann Coxon, *Louise Bourgeois* (London: Tate Publishing, 2010), p. 109. Rachel Cusk also draws attention to the conflicts bedevilling the figure of the 'artist-mother' in Bourgeois's work in an essay in her *Coventry* collection (Rachel Cusk, 'Louise Bourgeois: Suites on Fabric', in *Coventry* (London: Faber & Faber, 2019), p. 141).
45. This reading is especially advanced by Nixon, *Fantastic Reality*, p. 80.
46. See Coxon, *Louise Bourgeois*, p. 109.
47. Louise Bourgeois (1957, September 16). The Easton Foundation. LB-0141.
48. Wilson, *The Reclining Nude*, p. 16.
49. Louise Bourgeois (1959). The Easton Foundation. LB-0464.
50. In *Formless*, Bois and Krauss emphasis tactility in their account of 'the vision of animals focused on the horizontal ground on which they and their prey both travel, a vision that is therefore, in certain ways, merely an extension of the sense of touch' (p. 90).
51. Nancy, *La Naissance des seins*, p. 45.
52. Louise Bourgeois, cited in Thomas McEvilley, *Sculpture in the Age of Doubt* (New York: Allworth Press, 1999), p. 237.

53. See Nancy, *La Naissance des seins*, p. 42.
54. *Mamelles*'s defiant interpellation of the art-spectator here aligns with Bourgeois's statement that her sculptures should be encountered less as 'conversation pieces' than 'confrontation pieces' (cited in Deborah Wye, *Louise Bourgeois* (New York: MOMA Press, 1982), p. 30).
55. Nancy, *La Naissance des seins*, pp. 10, 44.
56. Ibid., p. 14.
57. Lana Lin, *Freud's Jaw and Other Lost Objects: Fractured Subjectivity in the Face of Cancer* (New York: Fordham University Press, 2017), p. 74. Lin also evokes how 'breast symmetry is a regulatory norm through which sex is materialized' (p. 75).
58. Nixon, for example, terms *Double Negative*'s ambivalent protrusions 'breast penises' (*Fantastic Reality*, p. 184).
59. See Nancy, *La Naissance des seins*, p. 29.
60. Siri Hustvedt has read this phase in Bourgeois's career as a form of 'love for the materials themselves' (*A Woman Looking at Men Looking at Women* (New York: Simon & Schuster, 2016), p. 28), resonant with Nancy's account of art as an 'amour des formes'.
61. See Coxon, *Louise Bourgeois*, p. 38.
62. Hervé Guibert, *Written in Invisible Ink: Selected Stories*, trans. by Jeffrey Zuckerman (Los Angeles: Semiotext(e), 2020), p. 66. Louise Bourgeois, cited in Emily Stokes, 'My Own World: A New Book Illuminates Louise Bourgeois' Relationship to Psychoanalysis', *Frieze* (October 2012) <https://frieze.com/article/my-own-world> [accessed 19 June 2020].
63. Nelson, '"I was not a Surrealist. I was an Existentialist"', p. 484.
64. See, for example, Louise Bourgeois, cited in Bryony Fer, *The Infinite Line: Remaking Art After Modernism* (New Haven, CT: Yale University Press, 2004): 'the poured form is stretched from the inside and obeys the laws of gravity' and 'hot wax poured into freezing water will assume a unique shape' (p. 110).
65. See Nixon, *Fantastic Reality*, p. 132. See also Mignon Nixon, 'Bad Enough Mother', in *October: The Second Decade, 1986–1996, Volume 76*, ed. by Rosalind E. Krauss (Cambridge MA: Mit Press, 1997), pp. 156–99 (p. 167), for whom 'the first object of aggression is not, as it is in the Oedipal-centred Freudian model, the father, and not even the mother, but a series of part-objects — breast, milk, penis, children, womb — to which the infant fantasizes the connection of other part-objects — mouth, teeth, urine, faeces — in frenzied attacks enacting, according to Klein, the force of the death drive'. Reading Bourgeois's work *The Destruction of the Father*, Nixon also makes reference to 'Bourgeois's oral-sadistic fantasy of dismembering and devouring her father's body' (p. 160).
66. See Fer, *Objects beyond Objecthood*, p. 110, who suggests that 'it was how the material seemed to perform — the viscosity of its pouring, the event of its malleable action' concerning Bourgeois in this period.
67. Nancy, *La Naissance des seins*, p. 45.
68. Jean-Luc Nancy, 'The Body of Pleasure', trans. by Anne O'Byrne, in *Corpus II: Writings on Sexuality*, ed. by Anne O'Byrne (New York: Fordham University Press, 2013), pp. 93–96 (p. 96).
69. Louise Bourgeois, *Destruction of the Father /Reconstruction of the Father: Writings and Interviews, 1923–1997*, ed. by Marie-Laure Bernadec and Hans-Ulrich Obrist (London: Violettes, 1998), p. 222.
70. See Peter Campbell, 'At Tate Modern: Louise Bourgeois', *London Review of Books*, 29.23 (29 November 2007), 32.
71. Nancy, *La Naissance des seins*, p. 30.
72. See Bois and Krauss, *Formless*, p. 32. Alyce Mahon has written, in relation to Courbet, similarly of the 'erotic pulses which permeate our existence' (*Eroticism and Art* (Oxford: Oxford University Press, 2007), p. 10).
73. Georges Bataille, 'L'Informe', cited in Bois & Krauss, *Formless*, pp. 5, 32.
74. Louise Bourgeois, cited in Francesco Bonami, 'Louise Bourgeois: In a Strange Way, Things are Getting Better and Better', *Flash Art 27*, 174 (January-February 1994), 36–39 (p. 38). For a reading of Bourgeois's art in terms of sensual horizontality, see Wilson, *The Reclining Nude*, 2019.
75. See Louise Bourgeois, 'On *Janus Fleuri* 1969', in *Louise Bourgeois*, ed. by Storr, Herkenhoff and Schwartzman, pp. 118–19 (p. 118).

76. See Coxon, *Louise Bourgeois*, p. 43.
77. Louise Bourgeois, cited in Deborah Wye and Carol Smith, *The Prints of Louise Bourgeois* (New York: MOMA Press, 1994), p. 225.
78. In so doing, I go against Fer's reading of the art of the 1960s as a move away from 'collage-based' practices to embrace a 'new aesthetics of seriality' (Fer, *The Infinite Line*, p. 2).
79. See Hannah Westley, *The Body as Medium and Metaphor* (Amsterdam: Rodopi, 2008), p. 167.
80. See Alex Potts, 'Louise Bourgeois: Sculptural Confrontations', *Louise Bourgeois*, special issue of *Oxford Art Journal*, 22.2 (1999), 39–53 (p. 44). Nancy, *La Naissance des seins*, p. 84.
81. See Nixon, *Fantastic Reality*, p. 71, for a reading of Bourgeois's re-appropriation of *Fillette* as fetishistic.
82. See Nancy, *La Naissance des seins*, p. 67, where the former warns against visions of the breast as a mere 'jouet d'une jouissance excitée, voyeuse et frôleuse' [voyeuristic toy of stimulated *jouissance*], and p. 82. Carol Mavor suggests that the breast might be understood as a 'soft object to become other things' ('Moeder, Maman, Mom', in *Chantal Akerman*, ed. by Schmid and Wilson, pp. 26–41 (p. 36)).
83. Lucy Lippard, cited in Fer, *The Infinite Line*, p. 104: 'Whilst Lippard's shift of focus to call a breast a breast was made in the nature of feminism, it lost something of the radical possibility of a more precarious subjectivity'. Maggie Nelson, praising Bourgeois's move away from a sculptural economy predicated mainly on subtraction, suggests in *The Art of Cruelty* that the artist's complex, vulvic, concave feminine forms undercut the heroism of penetration and 'the mythos of the devouring hole' (p. 174).
84. See Nancy, *La Naissance des seins*, p. 45.
85. Ibid., p. 37.
86. On 'the eroticisim of irregular morphology', see Wilson, *The Reclining Nude*, p. 188.
87. Bourgeois, in Herkenhoff, 'Interview', p. 14. Anna Zett, 'Sleeping in Public', *How to Sleep Faster*, 5 (Winter 2014), 6–25 (p. 12).
88. A small number of scholars who have engaged with the *Insomnia Drawings* read them through the optics of Surrealism and the movement's focus on the heightened state of dreams (see for example, Nancy Princenthal, 'Louise Bourgeois: The Insomnia Drawings', *Art on Paper*, 6.2 (November-December 2001), 98–99). A statement from Bourgeois herself might warn against such an interpretation: 'I have never mentioned the word dream in discussing my art, while [the Surrealists] talked about the dream all the time. I don't dream. You might say I work under a spell, I truly value the spell [...]. The spell and the dream are not the same. [The spell is] not a passive state, like a dream' (cited in Larratt-Smith, 'The Volcanic Unconsciousness', pp. 31–32).
89. See Nancy, *Le Plaisir au dessin*, p. 73.
90. Ibid., p. 49.
91. See Wayne Koestenbaum, *Figure It Out* (New York: Soft Skull Press, 2020), p. 13.
92. Marina Benjamin, *Insomnia* (London: Scribe, 2018), p. 4.
93. See Mieke Bal, 'Autotopography: Louise Bourgeois as Builder', *Biography*, 25.1 (Winter 2002), 180–202.
94. Nancy, *Le Plaisir au dessin*, p. 73; *Pleasure in Drawing*, trans. by Phillip Armstrong (Fordham: Fordham University Press, 2013), p. 57.
95. Ibid.
96. See Larratt-Smith, 'The Volcanic Unconsciousness', p. 639.
97. For Gary Indiana, in a psychoanalytically informed account, such an impulse hews to a quality of thriftiness within Bourgeois. He observes: 'Owing to a lifelong fear of abandonment, [Bourgeois] identified with the discarded and the rejected, and hence never threw anything out' ('On the Psychoanalytic Writings of Louise Bourgeois', *Ursula*, 4 (Fall 2019) <https://www.hauserwirth.com/magazine/25821-gary-indiana-psychoanalytic-writings-louise-bourgeois> [accessed 23 June 2020]).
98. Of the related, yet different 'dream diary' she kept in the 1950s, Bourgeois noted how the process was 'very time-consuming' but gave the artist 'the "joy of creation" that I used to have after working' (cited in Stokes, 'My Own World').
99. Louise Bourgeois, cited in *Louise Bourgeois*, ed. by Morris, p. 25.

100. Louise Bourgeois, cited in *Has the Day Invaded the Night or the Night Invaded the Day? Insomnia in the Work of Louise Bourgeois*, ed. by Phillip Larratt-Smith and Frances Morris (Edinburgh: Fruitmarket Gallery Press, 2014), pp. 132, 94, 21.
101. Ibid., p. 42; see Fig. 10.
102. See Amy Sillman, 'Ab-Ex and Disco Balls: In Defense of Abstract Expressionism II', in *Artforum:* Summer 2011, Available Online: <https://www.artforum.com/print/201106/ab-ex-and-disco-balls-in-defense-of-abstract-expressionism-ii-28354> [accessed 23 June 2020]. I am grateful to Aline Guillermet for making me aware of this essay.
103. Louise Bourgeois, cited in *Has the Day Invaded the Night or the Night Invaded the Day?*, ed. by Larratt-Smith and Morris, p. 132.
104. Louise Bourgeois, cited in Coxon, *Louise Bourgeois*, p. 91.
105. Louise Bourgeois: 'What is a drawing? It is a secretion, like a thread in a spider's web [...]. It is a knitting, a spiral, a spider web' (cited in *Louise Bourgeois*, ed. by Morris, p. 17).
106. In this sense the drawings' opening to luxury as plentitude; generosity of expression and incisive creative insight departs from the earlier-evoked hanging sculptures' languor; or their 'desire to give up, to sleep and be passive, to retreat' (Bourgeois, cited in *Destruction of the Father / Reconstruction of the Father*, ed. by Bernadac and Obrist, p. 222). In his account of the insomnia diaries and drawings, Larratt-Smith, further rescuing the drawings from indolent passivity, notes how in Bourgeois 'the passive state of the dreamer is contrasted with the *active process of the artist* waking under a "friendly spell"' ('The Volcanic Unconsciousness', p. 639, my emphasis).
107. Coxon, *Louise Bourgeois*, p. 118.
108. See Jean-Luc Nancy, *Être singulier pluriel* (Paris: Galilée, 1996).
109. See <https://www.moma.org/collection/works/98531> [accessed 27 August 2020].
110. Alain Badiou, cited in Nancy, *Le Plaisir au dessin*, p. 34.
111. Ibid., p. 108.
112. Of *Nature Study*, Rachel Cusk writes: '*Nature Study* enquires into this organic basis of form and finds at once menace and possibility in the *vegetable mechanics of growth*, which beget both flowers and monsters' ('Louise Bourgeois', p. 142, my emphasis).
113. Coxon, *Louise Bourgeois*, p. 93.
114. See Jean-Luc Nancy and Aurelien Barrau, *Dans quels mondes vivons-nous?* (Paris: Galilée, 2011), p. 89.
115. Louise Bourgeois, in Herkenhoff, 'Interview', p. 14.
116. Nancy, 'L'Excrit', p. 59; *Le Plaisir au dessin*, p. 58: 'la mise en jeu d'une sensibilité valant pour elle-même, dégagée de ses finalités opératoires ou informatives' [the putting into play of a sensibility on its own merit, emancipated from operational or informative ends].
117. For a reading of drawing as a 'veering away' from 'captive inscriptive systems', see Wayne Koestenbaum, 'On Doodles, Drawings, Pathetic Erotic Errands, and Writing', in *My 1980s & Other Essays* (London & New York: Farrar, Strass & Giroux, 2013), pp. 183–92 (p. 192).
118. Such was the assigned title of the exhibition of the *Insomnia Drawings* put together by the Fruitmarket Gallery in Edinburgh in 2014 (see <https://www.fruitmarket.co.uk/wp-content/uploads/2014/09/Louise-Bourgeois.pdf> [accessed 23 June 2020]).
119. In this manner the *Insomnia Drawings* display affinities with the Surrealist process of automatic writing, as Princenthal notes. In my reading I suggest that the drawings, while peripherally touching on such processes, overcome the merely automatic and exhibit both the pleasures of abandon and the intimacy of self-knowledge.
120. Louise Bourgeois, cited in *Has the Day Invaded the Night or the Night Invaded the Day?*, ed. by Larratt-Smith and Morris, p. 21.
121. Mary Hamel Schwultz, 'Louise Bourgeois: The Insomnia Drawings: Review', *Library Journal*, 126.13 (August 2001), 96.
122. Nancy, *Le Plaisir au dessin*, p. 83.
123. Louise Bourgeois, cited in *Has the Day Invaded the Night or the Night Invaded the Day?*, ed. by Larratt-Smith and Morris, p. 52.
124. See in particular Kristeva, *Black Sun*.
125. Jackie Wang, 'Oceanic Feeling and Communist Affect' <https://www.dropbox.com/s/gx8hmov33vss6fa/Oceanic%20Feeling%20%28Read%29.pdf?dl=0> [accessed 23 June 2020].

126. See Boyer, *The Undying*, p. 254.
127. Nancy, *La Naissance des seins*, p. 82.
128. Louise Bourgeois, cited in *Has the Day Invaded the Night or the Night Invaded the Day?*, ed. by Larratt-Smith and Morris, p. 18.
129. Ibid., pp. 60, 58.
130. In a statement from her journals Bourgeois twins the colour red to her depression, for example: 'Depth of depression is measured by your attraction to red' (Louise Bourgeois (1977). The Easton Foundation. LB-0017). See Jean-Luc Nancy, 'Icône de l'acharnement', *Trafic*, 39 (Autumn 2001), 58–64 (p. 62).
131. Jean-Luc Nancy, cited in Jacques Derrida, with Simon Hantai, *Le Toucher: Jean-Luc Nancy* (Paris: Galilée, 2000), p. 71.
132. Ibid.
133. See for example Kat Meads, *2.12AM: Essays* (Nacogdoches, TX: Stephen F. Austin State University Press, 2013), p. 96.
134. Louise Bourgeois, cited in *Has the Day Invaded the Night or the Night Invaded the Day?*, ed. by Larratt-Smith and Morris, p. 294.
135. On the question of the presence of an infinite demand within Nancy's work, see James, *The Fragmentary Demand.*
136. Louise Bourgeois, cited in *Has the Day Invaded the Night or the Night Invaded the Day?*, ed. by Larratt-Smith and Morris, p. 293.
137. See Nancy, 'The Body of Pleasure', trans. by O'Byrne, p. 16.
138. Bourgeois, cited in *Has the Day Invaded the Night or the Night Invaded the Day?*, ed. by Larratt-Smith and Morris, p. 293 ('une question d'intensité, de mesure et de contrôle').
139. A perspective on insomnia as a fertile realm of aesthetic insight has recently been offered by Samantha Harvey's memoir *The Shapeless Unease* (London: Jonathan Cape, 2020), which, as Katy Waldman has appraised, views 'awareness as a pure and abundant resource' ('The Late-night Revelations in a Memoir of Insomnia', *The New Yorker*, 4 June 2020 <https://www.newyorker.com/books/page-turner/the-late-night-revelations-in-a-memoir-of-insomnia> [accessed 17 June 2020]). This pathologisation of sleep is extensively discussed in Crary, *24/7*.
140. Koestenbaum, writing on the peripatetic lines of Paul Klee, Egon Schiele, and Picasso, further encounters drawing as an 'errancy fleeing captivity' (*Figure It Out*, p. 118)
141. Jean-Luc Nancy, *Tombe de sommeil* (Paris: Galilée, 2007), pp. 38, 13.
142. See <https://www.etymonline.com/word/luxury> [accessed 23 June 2020].
143. Louise Bourgeois, cited in *Has the Day Invaded the Night or the Night Invaded the Day?*, ed. by Larratt-Smith & Morris, p. 64.
144. Elisabeth Bronfen, 'Les Pouvoirs de l'insomnie', in *Louise Bourgeois: The Insomnia Drawings*, ed. by Marie-Laure Bernadec (Zurich: Daros Editions, 2000).
145. Louise Bourgeois, cited in Stokes, *My Own World.*
146. Nancy, *Tombe de sommeil*, p. 31.
147. Koestenbaum similarly writes of the line as a 'latent state, not quite shaped by describable intention', evoking 'the unformed, the not-yet, the reluctant' (*Figure It Out*, p. 115).
148. Nancy, *Tombe de sommeil*, p. 53.
149. Nancy, *Le Plaisir au dessin*, p. 55.
150. Louise Bourgeois, cited in Coxon, *Louise Bourgeois*, p. 92.
151. In her essay on Bourgeois, for example, Cusk sees the artist's gestures as a form of 'tracing the maternal form again and again' ('Louise Bourgeois', p. 143). Samantha Harvey, cited in Waldman, 'The Late-night Revelations in a Memoir of Insomnia'.
152. Harvey, *The Shapeless Unease*, p. 136.
153. Nancy, *Tombe de sommeil*, p. 74.
154. See Nancy, 'La Politique doit montrer ce qui la dépasse'.
155. See Vahni Capildeo, '"I Give Everything Away": A Parcel Containing Three (3) Sleeps (Customs & Resale Value Nil): Un cadeau pour Madame' <http://mollybloompoetry.weebly.com/vahnicapildeo.html> [accessed 23 June 2020].
156. For a brief account of why formalism is a feminist issue, see Eliza Apperly, 'Gentileschi: Let Us not Allow Sexual Violence to Define the Artist', *Psyche* (10 June 2020) <https://psyche.co/ideas/

gentileschi-let-us-not-allow-sexual-violence-to-define-the-artist> [accessed 18 June 2020]. Cusk also raises this issue, arguing that Bourgeois's works '[emanate] the power of form' ('Louise Bourgeois', p. 142).

157. See Louise Bourgeois, 'Ode à ma mère', cited in *Destruction of the Father /Reconstruction of the Father*, ed. by Bernadec and Obrist, p. 321.

158. See again Cusk, 'Louise Bourgeois', p. 143: 'She herself is unfixed, continually transmogifrying, she is a serpent, a spider, a sow-like field of breasts, an amputee, sometimes she fuses with man or exchanges characteristics with him, sometimes she is merely one enlarged aspect of herself'.

159. See Nancy, *Tombe de sommeil*, p. 14.

CHAPTER 4

Sophie Calle:
The Luxury of Taking Care

> La vraie façon d'étendre et de multiplier ses désirs est de vouloir lui imposer des bornes. — Marquis de Sade
>
> [The only way to prolong and multiply our desires is to impose limits on them.]
>
> We all know that there is a possibility of really immersing ourselves in non-lethal melancholy and loving it. We're nourished by the containment offered by the melancholic state. — Wayne Koestenbaum[1]

In an interview with the writer and critic Sheena Wagstaff, in response to questions about privacy, invasion, and identity appropriation, the visual and conceptual French artist Sophie Calle expresses a potential paradox within her *œuvre* of both wanting to 'have control' but also to relinquish mastery in the process of creating artworks. Speaking to the tension between will and contingency within her work, she states: 'I like to have control, and lose control'.[2] Experiences of self-loss, surrender, and sensations of release, but also strong desires for agency, aesthetic ordering, and ritualised constraint pattern all Calle's projects. In the course of this chapter I suggest that such a dialectic, applicable across Calle's multi-medial career, summons questions about luxury as craft, design, and artistic autonomy but also the experience of ecstatic acquiescence and subjective dissolution afforded by art. By making such an argument, I show how Calle's work speaks directly to debates about exposure, autofiction, and the performance of neoliberal sovereignty latent in the book as a whole. Encompassing visual, tactile, and auditory components, I suggest that Calle's work sources an exceptional fecundity in the platitudes of everyday life, and embellishes the texture of feminized, often heteropatriarchal tropes such as heartbreak, jealousy, depression, and desire to craft new paradigms of feminist self-actualisation and inscription.

In her work *Wilful Subjects*, Sara Ahmed suggests that will and wilfulness be thought as 'externalized' entities which 'acquire life by not being or at least staying within subjects'.[3] Such a formulation provides a useful starting point to think through these ideas of control, privilege, and luxury as artistic sovereignty in relation to Calle's *œuvre*. Poised on the fragile borderline between internal and external space, and public and private boundaries, works such as *Le Carnet d'adresses* (1983) or *L'Hôtel* (1984) interrogate what it means to 'own' a life, and how far that life

— under Calle's manipulation — might be circulated and distributed to consuming others.[4] Whilst such strategies are often cause for the reception of her *œuvre* as an abuse of power and as enacting a narcissistic exploitation of intimate materials, this subjecting of private life to external scrutiny is extended to the character of 'Sophie Calle' as well, whose personal relationships, failed marriages, interactions with her mother, and, at times, 'failure' to see projects fully through are all, in the course of works such as *No Sex Last Night* (1996), *Des histoires vraies* (1994–2013), 'Pas pu saisir la mort' (2007), and *Unfinished (*2005), held up to unflinching examination.[5] Whilst imprinting all her projects with her trademark aesthetic signature of kitsch stylisation, confessional disclosures, and generic promiscuity Calle also frequently subjects the integrity of her persona and identity to public consumption and dissemination. Her work showcases the pleasures to be found in the *effacement* of authorial identity so that the signifier 'Sophie Calle' can enter into what Bataille calls, in relation to his definition of sovereignty, 'une plus grande *disposition* de soi' [a larger disposition of the self].[6]

In the course of this chapter I focus on three works taken from diverse points in Calle's thirty-five year artistic career: *Suite vénitienne* of 1981, a project documenting Calle's decision to follow a man whom she had met the night before at a cocktail party on a subsequent trip to Venice; *Douleur exquise* of 2003, recounting the 'exquisite pain' of a romantic disappointment and Calle's ensuing attempts to heal, palliate, or distract herself by means of assembling other people's narratives of grief; and *Prenez soin de vous* of 2007, inviting a collective of 107 women of varying professions to respond creatively to a break-up email received by Calle from a lover that ended on the bewildering invective to 'take care'. All three, not by coincidence, adhere to highly formalised, highly circumscribed artistic *modes de emploi* or conceits.[7] Speaking to Calle's own observation in relation to her work that 'the rules of the game are always very strict', all three works start with an initial, tautly directed 'brief' before expanding out beyond such seemingly inflexible parameters.[8] *Suite vénitienne*, for example, initially ordains that Calle will not interact with the object of pursuit, the mysteriously named 'Henri B.', and yet soon departs from that imperative. *Douleur exquise* adopts a strategy of juxtaposing stories cataloguing the acute 'pain of others' in order to attain a straightforward healing of the self, yet as the stories amass and take shape, Calle finds her own subjectivity increasingly exposed and subject to erasure. Finally, *Prenez soin de vous*'s original stimulus — a one-page, clichéd, and banal break-up email — is, in the hands of a multiplicity of feminine subjectivities, abundantly transformed and creatively re-imagined in vertiginous excess of its original, flatly predictable premise. These surpluses of artistic intention extend Calle's project beyond conceptions of straightforward mastery and reveal, as Judith Butler notes in conversation with the work of Emmanuel Levinas, the unpredictable 'surfeit of others' which renders any project of the will vulnerable to radical and fracturing contact.[9]

Reading the evolution of Calle's art in terms of a successive opening to multiplicity and otherness, and in terms of a successive move away from narcissism and the entrancing pull of self-representation, allows for an expanded understanding of 'care' which the chapter — following its central presence in *Prenez soin de vous* — takes as a conceptual motif. Although typically aligned with Foucauldian ideas of 'le souci de soi' where the notion of caring for the self is ventured through an optic of self-discipline, mastery, and an obsessively ascetic cataloguing of internal consciousness, recent re-appropriations of the concept such as those ventured by Sandra Laugier have attempted to refashion *le souci* in intersubjective, ethical, and community-based terms.[10] Such contributions align *le souci* less with notions of 'self-care' than with more open-ended forms of attention to Otherness ('attention à autrui').[11] In my reading here, I argue that this notion of attention equally extends to Calle's meticulous, intricately crafted artworks to imagine care, co-extensively, as a quality of aesthetic and affective vigilance and as the luxury of making poetry out of everyday relationships and life.[12] Following Laugier's model, I suggest that Calle's work, despite its interest in ornamentation and details, traces a similar progression from overt concern with caring for the self to a more inclusive, open-ended caring for others. I also, with particular reference to the kinetic, multi-sensory, and indeed cinematic properties of *Prenez soin de vous*, suggest that in the span of these three works an evolution can be traced from the relative stasis of photography and the fetishised art-object to the more dynamic textures of the moving image.

In *Wilful Subjects*, Ahmed asserts that 'to wander away we must first recognise the path we are asked to follow', aptly conjuring the double-process of abandon and constraint, drift and discipline that I trace within Calle's work.[13] The discussion of *Suite vénitienne*, which opens the chapter, demonstrates the 'absolute concomitance' of her luxury: her radical commitment to subscribing to extraordinary formal frameworks while also seeking freedom at all costs.[14]

Suite vénitienne: Surrender, Submission, Failure

In January 1981, Sophie Calle, already in the habit of following strangers on the streets of Paris, decided to pursue a man whom she had met at a cocktail party.[15] Lingering in such a way to intrude upon his conversation, and hearing of his plans to take a train to Venice the next morning, she, resonating with her art's gravitation towards spontaneous experiences, resolved, on a whim, to join him.[16] In the published photo-textual account of the project in collaboration with the publisher *Actes Sud* the taking of such an impromptu decision is glossed by Calle follows:

> A la fin du mois de janvier 1980, dans les rues de Paris, j'ai suivi un homme dont j'ai perdu la trace quelques minutes plus tard dans la foule. Le soir même, lors d'une réception, tout à fait par hasard, il me fut présenté. Au cours d'une conversation, il me fit part d'un projet imminent de voyage à Venise. Je décidai alors de m'attacher à ses pas, de le suivre.[17]
>
> [At the end of January 1980, in the streets of Paris, I followed a man I lost track of a few minutes later in the crowd. The same evening, at a reception, quite by chance, he was presented to me. During a conversation, he told me about an imminent project to travel to Venice. I decided to trace his footsteps and follow him.]

Nonchalantly worded, the statement 'Je décidai alors', in its playfulness and easeful register, inscribes *Suite vénitienne*'s intention to forgo routine and everyday attachments in the name of instinct, desire, and singular artistic ambition. Forsaking the mundane rhythms of quotidian existence, the work presents itself — paraphrasing Baudelaire — as an exceptional 'invitation to a voyage', seducing both Calle and the spectator with its promise of displacement, sensual transport, and the abandonment of ordinary contexts in favour of more pleasurable practices of *dérive* and *flânerie* and related lines of flight.[18] In this way, as Joshua Armstrong has argued, *Suite vénitienne* engages with Situationist traditions engaged for the most part in creatively re-authoring the city and resisting the sterile effects of consumer culture.[19] It also, in a manner reminiscent of Chris Kraus's 1994 experimental novel *I Love Dick*, inverts the entrenched heterosexual model of 'the chase' — in which a man necessarily must always pursue the woman, as opposed to the other way around — to wield a canny feminist poesis in the process.[20] At the same time, resisting total control, *Suite vénitienne* enters into thrilling pacts with the unknown and with the Other, affirming an exposure to risk and contingency but also giving shape to the relief found in giving oneself over to another's path. In 'abandoning herself' to a stranger's habits and itineraries, Calle is pleasurably diverted from the pressures and demands of her own life, exempted from the imperatives of having to perform as an actor and an agent in the functioning world.[21] The decision, manifested in *Suite vénitienne*, to hand one's movements and chronologies over to a person whom one barely knows, permits in this way, as Jean Baudrillard observes in relation to the project, a liberating 'release' from personal responsibilities, accesses a state of 'dreamlike disengagement' where shadowing one's chosen Other is the only task at hand.[22] Attentive to the complex oscillation of intentions at play within Calle's work generally, I contend that *Suite vénitienne* both actualizes feminist ambitions to affectively remap the city and the terrain of heteropatriarchal courtship but also summons the desire to ecstatically disperse one's subjectivity by initiating an invitation to a voyage whose outcome is not pre-ordained. In *Le Plaisir au dessin*, Jean-Luc Nancy qualifies this as 'le plaisir de se rendre disponible pour cette chance, qui est la chance, le risque de l'existence. Le plaisir d'un certain abandon, de cet abandon à la grâce' [the pleasure of making oneself available to chance, which is the risk of existence. The pleasure of a certain abandon, of this abandonment to grace].[23]

In echo of Annie Ernaux's desires in *Se perdre* to 'lose herself' in the production of a story, the printed text of *Suite vénitienne* begins with a declaration of Calle's intention to submit herself entirely to her endeavour and to immerse herself completely in the singularities of her chosen task. In a statement highlighting Calle's total absorption and passivity before the project she dramatically recounts, 'Je me vois aux portes d'un labryinthe, prête à me perdre dans la ville et dans cette histoire. Soumise' [I see myself at the gates of the labryinth, ready to lose myself in the city and in this story. Submissive].[24] Such an admission, if in part playing on the clichéd trope of the romance genre's 'swooning woman', as Baudrillard writes, illuminates desires on Calle's part to yield to the pleasures of surrender but also exposes the syncopated dance of wilfulness at work in the piece.[25] Indeed, Calle's expressed readiness to 'lose herself' and surrender to the conditions of her self-imposed representational game indicates that this submission will remain at the mercy of autonomous decision, and, furthermore, that it will be bolstered by the privilege of having surplus leisure time and the financial means to embark on such a trip.[26]

A sense of art as leisure activity, or as pleasurable means of killing time removed from the debts and duties of the everyday is, on the eve of her departure to Venice, confirmed by Calle's evident delight in the burlesque, theatrical potential of her project. Making little reference to the man she has selected as her object of pursuit, or the potential ethical ramifications of the enterprise, her emphasis, as she boards a train from Paris, is instead placed on the project's capacities for noiresque parody, and on a fetishistic listing of the project's accessories.[27] Itemising the extravagant contents of her suitcase she writes,

> Dans ma valise: un nécessaire de maquillage qui m'aidera à modifier ma physionomie, une perruque blonde coupée au carré, des chapeaux, voilettes, gants, lunettes noires, un Leica et un Squintar (cet accessoire qui se vise sur l'objectif est muni d'un jeu de miroirs permettant de prendre des photos de coté, sans viser le sujet').[28]
>
> [In my suitcase: a toiletry bag of make-up which will help me alter my physiognomy, a blonde wig cut into a bob, hats, powder compacts, gloves, dark glasses, a Leica camera and a Squintar (that accessory which allows one to take photos from the side, without focusing on one's subject).]

Such excited recounting — mimicking Perec's conspicuous consumer litanies at play in *Les Choses*[29] — frames the project as an exercise in self-reinvention and amendment through fashion, relegating Henri B. in the process, as Sheena Wagstaff notes, to the background, positioning him as mere prop to a solo-authored voyage of self discovery.[30] Later in the work Calle will freely admit that she does not find her subject particularly interesting or attractive, corroborating this idea that Henri B. is incidental to what primarily is being staged as an exercise in self-actualisation and inscription. Mirroring Baudrillard's concept of the state of enchanting *rêverie* accessed by placing one's quotidian routines in the hands of another person, Calle writes 'Je suis seule à rêver' [I dream alone] and even states categorically that 'les sentiments d'Henri B ne font pas partie de mon histoire' [Henri B.'s feelings do not form part of my story].[31] Here, the sense that this is a trip principally in Calle's name and that, rather than Henri B. the city of Venice itself and its emotional cartography is the true object of desire, is fortified by Calle's mono-focused declaration 'Demain je verrai Venise pour la première fois' [Tomorrow I'll see Venice for the first time] (p. 43).

As Calle actually arrives in Venice, a desire for the hypnotic pleasures of self-transformation are prioritised over a more porous and diffuse pact with the city as a whole. On her first morning in the city, she begins her textual diary with a record of her outfit — 'Je porte un imperméable beige, un foulard et des lunettes noires' [I'm wearing a beige raincoat, a silk scarf, and dark glasses] (p. 44) — suggesting the extent to which the sartorial dimensions of the project are forefronted here.

Later that evening, having added a blonde wig to her outlandish get-up, Calle dedicates considerable narrative space to her change of silhouette at the expense of documenting the milieu around her. Rather than articulating the night as her first full evening in Venice, she writes, 'Ce soir, c'est ma première sortie en blonde' [Tonight is my first outing as a blonde] (p. 47). The emancipatory potential of self-transformation continues to fascinate Calle as the day's entry is concluded with 'Aujourd'hui, pour la première fois de ma vie, on m'a appelée "belle blonde"' [Today, for the first time in my life, I got called a 'beautiful blonde'] (p. 50).

Here, Calle's entrancement with her own modified appearance accords with Baudrillard's appointment of the act of following another person as a displaced means of seducing the self, or as a means of making oneself — by replacing one's habits and quotidian peregrinations with another's — an alluring stranger. In the opening sequences of the project, little interest, in contrast, is afforded to meeting or seducing Henri B., as Baudrillard writes, 'she expects nothing of him, she does not want to know him'.[32] This indifferent approach is confirmed by Calle's apparent lack of effort to devise a systematic method of encounter or retrieval, and by her aleatory and haphazard meandering through Venice's streets which, again, privileges non-possessive and non-teleological forms of *dérive* and *flânerie*, a kind of wandering for wandering's sake in alignment with luxury's 'purposeless excess'.[33] On her first morning in Venice Calle writes, 'Je marche au hasard dans les rues' [I walk haphazardly through the streets], and further signals to her circuitous, procrastinatory modus operandi when she terms her languid tours through the city 'mes allées et venues' [my comings and goings].[34]

Further implying that her peregrinations through the town are born of instinctual movement rather than cerebral objectives Calle forbids herself from overthinking the exercise as she writes, 'Je refuse de réfléchir à ma présence dans ces lieux. Je ne dois pas y penser. Je dois cesser d'imaginer les issues possibles et de me demander où me mène cette histoire' [I refuse to reflect upon my presence in these places. I shouldn't think about it. I should stop imagining the possible issues and asking myself where this story is leading].[35] Such a strategy enables the indulgence of digressive episodes, facilitates exposures to alternative experiences and encounters. To 'give up' becomes a signifier of intentional desire and wilfulness as, on one occasion, Calle forfeits the labour of trailing Henri B. in favour of accepting an invitation to have lunch with a barman, writing, 'J'abandonne. Je me rends place Saint-Marc. Au café "Florian", où je suis venue prendre un verre, je fais la connaissance de Jean, le barman. Il m'invite à déjeuner et j'accepte' [I give up. I take myself over to Saint-Mark's Square. At the 'Florian' cafe, where I came to have a drink, I make the acquaintance of Jean, the barman. He invites me to lunch and I accept] (p. 59). In a self-aware aside spotlighting the project as a leisurely itinerary, an ambulatory surrender, and a pleasurable exemption from everyday productivity Calle suggests that her chosen method 'est facile, élémentaire et reposante, même si elle s'est montrée jusque-là peu efficace' [is easy, elementary, and relaxing, even if so far it has proved barely efficient] (p. 83). Emancipated from all ordinary expectations, the goal is less to pounce on her target than to remain open to opportunities for pleasure.

In 'Please Follow Me', Baudrillard suggests that in order for the 'game' of circumspectly stalking another person to work, there must be no contact between the follower and the followed, at the risk of the exercise 'falling into banality'.[36] In order to maintain the enigma of the enterprise, the secret of the follower's pursuit, he writes, must not be broken. Calle subscribes to such a stipulation in expressing fears that she actually will come across Henri B. and in articulating reservations that a face-to-face encounter with her chosen subject will disrupt the easeful rhythms and leisurely temporalities of her voyage. Somewhat untethering the project from associations with romantic obsession, or the perceived voraciousness of feminine heterosexual desire, Calle, early on in her account, observes that 'Mon enquête se déroulait sans lui. Sa découverte risque de tout bouleverser, précipite l'échéance. J'ai peur' [My quest was unfolding without him. His discovery risks upsetting everything, precipitating failure. I'm scared] (p. 53).[37] Here, as in *Jeanne Dielman*, a certain desire for 'auto-immunity' and for the decadence of private ritual undisturbed by the external world is revealed.[38] Upon encountering a hotel porter who is able to reveal the intimate chronologies of Henri B.'s day, the fear of potentially having to relate to another person and of being forcibly ejected from a state of 'dream-like detachment' surfaces anew: 'à cette évocation si concrète des habitudes d'Henri B. la peur me saisit à nouveau' [at this extremely concrete evocation of Henri B.'s habits fear gripped me again] (p. 61). Taken together, such admissions underscore a reticence on Calle's part to completely forfeit her own agency. Cowed by the potentially disruptive force of alterity the sense is that Calle would prefer to remain within the dream-like abstract, within the conditional luxuries of 'what if'.

Despite early attempts to maintain the opacity of her project and not to be contaminated by the choices and decisions of others, an eventual sighting of Henri B. exiting his hotel with his wife breaks Calle's initial detachment and resolve to remain at one remove. Carried away by the excitement of finally having caught a glimpse of her subject, Calle immediately defers to doing as he does, to taking photographs of the same things that he deems worthy of documentation. The project's previously somewhat introspective passages of diaristic text give way to aphoristic captions as attention is displaced from Calle's own convoluted meditations onto being the best shadow she can be. This sudden concentration of attention and simplicity of focus speaks, as Baudrillard acknowledges, to the other's ability to furnish the meandering and aimless self with a template, with a *mode d'emploi* to adopt as one's own.[39] Yet, unwilling to relinquish sovereignty completely, Calle, after having sighted Henri B. ceases to track her object of pursuit after only one hour of surveillance.[40] With a sense of palpable relief and relaxation, she deploys 'abandonment' again, this time in the sense of leisurely excuse, as she writes permissively, 'J'abandonne. Je m'adosse à la façade de la Banco di Roma. J'ai surpris d'une heure dans la vie de Henri B.' [I give up. I slouch against the front of the Banco di Roma. I happened upon one hour in the life of Henri B.] (p. 72).

A similar approach is adopted later that same evening when Calle attempts to trail Henri B. and his wife eating dinner. When they do not emerge from their selected restaurant after a protracted period of time, Calle again, suspending her initial fears about the project's inadequacy and failure, submits to an early cessation of the day's work, writing, 'Cette fois c'est suffisant. A 21h30, je regagne mon hôtel' [This time it's enough. At 9.30 pm, I'm going back to my hotel] (p. 80). Such a policy of ease and comfort is carried over to the following day, which Calle devotes mainly to sitting in restaurants and arranging to meet friends and in which she freely admits, 'Je ne fais pas d'effort, je m'offre un répit — je l'ai vu' [I'm not making an effort, I'm giving myself a break — I saw him] (p. 81). In its slackened phenomenologies, such a policy maintains Nancy's account of the 'happiness' of the 'unprogrammed' rendez-vous which does not correspond to a fixed outcome.[41] It also, speaking to the role of levity within Calle's work, crucially forges a light, agile relation to the Other, conceiving Henri B. less as an ontological threat or burden whose traces must be violently erased than as a fellow habitant of Venice's enveloping and labyrinthine space whose sensual itineraries through the city can be followed, and dispensed of, at free will. Through such an optic, a 'graceful', indeed Nancean, view of surrender, submission, and abandon is offered as a counterpoint to a violent, masochistic, and 'impossible' portrayal of sexual difference that has typically persisted in contemporary Francophone production as a trope.[42]

Following her initial sighting a greater sense of receptivity to interaction with Henri B. is nonetheless expressed by Calle's speculation that 'peut-être m'invitera-t-il à m'asseoir dans son fauteuil, un verre de whisky à la main. J'aurai chaud' [maybe he'll invite me to sit with him in his armchair, a glass of whisky in hand. I will be warm] (p. 81). Such a projection of casual intimacy finds material correlation in Calle's running into Henri at a gallery, without his wife, a few days later, where they share a brief conversation and eventually embark on a walk around the city side by side. Here, in contrast to her early reticence Calle readily submits to Henri's suggestion that they leave together — 'Il propose: voulez-vous que nous marchions ensemble? Je fais signe que oui' [He suggests: would you like us to walk together? I indicate yes] (p. 91). Remaining silent as her muse begins reproaching her for not having adhered to certain rules of her own game more strictly, Calle's own prideful sovereignty appears to vanish as she, upon a further request from Henri that they take the vaporetto to Saint Mark's Square together, writes 'J'accepte. Je suis à sa disposition' [I accept. I am at his disposition] (p. 92). Such a declaration reverses the stakes of sovereignty at play in the project, replaces narcissistic self-interest with newfound 'attention à autrui'.

In keeping with the project's commitment to open-endedness and to intransitive modes of drifting which lead ultimately nowhere, such attention is however, not returned. Henri B. abandons Calle on disembarkation to attend his meeting, preventing her from taking photographs of his face which, as he reminds her, contravenes the project's ethical remove. Disappointed that their time together did not lead to further intimacy, Calle's tone is subsequently melancholic as she ruminates, 'Et si, en fait, j'avais été la victime inconsciente de son jeu, de ses trajets, de ses horaires?' [And what if, in fact, I had been the unconscious victim of his game, his journeys, his itineraries?] (p. 92), and reflects — as mastery and delight in an aesthetic game gives way to vulnerability and an experience of loss — on her newfound humbled state of exposure. Left to return to her hotel room alone, she recasts the project as a failure, writing 'Henri B. n'a rien fait, je n'ai rien découvert. Il fallait une fin banale à cette histoire banale' [Henri B. did nothing, I discovered nothing. There had to be a banal ending to this banal story] (p. 93).

Initially staged as an exceptional voyage, and as an indulgent dislocation of everyday routine, *Suite vénitienne*'s final stages re-orient the project as a meditation on obsession, loss, and, as Calle traces over the same routes, the voluptuous textures of depression. With her much deferred encounter with the object of her voyeuristic pilgrimage failing to inspire revelation or a *histoire d'amour* — 'Qu'est-ce que j'imaginais?' she writes, 'Qu'il allait me prendre avec lui, me défier, m'user?' [What did I imagine? That he was going to take me with him, challenge me, make use of me?] (p. 94) — Calle is invited to take a different path. Leisurely meandering is superseded by forensic retracings as she, in the remaining days of her stay in Venice, obsessively retraces their shared steps (p. 93). Dissolution and a sense of tenderness prevails, revealing how, as Butler writes, we are 'undone' by others, how they place forks in our routes'.[43]

In addition to an exercise in affective cartography and feminist re-authoring, then, *Suite vénitienne* explores the luxury of giving oneself over to another person and of focusing one's full attention on alluringly exotic strangers whilst acknowledging that objects of desire regularly disappoint, or exceed our grasp. A sense of 'dream-like disengagement' is indeed punctured as the reality of Henri B. overcomes Calle's expectations, thwarting the neatness of *Suite vénitienne*'s template, its game of doubling. Ideas of sovereignty as both the supreme exertion of a single will and the pleasurable dissolution of immutable identity are kept in balance as Calle, following the disillusioning meeting with Henri B., must come back to her senses and impose an artful end to the unresolved and underwhelming final stages of the project, 'take care' of its unexpected emotional and physical upheavals, so that ultimately she exercises the last word.[44] In the section of the chapter to follow on *Douleur exquise*, I show how as Calle's artistry evolves, her focus swells beyond the template of a highly cathected, often male Other to encompass a broader, more diverse range of subjectivities. Though more intentional in its design and scope, *Douleur exquise*, I argue, enacts a different kind of luxurious *dérive* in its drift away from self-obsession and affirmation of the exquisite solace of sharing stories.

Douleur exquise: Uncountable Experience

> My own language must break up and yield if I am to know you. You are what I gain through this disorientation and loss. — Judith Butler[45]

Douleur exquise, an expressive, striking project taking as stimulus a lover's sudden departure whilst Calle was in the middle of a research trip in Asia, builds on the interest in rituals, embellishment, and the collection of emotion into form which recurs throughout Calle's *œuvre*.[46] Exhibiting quasi-ethnographic photographs of Japan and Japanese culture (the products of Calle's research grant and the pretext for her leaving her lover behind in France) against short, startling accounts of other peoples' most singular moments of 'exquisite pain', the project is divided into two halves: 'Avant la douleur', which stages a retroactive countdown to the moment of rupture via superimposed, temporal stamps (see Fig. 4.1 below) that recede in number as the abandonment gets ever closer; and 'Après la douleur' which juxtaposes these other accounts of suffering and loss against Calle's own retellings of her personal bereavement, which diminish in length as the other stories take shape and accrue. As a result of these somewhat contrived templates, and, elsewhere in the artist's work, Calle's predilection for aestheticising the phenomenon of grief, the project has been interpreted as an attempt at mastery over an overwhelming affective experience, a purely cathartic or therapeutic exercise, and a narcissistic gorging on the misfortunes of other people as a means of purging or eliminating personal discomfort.[47] Taking distance from these readings, I am interested to read the project as, again utilising a term of Anne-Lise François, a successive opening to 'uncounted experience', or as an exposure to the shared multiplicity of loss and grief 'not of the order of observable action and measurable response'.[48] Emphasising the sensorial, textural qualities of the project which, in both installation and printed book format, folds between visual and haptic qualities, I show nonetheless how *Douleur exquise* gradually abandons interest in the fetish and in luxury's pleasures of displaying and arranging objects to instead develop empathy towards other stories of vulnerability and suffering, which open the work to a sense of the incalculable. In this way, I claim that *Douleur exquise* further mobilises the beginnings of a move away from narcissistic self-interest first initiated by *Suite vénitienne*. Offering a sensual experience of the work of art to the spectator-reader, I demonstrate how *Douleur exquise* modifies the former project's abstract interest in rituals, representational halls of mirrors and doublings, to engage with the affective terrains of grief and intersubjective relationships in innovative ways.

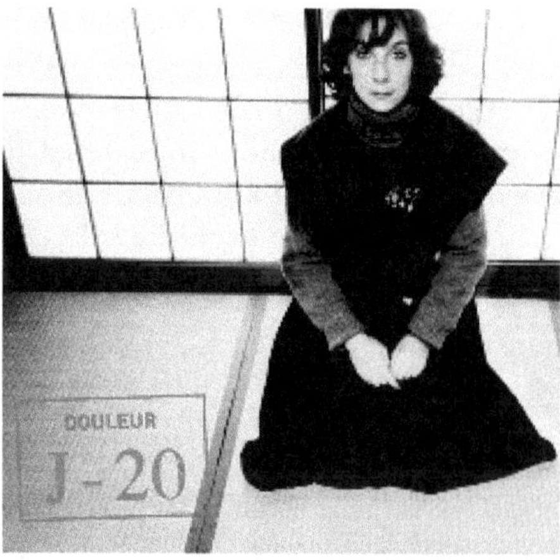

FIG. 4.1. Sophie Calle, *Douleur exquise* (Arles: Actes Sud, 2003)

Douleur exquise stages a spacious, multi-layered tour through a prior-lived traumatic happening, taking care by paying attention to the opaque textures of grief and memory. Both Wilson and Shirley Jordan have offered accounts of the experience of sensuous immersion invited by *Douleur exquise*'s exhibition as part of the wider Calle retrospective *M'as tu vue?* at the Centre Pompidou in 2004, noting how the piece's maze-like, enveloping construction worked to give material expression to the undercurrents of exposure, suffusion, and enclosure latent in the project as a whole.[49] In my reading here, I focus on the printed version of the project, published by Actes Sud in 2003, in order to unfold questions pertaining to the potential fetishisation of textual objects, their status as *objets de luxe* within Calle's *œuvre*, and the potential refuge granted by the 'thingness' of material textuality.[50] Despite the initial pleasures that the project takes in the sheen and lustre of the textual ornament, in its final stages I maintain that Calle surrenders a 'plaisir du texte' to the more immaterial — albeit, as Butler stresses, shared — experience of detachment, abandonment, and loss, however.

Measuring only 19.7 by 10.7 cm, *Douleur exquise* as textual object resists the scale and volume of the exhibition catalogue or *livre d'artiste* to become an *objet d'art* on its own miniature terms. Bound in grey cloth with its author's name and title stamped in red on the front cover, and a further passage of text embroidered on the back, the first encounter that it stages with the reader is textural and tactile, helping to displace Calle's work from its often unilateral insertion within visual or purely scopophilic economies.[51] With its patiently stitched, fabric cover, the effect, as Calle testifies herself in a recent interview with *France Culture,* is 'soigné' or, literally, 'cared for'.[52] Susan Stewart in her survey of miniaturised enactments of textuality has noted how 'minute writing is emblematic of craft and discipline; while the materiality of the product is diminished, the labor involved multiplies, and so does the significance of the total object'.[53] This concept of the 'total object' is derived from Jacques Derrida's distinction, in *De la grammatologie*, between the 'text' as an open field of semantic play and the 'book' as an 'idea of totality' or metaphor of containment and definitive enclosure.[54] In its gradual exposure to other accounts of bereavement and despair, it might be argued that *Douleur exquise* shifts from the latter to the former model, or that, in hosting and making space for additional stories and testimonies it forgoes the Derridian book's project of sequencing and closure to become a more porous forum of disclosure in which the self's story is dispersed.

In her account of melancholic 'restitutions' at work in Calle's project, Catherine Lemieux appoints the printed version of *Douleur exquise* a 'transubsantialisation' of grief and pain, or a means of transferring harmful affects onto a material and bounded object able to be possessed subsequently by a mourning subject. In such a context, Lemieux contends that 'l'art devient thérapeutique, car il permet de transubstantialiser la douleur et d'en faire un objet esthétique mis à distance' [art becomes therapeutic, since it allows for a transubstantialisation of pain].[55] In its emphasis on distancing, and transferential processes, such a reading speaks to the ontology of the fetish as a site of displaced lack, or a residue of unresolved absence. Resonating with *Douleur exquise*'s structuring in terms of a journey to the epicentre of a trauma, and investment in doubles, diptychs, and shadowing processes, fetishism, Emily Apter writes, 'records the trajectory of an idée fixe or noun in search of its materialist twin'.[56] For William Pietz, the fetish figures more explicitly as an exercise in situation and in fixing:

> The fetish is always a meaningful fixation of a singular event, it is above all a historical object, the enduring force and form of an unrepeatable event. This object is territorialized in material space (an earthly matrix) whether in the form of geographical locality, a marked site on the surface of the human body, or a medium of inscription or configuration defined by some portable or wearable thing.[57]

Here, Pietz's emphasis on inscription and on the fetishistic register's engraving of everyday patinas might speak to the techniques of embroidery and overlay at work in *Douleur exquise* which serve to elevate what Calle insists is essentially a 'banal story' into an object of design and craft, to imbue a potentially flat premise — man jilts woman, woman grieves — with thicker, more expansive aesthetic purchase.[58] On the occasion of their exhibition at the Centre Pompidou in 2003, Isabelle Décarie notes how the project's textual components, reproduced on large fabric panels had been 'patiemment brodé par Calle' [patiently stitched by Calle] adding sensory, material interest to the minimalist, visually-oriented tone of Calle's 'phototextual' narrative.[59] Such a technique has been carried over to Calle's most recent exhibitions and both valorises craft, historically derided as a 'female' mode of aesthetic production, as a worthy enterprise and embodies the idea of taking care as taking one's time, of luxury as the capacity to ornament the thin material of life as it is lived.[60] In the printed version of the project, texture is further expressed by the indentation of the text's titling on the front cover which invites the reader to run fingers over the words. Within the first half of the text, 'Avant la douleur', it is articulated by Calle's application of the above-mentioned 'countdown' stamp motif to the photos taken whilst she was in residency in Japan and estranged from her lover. Such overlays imprint and infuse a series of otherwise ethnographically clichéd photographs with a sense of imminent narrative upheaval. Such stencilling of hindsight or retroactive knowledge onto a superficially glossy and touristic account of time in Japan, countering Pietz's reading, crucially avoids the fetish's fixation onto one temporal event, or one locality, opening an otherwise sealed, hermetic text to other chronologies and orders of being. It avoids the text being used solely to therapeutic purpose so that it becomes sensual ecology rather than remedial instrument.

In an epigraph to the printed edition of *Douleur exquise*, Calle offers a definition of the concept as a 'douleur vive et nettement localisée' [acute, localized pain].[61] Such an inclusion affirms the projects as a whole magnetism towards visceral moments of affective intensity which, speaking to luxury's investment in exceptionality and in the dislocation of the ordinary, elevates quotidian flatness above everyday homogeneity. As the text progresses, specifically as Calle begins to collect and accumulate other narratives of pain, its representations and depictions become less vivid and delineated, substituting an economy of incisive statements of the self with a softer-focus aesthetics of effacement and ephemerality. Whilst the first half of

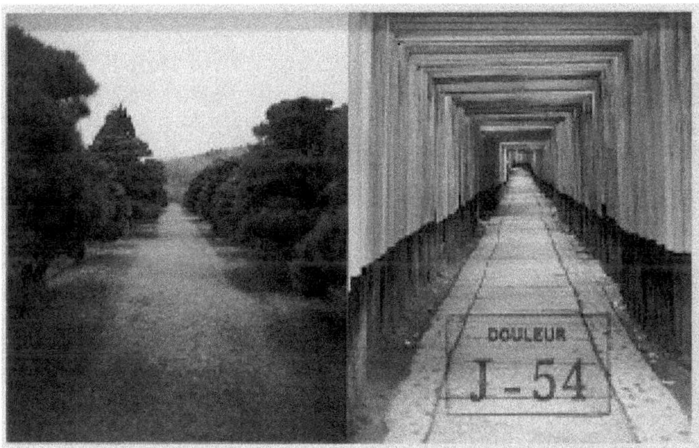

Fig. 4.2. Sophie Calle, *Douleur exquise* (Arles: Actes Sud, 2003)

the text — depicting Calle's trip to Japan — is indeed presented on glossy, coated paper, the second half is stripped of such lustre, its short texts and imagery matte, grainy pages, its colours noticeably duller. Such a progressive fading of the text's initial brightness leaves behind the order of the fetish and its' fantasies of possession to stage, instead, an incremental exposure to the unknown. It subjects an 'exquisite pain' to luxury's phenomenologies of calm suffusion and indolent spread. It replaces fetishistic grasping with an opening to others in all their incalculable singularity and multiplicity.

Defying such a reading, the text initially seems eager to insert itself within a more transactional exchange economy, however, and to suggest that its exhibition of the pain of others alongside its more plaintive song of the self is staged for pragmatic reasons: as a means of 'getting over', purging, or eliminating a romantic disappointment via ritualised consumption of other people's stories. In functional, prescriptive language Calle, in a long brief printed on the back cover of the printed edition, rehearses the preliminary genesis of the project as follows:

> Je suis partie au Japon le 25 octobre 1984 sans savoir que cette date marquait le début d'un compte à rebours de quatre-vingt jours qui allait aboutir à une rupture, banale, mais que j'ai vécue alors comme le moment le plus douloureux de ma vie. J'en ai tenu ce voyage pour responsable. De retour en France, le 28 janvier 1985, j'ai choisi, par conjuration, de raconter ma souffrance plutôt que mon périple. En contrepartie, j'ai demandé à mes interlocuteurs, amis ou rencontres de fortune: 'Quand avez-vous le plus souffert?'[62]

[I left Japan on 25 October 1984 without knowing that this date marked the beginning of a countdown of eighty days that would lead to a break-up, banal, but experienced as the most painful moment of my life. I held this trip responsible for it. On returning to France, on 28 January 1985, I chose, in a kind of spell, to narrate my suffering rather than my journey. In return, I asked my interlocutors, friends, or random encounters: 'When did you most suffer?']

Such a *constat* superficially appears to demonstrate Calle's exertion of her sovereignty, authorial design, and control. A language of choice and decision abounds as she abdicates responsibility for her abandonment and takes the executive decision to make her own *histoire*, rather than the observation of Japanese customs and lifestyle, the focus of her ensuing work of art. A process of exploration and potential self-discovery will be sacrificed, the generous consignment of a research grant deliberately squandered, in favour of (she suggests) a clinical process of cumulative numbing via the large-scale imbibing of testimonies of collective loss.[63] The terms of the contract, the rules of the game are envisaged as inflexible and fixed when she writes, 'Cet échange cesserait quand j'aurais épuisé ma propre histoire à force de la raconter, ou bien relativisé ma peine face à celle des autres' [This exchange would stop when I had exhausted my own story by means of recounting it, or rather relativised my pain faced with that of others].[64]

This conditional mode, and its projected hopes for a sense of luxurious calm which follows narrative over-exertion and consumption, is rendered present tense by the admission, in the sentence which directly follows, that 'La méthode a été radicale: en trois mois, j'étais guérie' [The method proved radical: in three months, I was cured].[65] On initial appearance, such a formulation risks embedding *Douleur exquise* in a curative, recuperative, and restoring register, positioning the piece's gradual accommodation of the 'pain of others' — to borrow a term from Susan Sontag — as a bald and calculated means of caring for the self.[66] Such a sentence, indeed, bears the cadences of a religious testimony, or an avowal of miraculous self-transformation. In contrast to the rest of the project's temporal compressions and suspensions, here the sequencing is exhibited as neat, teleological, and finite. The sentence is symmetrically structured like an equation, reinforcing Calle's prescription of the enterprise, at this point, as an exercise in compensation and reimbursement.

Here Calle's attempt to square *Douleur exquise* as a simple and unfussy process of replacement and of substitution, or to fit her multifarious and often opaque endeavours within certain fixed parameters undermines the project's protean and dislocating nature. It subjects it to a certain brand of 'mastery' which the nature of the assembled stories in themselves repeatedly exceed. Her insistence on the process's affective productivity and efficiency and quasi-scientific, methodological outlining of its functional procedures which, Jordan notes, likens the text's heterogeneous bazaar of painful testimonies to an exercise in 'data collection', defies elsewhere its melancholic wallowing and lingering in a 'banal' rupture, its transformation of the potentially empty acts of waiting and of suffering into a voluptuous *delectatio morosa*, steeped in, as Koestenbaum observes, the 'nourishing' affects of melancholy and grief.[67]

A theological concept originating from the second half of the twelfth century, the term *delectatio morosa* is composed etymologically of the Latin *delectatio* denoting pleasure and the epithet *morosa,* which, although close to the despondent, ruminating implications of 'moroseness' derives from the gerund *moratur* which refers to the act of waiting, or to a state of pause, stoppage, or delay. Attentive to the pleasure to be found within the process of desiring, rather than to the desire for conclusive or possessive pleasure in and of itself, *delectatio morosa* articulates the joy or delight 'that the imagination savours deliciously as it is expectantly waiting'. It bears witness, indeed, to the sensual, non-appropriative, and non-teleological luxury of lingering and wallowing 'in the desire for an object that remains absent because it is inaccessible or prohibited'. Within a state of *delectatio morosa*, 'the simple imaginary representation of the desired object' can procure an enjoyment analogous to that of actual possession.[68]

A sense of *delectatio morosa*, close to Freud's understanding of melancholia as a form of luxuriating in the vacancy created by the absent object, infuses the first half of *Douleur exquise*, which forgoes narrative direction to enact a festival of deep *attente* and anticipation.[69] (In such a way, the text is a feminist revision of Roland Barthes's baroque encyclopaedia of heartbreak, *Fragments d'un discours amoureux*.) Despite initially expressed intentions to make the most of the time and funds she has been given this initial conscientiousness is abandoned as Calle proceeds deliberately to fritter away her appointed resources.[70] Hoping to kill time and minimise the days spent in Japan as much as possible a decision to take the train — as opposed to flying — from Paris is reached, subjecting what would otherwise consist of a straightforward and efficient journey to willed expansion and protraction. Furthering this privileging of itinerant detours and digressions, once having arrived in Japan no definitive project or commentary on the country's singular customs is reached. Photos of cluttered hotel interiors in which Calle has presumably languished take precedence over documentations of exterior landscapes, and the minimal narrative space that does exist is given over to composing long, devoted letters to her ex. Throughout the section, the lustre of the laminated pages lavish this exercise in occupying time and diverting discomfort with a syrupy, romantic sheen. This sheen varnishes the narrative with a textural, and sensual, ambivalence which encourages luxuriating in the heartbreak, rather than dispatching it. For Anne Cheng, writing on the concept of the modern surface, 'Sheen, as that which both attracts and repels vision, plays hide-and-seek with visual satisfaction, and produces a sexy interplay between the scopic and the haptic: are we looking or are we feeling?'[71] Only the consistent imprint of the countdown stamps as narrative device belie efforts to impose sequencing and indexation on this otherwise amorphous time of waiting and apprehension.

Delaying the recounting of the devastating moment of *douleur* which inspires the project as a whole, Calle occasions an abrupt break in the narrative at the point of 'J-1' — the eve of the lover's expected return. In contrast to the project's hitherto policy of filling space the reader-spectator is offered little in the way of explanation as we learn, via the unannotated reproduction of the same curt telegram that Calle herself received, that her romantic partner did not reunite with her in Delhi. Such a blunt desertion impacts on the structure of the pages that will follow. The first section's meandering, unstructured, and indeed auto-affective spread is replaced by a tightly circumscribed diptych structure which directly juxtaposes Calle's own narratives — all tellings of the night in India that she realised that he wasn't coming, which fade and ultimately vanish from legibility as the other stories inflate in scale and size — with other testimonies of bereavement, now hosted and abundantly exposed. This structural re-scaffolding has been understood as an exercise in self-diminution, a means by which Calle obsessively attempts to flagellate herself for having indulged such an indeed 'banal' story, or alternatively as a deliberate 'contracting in' of other people as a means of 'soothing' the self.[72] Calle herself uses the language of relativisation, fuelling readings that *Douleur exquise* amounts to a numbers game: a dissolution of the singular by subjecting a romantic disappointment to the logic of the many.

In *Precarious Life*, Butler, in dialogue with the philosophy of Emmanuel Levinas, makes a case for the self as relational, as always already embedded in the lives of others. Such an understanding of subjectivity as enmeshed, by definition, in alterity, she writes, exposes grief as a collective experience, illuminates the universal sense of community which accompanies each singular loss.[73] Following such a reading, Calle's shift in *Douleur exquise* to integrating an account of the self alongside an acknowledgment of others might be seen less as a functional strategy substituting private pain for exploitative voyeurism than as a gesture towards cohabitation and sharing. Décarie, for example, sees the move towards a diptych layout as a broadening of the project's reach and intimacy shown towards the reader-spectator, suggesting how Calle 'invite les autres à venir coucher leur souffrance à droite avec elle' [invites Others to come and lay their suffering right alongside her].[74] To rehearse Butler's own terms, *Douleur exquise*'s double-bind might indeed expose how we are all 'bound' to one another, illustrating the deep 'bonds that compose us'.[75] In such a light the luxury of solipsistic melancholia might transmute into a form of 'communal luxury' in which the playing field is more even, in which many narratives of grief can co-exist.[76] A closed-off sense of self-containment and a striking quality of opaque, photographic hermeticism segues into an open and indeed caring sense of hospitality. By such means a 'narcissistic preoccupation of melancholia can be moved into a consideration of the vulnerability of others'.[77]

This sense of respect for the other stories which come to expand upon and amplify the affective resonances of Calle's own, and refusal to submit them to hierarchical criteria of value or judgment, is articulated by the heterogeneous nature of the accounts assembled, varying in tone, length, and subject. In keeping with François's definition of uncountable experience as that which eludes representational capture, possession, or mastery, some stories are elliptical and refuse to fit to expected templates of the tragic or dramatic, such as one participant's reticent and minimal account of a childhood afternoon spent on vacation in Arcachon with his family which is not further elaborated on or explained.[78] Extending this interest in what lies beyond the frame of representability, the illustration for one story solely appears as a blank square of white page, gesturing towards the accompanying text's vulnerable admission that the worst pain of the writer's life has yet to manifest, is still to come: 'J'espère, un jour, souffrir beaucoup, aller plus loin. Je n'ai pas encore rencontré mon histoire' [I hope, one day, to suffer a lot, to go further. I have not yet encountered my story].[79]

Butler writes in *Precarious Life* that 'suffering can yield an experience of humility, of vulnerability, of impressionability and dependence, and these can become resources, if we do not "resolve" them too quickly; they can move us beyond and against the vocation of the paranoid victim'.[80] *Douleur exquise* maintains a relationship of rapture and subjection before other accounts, other points of view, by refusing to provide a concluding statement on the collection of secondary narratives that it assembles. In what materialises as the last double-spread of the printed book, Calle's voice is completely effaced — the account of the night of 'la douleur' having been progressively diminishing, now totally erased, in its place only a blank page of grey. A table of contents is provided but at the very tail-end of the narrative, complicit in the project's temporal aneconomy of retroaction and spatial disorientation (even if this practice is habitual in French publishing). The final tract in the series offers a distinctive mix of the banal and the disquietingly poignant. Without much situating content, it tells of a woman, in her sixties, being led to commit suicide after having been accused of stealing a pot of *crème fraîche* from a supermarket.[81] This cohabitation of the gratuitous and the nonsensical with the truly tragic — with there being no sense to the order of events which ensue — maintains the reader and viewer of *Douleur exquise* in a state of unknowing and of humbled vulnerability. This account eludes understanding, eclipses Calle's fable of romantic disappointment. Inviting us to speculate upon the links between two seemingly unconnected events, the ending of the work preserves Derrida's understanding of the 'open work'.[82] In its concluding pages, the work preserves the mystery and non-calculability of the exceptional event which defies sequencing, understanding, and aesthetic compaction.

In my discussion of *Douleur exquise*, I have argued that luxury's implicit desire for the calm, serene, voluptuous order of things and privileging of a certain logic of the fetish yield, in the face of overwhelming and surprising pain, to vulnerability and humility which cannot be counted or measured. Whilst a contemplation of the other allows Calle (in line with Bataille's definition of luxury as the ability to 'dissolve' sovereignty) to sublimate her own romantic traumas, such a gesture, I have argued, exceeds self-interest to facilitate exposures to a larger community of suffering which prompts practices of care and the attentive framing of alterity. Luxury as auto-affective, photographic melancholy yields to a different understanding of the concept: to luxury as an acknowledgement of the exceptional events which elude understanding, to luxury as a recognition of the incalculable, of the immeasurable, which resists ultimate capture. In the next section of the chapter, focusing on *Prenez soin de vous*, I argue that an embrace of multiplicity and dispersal of sovereignty is explicit in the project from the beginning, further marking Calle's move towards co-operative practices in the evolution of her work. I suggest that while *Douleur exquise* traces an elaborate 'aneconomy' of absence, finding solace in the blind spots of the self, *Prenez soin de vous* is concerned from the outset with saturation, plenitude, and polyphonic presence to carve ultimately different paths. Though, like *Suite vénitienne*, eager to confect scenarios allowing respite from the pressures of self-representation, *Prenez soin de vous*'s aesthetics is defiantly immersive rather than avoidant, keen to upgrade yet another Callean encounter of romantic abjection into a spectacular production of community and creativity in which the desired object is a mere vehicle for women's multi-faceted expression.

Prenez soin de vous: Community, Excess, Spectacle

> Would there be any dance at all if one didn't exchange the sexes for an indeterminate number, and if one didn't exchange the law of the sexes for many variable rhythms? The desire remains one of escaping from the single combinatory and inventing incalculable choreographies. — JACQUES DERRIDA[83]

In the first two sections of this chapter I have argued that the evolution of Calle's work can be traced in terms of a cumulative opening to the unknown and to otherness in order to reframe luxury as an exposure to, and immersion in, difference and multiplicity as well as an experience of artistic control. I have argued that progressive movements towards otherness and a certain 'decreation of the self' replaces the accused 'narcissistic pleasure' of Calle's early works with increased practices of care and attentiveness towards other stories and narratives, which resonate with updated understandings of the concept of *le souci* as an affective stance which substitutes individual profit for collective responsibilities.[84] I turn more explicitly now to this term 'care' and its implications for a discussion of luxury in my analysis of Calle's multi-medial art project *Prenez soin de vous*. In a similar vein to my discussion of *Douleur exquise*, I argue that the project abdicates a story of the self before community and an innumerable 'swarm' of other narratives. In distinction to the first project's fetishistic stylisation careful symbiosis between text and image, and tendency towards sequencing and seriality, I suggest that *Prenez soin de vous* forgoes processes of listing, collecting, and arranging from the outset, immediately staging an aesthetics of elaborate excess, saturation, and plurality in its invitation to 107 women to expand upon a culturally thin and tired script — the break-up email. I argue that, in its embrace of a more multi-sensory and indeed cinematic approach to textual interpretation, *Prenez soin de vous* might affirm what Antoine Compagnon has termed 'la jouissance de la foule' [the *jouissance* of the crowd] to offer a re-reading of luxury as delight in an exuberance of meanings and interpretations and as a deliberately hyperbolic 'amplification of signs'.[85]

Affective Dispatch

In keeping with Calle's tendency to forage art from the scraps and traces of quotidian, personal documents, the large-scale, mixed media project *Prenez soin de vous*, exhibited at the 2007 Venice Biennale, the Bibliothèque nationale de France, the Whitechapel Gallery in London and later reproduced as a 400-page, glossy volume of photographs and texts in collaboration with the publisher Actes Sud, takes as stimulus a clichéd 'Dear Jane' letter, sent to the artist's email, from a romantic partner expressing his desire to end their relationship.[86] In both the exhibition and the book, this letter is cited in full, taking up a whole page in the printed volume and a dense panel of wall space in the installation. Calle's epigraph briefing readers as to the procedures of the project, the sole point at which the audience is granted access to her own thoughts or responses, is, in contrast, clipped and economical. In taut verse-like prose she writes:

> J'ai reçu un mail de rupture. Je n'ai pas su répondre.
> C'était comme s'il ne m'était pas destiné.
> Il se terminait par les mots: Prenez soin de vous.
> J'ai pris cette recommandation au pied de la lettre.
> J'ai demandé à 107 femmes — dont une à plumes
> et deux en bois — choisies pour leur métier, leur talent,
> d'interpréter la lettre sous un angle professionnel.
> L'analyser; la commenter, la jouer, la danser; la chanter:
> La disséquer: L'épuiser: Comprendre pour moi.
> Parler à ma place.
> Une façon de prendre le temps de rompre.
> A mon rythme.
> Prendre soin de moi.[87]

> [I received an email telling me it was over. I didn't know how to respond. | It was almost as if it hadn't been meant for me. | It ended with the words, 'Take care of yourself.' | I took this recommendation literally. | I asked 107 women — including two made from wood | and one with feathers) — chosen for their profession or skills, | to interpret this letter from a professional angle. | To analyse it, comment on it, play with it, dance it, sing it. | Dissect it. Exhaust it. Understand it for me. | Speak in my place. | It was a way of taking the time to break up. | At my own rhythm. | A way of taking care of myself.]

With its measured tone of detachment, and Calle's obvious desire to distance herself from or disown the letter, on initial reading such a preface appears shadowed by the cultural halo of shame which lingers over women's gendered performances as sexual subjects.[88] It seems, in its stated aim to 'exhaust' the enigmatic premise of the email, to fulfil appetites for feminine abjection, and indeed to satisfy entrenched expectations that self-identifying women subjects, condemned to over-analysing, 'luxuriate' in the fall-out of romantic loss. In *I Love Dick*, Chris Kraus questions whether formal strategies of distance and detachment when applied to women's 'confessional' narratives need be psychoanalysed as shame responses nonetheless. With trademark defiance she asks, 'Why do people still not get it when we handle vulnerability like philosophy, at some remove?'[89]

The desire to interpret and disseminate her lover's bracing sign-off 'at one remove' is at the conceptual heart of *Prenez soin de vous*'s wilful agenda. Calle's wish that her assembled professional collective of women 'understand' the letter in her place telegraphs a strong desire to retreat from the scene and to share the burden of emotional labour, effectively dispatching the work of a romantic trauma to professionalised second parties.[90] Writing on the Italian philosopher Adriana Caravero, Wilson traces 'a desire for another, or Others, to play the role of narrator for one's story, and concomitantly a desire for passivity, even in receptiveness and responsiveness'.[91] Still, the crowd-sourcing of an optimal response to a personal email so that Calle can take restorative leave of the situation, find rejuvenating space and time 'to break-up at [her] own rhythm', might position the luxury of taking care as the particular privilege of *self*-care. While thinkers such as Lorde and Ahmed have displayed how self-care, despite its increased co-opting for neoliberal purchase, can be utilised as a radical tactic for a feminist agenda, I contend that despite *Prenez soin de vous*'s intricate relationship to sovereignty, Calle's intention isn't to 'take care' of the self but to lose the self in a tumultuous array of other voices, which in tandem become sources of luxuriant collaboration and community.[92]

Independent of her preface, which expresses strong, executive desires to make the break-up email 'sing and dance' in a different way, Calle's own signature is consistently absent from the project. Her own response to the termination of her previous romantic contract is forfeited in order to accommodate and make space for a wealth of other fertile and abundantly creative readings. Such a tactic, as well as acknowledging the singular plurality of others and the communality of grief, of suffering, and of affective vulnerability, offers Calle reprieve from the universal impositions of the apology (and its subsequent expectation for a crafted response) and avoids her being fitted into the restrictive cultural trope of the 'jilted woman'. If Avital Ronell contends that 'feminism today has a parasitical, secondary territoriality, and if you respond to present conditions, you're subject to reactive, mimetic, and regressive posturings', then Calle's desired retreat from the scene of reading and outsourcing of the 'work' of interpretation to contracted others avoids this gendered and pernicious trap of reactivity.[93] Becoming a curator of conditional interpretations, rather than the primary respondent, Calle upscales the normative, heteropatriarchal territory of the romantic 'rupture' into a shared, inter-generational, and inter-disciplinary space of multi-layered resonance.[94]

In her own response to the invitation to perform the letter differently, the poet Anne Portugal observes that the silencing order which Calle places on herself becomes a 'constraint' or 'rule' in keeping with the Callean *œuvre*'s fetishistic following of patterns or restrictive orders.[95] While such motifs have been read by critics as predominantly formal traces of Calle's debt to Oulipo,[96] they can also, as in the work *Où et quand?* in which Calle simplifies her life to such an extent that all her options are decided by the psychic Maud Kirsten, be envisaged as methods of carving retreat from the overwhelming excess of 'choice capitalism' and its constant imperatives to 'profit' and 'enjoy'.[97] For Portugal, the concentration and reductionism of Calle's approach paradoxically allows 'infinite' occasions for expansion and revision, affords the luxury of letting things 'tourner autrement' [turn out differently].[98] In a preface to her seven-page, axiomatically composed and multiply sectioned poem she writes:

> La remède sera l'écriture.
> La règle oblige à s'empêcher
> d'autres dires, à entraîner
> les mêmes infiniment, à tenter
> qu'ils tournent autrement.
> De cette manière est devenu le soin d'aimer: plier l'écrit à
> volonté prolongera X
> à Sophie, comme avant.[99]

[The cure will be writing. | The rule obliges you to muffle | other sayings, to entertain | the same ones infinitely, to try | and make them turn out

> differently. | This is what the care of loving has become: voluntarily folding the written | text will distance X | from Sophie, as before.]

Identifying the project as an exercise in prolongation and 'unfoldings', Portugal's interpretation situates a mode of active authorship in Calle's ostensible evaporation from production. Challenging *Prenez soin de vous* as an open-ended dissemination of affective material, Portugal envisages Calle's ex or 'X' less as a function intent on expanding or transforming the field of textual contribution than as a mark or site of personal inscription.[100] In such a context, all 'returns' on Calle's original missive lead back to the self, to Sophie, even if Sophie exercises a deliberate response to mute herself amidst the tumult of responses. In the final section of the poem titled 'ipsos', Portugal assumes the letters of Calle's first name to offer a statement on the project as an exercise in ipseity, or as a serial reproduction of homogeneity and sameness.

In a very different, essayistic response to Calle's initial brief, the philologist Barbara Cassin echoes Portugal's ambivalent account, suggesting that the project stages an exploitative process of 'mettre en série par soi-même au moyen des autres' [serialising oneself by means of others] and showcases a desire to 'unfold, exhaust, integrate, and exhume a unique, cathected object'.[101] Introducing variation, texture, and rhythm into the rote clichés of an unforeseen romantic disappointment, this ability to 'exhaust' or reposition an event of trauma speaks to Barthes's more compassionate understanding of the need to formalise and 'manipulate' mourning, of the need to translate it into an active practice to avoid abject melancholy or victimhood. In an account resonating with Kraus's call for women artists to put formal parameters around vulnerability, Barthes observes:

> L'absence dure, il me faut la supporter. Je vais donc la manipuler: transformer la distorsion du temps en va-et-vient, produire du rythme, ouvrir la scène du langage [...]. L'absence devient une pratique active, un affairement (qui m'empêche de rien faire d'autre); il y a création d'une fiction aux rôles multiples (doutes, reproches, désirs, mélancolies). [...] Manipuler l'absence, c'est allonger ce moment retarder aussi longtemps que possible l'instant où l'autre pourrait basculer sèchement de l'absence dans la mort.
>
> [Absence persists — I must endure it. Hence I will *manipulate* it: transform the distortion of time into oscillation, produce rhythm, make an entrance onto the stage of language [...]. Absence becomes an active practice, there is a creation of a fiction which has many roles (doubts, reproaches, desires, melancholies). [...] To manipulate absence is to extend this interval, to delay as long as possible the moment when the other might topple sharply from absence into death.][102]

Such emphasis on manipulation, transformation, performativity, and syncopation ventures — in distinction from *Douleur exquise*'s aesthetics of effacement — an idea of luxury as the ability to ornament, expand upon, and multiply the vicissitudes and plateaus of banal, everyday existence. It conjures luxury as a certain mode of staying with an event in order to fully absorb and expand upon its affective potentialities. Such a practice feels less narcissistic or recessive than, as Edwards has observed, a means of making use of the master's tools to dismantle the master's house to become an immanent, oppositional practice.[103] Rather than deny the existence of the letter, Calle appropriates it for creative and aesthetic ends — contrives an elaborate production around the event of its receiving to disturb patriarchal culture's tendency to abject women as romantic failures or 'desperate'. For Kristeva, in her work on the abject and processes of horror, this is how the abject might creatively be exploited as a force for radicality, how indeed it might absorb *les règles du jeu* in order to deliberately overturn them:

> L'abject est pervers car il n'abandonne, ni n'assume un interdit, une règle ou une loi, mais il les détourne, fourvoie, corrompt, s'en sert, en use, pour mieux les denier [...]. Il réapprovisionne la souffrance de l'autre pour son propre bien, c'est le cynique (et le psychanalyste); il rassoit son pouvoir narcissique en feignant d'exposer ses abîmes: c'est l'artiste qui exerce son art comme une 'affaire'.
>
> [The abject is perverse because it neither gives up nor assumes a prohibition, a rule, or a law; but turns them aside, misleads, corrupts; uses them, takes advantage of them, the better to deny them. It retames the suffering of the other for its own good: it is the cynic (and the psychoanalyst); it re-establishes its narcissistic power while feigning to expose its abysses: it is the artist who practices his art as a 'business'.][104]

Mimicking the mechanisms that Kristeva highlights of calculated re-appropriations and entrepreneurial motives, the writer Christine Angot, in her interpretation of Calle's stimulus, nominates the project as a whole not as a game, exercise, or experiment in aesthetic variation but as 'une service que Sophie demandait à toutes ces femmes' [a service that Sophie demanded of all these women]. Claiming herself generally uneasy with the project and the texts produced according to its brief, Angot, in a postscript to the unfinished rough draft ultimately submitted to the endeavour terms all she has written 'stupid' and 'absurd'. With hints made towards neoliberalism's uneasy conflations between literal and emotional labour, all too frequently performed by women without recognition or reward, she chastises Calle for convoking 'un escradon de femmes' [a squadron of women] in order to displace the personal responsibility of healing from a break-up.[105]

A similar dynamic is revealed by the sociologist Nilufer Gole's reaction to Calle's request that other women take up the challenge of responding to the letter. In a long essay Gole expresses disbelief at the 'évidente transgression de la pudeur et de ses limites' [obvious transgression of modesty and limits] in work in the project yet, like Angot, confesses herself strangely entranced and drawn in by the enterprise, eager to submit to its extravagant and abstracted invitations.[106] Such ambivalence speaks to Kristeva's two-way logic of abjection which makes the object(s) of desired exploitation feel as if they are the ones intruding upon undisclosed material. It also illuminates the syncopated dance of 'seduction' Baudrillard identifies in relation to Calle's work, which calls experiences of submission and exposure into question. For Baudrillard the almost universal willingness of Calle's participants to subordinate themselves to projects which would usually inspire immediate resistance speaks, in the broadest sense, to people's desire 'to be seduced, that is to say not solicited within their raison d'être, but *drawn outside of their raison d'être*'. We are, he maintains, 'secretly flattered that something is asked or even demanded of us for no reason, or contrary to reason: It spares us the commonplace and honours us in a more profound complicity'.[107] In light of such a reading the pleasures of exemption or the luxury of abdicating from the 'duty to speak' works both ways: affording Calle herself relief from the pressures of self-representation and from the tired trope of the 'avengeful woman' but also granting the delegates contracted to the project the 'serene' effect of a brief or template to follow.[108] Through such a lens *Prenez soin de vous* might be viewed less as an exploitative or narcissistic exercise in caring for the self than as a means of expropriating and recycling personal grief, a means of 'outsourcing' the obsessional and involuted labouring of mourning to provide not only individual solace but pleasure to others. In the sub-section to follow I continue to explore how *Prenez soin de vous*'s collective approach to interpreting cultural documents can be encountered as multi-sensory and affirmative, embracing 'la jouissance de la foule' and exuberant modes of generic promiscuity to both expand the boundaries of the work of art and encourage states of radical hospitality in which multiple perspectives are received.

La Jouissance de la foule

> The exhaustion of material prescribes the infinite number of possible ways to form the signs of it. — Jean-Luc Nancy[109]

Prenez soin de vous dramatises both the desire to assert and exercise sovereignty and the desire to relinquish it. It outsources the affective labour of a romantic rupture to interpellated others as a means of finding rejuvenating space, time, and calm amidst a surfeit of inchoate emotions but also to set into motion a process of allowing oneself to be overwhelmed by the Other's unpredictable address. Such a process, of immersing in the saturation of alternative responses so as to drown out the petty calculations and negotiations of the ego, departs from *Suite vénitienne*'s meandering and contemplative *dérive*, or *Douleur exquise*'s favouring of frameworks, countdowns, and temporal compressions. Such a process forgoes representational mastery for a multivalent feminist sensorium and substitutes the two-dimensionality of the photographic image or the 'flatness' of transcribed, diaristic prose for the more kinetic, sonic, and dynamic ecosystems of the moving image.[110]

For Butler, the Other's address which can impinge on us at any time reveals the fundamental interrelatedness of bodily life which can be either a source of palpable joy or extensive suffering. That *Prenez soin de vous* indeed enacts a kind of pleasurable abdication or submission before an operatic, unruly, and decentralised 'swarm' of heterogeneous responses, affirming in the process not only the exorbitant excess of different subjectivities but a certain 'jouissance de la foule', will be my conclusive reading of this project. Expanding upon Butler's thinking, I suggest how Calle's abandonment or 'giving up' of authorial control and representational mastery, by encouraging the free circulation and interpretation of a private document, not only functions as a method of pleasurable self-dissolution but reinvents the site of aesthetic labour as a communal worksite or emotional laboratory, augmenting it as a jubilant, fecund, and non-hierarchical field of intersecting possibilities which affirms collaborative, multiply co-signed methods of invention.

In a 2015 volume on the political imaginary of the Paris Commune and its potential reverberations across today's disaffected, techno-saturated, and increasingly authoritarian political landscape, Kristin Ross cites selections from the 1871 Federation of Artists Manifesto, particularly focusing on the Communards' professed commitment to working co-operatively towards 'the birth of communal luxury, future splendors and the Universal Republic', here understanding 'communal luxury' in the sense of an opening up of access to art, spectacle, and beauty and of a revolutionary liberation of artistic production from centralised (here in the form of state) control.[III] Whilst eliding the historical dimension of Ross's account, I am interested to borrow such a concept for the purpose of discussing *Prenez soin de vous* in order to make sense of the project's joyful dissolution of the hierarchies between artist and audience and to better read its invitation to interpret or transform a private artefact irrespective of the profession, age, or class background of its headhunted recipients. Ross's account of the democratisation of luxury as aesthetic experience draws parallels with *Prenez soin de vous*'s hosting of a banquet of romantic deconstruction in which women from various walks of life are encouraged to partake.

A state of open hospitality and indiscriminacy is immediately gestured to by the non-sequential, random presentation of the printed book which proceeds without page numbers or a table of contents. The individual contributions are in similar fashion arrayed haphazardly without consideration of their varying degrees of prestige or professionalism. Consistent with the project's ambitions towards multiplicity, abundance, and profusion Calle gathers a prodigiously comprehensive range of skill sets — exhibiting the work of actors, singers, etiquette specialists, crossword puzzle composers, chess players, and proof readers, amongst others — yet refrains at any point from distinguishing between them or from casting aesthetic or evaluative judgment. Adolescents, academics, and even Calle's own mother are given equal footing, equal creative license to transform the initial stimulus as they see fit. This non-hierarchical exposition of the solicited responses accords to Ross's understanding of communal luxury as the unfettered dissemination of aesthetic ability, as the liberation of artistic production from centralised control.

Further nourishing this climate of profusion and plurality, the first three pages of the published edition of *Prenez soin de vous* are given over to rendering the original text in morse, hexadecimal code, and braille, signalling the text's ability to become beyond its initially clichéd, patriarchal premise, and cultivating its fecund capacities for interpretation and translation. As in *Douleur exquise*, an acknowledgment of the indecipherable and of what frustrates easy assimilation or capture in language is being made here, to position *Prenez soin de vous* as a new form of spectacle open to contingency and the incommensurable. Encompassing both visual and tactile mediations, such creative re-translations speak to the pleasure which the project locates in transforming an insipid contractual arrangement into a Babel-esque display of overlapping languages and sign-systems, of subjecting a flat, affectless email 'sans inscription' to textural, visual, and performative embellishment.

While the piece is formally impressive and even virtuosic, it also leaves an emotional imprint, 'taking care' of its spectators as much as its participants. By

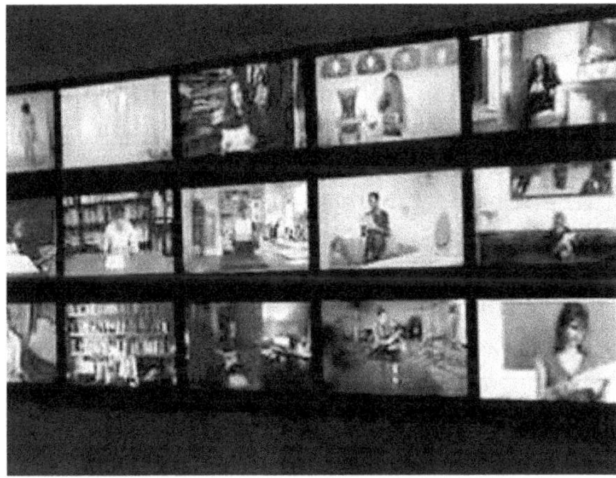

Fig. 4.3. Sophie Calle, *Prenez soin de vous*, 52nd Venice Biennale, 2007

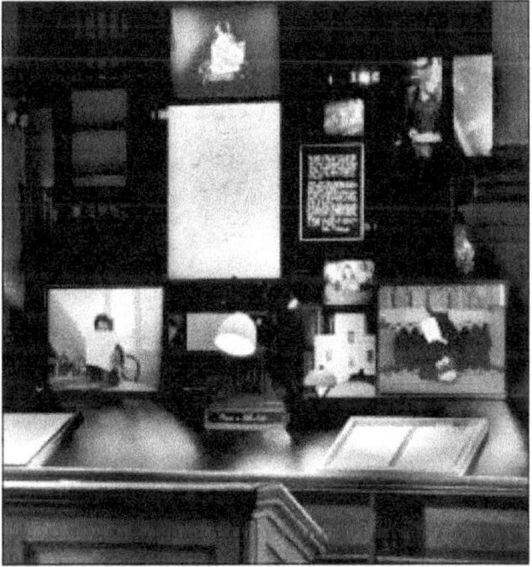

Fig. 4.4. Sophie Calle, *Prenez soin de vous*, Bibliothéque nationale de France, 2008

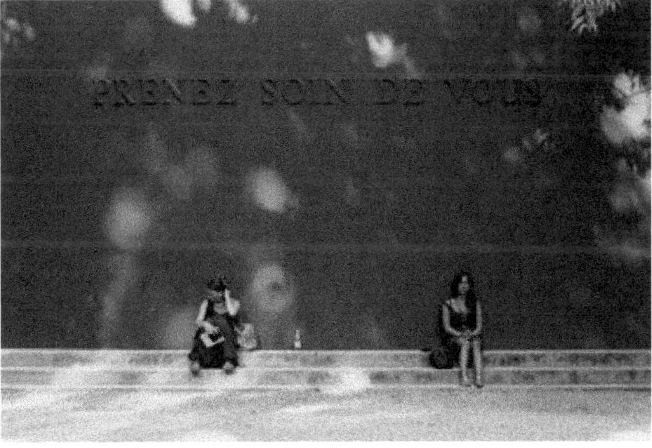

Fig. 4.5. Sophie Calle, *Prenez soin de vous*, 52nd Venice Biennale, 2007

means of its densely woven and multi-sensory ecosystem, it can be said that *Prenez soin de vous* 'cocoons' its audience and immerses it in different stratospheres of feeling: as suggested by, in Venice, the exterior of the installation version of the project being fashioned as a giant red spaceship (see Fig. 26, below), suggesting transport and transcendence, the elevation of participants to exotic, virtual new realms. In her writings on the moving image, Vivian Sobchack has argued that through film we are 'able to touch and be touched by the substance and texture of images; to feel a visual atmosphere envelop us'.[112] Yet *Prenez soin de vous*'s 'atmosphere' is not only visual — in fact it disrupts the reign of the purely scopic — but also auditory. At Venice, walking into the installation involved being met, as Shirley Jordan has written, with an overwhelming, if jubilant, 'cacophony' of sound.[113] For his part, Jean-Luc Nancy aligns the auditory with impulses towards participation and sharing, whereas the visual cleaves towards more static orders of representation and mimesis. 'Le visuel serait tendanciellement mimétique, et le sonore tendanciellement méthexique (c'est-à-dire dans l'ordre de la participation, du partage ou de la contagion)' [The visual regime tends towards the mimetic, and the sonorous tends towards the methectic (which is to say, to the logic of participation, sharing or contagion)], he writes.[114]

An emphasis on stature and amplification is further conveyed by the size of *Prenez soin de vous* as printed, textual object. Eclipsing Calle's other miniaturised publications, *Prenez soin de vous* in book form is a vast, encyclopaedic tome: close in size to an extravagant *livre d'artiste* or a retrospective exhibition catalogue. In a work on the connection between painting and poetry, Jean Khalfa has observed how the *livre d'artiste* functions primarily as a space of experimentation and of play rather than of narrative elucidation, and Stewart ventures how manifestations of 'the gigantic' serve to perform ideas of scale, significance, and exaggeration.[115] In *Prenez soin de vous*, strategies of stature and inflation are deployed in order to dramatise and make visible the luxury of 'making the most' of an otherwise phatic email but also to illuminate desires to exhaust it via deliberate practices of saturation.

By such means, surfeit and abundance might be deployed as political tools. Jordan notes the 'unrulinesss' of *Prenez soin de vous*'s non-linear assemblage of re-readings and focuses on the noisiness of the exhibited version of the project — hosting multiple videos and audio recordings in simultaneity — as a gesture engineered to 'drown out' the patriarchal arrogance of the initial note.[116] Iwona Blazwick similarly draws attention to the 'operatic scale' of the installation which, unfurling a 'labryinth of text, sound and image', functions to disarm the viewer, to subject our received ideas about what initially appears a humdrum exchange to burlesque play and creative re-purposings.[117] In a conclusion to the collection *Identities*, Butler poses, 'Can the exchange of speech or writing be the occasion for a disruption of the social ontology of positionality?'[118] *Prenez soin de vous* goes one step further, nonetheless, in exploding the dyadic contract of epistolary reciprocity, making disruption and dislocation primary mechanisms and subjecting the privilege of patriarchal positionality to multiplication and liberal disseminations.

In the printed book, the final contribution to Calle's invitation moves the original premise of the project even further. Suspending the predominantly feminist and humanistic bias of the enterprise, the invitation to partake in *Prenez soin de vous*'s mass production of interpretation is extended to Calle's pet parrot, Brenda, who is photographed taking a printed copy of the offending email in her beak before ripping it to shreds. Such an act returns the project to Calle's original entreaty that the email, as signalled by her early choice of the word *disséquer* [to dissect], be subjected to fragmentation, and expands the work's tolerance of alterity and difference in its inclusion not only of professional, feminized interpretations but of animal ones, too. Furthermore, the decision to let Brenda the parrot have the final word concludes the project on a comic note and exposes the work, in its final stages, to the luxury of levity, to the ability to make light of something, to 'transubstantiate' (to borrow a term of Annie Ernaux) a disappointing personal event into an opportunity for raucous creative cooperation and deconstruction.

Perhaps Calle's most ambitious and far-reaching work to date, *Prenez soin de vous* exploits an aesthetics of scale and multiplication to transform a 'short and repetitive text', in Cassin's words, into a fertile terrain for interpretative abundance.[119] Also figuring as Calle's most explicit opening to plural multiplicity and to the value of alternative, competing points of view, in the trajectory of her evolution as an artist thus far it illustrates the pleasures to be found in collaborative work. Whilst to some extent exerting a sovereign ability not to speak, and to vanish from the scene of reading to offload the burden of self-representation onto willing others, it moves beyond sovereignty to highlight the relational structures of being-in-common and invests in a creative form of 'communal luxury' to ultimately bask in a de-centered idea of art, which takes care in its attention to detail but also in its receptive accommodation of alterity. Through this accommodation, a cornerstone of everyday feminine experience — the ubiquity of patriarchal 'microaggressivity' — comes into view and is afforded, echoing Chantal Akerman's re-valorization of the domestic register, luxurious space and time via art.

Conclusion: A New Mode of Seduction

The work of Sophie Calle is broadly concerned to engineer exceptional situations and singular experiments out of which relationships to other people, intimacy, and the production and consumption of the lives of others can be reshaped and rethought. In this chapter, I have explored three discrete works by Calle and argued that each one exercises a specific privilege or entertains a certain fantasy outside what might usually be granted by the parameters of the quotidian. In my reading of *Suite vénitienne*, I showed how the indulgence of trailing a random stranger to Venice gratifies a certain view of art in the Callean *œuvre* as flight, escape, and the dislocation of the ordinary, speaking to ideas of luxury as sensual departure and affective remapping. In an analysis of *Douleur exquise*, I showed how impulses to soothe the self are measured against testimonies to the pain of others to enact the luxury of 'decreation' or of moving away from the self; and in *Prenez soin de vous*, how the experience of being held by a polyphonic, creative feminist sensorium can pleasurably overwhelm the age-old script of a romantic disappointment. Speaking to this study's broader efforts to affirm luxury as an experience of multiplicity, plurality, and the 'incalculable excess' of what cannot be thought or reduced to neat conceptual equations, in all three readings I have demonstrated how Calle's work, despite its fondness for constraint, often overcomes its own expressed limits. In its accommodation of and care for the unpredictable nature of the encounter with the Other, Calle's *œuvre* transcends solipsistic relief and conceives luxury as rapture, fascination, and as a surrender to communal experience.

In its work *Premiers matériaux pour une théorie de la jeune fille*, the writing and artistic collective Tiqqun suggests that:

> Nous sommes peu à peu passés, dans les trente dernières années, d'une séduction de type fordiste, avec ses lieux et ses moments désignés, sa forme-couple statique et proto-bourgeoise, à une séduction de type postfordiste, diffuse, flexible, précaire et déritualisée, qui a étendu l'usine à couples à la totalité du corps et de l'espace-temps social.
>
> [Over the past thirty years, we have passed, little by little, from Fordist seduction, with its designated sites and moments, its static and proto-bourgeois couple-form, to post-Fordist seduction, diffuse, flexible, precarious and deritualized, which has extended the couple factory to the entire body and the whole of social time-space.][120]

Also resonating with Ernaux's move away from the exclusive arena of the bourgeois couple to embrace the wider orbit of the outside world in *Passion simple*, such a statement provides ground for a revision of ideas about seduction in Calle's *œuvre*. For Baudrillard, seduction in Calle's work takes as primary object the seduction of the self. For Tiqqun, working out of the more virtual and immaterial context of digital neoliberalism, seduction, close to the free-floating, impersonal quality of Deleuze's concept of desire, no longer has an object and exists independently from subject-object targets to immerse participants in an ambient landscape of overlapping affects and intensities. This echoes the decentralised, kinetic, and polyphonic orchestra of voices on display in *Prenez soin de vous*.

In the preface to the work *Où et quand?* detailing her temporary trusting of her life decisions to the clairvoyant Maud Kirsten, Calle suggests that the process of devising meticulously designed templates through which to conduct her projects is 'reposant. L'obéissance aux règles, l'errance sous contrôle, le soulagement de ne pas avoir à juger les événements [...] Il n'est pas nécessaire de s'amuser. Être là suffit. La différence est que tout fait signe et s'en trouve auréolé de grâce' [relaxing. The obeying of rules, the controlled wandering, the relief at no longer having to judge events [...] It's not necessary to enjoy oneself. Being here is sufficient. The difference is that everything becomes a sign and finds itself haloed with grace].[121] Such a statement touches once again on questions of design, sovereignty, and wilfulness which I have traced throughout the chapter in order to explore ideas of luxury as the 'chameleonic' capability to revel both in the performance of the artist-as-character and, conversely, in the occasional desire to retreat from visibility, to oscillate between presence and absence, retreat and display.[122] Poised upon this threshold, Calle's projects take care to inhabit the threshold between self-assertion and self-disintegration, at once subjecting 'personal experience' to diffuse and precarious erasure while also asserting the persona of 'Sophie Calle'. At the same time, her works movingly and tenderly express the vulnerability articulated by Butler whereby 'no subject is its own point of departure' and where 'to be addressed is to be, from the start, deprived of will'.[123] Moving between sly auto-affection and profound empathy for the lives of others, Calle's work distills both the voluptuous activity of self-care via art and a devout attention to the textures of the outside world in which the self is always a relational, mediated composition.

Notes to Chapter 4

1. Donatien Alphonse François, marquis de Sade, *Les Cent Vingt Journées de Sodome*, in *Œuvres complètes*, ed. by Michel Delon, 3 vols (Paris: Gallimard/Pléiade, 1990–98), I, 66. Wayne Koestenbaum, cited in Nicole Miller, 'Following Sophie Calle', *Hyperallergic* <https://hyperallergic.com/305869/following-sophie-calle/> [accessed 7 August 2020].
2. Sophie Calle, cited in Sheena Wagstaff, 'Such Is My Pleasure, Such Is My Will', in *The Sophie Calle Reader*, ed. by Iwona Blazwick (London: Whitechapel Gallery Press, 2009), pp. 33–39 (p. 38).
3. See Sara Ahmed, *Wilful Subjects* (Durham. NC: Duke University Press, 2014), p. 2.
4. Michael Sheringham suggests that Calle's work 'tests the borders of what can and cannot be shared' (*Everyday Life: Theories and Practices from Surrealism to the Present* (Oxford: Oxford University Press, 2006), p. 344).
5. See Cécile Camart, 'Sophie Calle, alias Sophie Calle: le jeu d'un narcisse éclaté', *Art Press*, hors série, 5 (April 2002), 30–35; Michel Guerrin, 'Sophie Calle, fétichiste de sa propre vie', *Le Monde*, 11 September 2008; Johnnie Gratton, 'Sophie Calle's True Stories: More of the Same?', *Paragraph*, 26.3 (2003), 108–22; and Jonathan Romney, 'Double Exposure', *Guardian*, 19 March 1999.
6. See Bataille, *La Part maudite*, p. 151.
7. As Sheringham observes, Calle 'shares with Perec a fondness for inventory and enumeration, a love of constraints' (*Everyday Life*, p. 343).
8. Louise Neri, 'Sophie Calle', *Interview* (24 March 2009) <http://www.interviewmagazine.com/art/sophie-calle> [accessed 9 November 2015].
9. See Judith Butler, 'Precarious Life, Vulnerability and the Ethics of Cohabitation', *Journal of Speculative Philosophy*, 26.2 (2012), 134–51 <http://www.ccs.unibe.ch/unibe/philhist/ccs/content/e6912/e220286/e259083/e364031/TextworkshopButler_ger.pdf> [accessed 9 November 2015].
10. See Foucault, *Histoire de la sexualité, tome 3*. Sandra Laugier, 'Politiques du care', *Multitudes*, 2.38 (Autumn 2009), 74–75.
11. While the term 'self-care' has now become quasi-synonymous with consumer fetishism and commodity capitalism, originally the term was deployed by radical and intersectional feminists such as Audre Lorde as a means of making space for alterity and different forms of embodied subjectivity. See Audre Lorde, *A Burst of Light: Essays* (London: Sheba, 1988), p. 131; and Sara Ahmed, 'Self-care as Warfare', *Feminist Killjoys* blog, 25 August 2014 <http://feministkilljoys.com/2014/08/25/selfcare-as-warfare/> [accessed 9 November 2015]. Laugier, 'Politiques du care', p. 74.
12. For Bernard Stiegler, in *Ce qui fait que la vie vaut la peine d'être vécue: de la pharmacologie* (Paris: Flammarion, 2010), amidst the pressures imposed by the reign of capitalism, 'taking care' can take on the meaning of 'economising' ('Economiser signifie prendre soin'). See Sophie Calle, 'People Think They Know Me. But They Know Nothing', *Financial Times*, 10 January 2020.
13. Ahmed, *Wilful Subjects*, p. 9.
14. Giorgio Agamben's articulation of 'the absolute concomitance of subjectification and desubjectification, self-loss and self-possession, servitude and sovereignty' (*Remnants of Auschwitz*, trans. by Daniel Heller-Roazen (New York: Zone Books, 2002), p. 107) will be central to my reading of Calle's luxury here.

15. In the 'Préambule' to *A suivre*, Calle notes, prior to discovering her vocation as an artist for example, that 'Depuis des mois, je suivais des inconnus dans la rue. Pour le plaisir de les suivre et non parce qu'ils m'intéressaient' [For months, I followed strangers on the street. For the pleasure of following them and not because they interested me] ('Préambule', in *A suivre (Livre IV)* (Arles: Actes Sud, 1998), unpaginated).
16. McFadden goes so far as to appoint Calle, at the beginning of her career, an 'accidental artist' owing to the above-mentioned early practice of following people on the street in Paris (*Gendered Frames, Embodied Cameras*, p. 45). She cites Calle herself, who explained in an interview with Bice Curiger, 'I no longer knew how to occupy myself each day, so I decided that I would follow people on the street. [...] I just thought every morning that I would see where they went and let them decide what my day would be, since alone I could not decide' (Bice Curiger, 'Sophie Calle in Conversation', <https://sounds.bl.uk/Arts-literature-and-performance/ICA-talks/024M-C0095X0828XX-0100V0> [accessed 7 August 2020]).
17. Sophie Calle, *Suite vénitienne*, in *A suivre (Livre IV)*, pp. 37–110 (p. 38).
18. For a counter-cultural take on *flânerie* as feminist practice see Anne Friedberg, *Window Shopping: Cinema and the Postmodern* (Berkeley: University of California Press, 1994), and Lauren Elkin, *Flâneuse: Women Walk the City in Paris, New York, Tokyo, Venice and London* (London: Vintage, 2017). For an account of the term's historical associations with processes of specular consumption and with male-centred practices of occupying the city, see James Trainor, 'Walking the Walk: The Artist as Flâneur', *Border Crossings*, 88 (November 2003), 82–92.
19. See Joshua Armstrong, 'Annie Ernaux and Sophie Calle: Agency and the Ambient Language of Everyday Life', *French Review*, 90.4 (2017), 132–44.
20. For a reading of *I Love Dick*'s voracious vulnerability and its innovations in writing feminine shame, see Mitchell, *Writing Shame*, pp. 149–98.
21. In his essay 'Facticité et seduction', on the mechanisms of seduction at work in *Suite vénitienne* in collaboration with Marc Guillaume, Jean Baudrillard argues that in taking charge of others' lives, even for a stipulated and limited time, Sophie 'se vide de son propre personnage' [empties herself of her own character] (Jean Baudrillard and Marc Guillaume, 'Facticité et séduction', in *Figures de l'altérité* (Paris: Descartes, 1994), pp. 143–65 (p. 147) (NB an earlier version of this essay appeared in English under the title 'Please Follow Me', in *Suite vénitienne /Please Follow Me*, trans. by Dany Barash and Danny Hatfield (Seattle: Bay Press, 1988). I will refer to both in the course of my discussion here.
22. Baudrillard and Guillaume, 'Facticité et séduction', p. 81.
23. Nancy, *Le Plaisir au dessin*, p. 53.
24. Calle, *Suite vénitienne*, p. 44.
25. Baudrillard and Guillaume, 'Facticité et séduction', p. 87.
26. The privileged milieu of Calle's Parisian background, steeped in the community of the local intelligentsia, is well-documented by McFadden (*Gendered Frames, Embodied Cameras*), who tells of how Calle's father was an esteemed supporter and collector of artists and her mother an established book critic.
27. This elevation of the 'situation' over the story, to paraphrase Vivian Gornick in *The Situation and the Story* (New York: Macmillan, 2002), anticipates Calle's comment that her later work *Prenez soin de vous* 'responds more to the email than the man' (Curiger, 'Sophie Calle in Conversation').
28. Calle, *Suite vénitienne*, p. 43.
29. Georges Perec, *Les Choses: une histoire des années soixante* (Paris: Julliard, 1965).
30. Wagstaff, 'Such Is My Pleasure, Such Is My Will', p. 35.
31. Calle, *Suite vénitienne*, p. 61.
32. Baudrillard and Guillaume, 'Facticité et séduction', p. 80.
33. See Jean-Luc Nancy, *Sexistence* (Paris: Galilée, 2017), p. 6; 'Sexistence', trans. by Irving Goh, *diacritics*, 43.4 (2016), 110–18.
34. Calle, *Suite vénitienne*, p. 55. Such a praxis echoes Calle's practice of wandering the streets during her trip to Japan documented in *Douleur exquise*, in which one diary entry reads: 'Aujourd'hui, j'ai suivi un jeune couple dans la rue, pas longtemps, à peine une heure. Comme ça, juste pour nostalgie, pour retrouver des habitudes, des gestes. Pour le plaisir de les suivre. Pour les

souvenirs. Et aussi pour passer le temps, pour m'occuper' [Today, I followed a young couple in the street, not for a long time, scarcely an hour. Like that, just for nostalgia, to recover habits, gestures. For the pleasure of following them. For memories. And also to pass the time, to keep myself busy] (*Douleur exquise* (Arles: Actes Sud, 2003), pp. 180–81).

35. Calle, *Suite vénitienne*, p. 57.
36. Baudrillard, 'Please Follow Me', p. 78.
37. See Mitchell, *Writing Shame*, p. 161.
38. See Jacques Derrida, *Dissemination: la dissemination* (Paris: Seuil, 1972).
39. See Baudrillard, 'Please Follow Me.' p. 82.
40. Underscoring *Suite véntienne*'s luxury of disciplining strong emotions, Calle at a panel event in New York in 2016 suggested: 'What I liked about [the project] was that by this non-reciprocal relationship, I had the control to say, okay, I will stop being moved by this man or stop being obsessed with him on Monday at five o'clock. I had the possibility to create feelings and emotions by the ritual, the obsession — to be totally obsessed by somebody and to cut it off by a decision' (cited in Miller, 'Following Sophie Calle').
41. Nancy, *Le Plaisir au dessin*, p. 52.
42. See for example Crowley, *Duras, Writing and the Ethical*, for a discussion of Marguerite Duras's work through this lens.
43. See Judith Butler, *Precarious Life: The Powers of Mourning and Violence* (London & New York: Verso, 2004), p. 23: 'I tell a story about the relations I choose, only to expose, somewhere along the way, the way I am gripped and undone by these very relations. My narrative falters, as it must'.
44. This sense of the project continuing beyond Calle's intentions, producing a surplus of affective residues, can be supported by the fact that Henri B. threatened to sue Calle upon hearing of her publication intentions, prompting her to make a subsequent return trip to Venice in order to re-photograph all the project's original images using a decoy or fake object of interest. For a full account of this process, see Johnnie Gratton, 'Illustration Revisited: Phototextual Exchange and Resistance in Sophie Calle's *Suite vénitienne*', in *Textual and Visual Selves*, ed. by Edwards, Hubbell and Miller, pp. 139–67.
45. Butler, *Precarious Life*, p. 49.
46. In most of her projects, McFadden writes, Calle 'amplifies the activity to the point of hyperbole' (*Gendered Frames, Embodied Cameras*, p. 148).
47. For an excellent account of Calle's more recent explorations of grieving, see Emma Wilson, *Love Mortality and the Moving Image* (London: Palgrave Macmillan, 2012). See also accounts provided by Isabelle Décarie, 'Aimer souffrir: *Douleur exquise* de Sophie Calle', *Spirale: arts, lettres, sciences humaines*, 198 (2004), 34–35, or Catherine Lemieux, 'Mélancolie et restitutions dans *Douleur Exquise* de Sophie Calle', *Deuils sans fin dans la littérature contemporaine*, ed. by Mathilde Branthomme, special issue of *Post-scriptum*, 14 (July 2011) <http://post-scriptum.org/melancolie-et-restitutions-dans-douleur> [accessed 9 November 2015].
48. François, *Open Secrets*, p. 8. This argument of grief as an essentially collective structure is Butler's in *Precarious Life*, p. 23: 'What grief displays, in contrast, is the thrall in which our relations with others hold us, in ways that we cannot always recount or explain, in ways that challenge the very notion of ourselves as autonomous and in control'.
49. Wilson, *Love, Mortality and the Moving Image*. Shirley Jordan, 'Exhibiting Pain: Sophie Calle's *Douleur exquise*', *French Studies*, 61.2 (2007), 196–208. The retrospective, entitled *M'as-tu-vue?*, opened at the Centre Pompidou in Paris on 19 November 2003 and ran until 15 March 2004. The work was later published in book form as Sophie Calle, *M'as-tu-vue?* (Paris: Éditions du Centre Pompidou & Xavier Barral, 2005).
50. Calle, *Douleur exquise*. See Bill Brown, 'Thing Theory', *Critical Inquiry*, 28.1 (Autumn 2001), 1–22.
51. See particularly Robert L. Pincus's essay, 'Sophie Calle: The Prying Eye', *Art in America* (October 1989), 192–97, for a reading of Calle's work in terms of ocular surveillance and voyeurism.
52. Sophie Calle, 'Pour moi, un livre, c'est un objet qui parle avec une exposition', *France Culture*, 11 September 2020 <https://www.franceculture.fr/emissions/par-les-temps-qui-courent/par-les-temps-qui-courent-emission-du-vendredi-11-septembre-2020> [accessed 26 October 2020].

53. See Susan Stewart, *On Longing: Narratives of the Miniature, the Gigantic, the Souvenir, the Collection* (Durham, NC, & London: Duke University Press, 1993), p. 38.
54. See Jacques Derrida, *De la grammatologie* (Paris: Minuit, 1967), p. 30.
55. Lemieux, 'Mélancolie et restitutions dans *Douleur Exquise* de Sophie Calle'.
56. See Emily Apter, 'Introduction', in *Fetishism as Cultural Discourse*, ed. by Emily Apter and William Pietz (Ithaca, NY: Cornell University Press, 1993), pp. 1–14 (p. 4).
57. See William Pietz, 'The Problem of the Fetish', *Res*, 9.1 (Spring 1985), 5–17.
58. Calle, *Douleur exquise*, p. 13: 'Une rupture, banale, mais que j'ai vécue alors comme le moment le plus douloureux de ma vie'. In her reading of *Douleur exquise*, Jordan observes how 'Calle's narrative is extended, reiterative, heightened with (fictitious additions): in short, it is embroidered' ('Exhibiting Pain', p. 206).
59. Décarie, 'Aimer souffrir', p. 35.
60. See, for example, the focus on needlework in Calle's *Rachel, Monique*, exhibited at the Episcopal Church of the Heavenly Rest in Manhattan, 2014. For an account of how embroidery has been misogynistically attacked in art history institutions, see Roszika Parker, *The Subversive Stitch: Embroidery and the Making of the Feminine* (London: I. B. Tauris. 1984). For an advocation for 'crafting's redefinition of what counts as politics to include sensory interactions with highly tactile spaces and with other people, — or, in other words, feelings', see Ann Cvetkovich, *Depression: A Public Feeling* (Durham, NC, & London: Duke University Press, 2012), p. 177.
61. Calle, *Douleur exquise*, p. 9.
62. Ibid., back cover.
63. Speaking further to the clinical aspect of *Douleur exquise*'s enterprise, Calle explained in 2016, 'I interviewed people in exchange, asking what was exquisite pain in their own life. Exquisite pain is a medical term. When you break your arm, just where the break is: exquisite pain' (cited in Miller, 'Following Sophie Calle').
64. Calle, *Douleur exquise*, back cover.
65. Ibid., p. 203.
66. See Susan Sontag, *Regarding the Pain of Others* (New York & London: Penguin, 2003).
67. See Jordan, 'Exhibiting Pain', p. 197. See Koestenbaum, cited in 'Following Sophie Calle', where he also, relevant to *Douleur exquise,* elaborates on melancholy as 'a commitment to procedures of delving and a commitment to processes of emotional investigation, including of one's own melancholy, that are ultimately, if not cheaply cathartic, at least give some sort of structure to life'.
68. My definitions here are borrowed from the account of *delectatio morosa* offered in *Dictionary of Untranslatables: A Philosophical Lexicon*, ed. by Barbara Cassin, trans. by Emily Apter, Jacques Lezra and Michael Wood (Oxford & Princeton, NJ: Princeton University Press, 2014), p. 792. In *L'Érotisme*, Bataille defines *délectation morose* as a 'forme prolongée de tentation' (p. 245).
69. See Sigmund Freud, 'Mourning and Melancholia', in *The Standard Edition of The Complete Psychological Works of Sigmund Freud, Volume XIV (1914–1916)*, ed. by Alix Strachey and Alan Tyson (London: Vintage, 1999), pp. 243–59.
70. Calle, *Douleur exquise*, p. 16.
71. Anne Cheng, *Second Skin: Josephine Baker and the Modern Surface* (Oxford: Oxford University Press, 2011) p. 116.
72. Jordan, for example refers to the 'progressive self-effacement of Calle herself' that is staged via the piece ('Exhibiting Pain', p. 197). See Wilson, *Love, Mortality and the Moving Image*, p. 170.
73. Butler, *Precarious Life*, p. 20.
74. Décarie, 'Aimer souffrir', p. 35.
75. Butler, *Precarious Life*, p. 22.
76. In her discussion of the policies and decentralising impulse of the Paris Commune, Kristin Ross uses the term 'communal luxury' to denote an opening up of access to art and beauty, and a freeing of capital (*Communal Luxury* (New York & London, Verso: 2015)). Applicable to my thinking about luxury across the project, such a concept is particularly relevant to my discussion of Calle's work and its gradual move away from authorial intention to an embrace of heterogeneity and multiplicity.

77. Butler, *Precarious Life*, p. 30.
78. Calle, *Douleur exquise*, p. 247.
79. Ibid., p. 233.
80. Butler, *Precarious Life*, p. 150.
81. Calle, *Douleur exquise*, p. 275.
82. Derrida, *L'Écriture et la difference*, p. 30.
83. Christie V. McDonald and Jacques Derrida, 'Interview: Choreographies', *Cherchez la femme: Feminist Critique/Feminine Text, Diacritics*, 12.2 (Summer 1982), 66–76 (p. 76).
84. I borrow the term 'decreation of the self' from Simone Weil's *La Pesanteur et la grâce* (1947) (*Gravity and Grace*, trans. by Emma Crawford and Mario von der Rohr (London: Routledge, 2002)), where the objective of such an impulse is understood as a giving up of self-volition in order to irradiate God's will. Anne Carson, in her work *Decreation: Poetry, Essays, Opera* (New York: Vintage, 2006), builds on Weil's philosophy to understand 'decreation' as a sublime annihilation of the self, resonating with my reading of Calle's luxury in this chapter. For the 'narcissistic pleasure' of Calle's works, see Anna Kemp, 'Selling Yourself: The Commercialisation of Feeling in the Work of Sophie Calle', *Nottingham French Studies*, 52.3 (December 2013), 308–21 (p. 308). See also Laugier, 'Politiques du care', p. 74.
85. Antoine Compagnon, 'Baudelaire moderne et antimoderne', lecture given as part of the Collège de France, 'Littérature française moderne et contemporaine: histoire, critique, théorie' series <https://www.college-de-france.fr/media/antoine-compagnon/UPL3221135538535161 25_R1112_Compagnon.pdf> [accessed 12 November 2015]. Following Robin James's monograph, *Resilience and Melancholy* (London: Zero Books, 2015), it might be possible to read *Prenez soin de vous* as an exercise in the former rather than the latter, or as an enactment of a 'bouncing back' that overwrites melancholy's typical voluptuousness with effervescent feminist praxis and creativity. Echoing James, such a shift bespeaks neoliberalism's emphasis on activity over passivity, and might have implications for contemporary views of luxury as kinetic, transcending its historical associations with indolence and stasis. See Patrizia Calefato, *Luxury: Fashion, Lifestyle and Excess*, trans. by Lisa Adams (London: Bloomsbury Academic, 2014), p. 118.
86. For a reading of *Prenez soin de vous* as an accumulation of archival material, see Natalie Edwards, 'Accumulation and Archives: Sophie Calle's *Prenez soin de vous*', *Studies in 20th and 21st Century Literature*, 38.2–3 (January 2014), Article 3 (unpaginated). Furthering my discussion of Calle's textual fetishism and sensuous engagement with the materiality of relics, talismans, and objects I will mainly focus my discussion here on the printed version of the project. Whilst critical readings of *Prenez soin de vous* have tended to focus on the project's presentation as an installation (see Jordan, 'Exhibiting Pain', and Wilson's discussion of the work in *Love, Mortality and the Moving Image*, amongst others), I will focus on its secondary iteration as text and book in order to support my reading of the work as an animated swarm of different languages and sign systems which overwrite and amplify an initially banal missive.
87. Sophie Calle, *Prenez soin de vous* (Arles: Actes Sud, 2007), unpaginated.
88. For more on this see Mitchell, *Writing Shame*.
89. Chris Kraus, *I Love Dick* (Los Angeles: Semiotext(e), 2002) p. 208.
90. This strategy offers an ironic commentary on women's, in a post-Fordist context of production, gendered consignment to providing emotional or immaterial 'services' which are for the most part unremunerated (see Angela McRobbie, 'Reflections on Feminism and Immaterial Labor', in *New Formations*, 70 (2010), 60–76, for more on this relegation of women to the role of affective labourers).
91. Wilson, *The Reclining Nude*, p. 30.
92. See again Lorde, *A Burst of Light*, and Ahmed, 'Self-care as Warfare'.
93. See Avital Ronell, 'Interview', in *Angry Women*, ed. by Andrea Juno and V. Vale (New York: Juno Books, 1991), p. 127.
94. For an able discussion of the contemporary artist as curator rather than creator ex nihilo, see Hans Ulrich Obrist, *Ways of Curating* (London: Penguin, 2015). For a philosophical investigation into the semantic and cultural import of 'la rupture', see Claire Marin, *Ruptures* (Paris: L'Observatoire, 2019).

95. See Anne Portugal, 'La Contrainte', in Calle, *Prenez soin de vous*, unpaginated.
96. See for example Sheringham, *Everyday Life*, and Elkin, *Flâneuse*.
97. Sophie Calle, *Où et quand?* (Arles: Actes Sud, 2009).
98. Portugal, 'La Contrainte'.
99. Ibid.
100. For an account of Calle's ex qua X as a multiplying as opposed to self-affirming function, see Anna Watkins Fisher, 'Manic Impositions: The Parasitical Art of Chris Kraus and Sophie Calle', in *Women's Studies Quarterly*, 40.1–2 (Spring-Summer 2012), 223–35.
101. Barbara Cassin, cited in Calle, *Prenez soin de vous*, unpaginated: 'Une série à l'occasion d'un objet unique, érotico-mondain, la touchant par essence ou par accident, de manière à exhauster (dérouler, épuiser, intégrer et cathartique) cet objet'.
102. Roland Barthes, *Fragments d'un discours amoureux* (Paris: Seuil, 1977), pp. 21–22; *A Lover's Discourse: Fragments*, trans. by Richard Howard (New York: Farrar, Strass and Giroux, 1978), p. 16.
103. See Edwards, 'Accumulation and Archives'.
104. Julia Kristeva, *Pouvoirs de l'horreur: essai sur l'abjection* (Paris: Seuil, 1980), p. 23; *Powers of Horror: An Essay on Abjection*, trans. by Leon S. Roudiez (New York: Columbia University Press, 1982), p. 15.
105. See Christine Angot, in Calle, *Douleur exquise*, unpaginated.
106. Nilufer Gole in Calle, *Douleur exquise*, unpaginated. Cassin notes similarly that 'je n'ai pas pu cependant m'empêcher de m'impliquer davantage dans cette lecture, d'en donner une interprétation' [I couldn't however stop myself from becoming more involved in this reading, to give an interpretation of it] (in Calle, *Prenez soin de vous*, unpaginated).
107. Baudrillard, 'Please Follow Me', pp. 79, 80.
108. See François, *Open Secrets*, p. 22. See also Emmanuel Levinas who refers to 'my duty to respond to the other' (cited in Butler, *Precarious Life*, p. 159) and Nancy, who in 'Exscription', drawing heavily upon the work of Jacques Derrida, makes reference to "the *obligation* of responding", to the other' (p. 51).
109. Nancy, 'Exscription', p. 61.
110. In a conceptual piece narrating an interview with Calle from her imagined point of view, the writer Brian Dillon forefronts the artist's taste for 'flat modes of writing: the diary, the questionnaire, the list, the report' and 'resistance to metaphor' ('History Lessons No 5: Take Care of Yourself', *Art Review* (June 2007) <https://artreview.com/history-lessons-7-april-2020-brian-dillon-sophie-calle-interview/> [accessed 9 August 2020]).
111. Ross, *Communal Luxury*, p. 11.
112. See Vivian Sobchack, *Carnal Thoughts: Embodiment and Moving Image Culture* (Berkeley: University of California Press, 2004), p. 65.
113. Shirley Jordan, 'Performance in Sophie Calle's *Prenez soin de vous*', *French Cultural Studies*, 24.3 (2013), 249–63 (p. 251).
114. Jean-Luc Nancy, *À l'écoute* (Paris: Galilée, 2002), p. 27.
115. Jean Khalfa, 'Foreword', in *The Dialogue between Painting and Poetry: Livres d'artistes, 1874–1999*, ed. by Jean Khalfa (Cambridge: Black Apollo Press, 2001) pp. 7–37 (p. 9). Stewart, *On Longing*.
116. Jordan, 'Performance in Sophie Calle's *Prenez soin de vous*', p. 252.
117. See Iwona Blazwick, 'Talking to Strangers', in *The Sophie Calle Reader*, ed. by Blazwick, pp. 7–15 (p. 14).
118. See Judith Butler, 'Collected and Fractured: Response to Identities', in *Identities*, ed. by Kwame Anthony Appiah and Henry Louis Gates Jr. (Chicago: University of Chicago Press, 1995), pp. 441–42.
119. Cassin in Calle, *Douleur exquise*.
120. Tiqqun, *Premiers matériaux pour une théorie de la jeune fille* (Paris: Fayard, 2001), p. 140; *Preliminary Materials for a Theory of the Young Girl*, trans. by Ariana Reines (Los Angeles: Semiotext(e), 2012), p. 33.
121. Calle, *Où et quand?*, p. 117.
122. See Anne Sauvageot, *Sophie Calle: l'art caméléon* (Paris: Presses universitaires de France, 2007).
123. Butler, *Precarious Life*, pp. 41, 139.

CONCLUSION

Living Otherwise

In an article published at the peak of the 2020 coronavirus crisis, the scholar Benjamin H. Bratton, in response to worldwide demands that citizens 'work from home' indefinitely, deployed the curiously-worded concept 'Fully Automated Luxury Quarantine'.[1] The phrase was a wry reworking of Aaron Bastani's 'Fully Automated Luxury Communism', published as a book under the same title in 2019, which presented the audacious thesis that abundant wealth, resources, decadence, and joy should be opened up to all citizens regardless of class or status and prioritised as our urgent future political horizon.[2]

Bratton's ludically aware adjustment, highlighting the comfortable and relatively easeful quarantine enjoyed by the cultural and economic elite (in contrast to the highly risky, vulnerable, and exhausting 'confinement' suffered by essential and key workers) was intended to expose the relative utopia and pre-Covid naivety of Bastani's project.[3] Yet, the acute discrepancy between the two versions of the concept also bespeaks luxury's infinite plasticity and mutability as a signifier. Luxury means vastly different things in different contexts. Its signification is never static, immutable, or fixed. Luxury, it can be argued, sponsors the vibration of ongoing possibility rather than the firm telos of meaning.

Writing on the early impact of the pandemic for the journal *Artforum* in May 2020, the philosopher Paul B. Preciado argued further how:

> It is precisely because our bodies are the new enclaves of biopower and because our apartments are the new cells of biovigilance that it is more urgent than ever to invent new strategies of cognitive emancipation and release.[4]

With the private residence having now become the centre of the economy of what Preciado, resonating with the syntax of the moving image, calls 'tele-commuting', luxury's relation to enclosure, seclusion, withdrawal, and the privileged 'retreat' from normative economies has potentially been, in the wake of the pandemic, forever re-drawn.[5]

Paying close attention to experiences not available to constant surveillance and relentless consumption, in this study I have offered a distinct, contrarian account of luxury as both an alternative economy of pleasure and desire and an enriched, material relation to the world. Taking the work of Chantal Akerman, Annie Ernaux, Louise Bourgeois, and Sophie Calle as points of departure, I have shown how art and the aesthetic experience's longing for order, contemplation, relief, and transcendence can connect to luxury's project of voluptuous calm and desires to enhance and go beyond the repetitious circuits of the everyday. In the process, I have ventured a new concept of luxury as a form of sensual and aesthetic attention as opposed to insatiable commodity accumulation and possession.

In opening to the possibility of 'la vie du sens' [a life of sense] 'au-delà d'une existence correcte, digne et sereine' [which surpasses a merely dignified, correct, serene existence], the philosophy of Jean-Luc Nancy, a consistent presence throughout the book, avoids ideas of luxury as a passive mode of sedating comfort or restorative ease.[6] In *Le Plaisir au dessin*, Nancy argues convincingly that a Freudian account of pleasure and desire makes false oppositions between a satiated 'calme du repos' [calm of repose] and the still-yearning, ever-seeking 'frénésie de désir' [frenzy of desire].[7] Concepts of luxury, as, following Charles Baudelaire, an experience of calm voluptuousness, or as a state of containment which nonetheless exceeds its borders, avoids this stark polarisation, understanding luxury as both static and kinetic, moving and still, sated and restless. As Nancy implies, to go beyond the confines of a life merely dedicated to serene correctness entails singular, extraordinary contacts and exposures, entails encounters with exceptionality and with new singular models of thought and sensation, which all four of the artists under discussion have enabled. This model further distances ideas of luxury from notions of 'pure' excess, 'pure' transcendence, 'pure' escape, or sensible distraction. As Nancy suggests in his work *Sexistence* of 2017, the point is never to bask in a self-serving *jouissance* but to cultivate an ongoing existential 'incandescence', so as to develop a distinct ethics of sensation.[8] Keeping such a dynamic in mind, throughout this project I have explored how luxury both figures as a form of ecstatic dissolution — of the self, and of the restricted economies into which life is inserted — and a state, at the same time, of material connection. By such means I have suggested that to luxuriate is both to dream and imagine a life elsewhere or a life in excess of quotidian potentialities but also to immerse, take in, and embed oneself within already given sensual frameworks.

This balance of flight from the everyday and sensual immanence is scrupulously measured in the films of Chantal Akerman, the subject of the book's first chapter. In my discussion of Akerman, I suggested that the luxurious might be mapped onto three different modes of cinematic temporality: the durational, the incidental, and the entropic. In coalition with feminist film theory scholarship, I argued that Akerman's films give rise to moments of stunning insight and impact, and new ways of sensing and relating to the world, whilst avoiding, at the same time, any presentation of the female body as an easy item of consumption. I argued, with Bataille and Deleuze, that *Jeanne Dielman, 23 quai du Commerce, 1080 Bruxelles* and *Je, tu, il, elle* pursue experiences of losing control and sensual rebellion, to visually frame luxury as the active, resistant choice to not subscribe to certain generic and gendering economies.

In the next chapter on Annie Ernaux, I explored ideas of luxury through the lens of writing or *écriture* in dialogue with the thinking of Nancy, Derrida, and Bataille on the subject. Attentive to Ernaux's stylistic thrift and almost austere rationing of detail, but also to her frequent testimonies to the 'failure' of her projects to commit material experience to words, I argued that within her texts the sovereign (here in the sense of 'executive') ability to simplify, refine, and subject one's life to numerous rewritings competes with the excess and unaccountablility of relations to other people which elude writerly fixity. In such a manner, I suggested, Ernaux's projects open to the richness and fulfilment of having written, or to the 'luck and luxury', to borrow a phrase from the American poet Sharon Olds, of having dedicated oneself to an exercise or act in the complexities of lived, 'real' time.[9]

Moving from textual artefacts to plastic art and drawings in Chapter 3, discussing the production of the mixed media artist Louise Bourgeois, I examined luxury through the lens of aesthetic exuberance, creative insatiability, and the restless 'desire-pleasure' to be found in perpetually 'starting over' in artistic endeavours. Eager to emancipate Bourgeois's work from its enduring understanding in psychoanalytic terms, I suggested that Bourgeois's prolific output might be understood less as an exercise in anguished repetition than as a motif or gesture signalling the central role of play, curiosity, and enthusiasm in her practice. Emphasising Bourgeois's baroque shapes and sensuous modes of making art, I argued, in dialogue with Nancy's broad theoretical framework of opening and exposing, that the artist's drawings and sculptures might indeed bear pleasurable witness to the inchoate, fecund beginnings rather than the instrumental ends of a creative process.

A final chapter on contemporary artist Sophie Calle brought questions of luxury as agency, self-fashioning, and sovereignty subtending the book at large into closer relief. Working across three Callean projects (*Suite vénitienne*, *Douleur exquise*, and *Prenez soin de vous*) I suggested that Calle's art unfolds complex questions in relation to desires both to take care of and — via complex, inquisitive, and at times voyeuristic art experiments — to take leave of the self.

Whilst emphasising all four artists' frequent openings to otherness and to incommensurability, simultaneous attention to their shared fastidiousness of detail and vigilance before formal properties has avoided the type-casting of women artists as either passive consumers of art or excessive and 'uncensored' producers of narrowly confessional autobiographical material. If often refracted through autobiographical or autofictional generic tropes, a dominant aesthetics of refinement, and an intricate crafting of artistic materials, has made it difficult to argue for these artworks as opportunities, as Toril Moi writes, for 'indulging in the self'.[10] The breadth of interdisciplinary experimentation beyond the restrictive frames of self-portraiture evident within the work of all four artists and a certain consciousness of the artwork as discrete object avoids essentialising accusations while also not belittling the act of mining one's own life as material for art. Though themes such as surrender, prostration, and the pleasures of submission — particularly in the context of romantic and sexual relationships — recur across the book, models of abjection or of feminine passivity are carefully negotiated by Akerman, Bourgeois, Calle, and Ernaux. As Michel Foucault memorably counsels, 'The point is to invent oneself, to make one's body the place of production of extraordinarily polymorphous pleasures [...]. The point is to detach oneself from that virile form of pleasure'.[11] In most of the artworks that I have considered, experiences of giving oneself over, basking, and abandon consistently confront the risks and thresholds of such exercises to envisage luxury as a partial and precarious phenomenon, which forever teeters on the edge of fully accomplished sovereignty.

In his 2003 work *Le Luxe éternel: de l'âge du sacré au temps des marques*, Gilles Lipovetsky, in conversation with Elyette Roux, offers a definition of luxury as 'une réponse au désir de jouir du monde' [a response to the desire to take pleasure from the world].[12] While eager to imagine the luxurious as a form of closely relating to the finite textures of embodied life, I have sought throughout this study to avoid projecting it as an experience of straight enjoyment, uncomplicated pleasure, or uncompromising *jouissance*. As I have shown, luxury's semantic origins more closely refer to a queer process of dislocation, of defiantly twisting everyday, homogeneous situations out of shape.[13] As I have signalled throughout the project, luxury both speaks to a steeping in materiality, or a full 'using up' of and revelry in material sensuality, whilst also being at the same time haunted by desires 'greater than life', shadowed by this figure of the surplus or the 'incalculable excess' which suggests there always could be more. As Jacques Derrida suggests, indeed, in relation to this figure of the surplus, 'there is always a remainder that cannot be read, that must remain alien. This residue can never be interrogated as the same, but must be constantly sought out anew'.[14] In this book I have tried to speak to these residues, these surplus unknown values or traces of the incalculable, which subtend every instance of consumption or enjoyment, or, in relation to the moving image, illuminate the stillness of the frame. I have sought, in such a context, to offer luxury as an enlargement of the possible and as the design of new modes of being and living otherwise. In this questing of which Derrida speaks, in this resistance that luxury, in its constant search for the singular, the better, and the exceptional poses to absorption, we are, indeed, encouraged to continue thinking, and creating. We are encouraged to open ourselves up to difference rather than restrict ourselves to the banal production of the same. This process, lacking object or end-point, is inexhaustible. As Derrida and the artists I have studied suggest, it must continue to remain in question, and continue to be written.

Notes to the Conclusion

1. Benjamin H. Bratton, '18 Lessons of Quarantine Urbanism', *Strelka Mag* (3 April 2020) <https://strelkamag.com/en/article/18-lessons-from-quarantine-urbanism> [accessed 23 August 2020].
2. Aaron Bastani, *Fully Automated Luxury Communism: A Manifesto* (London: Verso Books, 2019).
3. For an elegant evisceration of how 'coronavirus has surfaced the care economy, broadly construed, as indispensable, and the perfidy and plunder of most other capitalist extraction and production as largely superfluous', see Wendy Brown, 'The Quarantine Files: Thinkers in Self-isolation', *The Los Angeles Review of Books* (14 April 2020) <https://lareviewofbooks.org/article/quarantine-files-thinkers-self-isolation/> [accessed 23 August 2020].
4. See Preciado, 'Learning from the Virus'.
5. Ibid.
6. See Nancy, 'La Politique doit montrer ce qui la dépasse'.
7. Nancy, *Le Plaisir au dessin*, p. 37.
8. Nancy, *Sexistence*.

9. Sharon Olds, 'A Week Later', in *Stag's Leap* (London: Random House, 2012) p. 46.
10. See Toril Moi, *Sexual/Textual Politics* (London: Routledge, 2002), p. 235.
11. Michel Foucault, cited in David Macey, *The Lives of Michel Foucault* (London: Verso Books, 2019), p. 365.
12. Lipovetsky and Roux, *Le Luxe éternel*, p. 40.
13. See again luxury's relation to *luctari* <https://www.etymonline.com/word/luxury> [accessed 23 August 2020].
14. Daniel Birnbaum and Anders Olsson, 'An Interview with Jacques Derrida on the Limits of Digestion', trans. by Brian Manning Delaney, *efflux*, 2 (January 2009) <http://www.e-flux.com/journal/an-interview-with-jacques-derrida-on-the-limits-of-digestion/> [accessed 25 October 2015].

BIBLIOGRAPHY

ACOCELLA, JOAN, 'The Spider's Web: Louise Bourgeois and her Art', *The New Yorker*, 4 February 2002

ADLER, AURÉLIE, 'Annie Ernaux: émiettement et consolidation du sujet auctorial', in *Éclats des vies muettes* (Paris: Presses Sorbonne Nouvelle, 2012) <http://books.openedition.org/psn/2174> [accessed 11 August 2020]

AGAMBEN, GIORGIO, *Nudities*, trans. by David Kishik and Stefan Pedatella (Stanford, CA: Stanford University Press, 2011)

—— *Remnants of Auschwitz*, trans. by Daniel Heller-Roazen (New York: Zone Books, 2002)

AHMED, SARA, 'Self-care as Warfare', *Feminist Killjoys* blog, 25 August 2014 <http://feministkilljoys.com/2014/08/25/selfcare-as-warfare/> [accessed 9 November 2015]

—— *Wilful Subjects* (Durham, NC: Duke University Press, 2014)

AKERMAN, CHANTAL, *Autoportrait en cinéaste* (Paris: Cahiers du Cinéma, 2004)

—— 'Chantal Akerman on *Jeanne Dielman, 23 quai du Commerce, 1080 Bruxelles*', *Camera Obscura*, 2 (Fall 1977), 115–21

AKERMAN, CHANTAL, and ANGELA MARTIN, 'Chantal Akerman's Films: A Dossier', *Feminist Review*, 3 (November 1979), 24–47

APPERLY, ELIZA. 'Gentileschi: Let us not Allow Sexual Violence to Define the Artist', *Psyche* (10 June 2020) <https://psyche.co/ideas/gentileschi-let-us-not-allow-sexual-violence-to-define-the-artist> [accessed 18 June 2020]

APTER, EMILY, 'Introduction', in *Fetishism as Cultural Discourse*, ed. by Emily Apter and William Pietz (London: Cornell University Press, 1993), pp. 1–14

—— *Unexceptional Politics* (London: Verso, 2018)

ARAUJO, MATEUS, 'Chantal Akerman, between the Mother and the World', trans. by Mark Cohen, *Film Quarterly*, 70.1 (Fall 2016), 32–38

ARMSTRONG, JOSHUA, 'Annie Ernaux and Sophie Calle: Agency and the Ambient Language of Everyday Life', *The French Review*, 90.4 (2017), 132–44

ARMITAGE, JOHN, *Luxury and Visual Culture* (London: Bloomsbury Academic, 2019)

ASHBERY, JOHN, 'Anxious Architecture', *New York Magazine*, 16 October 1978

ASSOULY, OLIVIER (ed.), *Le Luxe: essais sur la fabrique de l'ostentation* (Paris: Le Regard, 2011)

AUGÉ, MARC, *Non-lieux* (Paris: Seuil, 1992)

BAL, MIEKE, 'Autotopography: Louise Bourgeois as Builder', *Biography*, 25.1 (Winter 2002), 180–202

—— 'Narrative Inside Out: Louise Bourgeois's Spider as Theoretical Object', *Louise Bourgeois*, special issue of *Oxford Art Journal*, 22.2 (1999), 103–26

—— *Quoting Caravaggio: Contemporary Art, Preposterous History* (Chicago: University of Chicago Press, 2001)

BALL, STEVEN, and OTHERS (eds), *Expanded Cinema: Art, Performance, Film* (London: Tate Publishing, 2011)

BANET-WEISER, SARAH, *Empowered: Popular Feminism and Popular Misogyny* (Durham, NC, & London: Duke University Press, 2018)

Barradas Jorge, Nuno, and Tiago de Luca (eds), *Slow Cinema* (Edinburgh: Edinburgh University Press, 2015)

Barthes, Roland, *Fragments d'un discours amoureux* (Paris: Seuil, 1977)

——'Leaving the Movie Theater', in *The Rustle of Language*, trans. by Richard Howard (Irvine: University of California Press, 1989), pp. 345–49

——*A Lover's Discourse*, trans. by Richard Howard (New York: FSG, 1978)

——*Le Neutre: cours et séminaires au Collège de France (1977–1978)* (Paris: Seuil, 2002)

——*Le Plaisir du texte* (Paris: Seuil, 1973)

——*La Préparation du roman: cours au Collège de France (1978–1979 et 1979–1980)* (Paris: Seuil, 2019)

Bastani, Aaron, *Fully Automated Luxury Communism: A Manifesto* (London: Verso Books, 2019)

Bataille, Georges, *Le Bleu du ciel* (Paris: Fayard Pauvert, 1985)

——*L'Érotisme* [1957] (Paris, Minuit, 2011)

——*Œuvres complètes*, 12 vols (Paris: Gallimard, 1970–88)

——*La Part maudite* [1949] (Paris: Minuit, 2011)

——*The Accursed Share: An Essay on General Economy. Volume I: Consumption*, trans. by Robert Hurley (New York: Zone Books, 1988)

——*Théorie de la religion* (Paris: Gallimard, 1973)

Baudelaire, Charles, *Les Fleurs du mal* [1857] (Paris: Folio/Classique, 1996)

Baudrillard, Jean, *America* (London: Verso, 1989)

——'Please Follow Me', in *Suite vénitienne /Please Follow Me,* trans. by Dany Barash and Danny Hatfield (Seattle: Bay Press, 1988), pp. 75–87

Baudrillard, Jean, and Marc Guillaume, *Figures de l'altérité* (Paris: Descartes, 1994)

Baumbach, Nico, 'All that Heaven Allows: What is, or was, Cinephilia? (Part Three)' <https://www.filmlinc.org/daily/all-that-heaven-allows-what-is-or-was-cinephilia-part-three-cinephilia-2/> [accessed 18 February 2020]

Beckman, Frida (ed.), *Deleuze and Sex* (Edinburgh: Edinburgh University Press, 2011)

Béghin, Cyril, 'Light Out of Joint,' in *Chantal Akerman: Afterlives*, ed. by Marion Schmid and Emma Wilson, Moving Image, 9 (Cambridge: Legenda, 2019), pp. 139–49

Benaim, Laurence, 'Has Luxury become a Dirty Word in France?', *Business of Fashion* (March 2019) <https://www.businessoffashion.com/articles/opinion/has-luxury-become-a-dirty-word-in-france-gilets-jaunes-yellow-vests-protest> [accessed 23 August 2020]

Benjamin, Marina, *Insomnia* (London: Scribe, 2018)

Berlant, Lauren, 'Nearly Utopian, Nearly Normal: Post-Fordist Affect in La Promesse and Rosetta,' *Public Culture*, 19.2 (April 2007), 273–301 (p. 277)

Bernadec, Marie-Laure (ed.), *Louise Bourgeois: The Insomnia Drawings* (Zurich: Daros, 2000)

——*Louise Bourgeois & Pablo Picasso: Anatomies of Desire* (New York: Hauser & Wirth, 2019)

Beugnet, Martine. *Cinema and Sensation* (Edinburgh: Edinburgh University Press, 2007)

Birnbaum, Daniel, and Anders Olsson, 'An Interview with Jacques Derrida on the Limits of Digestion', trans. by Brian Manning Delaney, *efflux*, 2 (January 2009) <http://www.e-flux.com/journal/an-interview-with-jacques-derrida-on-the-limits-of-digestion/> [accessed 25 October 2015]

Blackhurst, Alice, 'The Defiant Muse', *Los Angeles Review of Books* (December 2019) <https://lareviewofbooks.org/article/the-defiant-muse/> [accessed 18 February 2020]

——'Is the Future of French Feminism Female?', *n+1* (February 2020) <https://nplusonemag.com/online-only/online-only/is-the-future-of-french-feminism-female/> [accessed 13 August 2020]

BLANCHOT, MAURICE, *La Communauté inavouable* (Paris: Minuit, 1983)
——*L'Écriture du désastre* (Paris: Gallimard, 1980)
——*L'Entretien infini* (Paris: Gallimard, 1969)
——*Le Livre à venir* [1959] (Paris: Folio, 1986)
BLAZWICK, IWONA, 'Talking to Strangers', in *The Sophie Calle Reader*, ed. by Iwona Blazwick (London: Whitechapel Gallery, 2009), pp. 7–15
BOIS, YVES-ALAIN, and ROSALIND KRAUSS, *Formless: A User's Guide* (New York: Zone, 1997)
BONAMI, FRANCESCO, 'Louise Bourgeois: In a Strange Way, Things are Getting Better and Better', *Flash Art*, 27.174 (January-February 1994), 36–39
BOURDIEU, PIERRE, 'Le Champ littéraire', *Actes de la recherche en sciences sociales*, 89 (September 1991), 3–46
——*La Distinction: critique sociale du jugement* (Paris: Minuit, 1979)
BOURGEOIS, LOUISE, 'A Merging of Male and Female 1974', in *Louise Bourgeois*, ed. by Robert Storr, Paulo Herkenhoff and Allan Schwartman (London: Phaidon, 2003), p. 120
——*Destruction of the Father /Reconstruction of the Father: Writings and Interviews, 1923–1997*, ed. by Marie-Laure Bernadec and Hans-Ulrich Obrist (London: Violette, 1998)
——'On Janus Fleuri 1969', in *Louise Bourgeois*, ed. by Robert Storr, Paulo Herkenhoff and Allan Schwartman (London: Phaidon, 2003), pp. 118–19
BOURRIAUD, NICOLAS, *Esthétique relationnelle* (Paris: Le Réel, 2001)
BOYER, ANNE, *The Undying* (New York: Farrar, Strass & Giroux, 2019)
BRAIDOTTI, ROSI, 'Affirmative Ethics and Generative Life', *Deleuze and Guattari Studies*, 13.4 (2019), 463–81
——*Nomadic Subjects* (New York: Columbia University Press, 1994)
BRATTON, BENJAMIN H., '18 Lessons of Quarantine Urbanism', *Strelka Mag* (3 April 2020) <https://strelkamag.com/en/article/18-lessons-from-quarantine-urbanism> [accessed 23 August 2020]
BRENEZ, NICOLE, 'Chantal Akerman: The Pajama Interview', *Devils, LOLA Journal*, 2 (2011) <http://www.lolajournal.com/2/pajama.html> [accessed 12 November 2015]
BREY, IRIS, *Le Regard féminin* (Paris: L'Olivier, 2020)
BRINKEMA, EUGENIE, *The Forms of the Affects* (Durham, NC: Duke University Press, 2014)
BRONFEN, ELISABETH, 'Les Pouvoirs de l'insomnie', in *Louise Bourgeois: The Insomnia Drawings*, ed. by Marie-Laure Bernadec (Zurich: Daros Editions, 2000)
BROWN, BILL, 'Thing Theory', *Critical Inquiry*, 28.1 (Autumn 2001), 1–22
BROWN, WENDY, 'The Quarantine Files: Thinkers in Self-isolation', *The Los Angeles Review of Books* (14 April 2020) <https://lareviewofbooks.org/article/quarantine-files-thinkers-self-isolation/> [accessed 23 August 2020]
BRUNO, GIULIANA, *Atlas of Emotion: Journeys in Art, Architecture and Film* (London & New York: Verso, 2007)
——'Projection: On Akerman's Screen, from Cinema to the Art Gallery', in *Chantal Akerman: Too Far, too Close*, exhibition catalogue (Antwerp: Ludion, 2012), pp. 15–26
BUTLER, JUDITH, 'Collected and Fractured: Response to Identities', in *Identities*, ed. by Kwame Anthony Appiah and Henry Louis Gates Jr (Chicago: University of Chicago Press, 1995), pp. 441–42
——*Precarious Life: The Powers of Mourning and Violence* (London & New York: Verso, 2004)
——'Precarious Life, Vulnerability and the Ethics of Cohabitation', *Journal of Speculative Philosophy*, 26.2 (2012), 134–51 <http://www.ccs.unibe.ch/unibe/philhist/ccs/content/e6912/e220286/e259083/e364031/TextworkshopButler_ger.pdf> [accessed 9 November 2015]
BUTLER, JUDITH, and CATHERINE MALABOU, 'You Be My Body for Me: Body, Shape and

Plasticity in Hegel's Phenomenology of Spirit', in *A Companion to Hegel*, ed. by Stephen Houlgate and Michael Baur (Oxford: Blackwell, 2011), pp. 611–40

Calefato, Patrizia, *Luxury: Fashion, Lifestyle and Excess*, trans. by Lisa Adams (London: Bloomsbury, 2014)

Calle, Sophie, 'Le Carnet d'adresses', in *Doubles-jeux (Livre VI)* (Arles: Actes Sud, 1998)

——*Des histoires vraies* (Arles: Actes Sud, 2013)

——*Douleur exquise* (Arles: Actes Sud, 2003)

——*L'Hôtel* (Paris: Editions de l'Etoile, 1984)

——*M'as-tu-vue?* (Paris: Éditions du Centre Pompidou & Xavier Barral, 2005)

——*Prenez soin de vous* (Arles: Actes Sud, 2007)

——*Où et quand?* (Arles: Actes Sud, 2009)

——'Pour moi, un livre, c'est un objet qui parle avec une exposition,' *France Culture* podcast (11 September 2020) <https://www.franceculture.fr/emissions/par-les-temps-qui-courent/par-les-temps-qui-courent-emission-du-vendredi-11-septembre-2020> [accessed 26 October 2020]

——'People Think They Know Me. But They Know Nothing', *Financial Times*, 10 January 2020

——*The Sophie Calle Reader*, ed. by Iwona Blazwick (London: Whitechapel Gallery, 2009)

——'Suite vénitienne', in *A suivre (Livre IV)* (Arles: Actes Sud, 1998), pp. 37–110

Camart, Cécile, 'Sophie Calle, alias Sophie Calle: le jeu d'un narcisse éclaté', *Art Press*, hors série, 5 (April 2002), 30–35

Campbell, Andy, 'Straight Sense', *Reviews in Cultural Theory*, 5.2 (1 August 2014) <http://www.reviewsinculture.com/?r=139> [accessed 8 November 2015]

Campbell, Peter, 'At Tate Modern: Louise Bourgeois', *London Review of Books*, 29.23 (29 November 2007), 32

Capildeo, Vahni, '"I give Everything Away": A Parcel Containing Three (3) Sleeps (Customs & Resale Value Nil): Un cadeau pour Madame' <http://mollybloompoetry.weebly.com/vahnicapildeo.html> [accessed 20 February 2015]

Caravero, Adriana, *Inclinations: A Critique of Rectitude* (Stanford, CA: Stanford University Press, 2016)

Carson, Anne, *Decreation: Poetry, Essays, Opera* (New York: Vintage, 2006)

——'Foam (Essay with Rhapsody) on the Sublime in Longinus and Antonioni', *Conjunctions*, 37 (2001), 96–104

Cassin, Barbara (ed.), *Dictionary of Untranslatables: A Philosophical Lexicon*, trans. by Emily Apter, Jacques Lezra and Michael Wood (Oxford & Princeton, NJ: Princeton University Press, 2014)

Cheng, Anne, *Second Skin: Josephine Baker and the Modern Surface* (Oxford: Oxford University Press, 2011)

Chamarette, Jenny, '*Jeanne Dielman, 23, Quai du Commerce, 1080 Bruxelles*', *Senses of Cinema*, 67 (May 2013) <http://sensesofcinema.com/2013/cteq/jeanne-dielman-23-quai-du-commerce-1080-bruxelles/#5> [accessed 25 September 2015]

Charpentier, Isabelle, 'La Littérature est une arme de combat', interview with Annie Ernaux, in *Rencontres avec Pierre Bourdieu*, ed. by Gérard Mauger (Paris: Le Croquant, 2005)

——'Une intellectuelle déplacée: enjeux et usages sociaux et politiques de l'œuvre d'Annie Ernaux (1974–1998)' (unpublished PhD thesis, Université d'Amiens, 1999)

Cixous, Hélène, *La Jeune Née* (Paris: Union générale d'Éditions, 1975)

——*Le Rire de la méduse et autres ironies* (Paris: Galilée, 2010)

Cohen, Joshua, *Not Working: Why We Have to Stop* (London: Granta, 2019)

Colebrook, Claire, 'Modernism without Women: The Refusal of Becoming-woman and Post-feminism', *Deleuze Studies*, 7.4 (November 2013), 427–55

COMPAGNON, ANTOINE. 'Baudelaire moderne et antimoderne', lecture given as part of the Collège de France, 'Littérature française moderne et contemporaine: histoire, critique, théorie' series <https://www.college-de-france.fr/media/antoine-compagnon/UPL3221135538535161 25_R1112_Compagnon.pdf> [accessed 12 November 2015]

COTILLE-FOLEY, NORA, 'L'Usage de la photographie chez Annie Ernaux', *French Studies*, 62.4 (October 2008), 442–54

COXON, ANN, *Louise Bourgeois* (London: Tate Publishing, 2010)

CRARY, JONATHAN, *24/7: Late Capitalism and the Ends of Sleep* (London: Verso, 2013)

CROWLEY, MARTIN, *Duras, Writing and the Ethical: Making the Broken Whole* (Oxford: Clarendon Press, 2000)

CURIGER, BICE, 'Sophie Calle in Conversation' <https://sounds.bl.uk/Arts-literature-and-performance/ICA-talks/024M-C0095X0828XX-0100V0> [accessed 7 August 2020]

CUSK, RACHEL, 'Louise Bourgeois: Suites on Fabric', in *Coventry* (London: Faber & Faber, 2019), pp. 141–46

CVETKOVICH, ANN, *Depression: A Public Feeling* (Durham, NC, & London: Duke University Press, 2012)

DAY, LORAINE. *Writing Shame and Desire: The Work of Annie Ernaux* (Oxford: Peter Lang, 2007)

DÉCARIE, ISABELLE, 'Aimer souffrir: *Douleur exquise* de Sophie Calle', *Spirale: arts, lettres, sciences humaines*, 198 (2004), 34–35

DEJEAN, JOAN E., *The Essence of Style: How the French Invented High Fashion, Fine Food, Chic Cafés, Style, Sophistication, and Glamour* (New York: Simon & Schuster, 2005)

DE LAURETIS, TERESA, 'Aesthetics and Feminist Theory: Rethinking Women's Cinema', in *Female Spectators: Looking at Film and Television*, ed. by E. Deirdre Pribam (London: Verso, 1988), pp. 178–79

DELEUZE, GILLES, *Cinéma 1: L'Image-mouvement.* (Paris: Minuit, 1983)

—— *Cinéma 2: L'Image-temps* (Paris: Minuit, 1985)

—— *Cinema II: The Time Image*, trans. by Hugh Tomlinson and Robert Galeta (London: Bloomsbury, 2013)

—— *Le Pli* (Paris: Minuit, 1988)

DELEUZE, GILLES, and FÉLIX GUATTARI, *L'Anti-Œdipe* (Paris: Minuit, 1972)

—— *Mille plateaux* (Paris: Minuit, 1980)

—— *A Thousand Plateaus*, trans. by Brian Massumi (London: Continuum, 2004)

DELEUZE, GILLES, and CLAIRE PARNET, *Dialogues* (Paris: Flammarion, 1977)

—— *Dialogues*, trans. by Hugh Tomlinson and Barbara Habberjam (New York: Columbia University Press, 1987)

DERCON, CHRIS, 'An Interview with Chantal Akerman about too Much and not Enough Cinema', *Contour* (2005) <http://www.contour2005.be/UK/ca.htm> [accessed 15 October 2015]

DERRIDA, JACQUES, *De la grammatologie* (Paris: Minuit, 1967)

—— *Dissemination: la dissemination* (Paris: Seuil, 1972)

—— *Donner le temps: la fausse monnaie* (Paris: Galilée, 1991)

—— *Given Time: Counterfeit Money*, trans. by Peggy Kamuf (Chicago: University of Chicago Press, 1994)

—— 'De l'économie restreinte à l'économie générale: un hégélianisme sans réserve', in *L'Écriture et la différence* (Paris: Seuil, 1967), pp. 369–407

—— *Glas* (Paris: Galilée, 1974)

—— *La Vie la mort: Séminaire (1975–1976)*, ed. by Pascale-Anne Brault and Peggy Kamuf (Paris: Seuil, 2019)

DERRIDA, JACQUES, WITH SIMON HANTAI, *Le Toucher: Jean-Luc Nancy* (Paris: Galilée, 2000)

Dika, Vera, *The (Moving) Pictures Generation: The Cinematic Impulse in Downtown New York Art and Film* (New York: Palgrave Macmillan, 2012)

Dillon, Brian, 'History Lessons No 5: Take Care of Yourself', *Art Review* (June 2007) <https://artreview.com/history-lessons-7-april-2020-brian-dillon-sophie-calle-interview/> [accessed 9 August 2020]

Dubroux, Daniele, 'Le Familier inquietant', *Cahiers du Cinéma*, 265 (March-April 1976), 17–20

Edwards, Natalie, 'The Absent Body: Photography and Autobiography in Hélène Cixous's *Photos des racines* and Annie Ernaux and Marc Marie's *L'Usage de la photo*', in *Textual and Visual Selves: Photography, Film and Comic Art in French Autobiography*, ed. by Natalie Edwards, Amy L. Hubbell and Ann Miller (Lincoln & London: University of Nebraska Press, 2011)

——'Accumulation and Archives: Sophie Calle's *Prenez soin de vous*', *Studies in 20th and 21st Century Literature*, 38.2–3 (January 2014), Article 3 (unpaginated)

Elkin, Lauren, *Flâneuse: Women Walk the City in Paris, New York, Tokyo, Venice and London* (London: Vintage, 2017)

Ernaux, Annie, *Les Années* (Paris: Gallimard, 2008)

——*L'Atelier noir* (Paris: Busclat, 2011)

——'Bourdieu: le chagrin', *Le Monde*, 5 May 2002

——'*La Distinction*: œuvre totale et révolutionnaire', in *Pierre Bourdieu: l'insoumission au heritage*, ed. by Édouard Louis (Paris: PuF, 2016), pp. 27–54

——*Écrire la vie* (Paris: Gallimard/Quarto, 2011)

——'Entretien avec Raphaelle Rérolle', Centre Pompidou, 8 February 2010 <http://editionsdelabibliotheque.bpi.fr/resources/titles/84240100911590/extras/Entretien_Annie_Ernaux.pdf> [accessed 7 November 2015]

——*L'Événement* (Paris: Folio, 2000)

——*La Honte* (Paris: Gallimard, 1997)

——*Je ne suis pas sortie de ma nuit* (Paris: Folio, 1997)

——*Journal du dehors* (Paris: Folio, 1993)

——*L'Occupation* (Paris: Folio, 2002)

——*Passion simple* (Paris: Folio, 1994)

——*La Place* (Paris: Gallimard, 1983)

——'Raisons d'écrire', in *Le Symbolique et le social: la réception internationale de Pierre Bourdieu*, ed. by J. Dubois, P. Durand and Y. Winkin (Liège: Presses universitaires de Liège, 2005)

——*Regarde les lumières mon amour* (Paris: Broché, 2014)

——'Sachez, Monsieur le Président, que nous ne laisserons plus nous voler notre vie...' <https://www.franceinter.fr/emissions/lettres-d-interieur/lettres-d-interieur-30-mars-2020> [accessed 15 August 2020]

——*Se perdre* [2001], in *Écrire la vie* (Paris: Gallimard/Quarto, 2011), pp. 697–876

——'Vers un je "transpersonnel" ', *RITM*, 6 (1993), 219–22

——*La Vie extérieure: (1993–1999)* (Paris: Folio, 2000)

——*Le Vrai Lieu: entretiens avec Michelle Porte* (Paris: Gallimard, 2014)

——*L'Écriture comme un couteau: entretien avec Frédéric-Yves Jeannet* (Paris: Folio, 2003)

Ernaux, Annie, and Marc Marie, *L'Usage de la photo* (Paris: Gallimard, 2005)

Fabre, Clarisse, 'Coronavirus: l'été meurtier du cinéma français', *Le Monde*, 6 August 2020 <https://www.lemonde.fr/culture/article/2020/08/06/coronavirus-l-ete-meurtrier-du-cinema-francais_6048265_3246.html> [accessed 23 August 2020]

Felski, Rita, 'Object Relations', *Contemporary Women's Writing*, 1.1–2 (December 2007), 185–91

Fer, Bryony, 'Objects beyond Objecthood', *Louise Bourgeois*, special issue of *Oxford Art Journal*, 22.2 (1999), 27–36

——*The Infinite Line: Re-making Art after Modernism* (New Haven, CT: Yale University Press, 2004)

FERGUSON, SAM, *Diaries Real and Fictional in Twentieth-century French Writing* (Oxford: Oxford University Press, 2018)

FISCHER, B. K., 'Shake Forth a Nest: Feminist Ekphrasis and the Example of Louise Bourgeois', *Los Angeles Review of Books*, 9 August 2014 <https://lareviewofbooks.org/essay/feminist-ekphrasis-example-louise-bourgeois> [accessed 8 November 2015]

FISHER, ANNA WATKINS, 'Manic Impositions: The Parasitical Art of Chris Kraus and Sophie Calle', *Women's Studies Quarterly*, 40.1–2 (Spring-Summer 2012), 223–35

FISHER, MARK, *Capitalist Realism: Is There No Alternative?* (London: Zero Books, 2009)

FISKE, COURTNEY, 'Louise Bourgeois: The Return of the Repressed', *Brooklyn Rail* (September 2012) <https://brooklynrail.org/2012/09/art_books/louise-bourgeois-the-return-of-the-repressed> [accessed 26 August 2020]

FLESCH, WILLIAM, 'Extravagance', *Oxford Literary Review*, 42.1 (2020), 52–75 <https://doi-org.ezp.lib.cam.ac.uk/10.3366/olr.2020.0293> [accessed 13 August 2020]

FLITTERMAN-LEWIS, SANDY, 'What's behind her Smile? Subjectivity and Desire in Germaine Dulac's *The Smiling Madame Beudet* and Chantal Akerman's *Jeanne Dielman, 23 Quai du Commerce, 1080 Bruxelles*', in *Identity and Memory: The Films of Chantal Akerman*, ed. by Gwendolyn Audrey (Carbondale: Southern Illinois University Press, 2003), pp. 27–40

FOUCAULT, MICHEL, *Histoire de la sexualité, tome 3: Le Souci de soi* (Paris: Gallimard, 1994)

——'Sade: Sergeant of Sex', in *Foucault Live: Collected Interviews, 1961–1984*, ed. by Sylvère Lottringer, trans. by Lysa Hochroth and John Johnston (Los Angeles: Semiotext(e),1996), pp. 186–87

——'Une esthétique de l'existence,' interview with A. Fontana, *Le Monde,* 15 July 1984, p. XI

FRANÇOIS, ANNE-LISE, *Open Secrets: The Literature of Uncounted Experience* (Stanford, CA: Stanford University Press, 2008)

FREUD, SIGMUND, 'Mourning and Melancholia', in *The Standard Edition of The Complete Psychological Works of Sigmund Freud, Volume XIV (1914–1916)*, ed. by Alix Strachey and Alan Tyson (London: Vintage, 1999), pp. 243–59

FRIEDBERG, ANNE, *Window Shopping: Cinema and the Postmodern* (Berkeley: University of California Press, 1994)

GALT, ROSALIND, *Pretty: Film and the Decorative Image* (New York: Columbia University Press, 2011)

GILLARD, BRYONY, and LOUIS HARTNOLL, 'Seeing Horizontally: Babette Mangolte Interviewed by Bryony Gillard and Louis Hartnoll', *The Moving Image Review & Art Journal*, 8.1–2 (1 September 2019), 138–47

GIRISH, DEVIKA, 'Letter to an Unknown Decade', *Film Comment* (January-February 2020) <https://www.filmcomment.com/article/letter-to-an-unknown-decade/> [accessed 18 February 2020]

GORFINKEL, ELENA, 'Against Lists', *Another Gaze* (9 December 2019) <https://www.anothergaze.com/elena-gorfinkel-manifesto-against-lists/> [accessed 18 February 2020]

——'Attachment Road: No Sex Last Night and American Honey', in *America: Films from Elsewhere*, ed. by Shanay Jhaveri (Mumbai: Shoestring Press, 2019), pp. 467–93

——'At the End of Cinema, This Thing Called Film', *Lola Journal*, 1 (January 2011) <http://www.lolajournal.com/1/end_of_cinema.html> [accessed 13 November 2015]

——'Wanda, Loden, Lodestone' (London: Institute for Contemporary Art London, May 2018) <https://kclpure.kcl.ac.uk/portal/files/96107025/ICA_Wanda_Loden_lodestone_v2.pdf> [accessed 24 August 2020]

——'*Wanda*'s Slowness: Enduring Insignificance', in *On Women's Films: Across Worlds and Generations*, ed. by Ivone Margulies and Jeremi Szaniawksi (London: Bloomsbury Academic, 2019), pp. 27–48

——'Weariness, Waiting: Enduration and Art Cinema's Tired Bodies', *Discourse*, 34.2–3 (Spring-Fall 2012), 311–47

Gornick, Vivian, *The End of the Novel of Love* [1998] (New York: Picador, 2020)

—— *The Situation and the Story* (New York: Macmillan, 2002)

Gorz, André, *The Immaterial* (Chicago: University of Chicago Press, 2010)

Goyer, Nicolas, and Walter Moser (eds), *Resurgences baroques: les trajectoires d'un parcours transculturel* (Brussels: La Lettre volée, 2001)

Gratton, Johnnie, 'Sophie Calle's True Stories: More of the Same?' *Paragraph*, 26.3 (2003), 108–22

——'Illustration Revisited: Phototextual Exchange and Resistance in Sophie Calle's *Suite vénitienne*', in *Textual and Visual Selves: Photography, Film, and Comic Art in French Autobiography*, ed. by Natalie Edwards, Amy L. Hubbel and Ann Miller (Lincoln & London: University of Nebraska Press, 2011), pp. 139–67

Guerrin, Michel, 'Sophie Calle, fétichiste de sa propre vie', *Le Monde*, 11 September 2008

Guibert, Hervé, *Written in Invisible Ink: Selected Stories*, trans. by Jeffrey Zuckerman (Los Angeles: Semiotext(e), 2020)

Halberstam, Jack, *In a Queer Time and Place: Transgender Bodies, Subcultural Lives* (New York & London: New York University Press, 2005)

Hardt, Michael, 'Affective Labor', *boundary:2*, 26.2 (Summer 1999), 89–101

Hartman, Saidiya, 'Extended Notes on the Riot', *e-flux*, 105 (December 2019) <https://www.e-flux.com/journal/105/302565/extended-notes-on-the-riot/> [accessed 25 August 2020]

—— *Wayward Lives, Beautiful Experiments: Intimate Histories of Riotous Black Girls, Troublesome Women and Queer Radicals* (New York: Serpent's Tail, 2019)

Harvey, David, 'The Body as an Accumulation Strategy', *Society and Space*, 16 (1998), 401–21

Harvey, Samantha, *The Shapeless Unease* (London: Jonathan Cape, 2020)

Havercroft, Barbara, 'Dire l'indicible: trauma et honte chez Annie Ernaux', *Roman 20–50*, 40 (December 2005), 119–31

Herkenhoff, Paulo, 'Interview: Paulo Herkenhoff in conversation with Louise Bourgeois, transcribed and edited by Thyrza Nichols Goodeve', in *Louise Bourgeois*, ed. by Robert Storr, Paulo Herkenhoff and Allan Schwartman (London: Phaidon, 2003), pp. 6–25

Hogg, Joanna, and Adam Roberts, 'Chantal Akerman: Extraordinary Artist of the Everyday', *Guardian*, 8 October 2015

Hornstein, Shelley, 'Ornament, Boundaries and Mourning After Auschwitz', in *Reading Charlotte Saloman*, ed. by Michael P. Steinberg and Monica Bohm-Duchen (Ithaca, NY: Cornell University Press, 2006), pp. 126–40

Hustvedt, Siri, *A Woman Looking at Men Looking at Women* (New York: Simon & Schuster, 2016)

Indiana, Gary, 'On the Psychoanalytic Writings of Louise Bourgeois', *Ursula*, 4 (Fall 2019) <https://www.hauserwirth.com/magazine/25821-gary-indiana-psychoanalytic-writings-louise-bourgeois> [accessed 23 June 2020]

Irigaray, Luce, *Ce sexe qui n'en est pas un* (Paris: Minuit, 1977)

Jackson, Anna, *Diary Poetics: Form and Style in Writers' Diaries, 1915–1962* (London: Routledge, 2010)

Jacobs, Steven, 'Semiotics of the Living Room: Domestic Interiors in Chantal Akerman's Cinema', in *Chantal Akerman: Too Far, Too Close*, exhibition catalogue (Antwerp: Ludion, 2012), pp. 73–87

JAMES, IAN, *The Fragmentary Demand: An Introduction to the Philosophy of Jean-Luc Nancy* (Stanford, CA: Stanford University Press, 2005)

—— *The New French Philosophy* (Cambridge: Polity, 2012)

JAMES, ROBIN, *Resilience and Melancholy* (London: Zero Books, 2015)

JAMSHAID, ZAIN, '"Invested in Expression or in Its Destruction?" The Politics of Space and Representation in Chantal Akerman's Cinema', *Senses of Cinema*, 64 (September 2012) <http://sensesofcinema.com/2012/feature-articles/invested-in-expression-or-in-its-destruction-the-politics-of-space-and-representation-in-chantal-akermans-cinema/> [accessed 25 September 2015]

JARDINE, ALICE, 'Woman in Limbo: Deleuze and his Br(others)', *SubStance*, 13.3–4 (1984), 46–60

JOHNSON, SAMUEL, *The Fatal Effects of Luxury and Indolence* (London: J. Bradley, 1778)

JOHNSTON, CLAIRE, 'Towards a Feminist Film Practice: Some Theses', in *Movies and Methods Volume II*, ed. by Bill Nichols (Berkeley: University of California Press, 1985), pp. 315–27

JORDAN, SHIRLEY, 'Exhibiting Pain: Sophie Calle's *Douleur exquise*', *French Studies*, 61.2 (2007), 196–208

—— 'Performance in Sophie Calle's *Prenez soin de vous*', *French Cultural Studies*, 24.3 (2013), 249–63

KAWAKAMI, AKANE, *Photobiography: Photographic Self-writing in Proust, Guibert, Ernaux, Mace* (Oxford: Legenda, 2013)

KEMP, ANNA, 'Selling Yourself: The Commercialisation of Feeling in the Work of Sophie Calle', *Nottingham French* Studies, 52.3 (December 2013), 308–21

KEMP, SIMON, 'Contamination Anxiety in Annie Ernaux's Twenty-first-century Texts', in *Women's Writing in Twenty-first-century France: Life as Literature*, ed. by Amaleena Damlé and Gill Rye (Cardiff: University of Wales Press, 2013), pp. 168–79

KHALFA, JEAN (ed.), *The Dialogue Between Painting and Poetry: livres d'artistes, 1874–1999* (Cambridge: Black Apollo Press, 2001)

KINDER, MARSHA, 'Reflections on "Jeanne Dielman"', *Film Quarterly*, 30.4 (Summer 1977), 2–8

KINSMAN, R. PATRICK, 'She's Come Undone: Chantal Akerman's *Jeanne Dielman, 23 Quai du Commerce, 1080 Bruxelles* (1975) and Countercinema', *Quarterly Review of Film and Video*, 24 (2007), 217–24

KOEPNICK, LUTZ, *The Long Take: Art Cinema and the Wondrous* (Minneapolis: University of Minnesota Press, 2017)

KOESTENBAUM, WAYNE, *Figure It Out* (New York: Soft Skull Press, 2020)

—— *My 1980s & Other Essays* (London & New York: Farrar, Strass & Giroux, 2013)

KOIS, DAN, 'Eating Your Cultural Vegetables', *New York Times*, 29 April 2011 <https://www.nytimes.com/2011/05/01/magazine/mag-01Riff-t.html> [accessed 23 August 2020]

KOWALESKI-WALLACE, ELIZABETH, *Consuming Subjects: Women, Shopping and Business in the Eighteenth Century* (New York: Columbia University Press, 1997)

KRAUS, CHRIS, *Aliens and Anorexia* (Los Angeles: Semiotext(e), 2000)

—— *I Love Dick* (Los Angeles: Semiotext(e), 2002)

KRAUSS, ROSALIND E., *Bachelors* (Cambridge, MA: MIT Press (October Books), 2000)

KRISTEVA, JULIA, *Black Sun: Depression and Melancholia* (New York: Columbia University Press, 1989)

—— *Pouvoirs de l'horreur: essai sur l'abjection* (Paris: Seuil, 1980)

—— *Powers of Horror: An Essay on Abjection*, trans. by Leon S. Roudiez (New York: Columbia University Press, 1982)

—— 'Women's Time', in *The Kristeva Reader*, ed. by Toril Moi (New York: Columbia University Press, 1986), pp. 187–213

KUSPIT, DONALD, *Louise Bourgeois* (New York: Random House, 1988)

LACORE-MARTIN, EMMANUELLE, 'Le Cerceau de papier: mémoire, écriture et circularité dans *Passion simple* et *Se perdre* d'Annie Ernaux', *French Forum*, 33.1–2 (Winter-Spring 2008), 179–93

LARRATT-SMITH, PHILLIP, 'The Volcanic Unconsciousness: Ten Dreams of Louise Bourgeois', *Psychoanalytic Review*, 105.6 (December 2018), 639–56

LARRATT-SMITH, PHILLIP (ed.), *Petite maman* (Mexico City: Instituto Nacional de Bellas Artes, 2014)

LARRATT-SMITH, PHILLIP, and FRANCES MORRIS (eds), *Has the Day Invaded the Night or the Night Invaded the Day? Insomnia in the Work of Louise Bourgeois* (Edinburgh: Fruit Market Gallery Press, 2014)

LAUGIER, SANDRA, 'POLITIQUES DU CARE', *Multitudes*, 2.38 (Autumn 2009), 74–75

LAUWAERT, DIRK, '23, quai du Commerce, Brussels: On Chantal Akerman', *Sabizian* (February 2019) <https://sabzian.be/article/23-quai-du-commerce-brussels> [accessed 23 August]

LAZZARATO, MAURIZIO, *The Making of the Indebted Man* (Los Angeles: Semiotext(e), 2012)

——*Marcel Duchamp and the Refusal of Work* (New York: Semiotext(e), 2014)

LEBOVICI, ÉLISABETH, 'No Idolatry and Losing Everything that Made You a Slave: Interview with Chantal Akerman', *Mousse*, 31 (November 2011)

LEBOW, ALISA, 'Identity Slips: The Autobiographical Register in the Work of Chantal Akerman', *Film Quarterly*, 70.1 (Fall 2016), 54–60

LEHMAN, BORIS, 'Non-éloge (aujourd'hui je dirais)', *Sabzian* (September 2019) <https://sabzian.be/text/non-%C3%A9loge-aujourd%E2%80%99hui-je-dirais> [accessed 24 August 2020]

LEHRER-GRAIWER, SARAH, 'Optical Drive: Sarah Lehrer-Graiwer talks with Laura Owens', *Artforum* (March 2013), 231–39

LEMIEUX, CATHERINE, 'Mélancolie et restitutions dans *Douleur Exquise* de Sophie Calle', *Deuils sans fin dans la littérature contemporaine*, ed. by Mathilde Branthomme, special issue of *Post-scriptum*, 14 (July 2011) <http://post-scriptum.org/melancolie-et-restitutions-dans-douleur> [accessed 9 November 2015]

LINDNER, KATHARINA, 'Queer-ing Texture: Tactility, Spatiality, and Kinesthetic Empathy in *She Monkeys*', *Camera Obscura*, 32.3.96 (2017), 121–54

LIPOVETSKY, GILLES, and ELYETTE ROUX, *Le Luxe éternel: de l'âge du sacré au temps des marques* (Paris: Gallimard, 2003)

LIPPARD, LUCY R., 'Eros Presumptive', *The Hudson Review*, 20.1 (Spring 1967), 91–99

——'Louise Bourgeois: From the Inside Out', *Artforum*, 13 (March 1975), 26–33

LIN, LANA, *Freud's Jaw and Other Lost Objects: Fractured Subjectivity in the Face of Cancer* (New York: Fordham University Press, 2017)

LOADER, JAYNE, 'Jeanne Dielman: Death in Installments', *Jump Cut*, 16 (1977), 10–12

LODGE, GUY, 'How the Coronavirus Hit Cinema', *Sight & Sound* <https://www2.bfi.org.uk/news-opinion/sight-sound-magazine/comment/cinema-impact-coronavirus> [accessed 23 August 2020]

LONGFELLOW, BRENDA, 'Love Letters to the Mother: The Works of Chantal Akerman', *Canadian Journal of Political and Social Theory*, 13.1–2 (1989), 73–90

LORDE, AUDRE, *A Burst of Light: Essays* (London: Sheba, 1988)

LOUIS, ÉDOUARD (ed.), *Pierre Bourdieu: l'insoumission au héritage* (Paris: PuF, 2016)

LOWE, SARAH M., *The Diary of Frida Kahlo: An Intimate Self-portrait* (New York: Abrams, 2006)

MACEY, DAVID, *The Lives of Michel Foucault* (London: Verso Books, 2019)

MAHON, ALYCE, *Eroticism and Art* (Oxford: Oxford University Press, 2005)

MALLON, THOMAS, *A Book of Their Own: People and their Diaries* (London: Picador Books, 1984)

MARGULIES, IVONE, 'A Matter of Time: *Jeanne Dielman, 23, quai du Commerce, 1080 Bruxelles*', *Current: Criterion Collection* blog (August 2009) <https://www.criterion.com/current/posts/1215-a-matter-of-time-jeanne-dielman-23-quai-du-commerce-1080-bruxelles> [accessed 6 November 2015]

—— *Nothing Happens: Chantal Akerman's Hyperrealist Everyday* (Durham, NC: Duke University Press, 1996)

MARIN, CLAIRE, *Ruptures* (Paris: L'Observatoire, 2019)

MARKS, LAURA U., *The Skin of the Film: Intercultural Cinema, Embodiment, and the Senses* (Durham, NC: Duke University Press, 1999)

—— 'Thinking Multisensory Culture', *Cinema and the Senses*, ed. by Emma Wilson, special issue of *Paragraph*, 31.2 (July 2008), 123–37

—— *Touch: Sensuous Theory and Multisensory Media* (Minneapolis: University of Minnesota Press, 2002)

MARTIN, ADRIAN, 'A Theory of Agitation, or, Getting Off in the Cinema', *Continuum: Journal of Media & Cultural Studies*, 26.4 (2012), 519–28

MAUSS, MARCEL, *Essai sur le don* (Paris: Seuil, 1925)

MAVOR, CAROL, 'Moeder, Maman, Mom', in *Chantal Åkerman: Afterlives*, ed. by Marion Schmid and Emma Wilson, Moving Image, 9 (Cambridge: Legenda, 2019), pp. 26–41

—— *Reading Boyishly: Roland Barthes, J. M. Barrie, Jacques Henri Lartigue, Marcel Proust, and D. W. Winnicott* (Durham, NC: Duke University Press, 2008)

MAYNE, JUDITH, *The Woman at the Keyhole: Feminism and Women's Cinema* (Bloomington: Indiana University Press, 1990)

MCBANE, BARBARA, 'Walking, Talking, Singing, Exploding... and Silence: Chantal Akerman's Soundtracks', *Film Quarterly*, 70.1 (Fall 2016) <https://filmquarterly.org/2016/09/16/walking-talking-singing-exploding/> [accessed 24 August 2020]

MCDONALD, CHRISTIE V., and JACQUES DERRIDA, 'Interview: Choreographies', *Cherchez la femme: Feminist Critique/Feminine Text, Diacritics*, 12.2 (Summer 1982), 66–76

MCEVILLEY, THOMAS, *Sculpture in the Age of Doubt* (New York: Allworth Press, 1999)

MCGOWAN, TODD, *Out of Time: Desire in Atemporal Cinema* (Minneapolis: University of Minnesota Press, 2011)

MCGRATH, MERCEDES, 'Lesbian Gestures in the Cinema of Chantal Akerman' (unpublished MPhil thesis, University of Cambridge, June 2019)

MCILVANNEY, SIOBHAN, *Annie Ernaux: The Return to Origins* (Liverpool: Liverpool University Press, 2001)

MCFADDEN, CYBELLE, *Gendered Frames, Embodied Cameras: Varda, Akerman, Cabrera, Calle, and Maïwenn* (Lanham, MD: Rowman & Littlefield, 2014)

MCMAHON, LAURA, 'Animal Worlds: Film, Philosophy and Time', talk given at the University of Cambridge, 30 October 2019

—— 'Touching Intact: Sophie Calle's Threat to Privacy', in *Threat: Essays in French Literature, Thought and Visual Culture*, ed. by Georgina Evans and Adam Kay (Oxford: Peter Lang, 2010), pp. 69–81

MCROBBIE, ANGELA, 'Reflections on Feminism and Immaterial Labor', *New Formations*, 70 (2010), 60–76

MEADS, KAT, *2.12 AM: Essays* (Nacogdoches, TX: Stephen F. Austin State University Press, 2013)

MERLEAU-PONTY, MAURICE, *The Phenomenology of Perception*, trans. by Colin Smith (London: Routledge, 1962)

MILLER, NICOLE, 'Following Sophie Calle', *Hyperallergic* <https://hyperallergic.com/305869/following-sophie-calle/> [accessed 7 August 2020]

Mitchell, Kaye, *Writing Shame: Contemporary Literature, Gender and Negative Affect* (Edinburgh: Edinburgh University Press, 2020)

Moi, Toril, *Sexual/Textual Politics* (London: Routledge, 2002)

Momcilovic, Jérôme, *Chantal Akerman: Dieu se reposa, mais pas nous* (Paris: Capricci, 2018)

Morgan, Frances, 'Afterword,' in Chantal Akerman, *My Mother Laughs*, trans. by Daniella Shreir (London: Silver Press, 2019), pp. 191–203

Morris, Frances (ed.), *Louise Bourgeois* (London: Tate Publishing, 2007)

Moulier-Boutang, Yann, *Cognitive Capitalism* (Cambridge: Polity, 2012)

Mulvey, Laura, *Afterimages: On Women, Cinema and Changing Times* (London: Reaktion Books, 2019)

——*Death 24x a Second: Stillness and the Moving Image* (London: Reaktion Books, 2006)

——'Visual Pleasure and Narrative Cinema', *Screen*, 16.3 (Autumn 1975), 6–18

Murray, Raymond, *Images in the Dark: An Encyclopedia of Gay and Lesbian Film and Video* (New York: Titan Books, 1998)

Murray, Ros, 'The Radical Politics of Possibility: Towards a Queer Existential Phenomenology through Chantal Akerman's *Je, tu, il, elle*', *feral feminisms*, 5 (Spring 2016) <https://feralfeminisms.com/radical-politics-of-possibility/> [accessed 17 September 2020]

——'Revisiting Jeanne Dielman: *Autour de Jeanne Dielman* (2004), *Woman Sitting After Killing* (2001) and Akerman's "cinéma de ressassement"', *The Moving Image Review & Art Journal* (MIRAJ), 8.1–2 (1 September 2019), 54–66

Myles, Eileen, 'Introduction', in Chantal Akerman, *My Mother Laughs*, trans. by Daniella Shrier (London: Silver Press, 2019), pp. i–vi

Nancy, Jean-Luc, *L'Adoration* (ïris: Galilée, 2010)

——*À l'écoute* (Paris: Galilée, 2002)

——'The Body of Pleasure', trans. by Anne O'Byrne, in *Corpus II: Writings on Sexuality*, trans. by Anne O'Byrne (New York: Fordham University Press, 2013)

——*La Communauté désœvrée* (Paris: Christian Bourgeois, 1986)

——*The Inoperative Community*, trans. by Peter Connor (Minneapolis: Minnesota University Press, 1991)

——*Être singulier pluriel* (Paris: Galilée, 1996)

——'L'Excrit', in *Une pensée finie* (Paris: Galilee, 1990), pp. 55–64

——'Exscription', trans. by Katherine Lydon, *Yale French Studies*, 78 (1990), 47–65

——'Icône de l'acharnement', *Trafic*, 39 (Autumn 2001), 58–64

——'Il y a du rapport sexuel — et après', *Littérature*, 142.2 (2006), 30–40

——*La Naissance des seins* (Paris: Galilée, 2006)

——'L'Offrande sublime', in *Du sublime*, ed. by Jean-François Courtine (Paris: Belin, 2009), pp. 62–95

——*Le Partage des voix* (Paris: Galilée, 1982)

——*Le Plaisir au dessin* (Paris: Galilée, 2009)

——*The Pleasure in Drawing*, trans. by Phillip Armstrong (Oxford: Oxford University Press, 2013)

——'La Politique doit montrer ce qui la dépasse', *Le Monde*, 12 April 2012 <https://www.lemonde.fr/idees/article/2012/04/12/la-politique-doit-montrer-ce-qui-la-depasse_1684455_3232.html> [accessed 23 August 2020]

——*Sexistence* (Paris: Galilée, 2017)

——'Sexistence', trans. by Irving Goh, *diacritics*, 43.4 (2016), 110–18

——*Tombe de sommeil* (Paris: Galilée, 2007)

Nancy, Jean-Luc, and Aurélien Barrau, *Dans quels mondes vivons-nous?* (Paris: Galilée, 2011)

Nancy, Jean-Luc, and Abbas Kiarostami, *L'Évidence du film* (Brussels: Yves Gevaert, 2001)

Nelson, Maggie, *The Art of Cruelty: A Reckoning* (New York & London: W. W. Norton, 2011)

Nelson, Saul F., '"I Was not a Surrealist. I Was an Existentialist": Louise Bourgeois Reconsidered', *Oxford Art Journal*, 40.3 (December 2017), 469–90

Neri, Louise, 'Sophie Calle', *Interview* (24 March, 2009) <http://www.interviewmagazine.com/art/sophie-calle> [accessed 9 November 2015]

Nigianni, Chrysanthi, 'Butterfly Kiss: The Contagious Kiss of Becoming-Lesbian', in *Deleuze and Queer Theory*, ed. by Chrysanthi Nigianni and Merl Storr (Edinburgh: Edinburgh University Press, 2012), pp. 168–83

—— 'Chantal Akerman's *La-bàs:* The Suspended Image and the Politics of Anti-messianism', *Senses of Cinema*, 67 (July 2013) <http://sensesofcinema.com/2013/feature-articles/chantal-akermans-la-bas-the-suspended-image-and-the-politics-of-anti-messianism/> [accessed 25 September 2015]

Nixon, Mignon, 'Bad Enough Mother', in *October: The Second Decade, 1986–1996, Volume 76*, ed. by Rosalind E. Krauss (Cambridge, MA: MIT Press, 1997), pp. 156–99

—— *Fantastic Reality: Louise Bourgeois and a Story of Modern Art* (Cambridge, MA: MIT Press, 2005)

Nixon, Rob, *Slow Violence and the Environmentalism of the Poor* (Cambridge, MA: Harvard University Press, 2011)

Nochlin, Linda, 'Don't You cut your Lunch up when You're Ready to eat it?', *London Review of Books*, 24.7 (4 April 2002), 12–13

Obrist, Hans Ulrich, *Ways of Curating* (London: Penguin, 2015)

Olds, Sharon, *Arias* (London: Jonathan Cape, 2019)

—— *Stag's Leap* (London: Random House, 2012)

Orange, Michelle, 'Femme vérité: The Films of Chantal Akerman', *Virginia Quarterly Review* (Spring 2016) <https://www.vqronline.org/tv-film-criticism/2016/03/femme-verit%C3%A9> [accessed 24 August 2020]

Parker, Roszika, *The Subversive Stitch: Embroidery and the Making of the Feminine* (London: I. B. Tauris, 1984)

Patterson, Patricia, and Manny Farber, 'Kitchen without Kitsch', *Film Comment* (November-December 1977) <https://akephale.com/2016/06/20/kitchen-without-kitsch/> [accessed 20 March 2020]

Paulin, Tom, 'Writing to the Moment', in *Writing to the Moment: Selected Critical Essays, 1980–1986* (London: Faber & Faber, 1996)

Perec, Georges, *Les Choses: une histoire des années soixante* (Paris: Julliard, 1965)

Phelan, Penny, 'Survey', in *Art and Feminism*, ed. by Helena Reckitt (London & New York: Phaidon, 2006), pp. 14–49

Pietz, William, 'The Problem of the Fetish', *Res*, 9.1 (Spring 1985), 5–17

Pincus, Robert L., 'Sophie Calle: The Prying Eye', *Art in America* (October 1989), 192–97

Pollock, Griselda, *After-affects /After-images: Trauma and Aesthetic Transformation in the Virtual Feminist Museum* (Manchester: Manchester University Press, 2013)

—— 'The Long Journey: Maternal Trauma, Tears and Kisses in a Work by Chantal Akerman', *Studies in the Maternal*, 2.1 (2010), 1–32

Potts, Alex, 'Louise Bourgeois: Sculptural Confrontations', *Louise Bourgeois*, special issue of *Oxford Art Journal*, 22.2 (1999), 39–53

Preciado, Paul B., 'Learning from the Virus', *Artforum* (May-June 2020) <https://www.artforum.com/print/202005/paul-b-preciado-82823> [accessed 23 August 2020]

Princenthal, Nancy, 'Louise Bourgeois: The Insomnia Drawings', *Art on Paper*, 6.2 (November-December 2001), 98–99

Rales, Emily Wei (ed.), *Louise Bourgeois: To Unravel a Torment* (Potomac, MD: Glenstone Museum, 2018)

Rennebohm, Kate, 'La Ressasseuse: Chantal Akerman, 1950–2015', *Cinema Scope*, 64 (2015) <https://cinema-scope.com/columns/deaths-of-cinema/> [accessed 24 August 2020]

Resmini, Mauro, 'Reframing the New French Extremity: Cinema, Theory, Mediation', *Camera Obscura*, 30.3.90 (2015), 161–87

Rhodes, John David, 'Art Cinema's Immaterial Labors', *Diacritics*, 46.4 (2018), 96–116

—— 'Belabored: Style as Work', *Framework*, 53.1 (2012), 189–96

Rich, B. Ruby, 'Chantal Akerman Interview, Chicago: 1976/2016', *Film Quarterly*, 70.1 (Fall 2016), 16–24

—— 'Designing Desire: Chantal Akerman (1983)', in *Chick Flicks: Theories and Memories of the Feminist Film Movement* (Durham, NC: Duke University Press, 1998), pp. 169–207

Roberts, Adam, 'Preparing to See *Jeanne Dielman*', *ICA Bulletin* <https://archive.ica.art/bulletin/preparing-see-jeanne-dielman> [accessed 24 August 2020]

Robertson, Lisa, *The Baudelaire Fractal* (Toronto: Coach House Books, 2020)

—— *Cinema of the Present* (Toronto: Coach House Books, 2014)

—— *Nilling: On Noise, Pornography, The Codex, Melancholy, Lucretius, Folds, Cities, and Related Aporias* (Toronto: Bookthug Press, 2012)

—— 'Rose: A Carnal Becoming', *Cabinet Magazine*, 48 (Winter 2012–13) <http://www.cabinetmagazine.org/issues/48/robertson.php> [accessed 23 August 2020]

Romney, Jonathan, 'Double Exposure', *Guardian*, 19 March 1999

Ronell, Avital, 'Interview', in *Angry Women*, ed. by Andrea Juno and V. Vale (New York: Juno Books, 1991)

Ross, Kristin, *Communal Luxury: The Political Imaginary of the Paris Commune* (New York & London: Verso, 2015)

Sade, Donatien Alphonse François, marquis de, *Œuvres complètes*, ed. by Michel Delon, 3 vols (Paris: Gallimard/Pléiade, 1990–98)

Sartre, Jean-Paul, *La Nausée* (Paris: Gallimard, 1938)

Sauvageot, Anne, *Sophie Calle: l'art caméléon* (Paris: Presses universitaires de France, 2007)

Scanlan, Kathryn, 'There is the Sound, too, of a Ticking Clock: A Time-based Reading of Anne Charlotte Robertson's "Five Year Diary"', *Another Gaze* (10 August 2020) <https://www.anothergaze.com/sound-ticking-clock-time-based-reading-anne-charlotte-robertsons-five-year-diary/> [accessed 15 August 2020]

Schiller, Britt-Marie, 'Hair, Threads, and Umbilical Cords: Louise Bourgeois's Dream of Connection', *Psychoanalytic Review*, 105.6 (December 2018), 657–73

Schmid, Marion, *Chantal Akerman* (Manchester: Manchester University Press, 2010)

Schmid, Marion, and Emma Wilson (eds), *Chantal Akerman: Afterlives*, Moving Image, 9 (Cambridge: Legenda, 2019)

Schoonover, Karl, 'Wastrels of Time: Slow Cinema's Laboring Body, the Political Spectator, and the Queer', *Framework*, 53.1 (2012), 65–78

Schor, Naomi, *Bad Objects: Essays Popular and Unpopular* (Durham, NC: Duke University Press, 1989)

—— *Reading in Detail: Aesthetics and the Feminine* (London: Routledge, 2013)

Schwartz, Madeleine, 'A Memoirist who Mistrusts her Own Memories', *New Yorker*, 20 April 2020

Schwultz, Mary Hamel, 'Louise Bourgeois: The Insomnia Drawings: Review', *Library Journal*, 126.13 (August 2001), 96

Shambu, Girish, 'For a New Cinephilia', *Film Quarterly*, 72.3 (Spring 2019), 32–34

Shaviro, Steven, *Post-cinematic Affect* (London: Zero Books, 2010)

Sheringham, Michael, *Everyday Life: Theories and Practices from Surrealism to the Present* (Oxford: Oxford University Press, 2006)

SHRIER, DANIELLA, 'Another Gaze: Feminist Filmmaking and the Work of Chantal Akerman', *Suite 212* podcast <https://podcasts.apple.com/ie/podcast/another-gaze-feminist-filmmaking-work-chantal-akerman/id1366889715?i=1000436833971> [accessed 24 August 2020]

SILLMAN, AMY, 'Ab-Ex and Disco Balls: In Defense of Abstract Expressionism II', in *Artforum* (Summer 2011) <https://www.artforum.com/print/201106/ab-ex-and-disco-balls-in-defense-of-abstract-expressionism-ii-28354> [accessed 23 June 2020]

SOBCHACK, VIVIAN, *Carnal Thoughts: Embodiment and Moving Image Culture* (Berkeley: University of California Press, 2004)

SONTAG, SUSAN, 'The Decay of Cinema', *The New York Times*, 25 February 1996 <http://movies2.nytimes.com/books/00/03/12/specials/sontag-cinema.html> [accessed 17 February 2020]

—— *Regarding the Pain of Others* (New York & London: Penguin, 2003)

STEWART, KATHLEEN, *Ordinary Affects* (Durham, NC: Duke University Press, 2007)

STEWART, SUSAN, *On Longing: Narratives of the Miniature, the Gigantic, the Souvenir, the Collection* (Durham, NC, & London: Duke University Press, 1993)

STIEGLER, BERNARD, *Ce qui fait que la vie vaut la peine d'être vécue: de la pharmacologie* (Paris: Flammarion, 2010)

STOKES, EMILY, 'My Own World: A New Book Illuminates Louise Bourgeois' Relationship to Psychoanalysis', *Frieze* (October 2012) <https://frieze.com/article/my-own-world> [accessed 19 June 2020]

STORR, ROBERT, 'A Sketch for a Portrait: Louise Bourgeois', in *Louise Bourgeois*, ed. by Robert Storr, Paulo Herkenhoff and Allan Schwartzman (London: Phaidon, 2003), pp. 28–93

SZCZEPANIAK-GILLECE, JOCELYN, 'Smoke and Mirrors: Cigarettes, Cinephilia, and Reverie in the American Movie Theater', *Objects, Exhibition, and the Spectator*, special issue of *Film History*, 28.3 (2016), 85–113

TALIJAN, EMILIJA, 'Minimalism's Radical Quiet: Chantal Akerman's *Jeanne Dielman*', *Four by Three Magazine* (2016) <http://www.fourbythreemagazine.com/issue/silence/chantal-akermans-jeanne-dielman> [accessed 24 August 2020]

TAYLOR, KEIFER, '*Jeanne Dielman*: A Soundtrack of the Everyday', *A Nos Amours* blog (2014) <https://anosamoursblog.weebly.com/blog/category/jeanne-dielman> [accessed 25 August 2020]

THAIN, ALANNA, *Bodies in Suspense: Time and Affect in Cinema* (Minneapolis: University of Minnesota Press, 2017)

THIELE, KATHRIN, '"To Believe in this World, as It Is": Immanence and the Quest for Political Activism', *Deleuze Studies*, 4. suppl. (November 2010), 28–45 <https://www-euppublishing-com.ezp.lib.cam.ac.uk/doi/10.3366/dls.2010.0204> [accessed 23 August 2020]

TIQQUN, *Premiers matériaux pour une théorie de la jeune fille* (Paris: Fayard, 2001)

—— *Preliminary Materials for a Theory of the Young Girl*, trans. by Ariana Reines (Los Angeles: Semiotext(e), 2012)

TRACZ, TAMARA, 'Je tu il elle', *Senses of Cinema*, 67 (May 2013) <http://sensesofcinema.com/2013/cteq/je-tu-il-elle/> [accessed 25 August 2020]

TRAINOR, JAMES, 'Walking the Walk: The Artist as Flâneur', *Border Crossings*, 88 (November 2003), 82–92

VAN REETH, ADÈLE, and JEAN-LUC NANCY, *La Jouissance* (Paris: Plon, 2014)

VEBLEN, THEODOR, *The Theory of the Leisure Class: An Economic Study in the Evolution of Institutions* [1899] (Lenox, MA: Hard Press, 2010)

WAGSTAFF, SHEENA, 'Such is my Pleasure, Such is my Will', in *The Sophie Calle Reader*, ed. by Iwona Blazwick (London: Whitechapel Gallery, 2009), pp. 33–39

Waldman, Katy, 'The Late-night Revelations in a Memoir of Insomnia', *The New Yorker*, 4 June 2020 <https://www.newyorker.com/books/page-turner/the-late-night-revelations-in-a-memoir-of-insomnia> [accessed 17 June 2020]

Walsh, Maria, 'News from Home the Redux Version: Amodal Perception and 'la jouissance du voir', *The Moving Image Review & Art Journal*, 8.1–2 (1 September 2019), 28–38

Wang, Jackie, 'Oceanic Feeling and Communist Affect' <https://friendship-as-a-form-of-life.tumblr.com/post/162453258727/friendship-as-a-form-of-life-friendship-as-a> [accessed 23 June 2020]

Weil, Simone, *Gravity and Grace*, trans. by Emma Crawford and Mario von der Rohr (London: Routledge, 2002)

Weiss, Andrea, *Vampires and Violets: Lesbians in the Cinema* (London: Jonathan Cape, 1992)

Westley, Hannah, *The Body as Medium and Metaphor* (Amsterdam: Rodopi, 2008)

Wiegman, Robyn, 'Sex and Negativity; or, What Queer Theory Has for You', *Cultural Critique*, 95 (Winter 2017), 219–43

Wiesing, Lambert, 'Toward a Phenomenology of Luxury', *Cultural Politics*, 14.1 (2018), 78–89

Willging, Jennifer, 'Annie Ernaux's Shameful Narration', *French Forum*, 26.1 (2001), 83–103

Wilson, Emma, *Love, Mortality and the Moving Image* (London: Palgrave Macmillan, 2012)

—— *The Reclining Nude* (Liverpool: Liverpool University Press, 2019)

Winnicott, D. W., *Playing and Reality* (Harmondsworth: Penguin Books, 1971)

—— 'Transitional Objects and Transitional Phenomena: A Study of the first not-me possession', *The International Journal of Psychoanalysis*, 34 (1953), 89–97

Wye, Deborah, *Louise Bourgeois* (New York: MOMA Press, 1982)

Wye, Deborah, and Carol Smith, *The Prints of Louise Bourgeois* (New York: MOMA Press, 1994)

Zambreno, Kate, *Heroines* (Los Angeles: Semiotext(e), 2012)

Zett, Anna, 'Sleeping in Public', *How to Sleep Faster*, 5 (Winter 2014), 6–25

Žižek, Slavoj, *The Fragile Absolute: Or, Why Is the Christian Legacy Worth Fighting For?* (London: Verso, 2009)

—— 'Surplus-enjoyment: Between the Sublime and the Trash', *Lacanian Ink*, 15 (1999) <http://www.lacan.com/frameXV6.htm> [accessed 4 October 2015]

Artworks, Installations, Exhibitions and Films

Chantal Akerman

Chantal Akerman par Chantal Akerman (1996)

Chantal Akerman, Maniac Shadows, [installation] 2013, The Kitchen, New York

Chantal Akerman, Moving Through Time and Space, [exhibition] 2008, MIT Visual Arts Centre, Cambridge, MA

Entretien avec ma mère, Natalia Akerman (2007)

J'ai faim j'ai froid (1984)

Je, tu, il, elle (1974)

Jeanne Dielman, 23 quai du Commerce, 1080 Bruxelles (1975)

La Chambre (1972)

Là-bas (2006)

Les Rendez-vous d'Anna (Chantal Akerman, 1978)

No Home Movie (2016)

Saute ma ville (Chantal Akerman, 1968)

Woman Sitting After Killing, [installation] 2001, Venice Biennale, Venice.

Annie Ernaux

Les Mots comme des pierres (2019)

Sophie Calle

Douleur exquise (2003)
Le Carnet d'adresses (1998)
L'Hôtel (1984)
M'as-tu-vue?, [exhibition] 2004, Centre Pompidou, Paris
No Sex Last Night (with Greg Shephard, 1996)
Où et quand? (2009)
Prenez soin de vous, [installation] 2007, French International Pavilion, Venice Biennale, Venice
Prenez soin de vous, [installation] 2008, Bibliothèque nationale de France, Paris
Rachel, Monique, [installation] 2014, Episcopal Church of the Heavenly Rest, New York City

Louise Bourgeois

Double Negative (1963)
Eccentric Abstraction, [group exhibition], 1966, Fischbach Gallery, New York City
Fillette (1968)
Janus Fleuri (1968)
Louise Bourgeois: Le Jour la nuit le jour, [exhibition] 2002, Palais de Tokyo, Paris
Louise Bourgeois: The Insomnia Drawings, [exhibition] 2003, Whitney Museum of American Art, New York City
Louise Bourgeois: I Give Everything Away, [exhibition] 2013–14, Fruitmarket Gallery, Edinburgh
Louise Bourgeois: A Woman Without Secrets, [exhibition] 2013–14, National Gallery of Scotland, Edinburgh
Louise Bourgeois: Works on Paper, [exhibition] 2014, Tate Modern, London
Mamelles (1991)
Ode à L'Oubli (2004)
Personnages, [exhibition] 1950, Peridot Gallery, New York City
Soft Sculpture, [exhibition] 1986, American Federation of Arts, New York City
The She-Fox (1985)
Unconscious Landscape (1967)

INDEX

abandon 1, 8, 18, 20, 22–23, 25, 27, 30, 36–37, 52, 56–57, 59, 64–66, 70, 72, 74, 88, 90, 94–95, 97, 103, 111, 115, 120, 125–26, 129–40, 132–33, 136–37, 144–45, 160
abjection 30, 59, 83, 92, 140–41, 143–44, 156, 159
absorption 10, 16, 18, 24, 27, 29–31, 34–35, 40, 45, 60, 77, 97, 126, 143–44, 160
abundance 1–2, 4, 25, 28, 31, 57, 82–83, 85, 100, 111–12, 121, 124, 146, 148–49, 157
accumulation 4, 6–7, 18–19, 24, 36, 48, 107, 155–56, 158, 168, 170
(self)-actualisation 3, 28, 123, 127
adornment 2, 8, 62, 67
affect 1, 3–8, 10–11, 15, 17, 14–15, 27–31, 37–39, 42–43, 49–51, 53–56, 59, 64, 67–68, 73–75, 78, 94–95, 99, 105, 108, 110–11, 114–16, 121, 125–26, 131–34, 136–40, 142–45, 146–47, 149–53, 155, 164, 177
affection-image 28–29, 43
Agamben, Giorgio 62, 77, 151
agency 30, 39, 48, 52–54, 123, 126, 129, 152, 159, 163
Ahmed, Sarah 123, 125, 141, 151, 155, 163
Akerman, Chantal 6, 15–54, 79, 119, 149, 157, 158, 159
  films:
    Chantal Akerman par Chantal Akerman 6
    Entretien avec ma mère 46
    J'ai faim, j'ai froid 178
    Je, tu, il, elle 7, 15–17, 21–38
    Jeanne Dielman: 23 quai du Commerce, 1080 Bruxelles 7, 17–34, 37, 40, 43–44, 46–52, 54, 129, 158, 163, 166, 169, 171–74, 176–78
    La chambre 16, 26–27, 34, 178
    Là-bas 34, 44, 46, 52, 54, 175, 178
    Les rendez-vous d'Anna 6, 178
    No Home Movie 6, 178
    Saute ma ville 6, 26, 41, 50, 178
  installations:
    'Maniac Shadows' 54, 178
    'Moving Through Time and Space' 178
    'Woman Sitting After Killing' 49, 51, 174, 178
  writings:
    Autoportrait en cineaste 16, 26, 36, 37, 40, 47, 50–51, 53, 72, 79, 163
    My Mother Laughs 48–49, 174
amplification 1, 5, 9, 16, 65, 69, 138, 140, 148, 153, 155
aneconomy 43, 139
artistic control 1, 8, 66, 73, 92, 107, 109, 111, 121, 123, 126, 136, 140, 145–46, 150, 153, 158
attention 1, 2, 8, 10, 15–17, 21, 24–25, 29, 31, 34, 36, 45–46, 48, 60, 61, 63, 66, 73, 78, 87, 92, 116, 125–26, 129, 130–31, 133, 136–37, 139, 140, 149, 151, 157, 158–59
autobiography 7, 53–54, 72, 76, 110, 159, 168, 170
autoeroticism 32, 34, 36
autofiction 7, 11, 123, 159
availability 3, 58, 98, 113, 126, 157

baroqueness 8, 85, 105, 117, 159, 170
Barthes, Roland 1, 9, 19, 46, 48, 56, 59, 61, 75–76, 77, 137, 143, 164, 173
Bataille, Georges:
  Overview 6
  La part maudite 6, 12, 16, 24, 36, 49, 51, 53–54, 76, 151, 164
  L'érotisme 6, 11–12, 16, 20, 24–25, 42, 48–51, 57, 59, 78, 154, 164
  Oeuvres complètes 9, 76, 151, 164, 176
  Théorie de la religion 12, 51, 164
  Le Bleu du ciel 25, 50, 148, 164
Baudrillard. Jean 38–39, 53, 126–29, 144, 150, 152–53, 156
beauty 8, 20, 33, 49, 64, 70, 74, 109, 128, 146
becoming-woman 31, 38
being-with 17, 47
  see also feeling-with
Berlant, Lauren 29, 51, 164
Blanchot, Maurice 57–60, 62, 65, 67, 70, 76, 77–78, 165
Bourdieu, Pierre 4, 7, 11, 55–56, 63, 75, 77, 165, 166, 168, 172
Bourgeois, Louise 7–8, 91–122, 157, 159
  artworks:
    Double Negative 90–92, 118, 179
    Fillette 95–98, 119, 179
    Janus Fleuri 93–95, 118, 165, 179
    Mamelles 88–90, 118, 179
    Ode à L'Oubli 105, 179
    The She Fox 85–88, 91, 179
    Unconscious Landscape 90–92, 179
  exhibitions:
    'Eccentric Abstraction' 179
    'Louise Bourgeois: Le Jour La Nuit Le Jour' 179

'Louise Bourgeois: I Give Everything Away' 107, 121, 166, 179
'Louise Bourgeois: A Woman Without Secrets' 179
'Louise Bourgeois: Works on Paper' 179
'Personnages' 82, 90, 116, 179
'Soft Sculptures' 83–98
writings:
The Insomnia Drawings 98–114
Boyer, Anne 5, 11, 121, 165
Butler, Judith 12, 124, 131, 133, 138, 145, 148, 151, 153, 154, 155, 165

Calle, Sophie 3, 8, 13, 39, 44, 51, 53, 78, 83, 91, 103, 123–56, 157, 159
artworks:
Des histoires vraies 124, 151, 166, 170
Douleur exquise 8, 124, 131–40, 143, 145–47, 149, 152–56, 159, 166–67, 171–72, 179
Le carnet d'adresses 123, 166, 179
L'Hôtel 123, 166, 179
Où et quand? 142, 150, 156, 166, 179
Prenez soin de vous 8, 124–25, 133–34, 139–52, 155–56, 159, 166, 168, 171, 179
Suite vénitienne 8, 78, 124, 125–31, 132, 139, 145, 149, 152–53, 159, 164, 166, 170
films:
No Sex Last Night 39, 53, 124, 169
installations:
'M'as-tu-vue?' 133, 153, 166, 179
'Prenez soin de vous' (Venice) 139–52
'Prenez soin de vous' (Paris) 139–52
'Rachel Monique' 154, 179
capitalism 1–6, 10, 11, 13, 17, 30, 33, 44, 52, 54, 57, 63, 82, 111, 112, 116, 142, 151, 154, 160, 167, 169, 174
cognitive capitalism 3, 10, 157, 174
Caravero, Adriana 115, 141, 166
care 8, 20, 21, 27, 34, 36, 42, 45, 46, 53, 60, 74, 81 97–98, 107, 123–56, 159, 160, 163
self-care 123–56
see also souci
see also Prenez soin de vous
Carson, Anne 66, 77, 155, 166
Cassin, Barbara 143, 154, 156, 166
cinema 1–3, 6–10, 12–13, 15–54, 55, 58, 60, 62, 70, 74, 82, 125, 140, 152
cinema of sensation 3
slow cinema 2
cinephilia 2, 9, 10, 16, 45
Cixous, Hélène 4, 11, 57, 76
collaboration 3, 8, 11, 33, 125, 140, 142, 152
see also community, connection, sharing
comfort 2, 21, 35, 45, 64, 85, 109, 130, 132, 137, 157–58
commodity 3, 5–10, 17, 34, 36, 55–56, 62, 65, 82, 114, 151, 158
Communism 157, 160, 164
community 6, 7, 57, 58–66, 88, 125, 138–40, 140–45, 152
community of lovers 58–66
inoperative community 62
see also désoeuvrement
connection 5, 34, 62, 92, 98, 105, 107, 115, 118
see also community, sharing, collaboration
consumption 1–6, 16, 18, 20, 33–36, 45–46, 52, 54–56, 59, 62, 97, 115, 124, 135–36, 149, 152, 157, 158, 160
conspicuous consumption 1, 4, 55–56, 62, 127
containment 1, 21, 65–66, 90–91, 98, 103, 123, 133, 138, 158
contingency 20, 30, 40, 57, 65, 72, 82–83, 91, 99, 100, 113, 123, 126, 146
co-presence 3
see also being-with, feeling-with
Coronavirus crisis 1, 157, 160, 168, 172
craft 8, 45, 58, 66, 68, 123, 125, 133–34, 142, 154, 159
creativity 1, 3–9, 17, 32–33, 35, 54, 67, 70, 73, 81, 83, 85, 89, 92, 98, 99, 100, 103, 105, 107–11, 113–15, 117, 120, 124, 126, 140, 142, 144, 146, 148, 149, 155, 159
curation 5, 8, 99, 105, 115, 136, 142, 155, 163, 172, 175
Cusk, Rachel 117, 120–22

decadence 5, 15, 20, 52, 57, 63, 73, 92, 129, 157
Delectatio morosa 136–37, 154
Deleuze, Gilles:
Overview 5
'Désir et Plaisir' 15, 25, 41, 44, 54, 150
Dialogues 52, 167
L'Anti-Oedipe 11, 52, 167
L'image-mouvement. Cinéma 1 27, 49, 167
L'image-temps. Cinéma 2 10, 16, 46
Le pli 37, 44, 53
Mille plateaux 38, 41, 43, 46, 51–54, 116, 167
dépense 11, 24, 57, 59, 63, 66, 69
Derrida, Jacques 6
Dissemination 153
Donner le temps: la fausse monnaie 49
L'écriture et la différence 12, 48, 57, 76, 155, 167
Glas 76
De la grammatologie 133, 154, 167
Le toucher, Jean-Luc Nancy 87
La Vie la mort: Séminaire (1975–1976) 75
dérive 89, 99, 126, 128, 131, 145
design 47, 107, 113, 123, 131, 134, 136, 150, 160
desire 1, 2, 3, 5, 8, 9, 10, 12, 15, 19, 24, 25, 29, 31, 33, 36, 37, 38, 39, 40–44, 47, 51–57, 60–62, 64, 66–69, 71, 73–75, 77–78, 85, 88, 90–91, 97, 99, 103, 105, 109–11, 120, 123, 126–29, 131, 136–37, 139–45, 148, 150, 157, 158–60, 164
désoeuvrement 76
detail 8, 9, 15, 18, 19, 29, 40, 45, 48, 60, 76, 81, 110, 125, 149, 150, 159

difference 8, 12, 36, 48, 57, 67, 69, 82, 83–85, 89–90, 95, 98, 103, 108–11,113–15, 130–31, 139–40, 142–43, 145, 148–49, 150, 155, 160, 167
digital age 5, 8, 13, 150
dislocation 17, 23, 49, 102, 131, 134, 136, 148–49, 160
dissolution 24, 38, 40, 43, 68–71, 75, 78, 92, 94, 107, 109, 123, 131, 138, 145–46, 158
distinction 4, 7, 11, 55–56, 60, 75, 77, 90, 111, 114
see also Bourdieu, Pierre
Duras, Marguerite 9, 26, 83, 116, 153
duration 2, 10, 15–54, 94, 113, 158

ease 68, 121, 126, 129–30, 157, 158
écriture 7, 22, 35, 55–80, 107, 162, 155, 158, 165
see also writing
ecstasy 29, 64
embodiment 1, 3–7, 9, 16, 18, 20, 24, 27, 32, 44–45, 49, 51, 53–55, 78, 81–82, 85, 94, 103, 108, 111, 113–14, 117, 151–53, 156, 160
embodied spectatorship 1, 3, 7, 18, 27, 32
enjoyment 4, 7, 8, 11, 31, 59, 81, 103, 137, 142, 150, 157, 160, 178
see also pleasure
entropy 6, 24, 29, 31, 43, 57, 59, 82, 83, 90–95, 110, 115
Ernaux, Annie 3, 7, 29, 39, 44, 51, 55–79
La place 56, 75, 79
'Vers un je "transpersonnel"' 7, 13, 76
Journal du dehors 76–77
Passion simple 7, 13, 55, 56, 57, 58–66, 67, 68, 69, 70, 71, 73, 74, 75, 76, 77, 78, 79, 150
Je ne suis pas sortie de ma nuit 12, 78
L'événement 12, 75
La Vie extérieure: (1993–1999) 76
Se perdre 7, 58, 65, 66–73, 74, 75, 76, 77, 78, 79, 126
'Bourdieu: le chagrin' 75
L'occupation 75
L'écriture comme un couteau 75, 78
L'Usage de la photo 12, 76
'Raisons d'écrire' 75
'La littérature est une arme de combat...' 75
Les années 70, 74, 79
L'atélier noir 74, 79
Ecrire la vie 75
Regarde les lumières mon amour 12, 76
Le vrai lieu: Entretiens avec Michelle Porte 56, 75–76
'Sachez, Monsieur le Président, que nous ne laisserons plus nous voler notre vie...' 79
eroticism 2, 8, 9, 17, 19, 20, 21, 32–34, 36, 39, 40–42, 44, 49, 54, 56–62, 65, 68, 81–84, 89, 98–99, 118–19, 120, 156, 172
see also Bataille, Georges
escape 1, 15, 18, 29, 30, 38, 44–45, 73, 140, 149, 158
see also flight
ethics 3, 9, 11, 21, 30, 31, 51, 71, 76, 125, 127, 130, 151, 153, 158, 165, 167
everyday 5, 8, 9, 12, 15–16, 44, 48, 56–57, 82, 107, 114, 123, 125–28, 131, 134, 143, 149, 151–52, 158, 160
exceptionality 8, 17, 23, 27, 29, 43, 45, 49, 50, 57, 61, 64, 77, 113, 123, 126, 131, 134, 139, 149, 158, 160, 163
see also extraordinary
excess 1, 4–6, 10, 15, 19, 22, 29, 37, 42, 47, 55–56, 73, 128, 140–49, 150, 155, 158–60, 166
exhibition 4, 8, 59, 62, 67, 69, 83, 87, 97, 100, 105, 120, 153–55, 171, 177
expansion 1–4, 7–9, 16–17, 30, 34, 40, 44–47, 52, 54, 61, 64–65, 67–68, 74, 78, 82, 92, 95–98, 107–08, 112, 124, 134, 137–38, 140, 142–43, 145, 149
experimentation 3–4, 7–8, 11, 13, 19, 26, 32, 58, 67, 70–72, 83, 85, 92, 99, 103, 105, 126, 144, 148–49, 159, 170
exscription 57, 65, 73, 156
exteriority 21, 36, 46, 81, 87, 94–95, 137, 148
extraordinary 47, 64, 125, 158–59

failure 72, 124 125–31, 144, 159
feminism 2–4, 8–9, 10–12, 16–17, 24, 27, 31–33, 36, 38, 40–41, 43, 47–54, 58–59, 69, 72, 75, 76, 78, 97, 114–15, 117, 119, 122–23, 126, 131, 137, 142
femininity 4, 11, 16, 24, 31, 32–33, 36, 38, 40–41, 43, 47, 49–51, 53–54, 5963, 75–76, 84, 94, 119, 124, 129, 141, 149, 152, 154, 155, 159
festivity 6, 20, 26, 52, 59, 62, 69, 127
fetishism 1, 4, 7–9, 56, 42, 57, 63, 71, 81, 83–84, 88, 92, 97, 114, 116, 119, 125, 127, 132–35, 139, 140, 142
flânerie 70, 126, 128, 152, 156
flight 45, 67–68, 94, 103, 105, 126, 149, 158
formalism 2–4, 7, 10, 15–17, 19–21, 23, 26, 29, 47, 92, 24, 108–09, 111, 114, 122, 124–25, 141–43, 146, 159
Foucault, Michel 11, 13, 116, 151, 159, 161, 169, 172
Freud, Sigmund 49, 108, 118, 137, 154, 158, 169
fulfilment (*pouvoir-vivre*) 1, 51, 55–56, 68, 74, 141, 159

gaze 3, 16, 34, 44–46, 47, 60, 62, 75–76, 85, 94, 98, 115
male gaze 3, 16
female gaze 44, 47, 51, 53, 64
gender 4, 8, 11, 17, 51, 56, 62, 68, 78, 84, 141–42, 155, 158
general economy 20, 25, 48, 54, 57, 63, 70, 72, 77, 79
see also Bataille, Georges
gift 23, 49, 64, 71–72, 77
see also Derrida, Jacques
gilets jaunes 5, 11, 164
Gorfinkel, Elena 2, 10, 17, 39, 40, 46–47, 52–53
Gornick, Vivian 77, 152
Guibert, Hervé 76, 91, 118

haptic 15, 17, 19, 33, 36–37, 42, 45, 60, 81, 85, 88, 97, 100, 105, 108, 114, 132, 137

Hartman, Saidiya 8, 13, 36, 53

immanence 3, 5–6, 12, 15–16, 29, 34, 36, 44–46, 58, 74, 85, 94, 144, 158, 177
immateriality 3, 5, 8–10, 17, 46, 48, 55, 63, 133, 150, 155
immersion 1–2, 9, 15–54, 65–67, 70, 73–74, 81, 85, 112, 114–15, 123, 126, 133, 139–40, 145, 148, 150, 158
incalculable 6, 32, 73, 84, 113, 132, 135, 139–40, 150, 160
inter-disciplinary 3, 4, 12, 38, 142, 159
intransitivity 5–6, 21, 24, 35–36, 57, 60, 64, 71, 77, 111, 130
Irigaray, Luce 24, 50

jouissance 4–5, 11, 17, 19, 24–25, 29, 43, 47, 59, 68, 97, 110, 114, 119, 140, 145–49, 158, 160

kinesis 3, 10, 21, 31, 37, 42, 58, 65, 70, 82, 95, 108, 125, 145, 150, 155, 158
Koestenbaum, Wayne 99, 119–21, 123, 136, 151, 154
Kraus, Chris
Krauss, Rosalind 13, 24, 60, 62, 85, 94–95, 115–18, 126, 141, 143, 155–56
Kristeva, Julia 50, 53, 84, 108, 117, 120, 144, 156

languor 2, 17, 19, 24, 26–27, 30, 31–44, 52, 109, 120
Laugier, Sandra 125, 151, 155, 172
Lazzarato, Maurice 10–11, 32, 52
light 9, 19, 20, 22, 27, 30, 35, 44, 48, 91, 112–14, 138, 151, 155, 164
limit-experience 7, 29
Lipovetsky, Gilles 9, 160–61
Lippard, Lucy 40, 49, 50, 52–53, 82, 87, 98, 116, 119, 141, 172
Lorde, Audre 141, 151, 155
loss 31, 58, 61, 69, 70–72, 75, 83, 108, 131–32, 133, 136, 138, 141
  self-loss 70, 123, 151
  see also Se perdre, abandon
Louis, Edouard 77

Mangolte, Babette 21, 50
Margulies, Ivone 10, 12, 15, 18–19, 37, 42, 46–51, 53–54
materiality 1, 3–10, 15–18, 23, 27, 33, 37, 42, 44–48, 53, 56–57, 59–64, 68, 73–74, 78, 81–85, 87–88, 90–92, 95, 97–100, 105, 107–11, 113–15, 118, 124, 130, 133–34, 143–45, 155–60
maternity 7, 12, 21, 26, 42, 46–49, 51, 54, 69, 71–72, 78, 83, 85, 87–88, 98 116–18, 121, 124, 146, 152
melancholy 8, 13, 31, 37, 49, 53, 81–83, 92, 114, 115–17, 121, 123, 130–31, 133, 136–39, 143, 145, 153, 154–55, 165, 167, 169, 170–72
Merleau-Ponty, Maurice 82, 116
metamorphosis 82, 88, 98, 114–15, 157
movement-image 27, 49, 167
multiplicity 44, 50, 60, 71, 82, 85, 87–90, 94–95, 99–100, 108–09, 113–14, 116, 123–25, 132, 135–36, 139–40, 142–43, 145–46, 148–49, 151, 155–56
multi-sensuality 36, 81, 85, 99, 105, 108, 142, 145
Mulvey, Laura 2, 10, 13, 16, 18, 46, 48, 50

Nancy, Jean-Luc 4–6, 12, 57–59, 82
  Le partage des voix 76
  La communauté désoeuvrée 47, 59, 61, 76–77
  'L'excrit' 65–66, 68, 70, 73, 76–78
  Être singulier pluriel 120
  Corpus II: Writings on Sexuality 118
  L'"il y a" du rapport sexuel 31
  'Icône de l'acharnement'
  L'Evidence du film 45–46, 50, 54
  À l'écoute 156
  La Naissance des seins 81, 83–98
  'Il y a du rapport sexuel — et après' 51
  Tombe de sommeil 111–14
  Le Plaisir au dessin 81, 99–114
  'L'offrande sublime' 65, 72, 74, 77, 79
  L'Adoration 111
  Dans quels mondes vivons-nous? 120
  'La politique doit montrer ce qui la dépasse' 76
  La jouissance 11
  Sexistence 152, 158, 160
negativity 5–6, 9–11, 78, 81, 85, 90–92, 111, 114, 118, 174, 178–79
Nelson, Maggie 81, 92, 115, 119
nomadism 12, 17, 31–32, 36, 37–40, 51, 53–54
non-human 41, 71, 100, 145, 148

Olds, Sharon 50, 159, 161
ontology 4, 54, 105, 130, 133, 148
opening 1, 4, 7, 11, 16, 22–23, 25, 27, 34, 36, 38, 45, 50, 52, 55, 65–68, 72–74, 77, 81–83, 85, 87–88, 95, 99, 103, 107, 110, 111, 125, 128, 130, 132, 133–35, 138–40, 143, 146, 149, 153, 154, 156–60, 169
order 1, 8, 20–21, 23–26, 29, 61–62, 66–67, 76, 78, 90, 103, 107–08, 123, 134, 139, 142, 148, 157–58
orgasm 17, 24, 32, 39–41, 43, 50, 52
  see also jouissance
otherness 4, 7–8, 11, 25, 36–37, 39, 41–43, 57, 60, 64–68, 71, 73–74, 76, 84, 88, 92, 105, 107, 108, 128–29, 124–46, 148–61, 163–64
Owens, Laura 40, 54, 172

partage 58, 76, 114, 148
  see also sharing
participation 2, 33, 52, 114, 138, 144, 146, 148, 150
passion 7, 13, 18, 25, 50, 55–57, 58–71, 73–79, 150
passivity ,2, 4, 11, 16, 24, 33, 36, 56–57, 71, 85, 87, 98, 113, 119, 120, 126, 141, 155, 158–59
pause 27, 31, 40, 136
  see also suspension

Perec, Georges 127, 151–52
performance 3, 6, 8, 21–22, 39, 46, 69, 72, 83, 95, 123, 126, 141–44, 146, 148, 150, 152, 156, 163, 167, 171
phenomenology 1, 3, 6, 9–10, 12, 15–16, 18, 39, 50, 52, 62, 81, 103, 114, 116, 130, 132, 135
plasticity 3, 7, 9, 12, 88–91, 95, 157, 159
play 6, 17, 19, 26, 31, 34, 41, 43, 50, 66–67, 70, 72, 81, 97, 107–08, 110–11, 114, 117, 120, 124, 126–27, 129, 130–31, 133, 136–38, 141–42, 144, 146, 148, 150, 153, 159
pleasure 1–2, 4, 9–10, 12, 15–19, 22, 27, 30–32, 34, 36, 38–40, 43–45, 48, 50, 53–56, 58–59, 62, 69–70, 78, 81, 95, 97–98, 98–115, 118–21, 124, 126–28, 132–33, 136–37, 140, 145–46, 149, 151–53, 155, 157, 158–60, 174
see also visual pleasure
plurality 1, 8–9, 71, 82, 90, 105, 140, 142, 146, 149–50
possibility 1–3, 5, 7–9, 16–17, 21, 23, 25, 27–28, 30, 39, 44, 46, 53, 55–56, 64, 66, 71, 89, 94, 97, 99, 103, 105, 108–09, 111–14, 117, 123, 128–29, 133–36, 143–46, 157–58, 160
see also fulfilment
potlatch 6, 57
Preciado, Paul B. 11, 46, 157, 160
process. 1, 3–4, 6, 8, 20, 22–23, 33, 35, 36–38, 46, 58, 60–61, 65–66, 73, 85, 91–92, 97–98, 103, 105, 109–14, 117, 119–20, 123, 125–27, 133, 136, 140, 143–45, 150, 152–54, 159, 160
production 3–5, 10–11, 16, 17, 21, 27, 31–37, 46, 52, 56–57, 59, 68, 73, 82–83, 85, 87, 89, 91–92, 99, 103, 113, 116, 126, 130–31, 134, 140, 143–44, 146, 149, 155, 159, 160
productivity 5, 8, 11, 17, 20, 29, 31–37, 40, 44, 52, 54, 57, 61, 64, 100, 109, 111, 128, 136, 149, 159–60
psychoanalysis 7, 11, 13, 49, 81, 83, 85, 108, 114–19, 122, 141, 144, 159
purposelessness 1, 31–37, 128

queerness 2, 8–10, 12–13, 32, 40, 52–54, 78, 160

relationality 1–13, 18, 23, 28, 30, 34, 39, 41–45, 52, 54, 56, 58–59, 61, 64, 66–68, 70–71, 75, 88, 105, 111, 112–13, 118, 124–26, 130, 132, 138–40, 142, 144, 149, 151, 153, 157, 159
see also non-relationality
restricted economy 20–21, 24, 30, 44, 70, 158
retreat 17–18, 26, 30, 33–34, 36, 48, 53, 61, 74, 84, 99, 120, 141–42, 150, 157
rhythm 15, 17, 19, 24, 45, 48–49, 57, 66, 81, 94, 107–09, 112–15, 126, 129, 140–41, 143
ritual 9, 12, 17, 18, 21, 31, 35, 46, 62, 64, 69, 123, 129, 131–32, 135, 150, 153
Robertson, Lisa 6, 12–13, 44, 48, 53–54, 78
Ross, Kristin 146, 154, 156

sacrifice 6, 25, 29–30, 59, 60, 68, 72, 136
Sade, Marquis de 116, 123, 151
Sartre, Jean-Paul 71, 79
scopic 19, 137, 148
sensation 3, 5–6, 9–10, 13, 16–17, 19, 24, 25, 27, 29, 38, 43, 50, 56, 73–75, 85, 98, 112, 123, 158
sense 84, 87, 89, 92, 100, 107, 110–12, 116–17, 138–39, 146, 158
sensuousness 1, 3–5, 7, 12, 17, 32, 37, 44, 50, 54, 56, 60, 64, 81–122, 133, 155, 159
sensuous scholarship 3
see also multi-sensuality
servitude 25, 151
sexuality 1, 4, 7, 12–13, 15–17, 19–21, 23, 29–32, 39–41, 43–45, 52, 60, 62–63, 66, 69–70, 81–82, 84–85, 94–95, 97–98, 114, 118, 122, 126, 129, 130, 141, 151, 159, 161
sharing 3–9, 44, 47, 49, 57–58, 66, 92, 107, 114, 130–33, 138, 141–43, 148, 151, 159
see also partage
simplification 8, 33–34, 38 42, 57–66, 68, 73, 88, 113, 129, 136–37, 142, 150, 159
singularity 6, 8, 15, 24–26, 39, 49, 58, 61, 64, 71, 73, 89, 105, 113, 126, 132, 134, 135, 137–38, 142, 149, 158, 160
singular plural 105, 142, 158
sleep 16, 98–114, 116, 119–21
slowness 9–10, 24, 26, 31–32, 34, 43, 49, 53, 109, 116
see also slow cinema
solitude 3, 9, 15–17, 30, 34, 36, 44, 114, 157
Sontag, Susan 9, 136
souci 8, 13, 27, 60, 63, 68, 103, 125, 140, 169
see also care
sovereignty 3, 11–12, 20, 22, 27, 29, 30, 40, 43, 66, 69, 71–72, 88, 123–24, 129, 130–31, 136, 139, 142, 145, 149–51, 159–60
squander 6, 36, 44, 57, 59, 70–71, 136
Stiegler, Bernard 151
stillness 1, 9, 13, 21, 24, 27, 31, 36–37, 40, 45, 47, 50–51, 82, 109, 113, 155, 158, 160
structure/structuralism 2, 6–7, 15, 17, 19–20, 23, 27, 35, 37, 40, 50, 58, 65, 83, 88, 98, 100, 105, 133, 136–38, 149, 153, 154
see also formalism
submission 41, 125–31, 138, 144–45, 159
surface 2, 10, 15–18, 21–24, 31, 37, 47, 49, 51–53, 59, 74, 77, 83, 87, 92, 95, 97, 129, 134, 137
surplus 4, 11, 19, 22, 73, 107, 110, 115, 124, 127, 153, 160
surrender 2, 11, 36, 38, 59, 66, 78, 83, 87, 91, 95, 97, 123, 125–31, 133, 150, 159
suspension 1, 3, 10, 17, 23, 26, 30, 32, 40, 44–46, 58, 60–62, 68, 70–71, 83, 85, 94–95, 97, 107, 110–12, 130, 136, 148
see also pause

temporality 2, 7, 10, 16, 17–18, 20, 23, 25–26, 28–29,

31–32, 34, 37, 40, 45, 50, 53–54, 63, 67, 82, 109, 129, 132, 134, 136, 139, 145, 158
see also time
texture
time 1–5, 7–9, 10, 12–13, 15–19, 21–27, 29, 30–32, 34–38, 40, 42–46, 48–54, 56–65, 67–70, 72–74, 76, 78, 82, 85, 89, 91, 98, 103, 107–08, 110, 112–14, 116, 119, 122, 124, 126–27, 128–29, 130, 134, 137, 141, 143, 145, 149, 150–53, 158–60
time-image 10, 16, 46
Tiqqun 150, 156
transgression 1, 73, 78, 144

uncountable experience 131–50
unproductivity 11, 17, 31–44, 52, 54
see also non-production

Veblen, Theodor 9
visual pleasure 10, 16, 18–19, 27, 31, 39, 48
voluptuousness 1, 7, 16, 17–31, 35, 37, 40, 48, 52, 56, 74, 78, 95, 98–100, 117, 131, 136, 139, 151, 155, 158
vulnerability 22, 45, 82, 84–85, 88, 91, 97, 99–100, 105, 124, 131–32, 138, 139, 141–43, 151–52, 157, 165

waste 1, 9, 20, 35–36, 44, 49, 57, 59, 70–71, 110, 176
Weil, Simone 155, 178
Wilson, Emma 10, 12, 39, 48, 52–54, 87, 116–19, 133, 141, 153–55, 164
Winnicott, D. W. 46, 117
withdrawal 32, 34, 36, 50, 52, 61, 73–74, 82, 84, 87, 91, 95, 97, 99, 111, 116

Žižek, Slavoj 4, 11, 29, 51

www.ingramcontent.com/pod-product-compliance
Lightning Source LLC
LaVergne TN
LVHW081259100826
845148LV00005B/924